VOLATILE LANDSCAPE

IRAQ AND ITS INSURGENT MOVEMENTS

Edited By Ramzy Mardini

The Jamestown Foundation
Washington, DC

THE JAMESTOWN FOUNDATION

Published in the United States by
The Jamestown Foundation
1111 16th Street NW
Suite 320
Washington, DC 20036
http://www.jamestown.org

For more information on this book of the Jamestown Foundation, email pubs@jamestown.org

ISBN 978-0-9816905-4-4

Cover art provided by Peggy Archambault of Peggy Archambault Design

Jamestown's Mission

The Jamestown Foundation's mission is to inform and educate policy makers and the broader policy community about events and trends in those societies which are strategically or tactically important to the United States and which frequently restrict access to such information. Utilizing indigenous and primary sources, Jamestown's material is delivered without political bias, filter or agenda. It is often the only source of information which should be, but is not always, available through official or intelligence channels, especially in regard to Eurasia and terrorism.

Origins

Launched in 1984 after Jamestown's late president and founder William Geimer's work with Arkady Shevchenko, the highest-ranking Soviet official ever to defect when he left his position as undersecretary general of the United Nations, The Jamestown Foundation rapidly became the leading source of information about the inner workings of closed totalitarian societies.

Over the past two decades, Jamestown has developed an extensive global network of experts – from the Black Sea to Siberia, from the Persian Gulf to the Pacific. This core of intellectual talent includes scientists, journalists, scholars and economists. Their insight contributes significantly to policy makers engaged in addressing today's new and emerging global threats, including that from international terrorists.

Volatile Landscape

Iraq and its Insurgent Movements

Table of Contents

Chapter 4: Faces of the Insurgency

Chapter 6: Iraq's Dangerous Kurdish-Arab Rivalry

Part III: Iraq since the June 30, 2009 Withdrawal

Chapter 7: A Volatile Security Environment

Chapter 8: Insurgent Strategies Since the U.S. Withdrawal

Map of Iraq*

*Map created by Nations Online Project,
http://www.nationsonline.org/oneworld/map/iraq_map.htm

Acknowledgements

The list of those who have contributed to this volume of writings about Iraq and its insurgent groups is quite extensive. Given that many of the contributors to this compilation of Jamestown's writings on Iraq are the analysts themselves, we owe our gratitude for their research and analysis without which this volume would not be possible. Many of these experts have spent a decade or more covering developments in this important Middle Eastern country which was once the flank of the Arab world. With the change of events that occurred after 2003, analysis of Iraq has gone from writing about Saddam Hussein and his henchmen, to the various actors shaping the political and security environment of the new state. Toward this goal, Jamestown has continued to fill the void by providing timely fact-based research and analysis on the security situation in Iraq since 2003.

Whereas most Western analysis in the Washington, D.C. think-tank community mostly addressed the political-military issues related to the 'surge' in Iraq, this book focuses on the insurgent groups that have fought for power in post-Saddam Iraq, and who will continue playing a major role in shaping the post-U.S. security environment. With the overwhelming shift in U.S attention to Afghanistan, this work comes at an even more opportune time. Attention to Iraq has slipped in the past twelve months and declined noticeably from the pages of the western media. *Volatile Landscape: Iraq and its Insurgent Movements,* seeks to reverse this trend by refocusing Western attention on this important country and the insurgent groups shaping the debates on security.

As with most books published by The Jamestown Foundation, this volume is designed to be a reference volume for the policymaking community and is not designed to be the final word on militant movements in Iraq. What it does offer its readers is a reference tool to read about the key actors and groups making up the militancy. No organization in the world is better suited to address this issue than the analysts who write for The Jamestown Foundation and its flagship publication *Terrorism Monitor.* This group represents a truly global network of analysts and experts that extends to over fifty different countries. It is their insight that makes our analysis on terrorism unique and a key source of timely information to the U.S. policymaking community. We owe a deep debt of gratitude to these writers who have helped Jamestown continue to offer a diverse array of perspectives on conflict and instability which remains sorely lacking in the mainstream Western media.

This book would not be possible without the assistance of Ramzy Mardini. We owe him a special note of thanks for the endless hours he spent in editing the articles that make up this book. He has played a critical role in the past several months liaising with analysts around the world and in making this compilation of Jamestown writings on Iraq come all together. A special note of thanks also is due to Julianne Opet of Jamestown staff who assisted this project and played, as always, a crucial role in all the various logistical aspects in the printing of this book.

I would like to thank the Jamestown Board of Directors, in particular, our outgoing Chairman, Willem de Vogel, for his support, guidance, and boundless energy. Under his leadership Jamestown, continued to expand and regenerate in this age of uncertainty in Eurasia and the Middle East.

Finally, The Jamestown Foundation owes its gratitude to our generous donors who support our activities. Without their support, our research would simply not be possible. And lastly we would like to thank the readers of Jamestown's publications for their continuing support, feedback and encouragement.

Glen E. Howard
President
The Jamestown Foundation

Timeline of Key Events (2003-2010)[1]

* *Timeline compiled by BBC News*

2003

March 17 – U.S. President George W. Bush gives Saddam Hussein and his sons 48 hours to leave Iraq or face war.

March 20 – American missiles hit targets in Baghdad, marking the start of a US-led campaign to topple Saddam Hussein.

April 9 – U.S. forces advance into central Baghdad. Saddam Hussein's grip on the city is broken. In the following days Kurdish *peshmerga* fighters and U.S. forces take control of the northern cities of Kirkuk and Mosul. There is looting in Baghdad and elsewhere.

May 22 – United Nations Security Council backs U.S.-led administration in Iraq and lifts economic sanctions.

May 23 – U.S. Administrator Paul Bremer abolishes the ministries and institutions of the former regime. The Iraq Army is also disbanded.

July 16 – Head of U.S. Central Command General John Abizaid claims Iraq bears the hallmarks of a "classic guerrilla-type campaign."

July 22 – Saddam's sons Uday and Qusay are killed in a gun battle in Mosul.

August 7 – Jordan's Embassy in Baghdad is bombed, killing and wounding dozens of people.

August 19 – A bomb demolishes the United Nations Baghdad headquarters, killing at least 20 people, including the top U.N. envoy Sergio Vieira de Mello. A number of international agencies decide to pull their staff out of the Iraqi capital following the attack.

August 29 – A large bomb in Najaf kills 125 people, including Shi'a leader Ayatollah Mohammad Baqr al-Hakim, the head of the Supreme Council for

---

[1] "Timeline: Iraq: A Chronology of Key Events," BBC News, February 11, 2010 (Last Updated): http://news.bbc.co.uk/2/hi/middle_east/737483.stm. Also, "Timeline: Iraq after Saddam," BBC News, March 20, 2007 (Last Updated): http://news.bbc.co.uk/2/hi/middle_east/4192189.stm.

Islamic Revolution in Iraq (SCIRI). His younger brother, Abdul Aziz al-Hakim, becomes the new leader of SCIRI.

December 13 – Saddam Hussein is captured in Tikrit by U.S. special forces.

2004

March 2 – Suicide bombers attack Shi'a festival-attendees in Karbala and Baghdad, killing more than 180 people. U.S. officials blame the attacks on Abu Musab al-Zarqawi.

April-May – Shi'a militiamen loyal to radical cleric Muqtada al-Sadr take on coalition forces in uprisings in several cities in southern Iraq; Hundreds are reported killed in fighting during the month-long U.S. military siege of the Sunni Arab city of Fallujah.

June 28 – U.S. hands sovereignty to Iraq's Interim Government headed by Prime Minister Ayad Allawi, a secular Shi'a.

August - Fighting erupts in Najaf between U.S. forces and the *Jaysh al-Mahdi* militia of radical Shi'a cleric Muqtada al-Sadr. An agreement was brokered by Grand Ayatollah Ali al-Sistani, requiring al-Sadr's militia to leave the Imam Ali Mosque and U.S. forces to pull back.

November – A major U.S.-led offensive is undertaken against insurgents in the city of Fallujah, which had been under insurgent control since April.

2005

January 30 - An estimated eight million people vote in the elections for a Transitional National Assembly. The Shi'a United Iraqi Alliance wins a majority of assembly seats. The Kurdish Alliance comes in second.

February 28 - At least 114 people are killed by a massive car bomb in Hilla, south of Baghdad, in the worst single incident since the U.S.-led invasion.

April - Amid escalating violence, parliament selects Kurdish leader Jalal al-

Talabani as President of Iraq. Ibrahim al-Jaafari, a Shi'a, is named as Prime Minister.

May - Surge in car bombings, bomb explosions and shootings: Iraqi ministries put the civilian death toll for May at 672, up from 364 in April.

June - Masoud Barzani is sworn in as President of the Kurdish Regional Government.

August - Draft constitution is endorsed by Shi'a and Kurdish negotiators, but not by Sunni representatives; More than 1,000 people are killed during a stampede at a Shi'a ceremony in Baghdad.

September - 182 people are killed in attacks in Baghdad.

October - Saddam Hussein goes on trial on charges of crimes against humanity; Voters approve a new constitution, which aims to create an Islamic federal democracy.

December - Iraqis vote for the first, full-term government and parliament since the U.S.-led invasion.

2006

January - The Shi'a-led United Iraqi Alliance emerges as the winner of the December 2005 parliamentary elections, but fails to gain an absolute majority.

February 22 - A bomb explodes at the al-Askari Mosque in Samarra, a significant shrine in Shi'a Islam, igniting reprisals against Sunnis and sectarian violence.

April 22 - The newly re-elected Iraqi President Jalal al-Talabani asks the Shi'a compromise candidate, Nouri al-Maliki, to form a new government, ending months of deadlock.

May and June - The United Nations states that an average of more than 100 civilians per dayare killed in violence in Iraq.

June 7 - Al-Qaeda in Iraq leader, Abu Musab al-Zarqawi, is killed in a U.S. air strike. Abu Ayyub al-Masri, also known as Abu Hamza al-Muhajir, was later named as the new leader of al-Qaeda in Iraq.

November - Saddam Hussein is found guilty of crimes against humanity and sentenced to death; Iraq and Syria restore diplomatic relations after nearly a quarter century.

November 23 - More than 200 Iraqis are killed in car bombings in the mostly Shi'a area of Sadr City in Baghdad, in what was the worst attack on the capital since the U.S.-led invasion of 2003.

December - In making recommendations to President Bush on policy options in Iraq, the Iraq Study Group Report describes the situation as grave and deteriorating.

December 30 - Saddam Hussein is executed by hanging. In response, the formation of the Ba'athist insurgent group "Men of the Army of al-Naqshbandia Way" (JRTN) is announced.

2007

January - U.S. President Bush announces a new Iraq strategy; thousands more of U.S. troops will be dispatched to shore up security in Baghdad and al-Anbar province; the United Nations says more than 34,000 Iraqi civilians were killed in violence during 2006, surpassing official Iraqi estimates by threefold.

February - A bomb in Baghdad's Sadriya market kills more than 130 people. It is the worst single bombing since 2003.

March - Insurgents detonate three trucks with toxic chlorine gas in Fallujah and Ramadi, injuring hundreds.

April 18 - Multiple bombings in Baghdad targeting Shi'a kill nearly 200 people.

August 1 - Six members of the main Sunni Arab political bloc in Iraq, the Iraqi Accordance Front, withdraw from the cabinet following a dispute over power-sharing;

August 14 - Truck and car bombs hit two villages of Iraq's Yazidi community, killing at least 250 people - the deadliest attack since 2003;

August 16 - Kurdish and Shi'a leaders form an alliance to save Prime Minister

Nouri al-Maliki's government from political paralysis, but fail to bring in any Sunni leaders.

December - Turkey launches an air raid inside northern Iraq on fighters from the Kurdish PKK rebels; Great Britain hands over security of Basra province to Iraqi forces, effectively marking the end of nearly five years of British control of southern Iraq.

2008

January - Parliament passes legislation allowing former officials from Saddam Hussein's Ba'ath party to return to public life; Turkish forces mount a ground offensive against Kurdish rebels in northern Iraq.

March - Unprecedented two-day visit to Iraq by Iran's President, Mahmoud Ahmadinejad; Prime Minister Nouri al-Maliki orders crackdown on militias in Basra, sparking pitched battles with radical Shi'a cleric Muqtada al-Sadr's *Jaysh al-Mahdi* militia.

July - Prime Minister Nouri al-Maliki raises the prospect for the first time of setting a timetable for the withdrawal of U.S. troops as part of negotiations over a new security agreement with the United States; The main Sunni Arab bloc, the Iraqi Accordance Front, rejoins the Shi'a-led government almost a year after it pulled out.

September – U.S. forces hand over control of the western province of al-Anbar – once an insurgent and al-Qaeda in Iraq stronghold – to the Iraqi government. It is the first Sunni province to be returned to the Shi'a-led government; Iraqi parliament passes provincial elections law. Issue of contested city of Kirkuk is set aside so elections can go ahead elsewhere.

October 1 - Members of the Baghdad Awakening Council, estimated to number about 54,000, move to the Iraqi government payroll, with other members of the councils set to follow; The U.S. military says al-Qaeda in Iraq's second-in-command has been killed during a raid in the northern city of Mosul.

November - The Iraqi parliament approves a security pact with the United States under which all U.S. troops are due to leave Iraq by the end of 2011.

2009

January - Iraq takes control of security in Baghdad's fortified Green Zone and assumes more powers over foreign troops based in the country.

February - The political bloc headed by Prime Minister Nouri al-Maliki scores big wins in the January 2009 provincial elections.

March – U.S. President Barack Obama announces the withdrawal of all U.S. combat troops by the end of August 2010. Up to 50,000 U.S. troops will stay on into 2011 to advise Iraqi forces and protect U.S. interests, leaving by the end of 2011.

April - Parliament elects Ayad al-Samarraie, a Sunni Arab, as its Speaker, filling the vacancy left when Mahmoud al-Mashhadani stepped down in December 2008. The post is reserved for Sunni Arabs by agreement among political leaders.

June 30 - US troops withdraw from towns and cities in Iraq, six years after the invasion, having formally handed over security duties to new Iraqi forces.

July 25 - New opposition forces make strong gains in elections to the Kurdistan Regional Government's parliament. Masoud Barzani is re-elected in the presidential election.

August 19 – Known to Iraqis as "Bloody Wednesday," multiple coordinated explosions had rocked downtown Baghdad, resulting in over 120 deaths, and over 600 wounded. The Iraq government claims the attacks indicated an alliance between al-Qaeda in Iraq and Ba'athists based in Syria.

August 26 – Shi'a political leader Abdul Aziz al-Hakim, head of the Islamic Supreme Council of Iraq, dies in a hospital in Tehran. His son, Ammar al-Hakim, takes leadership of the party.

October - Prime Minister Nouri al-Maliki announces the formation of a new political grouping of 40 parties, called the State of Law, after a split in the Shi'a

United Iraqi Alliance that won the 2005 elections.

October 25 - Two car bombs near the Green Zone in Baghdad kill at least 155 people, in Iraq's deadliest attack since April 2007.

December - Vice-President Tariq al-Hashimi withdraws his veto to the new election law after parliament unanimously approves an amendment to protect the rights of the Sunni Muslim and other minorities.

December 8 - The al-Qaeda-linked Islamic State of Iraq claims responsibility for five connected suicide bombings in Baghdad that leave at least 127 people dead and 400 wounded. The group also claimed attacks in the August 19 and October 25 bombings that killed 240 people; Tensions emerge as Iraq accuses Iranian troops of occupying an oilfield in Iraqi territory.

2010

January - Controversy emerges as candidates with alleged links to the Ba'ath Party are banned from participating in the March 7 parliamentary election.

INTRODUCTION

The Surge, the Leap, and the Great Fall: Sectarianism and Nationalism during the al-Maliki Government, 2006–2010

By Reidar Visser

On April 14, 2009, following the local elections earlier in the year, Iskandar Witwit, a former Iraqi general affiliated with the secular *al-Iraqiya* movement, was elected as Deputy Governor of Babel. Witwit received no less than 20 out of 23 votes in an assembly otherwise dominated by the State of Law list of Nouri al-Maliki and smaller Shi'a Islamist groups after al-Maliki had opted to exclude the Islamic Supreme Council of Iraq (ISCI) from his coalition. Developments in Babel reflected similar tendencies at the national level, where al-Maliki in a bid to emerge as a national leader for all of Iraq was discussing the prospect of a wider electoral alliance with *al-Iraqiyya* and similar secular forces – including the Hiwar front headed by Saleh al-Mutlaq, a figure supported by the secular establishment that had existed in Iraq before 2003.

On February 10, 2010, Iskandar Witwit was de-Ba'athified and removed from the post as deputy governor that he had won with such overwhelming margins just eight months earlier. Those who carried out his abrupt demotion were the same allies of al-Maliki in the governorate council that had previously supported him. Earlier in the year, Witwit had been one of 511 candidates for the parliamentary election that had been banned from standing as candidates by the Accountability and Justice Commission. That board, in turn, was dominated by the influential figures of Ahmad Chalabi and Ali al-Lami, both candidates for the Shi'a-dominated Iraqi National Alliance which Chalabi had put together by re-uniting the Sadrists and ISCI at a series of meetings in Tehran in May 2009. Witwit's case was appealed and whereas he was actually one of a small number of candidates that were eventually reinstated as candidates nationally, the damage at the local level had already been done. Indeed, similar acts followed elsewhere: In an outburst of vigilantism across Iraq south of Baghdad, tentative alliances that had been entered into between al-Maliki and various secular figures in 2009 were abruptly torn apart as al-Maliki adherents – this time with the support of fellow Shi'as in ISCI – moved to purge the bureaucracy of people suspected of having ties to the former Ba'ath party.

VOLATILE LANDSCAPE

Three factors help explain the rapidity of Iraq's political decline between 2009 and 2010, and more generally why the Iraq from which the United States is withdrawing is looking increasingly similar to the situation in 2005 and can create situations identical to that seen in Babel. The first concerns the essentially tentative and limited character of al-Maliki's transformation from a sectarian to a national figure following the US-led "surge" in Iraq from 2007 onwards. The real start of that transformation came in March 2008, with the "Charge of the Knights" operation in Basra. The "charge" was indeed the kind of "leap" that the multi-vocal Arabic concept *sawla* signifies: To many Iraqis, al-Maliki instantly became something of a national hero by going after fellow Shi'a Sadrists, thereby emerging the first of the post-2003 leaders to handle the sensitive security file in a manner that was seen as truly non-sectarian. He later followed up with a return to a rhetoric of centralism that was more familiar to ordinary Iraqis than foreign concepts of federalism that had been introduced with the new constitution in 2005, and went on to prosecute an election campaign for the governorate councils in January 2009 where for the first time the focus was on bread-and-butter issues and candidate qualities instead of the sectarian rhetoric of the past. Nonetheless, whereas the performance of al-Maliki's list, State of Law, was impressive in urban areas like Basra and Baghdad, it should be noted that even with the increased sympathy for him among Sunnis, his list generally fared poorly throughout the Sunni-majority areas north of Baghdad.

The second factor has to do with chronology. As the provincial election results showed, al-Maliki's transformation to a national leader still had considerable geographical limitations as of January 2009. Perhaps the bravest features of his "leap" actually came after the elections, during the coalition-forming process in the spring of 2009 – when he for some weeks systematically tried to turn against ISCI and instead reached out to other parties, including secular lists. But equally important, this trend was very soon reversed. Following a visit to Iraq by Iran's Ali Larijani in late March 2009, as well as a string of unexplained bombings in what was considered "safe" Shi'a areas, al-Maliki agreed in early April to include ISCI in the local councils in both Maysan and Wasit provinces despite the fact that his allies there did not strictly speaking depend on ISCI's support to form coalitions. His efforts to create a new alliance between his own Shi'a Islamist core and secularists suffered another setback on April 19, 2009 in parliament (whose deputies reflected the results of the 2005 election), when Ayad al-Samarraie of the *Tawafuq* bloc – largely seen as the anti-Maliki candidate at the time – was finally elected as new speaker of the parliament to replace Mahmoud al-Mashhadani. Echoing the still fragile and exploratory character of the emerging bonds between themselves and the secularists in places like Babel, the Da'awa deputies in parliament voted blank instead of openly supporting the challenger to al-Samarraie, Mustafa al-Hiti of the Hiwar front.

Already from that point in mid-April 2009 and onwards, al-Maliki increasingly retreated from his experiment with Iraqi nationalism. True, he did resist attempts by Iran and ISCI to have him join their list for the 2010 parliamentary election in what would have been a carbon copy of 2005. But in all other respects, his image as a national leader received blows. The coalition that he presented in October 2009 was certainly superior to that of ISCI in terms of its inclusion of some independent Sunni figures with more than merely ceremonial roles. However, no major secular or Sunni politicians were co-opted. With respect to his Kurdistan/Kirkuk policy, another important area as far as Iraqi nationalist credentials are concerned, al-Maliki simply chose to fade into the background after having previously (especially in 2008) made lots of noise, if not much else. In November 2009 he authorized his parliamentary allies to sign off on an electoral law that basically gave the Kurds everything they asked for with respect to Kirkuk.

Perhaps even more crucially, al-Maliki in this period also strayed from his "state of law" concept and increasingly came to be seen as sectarian in his approach to questions about the constitutional order in Iraq. This was highlighted first in the debate about the veto of the elections law by (the Sunni) Vice-President Tariq al-Hashimi in November 2009. Al-Hashimi's veto was problematic for many reasons (including the apparent hope that it would rectify certain issues without re-opening the general debate about the law); however it was never "unconstitutional," which was what al-Maliki's allies in parliament acrimoniously tried to label it. Later, and in an even more marked departure from his erstwhile attempts at being "national," al-Maliki in early 2010 ended up embracing the de-Ba'athification policy of the Accountability and Justice Commission that was directed by his main Shi'a "competitors" in the parliamentary elections, the Iraqi National Alliance. The decision by the committee to exclude hundreds of secular and nationalist candidates was based on a catalogue of infractions of basic principles of due process and made a mockery of the idea of "rule of law" in Iraq; its support by al-Maliki marked the decisive end of his era as an Iraqi nationalist. Even if there are still signs of intra-

Shi'a competition on the political scene, the 2010 parliamentary election now looks set to be a competition in de-Ba'athification, rather than a competition in national leadership. In fact, an outright return to the all-Shi'a alliance of 2005 is increasingly being talked about.

The third factor of relevance here relates to the extent to which external powers have been driving the process forward. Few question the Iranian desire to see a return to sectarian fronts in Iraq – an aim that in fact is being publicly confirmed by Iranian think tanks and commentators like Kayhan Barzegar. The basic idea is that given the demographic realities of Iraq, Tehran will be best served with a type of politics where ethno-sectarian labels – Sunnis, Shi'as, and Kurds – are at the top of the agenda. This, it is believed, will forever prevent the emergence of the scenario that is most feared by Iran: a nationalist government in Iraq without sectarian loyalties that can influence its foreign policy in a pro-Iranian direction. Accordingly, Tehran has eagerly supported the attempts to reconstitute an all-Shi'a alliance (much of the diplomacy that led to the creation of the Iraqi National Alliance was actually conducted on Iranian soil in the spring of 2009), and has welcomed the re-emergence of de-Ba'athification as a defining issue in Iraqi politics (it should be remembered how central the image of the Ba'ath as the number one enemy was to the Shi'a alliance in 2005, when they placed a picture of their secular opponent Ayad Allawi on election posters, and asked voters whether they wanted the return of the Ba'ath). Many also find it plausible that Iran may have played a role, directly or indirectly, in at least some of the many attacks in 2009 that served to corner al-Maliki and left him with few options except a return to the sectarian fold, although this kind of involvement is much harder to document beyond allegations from defected Iraqi intelligence chiefs and unnamed U.S. military officials talking to the press.

Less attention has been given to the way in which U.S. Iraq policy for the past year or so has had exactly the same effect of pushing Iraq into a more sectarian direction. Al-Maliki's finest hour as an Iraqi nationalist happened to coincide with the first months of the U.S. presidency of Barack Obama, but it also collapsed in that period.

The U.S. government approach to Iraq in early 2009 seemed to be characterized first and foremost by passivity, perhaps coupled with general optimism concerning the prospect of rapprochement with Iran, which may have served to deflect attention from the intense efforts by Tehran to regain the initiative in Iraq by creating trouble for al-Maliki. At any rate, to the extent that there was any American "Iraq policy" in early 2009, the dominant trends seemed to be fear of al-Maliki becoming too strong and centralist, unease about his policies towards the Kurds, and conversely, a general tendency of classifying the still fragile sectarian situation in the rest of Iraq as a bygone problem. Accordingly, the limited U.S. interference in Iraq in this period mostly served to weaken al-Maliki and deprive him of whatever embryonic nationalist credentials he had managed to amass in the wake of the surge. This was seen first in April 2009 in the general U.S. government support for the anti-Maliki candidate for Speaker of parliament, Ayad al-Samarraie.

Also were the multiple visits by U.S. Vice-President Joseph Biden that were reportedly aimed at making al-Maliki back down from his attempts to take a strong centralist position in relations with the Kurds and the Baghdad-Arbil dispute over Kirkuk. Similarly, the initiative by U.S. General Raymond Odierno in early autumn 2009 to involve al-Maliki in joint patrols in territories considered "disputed" by the Kurds, served to kill off any chances of an alliance between al-Maliki and the nationalist/secularists for the 2010 election since the nationalists do not recognize the designation of "disputed territories" used by the Kurds and the Americans (Kirkuk being the only *constitutionally* recognized territory of this kind). Reportedly, the Iraqi secularist leaders who visited Washington, DC during Ramadan were even denied meetings they sought with the Obama administration. Conversely, U.S. officials had met frequently with Kurdish officials throughout autumn 2009 and also received Iraqi Kurdistan President Masoud Barzani – all apparently without achieving the slightest change in the Kurdish position in key questions of national reconciliation.

Throughout the growing estrangement between al-Maliki and the secular Iraqi nationalists, the U.S. Embassy in Baghdad – often supported by the United Nations Assistance Mission for Iraq – have quite consistently been on the opposite side of the nationalists. This was seen clearly in the debate about Kirkuk in the elections law – an issue that had previously served to create rapprochement between al-Maliki and these groups. However, the message from the U.S. Embassy about the undesirability of linking the Kirkuk issue to the elections was expressed early on, thereby effectively supporting voting patterns in the Iraqi parliament on the election law that were strangely reminiscent of 2005 – a Kurdish-Shi'a alliance defined in ethno-sectarian terms, with only token Sunni support. An even more serious alienation of the secularist/nationalist element occurred when the de-Ba'athification issue came on the agenda in January 2010.

Despite apparent reactions against the de-Ba'athification commission, especially from the U.S. military, President Obama and Vice President Biden have expressed full confidence in the Iraq government and its handling of the election process in key public addresses. The hopes of Iraqi nationalists received another blow after public remarks by U.S. Ambassador Christopher Hill during his visit to Washington, DC in February 2010, when he essentially minimized the problem of the de-Ba'athification issue and went as far as effectively embracing Ahmad Chalabi's legal argument in using Article 7 of the Iraq constitution to exclude electoral candidates (the argument is flawed because Article 7 refers to a law which has so far yet to be adopted and which must also handle sectarianism and racism as a basis for the exclusion of candidates). Instead of a repeat of the positive tendencies of January 2009, we are therefore suddenly looking at a situation in which a low voter turnout or even organized boycotts among secular Iraqi nationalists and Sunnis are distinct possibilities.

In sum, then, with the tentative nature of al-Maliki's transformation to an Iraqi nationalist, its limited extension in time (basically January–April 2009), and the robust moves by both Iran and the United States to prevent him from holding on to it (or returning to it), the final outcome of the March 7 election – at least in terms of coalition-forming for the next government – may well turn out to be more similar to 2005 than many had hoped just a year ago. In that sort of context, knowledge about the Byzantine complexities of Iraq's insurgent landscape may also remain relevant for much longer than expected.

Reidar Visser *is a Research Fellow at the Norwegian Institute of International Affairs. Many of his writings are available from his widely cited Iraq website, www.historiae.org.*

PART I

The Counterinsurgency Years

Chapter 1

Before Counterinsurgency

Post-2005 Provincial Election Terrorist Trends in Iraq

By Mahan Abedin
March 10, 2005
Terrorism Monitor 3 (5)

Half-heartedly trumpeted as a potential breakthrough against the insurgency, the 2005 Iraq provincial elections – in the short-term at least – seem to have made the security difficulties even more intractable. Indeed, any wishful thinking by the U.S. military, political planners in Iraq, and their local allies was summarily dismissed by then Air Force General Richard Meyers, who predicted that the insurgency could last for more than 10 years.

Tracking the evolution of the Iraqi insurgency from its opening shots in May 2003 to the present yields some interesting generalizations. The most important development revolves around the identity and ultimate objectives of the insurgents. Indeed, what started as a low-key campaign by remnants of the former regime and outraged Iraqi nationalists, in due course, evolved into a serious conflict largely dominated by Islamic and jihadist organizations. This is not to ignore or understate the continuing role of Ba'ath remnants and secular Arab/Iraqi nationalists in the insurgency, but to emphasize that the overall character and theme of the resistance is now Islamic.

Moreover, insofar as the Ba'ath/nationalist and Islamic/jihadist dichotomy is concerned, a clear division in operational tactics is evident. While the dominant Islamic insurgent organizations have opted for mass-casualty bombings and the whole-sale slaughter of members of the new Iraqi military and security forces, the Ba'ath network has largely confined its attacks to coalition armies and leaders of prominent Shi'a Islamic organizations. The Ba'ath network also allegedly planned for the post-occupation insurgency, with sabotage of key installations and penetration of the new power structures constituting key priorities [1].

While there is a proliferation of small insurgent organizations, four groups have emerged as the largest and most active. They all profess to be Islamic and all but one of them can easily be categorized as Salafi/jihadi. While all of them share certain core objectives – the most important being the ejection of foreign armies from Iraq – there are important differences amongst them.

Army of Ansar al-Sunna

Jaysh Ansar al-Sunna (Army of the Protectors of the Traditions) has emerged as arguably the most active and lethal of the insurgent organizations. It specializes in suicide bombings, spectacular attacks against coalition armies and Iraqi security forces, and the seizing and beheading of Iraqi government agents and foreigners.

Ansar al-Sunna officially declared its formation in an Internet statement on September 20, 2003. Western analysts have often assumed that Ansar al-Sunna is a splinter group from the largely Kurdish Ansar al-Islam, with Sunni Arabs and foreign al-Qaeda linked militants at its core. Despite the plausibility of these assumptions, there is no real evidence to validate them. The group's activities in the Arab regions of northern Iraq (particularly around Mosul) have been seized upon to hypothesize a link with Ansar al-Islam. But the fact is that Ansar al-Sunna is active throughout the entire Sunni heartland of Iraq – from the lawless areas immediately to the south of Baghdad to the epicenter of the insurgency in the al-Anbar province.

Ansar al-Sunna has carried out dozens of major suicide bombings, one of the most spectacular being the suicide bombing at a U.S. Army base near Mosul on December 21, 2004 that killed 22 people, including 14 U.S. military personnel. In August 2004 the group seized and killed 12 Nepalese hostages. It posted the video of the massacre on its website with the group's emir, Abu Abdullah al-Hassan bin Mahmoud (wrongly identified as a Jordanian) claiming the Nepalese were slaughtered for "fighting the Muslims and serving the Jews and the Christians" and "believing in Buddha as their God." The group has released dozens of gruesome videos showing the last moments of hostages, with graphic pictures of beheadings and shootings. For instance in early November 2004 Ansar al-Sunna released a video showing the beheading of Iraqi Major Hussein Shunun in Mosul, claiming that he had been slaughtered "after confessing to collaborating with the enemy."

The Islamic Army in Iraq

Al-Jaysh al-Islami fi'l Iraq differs from the other jihadist insurgent organizations insofar as it does not belong to the salafist tendency. Broadly speaking, it is an inclusive Islamic organization with Iraqi nationalist tendencies. Despite being overwhelmingly Sunni in composition and ideology there are believed to be some Shi'as in its ranks. The precise circumstances around its emergence are unclear, but it is assumed that the group was established in the summer of 2003.

In terms of operational tactics, the Islamic Army avoids bombings (suicidal or otherwise) and instead specializes in targeted assassinations of Iraqi government agents and low profile attacks on coalition forces. Its operations are predominantly centered on the lawless regions immediately to the south of Baghdad and in the capital itself. The Islamic Army also seizes hostages, but unlike other Islamist organizations it seems to specialize in intensively interrogating its captives. For instance, the group seized an Iranian diplomat in August 2004 on the road from Baghdad to Karbala. It released the diplomat the following month after ascertaining his "piety" and "that the Iranian government did not intend to interfere in Iraqi matters." Previously the group had demanded the Iranian government release 500 Iraqi POW's from the 1980-1988 Iran-Iraq War. Also in July 2004, an Egyptian embassy official was seized and held for three days by a group calling itself the Lions of Allah Brigade – likely a unit affiliated to the Islamic Army. Like the Iranian diplomat, the Egyptian embassy official was subjected to intensive interrogations – an indicator, perhaps, that the Islamic Army has former Iraqi security agents in its ranks. In late December 2004, the Islamic Army released two French hostages that had been seized earlier that August.

Nonetheless the Islamic Army can be as ruthless as the other insurgent organization when it comes to the ultimate fate of hostages. In late August 2004 the group executed Enzo Baldoni, an Italian journalist and a volunteer for the Red Cross in Iraq, after the Italian government refused to withdraw its forces from Iraq. Moreover on April 15, 2004, the Islamic Army in Iraq assassinated Khalil Naimi, first secretary to the Iranian embassy in Baghdad. Naimi was accused of being a senior Iranian intelligence officer in charge of collecting information on the Iraqi "resistance."

The Islamic Army is also active on the propaganda front. For instance on January 2, 2005 it issued a message to the American people, in which it underlines its principles and credentials thus: "The whole world sees that clearly in the crimes committed by your army, every time they have imprisoned our sons with no right when compared to the actions of our army, which questions anyone it seizes before they are even charged."

The al-Zarqawi Network

The terror group al-Qaeda in Iraq, led by the notorious Jordanian Abu Musab al-Zarqawi, has received most of the attention of the western media. Openly loyal to Osama bin Laden and operating under the name al-Qaeda in the Land of the Two Rivers, the al-Zarqawi network is most likely behind the recent spate of bombings against Shi'a mosques and other sectarian targets. Another distinctive feature of this organization is that it is the only insurgent group with substantial numbers of non-Iraqi Arabs at its core.

While the al-Zarqawi network has stepped up its terrorist campaign in the weeks after the 2005 provincial elections – probably in the hope of exacerbating the current political stalemate – there are also signs that it could be in serious trouble. The Iraqi Hizballah Movement has recently reported that Syrian security officials have handed over useful information on the senior operatives and safe houses of the al-Zarqawi network to Iraqi and American security agents [2]. While the Iraqi media (particularly those run by Shi'a Islamic parties) generally exaggerate the Syrian connection, it is nonetheless interesting that these allegations coincide with the recent handover of Sabawi Ibrahim al-Hassan by the Syrian government to Iraqi and U.S. officials. It is also worth noting that the al-Zarqawi network has lost a string of senior operatives in recent months, the latest being the capture of Taleb al-Dulaymi in late February 2005. Whether the al-Zarqawi network is eclipsed in the near future – in terms of lethality and visibility – by the other insurgent organizations, remains to be seen.

Ansar al-Islam

Ansar al-Islam is the oldest of the Islamic insurgent groups in Iraq. The rise of the Army of Ansar al-Sunna was generally viewed as signaling the demise of Ansar al-Islam. Surely enough, little has been heard of the activities of the group since late 2003. Most recent open-source materials on Ansar al-Islam concentrate on its alleged European networks and trafficking of would-be mujahideen from countries like Italy to Iraq.

However any predictions of the demise of this complex organization are likely to prove premature. While most of its senior and quality members have been killed, detained or dispersed, Kurdish security officials have consistently maintained that the battle against this organization is likely to prove a long-term one. Indeed, in the event of deteriorating relations between regional Kurdish parties and the emerging new central authority in Baghdad, Ansar al-Islam could stage a full revival and might even be manipulated by forces anxious to suppress Kurdish nationalism.

Conclusion

The Iraqi insurgency initially deteriorated sharply after the handover of limited power to Prime Minister Ayad Alawi and his government in late June 2004. The catalyst for this was the blunting of the "de-Ba'athification" process and the appointment of former Ba'athists to key positions. The most controversial of these is Alawi's Defense Minister, Hazem Shaalan, whose chief mission over the past eight months has been to make statements and allegations that are largely irrelevant to the situation on the ground. Shaalan has routinely blamed Syria and Iran for the insurgency, in addition to implicating Shi'a parties in the violence (an odd allegation given that these organizations have borne the brunt of the relentless terrorist campaign). Shaalan had also repeatedly predicted the capture of al-Zarqawi, most recently in late February 2005 [3].

The new Iraqi government that would likely form in the coming weeks has one very important advantage over the Alawi government: It is an elected government and can capitalize on all the benefits that this brings. However, whether it can undermine the insurgency and improve the security situation rests on its ability to develop a committed and loyal security and intelligence system. Alawi is widely accused of bringing back former Ba'ath intelligence officers who were not only incompetent as intelligence operatives but whose loyalty to the new Iraq was not beyond dispute.

The largely Shi'a coalition that will likely dominate the next government has promised to re-institute the rigorous "de-Ba'athification" system put in place by former U.S. Administrator in Iraq, Pual Bremer. But to have a meaningful impact on the insurgency, it will have to confront the emerging political representatives of the insurgents. In this respect, two organizations are of particular interest. The first is the Association of Muslim Scholars (AMS), a grouping that brings together Sunni clergy, has links to several Islamic insurgent groups and has often used its influence to free foreign hostages. However, its widespread links with the insurgents is clearly problematic and needs to be addressed accordingly. The Iraqi National Congress recently published an editorial demanding the AMS clarify its position on the terrorist campaign [4]. The other organization is the Iraqi Islamic Party led by Muhsin Abdul Hamid. While this Sunni party's links with the insurgents has not been established beyond doubt, it nonetheless has an ambiguous stance on the insurgents. While it condemns the more outrageous terrorist incidents, it refuses to denounce attacks on coalition forces.

Given the proliferation of insurgent organizations and the substantial support these groups enjoy in the Arab Sunni heartlands of Iraq, the most that can be expected of the new government and its western backers is the partial containment of the violence. However, there is ample scope for the insurgency to become much worse in the decisive months ahead, especially if the insurgent organizations continue to develop their connections with sympathetic political and religious organizations.

Notes

1. *Al-Mu'tamar*, November 4, 2004, (Baghdad daily belonging to the Iraqi National Congress).
2. *Al-Bayyinah* (Baghdad), March 5, 2005.
3. Al-Sharqiyah TV (Baghdad), February 27, 2005.
4. *Al-Mu'tamar*, February 16, 2005.

Foreign Involvement in the Iraqi Insurgency

By Ahmed Hashim
May 10, 2005
Terrorism Monitor 2 (16)

The Iraqi insurgency spiked again in August 2004 when radical Shi'a cleric Muqtada al-Sadr took the offensive against the transitional Iraq government of then Prime Minister Ayad Allawi and the Multi-National Force–Iraq. It was optimistically believed that following the return to Iraqi sovereignty at the end of June 2004, the insurgency by both Sunni and Shi'a groups would wither away. It has not, and the issue of foreign involvement with insurgent groups – which has hovered in the background since the insurgency began – came to the foreground in the summer of 2004. U.S. General Richard Myers, then chairman of the Joint Chiefs of Staff, highlighted the issue with regard to Syria when he adamantly stated: "We know that the pathway into Iraq for many foreign fighters is through

Syria. It's a fact. We know it. The Syrians know it" [1]. In July 2004, the Iraqi Defense Minister Hazem Shaalan claimed that Iran was interfering in Iraqi domestic affairs by allowing or promoting infiltration into Iraq, which has led to a significant contretemps between the two neighbors.

The question of foreign insurgents in Iraq presents a particularly tangled problem. Layers of complexity beneath a seemingly simple surface make it difficult to untangle fact from fiction when discussing the issue. Though the Bush administration has maintained that attacks are the work of "regime dead-enders" and foreign infiltrators, hard empirical evidence – often from the U.S. military forces – indicates that the foreign element is minuscule. Evidence which shows that of 8,000 suspected insurgents detained in Iraq, only 127 hold foreign passports, supports this latter claim. But a simple head-count does not tell the whole story. The insurgency's foreign element has had a greater impact than mere numbers would lead us to believe.

Un-sponsored Foreign Insurgents

This insurgency has seen its share of outraged and disgruntled individuals, Arab nationalists, and "unsponsored" religious extremists make their way into Iraq to fight the foreign occupation. Many Palestinians were recruited to fight in Iraq in 2002, and some joined the regime's irregular force, the *Fedayeen* Saddam [2]. Similarly, large numbers of Syrian volunteers with close tribal and cultural links to Iraqis across the border felt it was their duty to fight. These individuals received no encouragement from their government. One such fighter, a 26-year-old Syrian named "Abed," decided to fight in Iraq barely a week after the war began because, as he put it, "there was something inside that made me explode." Another, a Saudi captured in Iraq named Mohammad Qadir Hussein, was a poor, disgruntled individual who had no military training, but who was motivated by an abiding desire to help other Muslims in distress [3].

The collapse of Iraqi border controls facilitated the entry of un-sponsored insurgents into Iraq, while Iraqi middlemen or facilitators provided logistical support (i.e. food, directions, and weapons and ammunition) once these individuals had gained entry into the country. Unsponsored foreign infiltrators are then "passed on" to Sunni *imams* who became their mentors. Many of these foreign infiltrators entered Iraq before the start of Operation Iraqi Freedom (OIF). While poorly trained and ill-equipped, a substantial number of them fought doggedly and to the death in some of the battles between Iraqi irregular forces and the Coalition advancing from the south. After the end of OIF, some returned home, while others remained and fought in the insurgency. Many of these gravitated towards the more disciplined jihadist insurgents.

Non-State Actors and Organizations

Foreign insurgents who come in as part of a "package" sent into Iraq by non-state actors are a more formidable force than un-sponsored foreign infiltrators. There is growing evidence that Iraq has begun to attract foreign Islamists and anti-American groups such as al-Qaeda and the Tawhid organization of the elusive and enigmatic Jordanian-Palestinian terrorist, Abu Musab al-Zarqawi, for whom Iraq is a new and easily accessible battlefield.

Uncertainty regarding the level or depth of al-Qaeda presence in Iraq remains due to a lack of non-politicized intelligence on its activities in that country. Osama bin Laden and his subordinates did not think much of Saddam Hussein and his regime, with evidence showing that the feelings were mutual. In the early days of the war, when there was an influx of foreign volunteers into Iraq, Saddam apparently warned the Ba'ath party against close links with outsiders, especially religious extremists [4]. A senior Islamist operative (now deceased) allegedly authored a text entitled "The Future of Iraq and the Peninsula After Baghdad's Fall: The Religious, Military, Political and Economic Future." The work argues that the fall of the Ba'athist regime was "better for the Islamists than the victory of the Iraqi Ba'athists, because the collapse of Arab Ba'athism means the collapse of the atheist, pan-Arab slogans that swept the Muslim nation…the demise of the Ba'ath government in Iraq heralds the hoisting of the Islamic banner over the debris" [5]. Such fighters were attracted to Iraq following the war precisely in order to fight the U.S. presence in that country for the sake of Islam.

Once in Iraq, "sponsored" jihadists needed to create a logistical infrastructure, as infiltrating heavy weapons and explosives across the borders of Iraq's neighbors is difficult [6]. For this they needed the help of Iraqis. Mutual suspicion between Sunni Islamists and former regime loyalists, secular-minded nationalists, and tribal elements actively opposing the Coalition does not mean that the latter groups are averse to providing logistical support for the former. Attempts by foreign jihadist organizations to operate in Iraq depend on the resources, protection and concealment provided to their fighters by Iraqis. Unable to enter into Iraq with the resources they need or blend in with the local population, these foreign elements would be lost without support from within Iraq.

Salafists in Iraq

The importance of the foreign jihadists who adhere to a strict interpretation of Sunni Islam (known properly as Salafism but popularly as Wahhabism) lies in three distinct areas. Firstly, these foreign jihadists have coupled with local Iraqi Salafists – who emerged into the open following the downfall of the Saddam regime – to successfully introduce a cohesive and extreme ideology to the public. While many of these groups, like the Mujahideen al-Salafiyah in Balad, have even reached out to members of the former Fedayeen Saddam as long as the latter drop their allegiance to Saddam.

Secondly, they have increased the prospects for communal violence by waging a campaign of deliberate and focused attacks against leaders of other Muslim communities, promoters of "moral laxity," and non-Muslims. In the fall of 2003, Islamists were particularly active in Mosul, where they attacked a nunnery, killed a well-known writer, bombed a popular cinema, and torched four liquor stores. Some of the worst atrocities came with the bombings of Christian churches in Iraq.

Thirdly, they have been responsible for the suicide bombing campaigns in Iraq between early fall 2003 and summer 2004. August 2003 saw three massive car bombings. Some of the most devastating suicide attacks came in mid-November 2003 against Italians in Nasiriyah and in mid-January 2004 outside a Coalition Provisional Authority (CPA) compound in Baghdad. In March 2004, the Shi'a religious celebration of Ashura witnessed multiple suicide bombings, which had killed hundreds [7].

However, as of summer 2004, it is increasingly evident that the different agendas and modus operandi of the nationalist Iraqi insurgency and their ostensible jihadist allies have caused considerable tensions between these groups. While they admire the motivation and skills of the foreigners, many mainstream Islamist and tribal insurgents resent an ideological agenda, which has resulted in the killing of Iraqis simply for not adhering to a strict religious line. The foreign fighter's apparent blood lust, which has led to indiscriminate attacks and the beheading of abductees, also angers Iraqi nationalists [8]. In early summer 2004, nationalist insurgents in Fallujah were about to assault a group of foreign jihadists based in the Jolan suburb, led by a Saudi with the nom de guerre of Abu Abdullah. Later, insurgent "authorities" in Fallujah – largely made up of former military personnel and Iraqi police and led by clerics – succeeded in evicting a number of non-Iraqi terrorists from the area.

State Support for the Insurgency

The Bush Administration has accused two of Iraq's neighbors, Syria and Iran, of facilitating or actively encouraging foreign fighters to cross the Iraqi border. The singling out of these two countries, despite the fact that Jordan, Saudi Arabia and Turkey also maintain porous borders with Iraq, reflects the political dynamics at play as the U.S. tries to stabilize the greater Middle East.

Syria and Iran fear the U.S. will succeed in its (unstated) goal of implementing a pro-American "puppet regime" in Baghdad. Such a regime would allow U.S. bases to operate in Iraq, giving U.S. forces the ability to threaten these countries. Both Tehran and Damascus see each other as the next U.S. target for regime change. The logical response is to support anti-American operations in Iraq, thereby ensuring that the Bush Administration remains mired there. However, this is a very risky endeavor on many levels.

Both countries understand that to overtly support anti-American forces in Iraq risks incurring America's wrath. Not long after the end of OIF, warnings from the Bush administration to Syria and Iran not to help the nascent insurgency were issued from a position of strength. Both Syria and Iran bent over backwards to avoid irritating a U.S. that was itching for a fight. Indeed, there were reports that U.S. Special Operations Units undertook actions across the border into Syria and actually clashed with Syrian border guards. Therefore, the growing U.S. problems in Iraq by fall 2003 must have been a source of considerable satisfaction to both Tehran and Damascus.

While neither could overtly support the insurgency, it is not too far-fetched to assume that they did so covertly or turned a blind eye to pro-insurgent activities conducted by elements within their respective countries. Both Syria and Iran have domestic constituencies that are thoroughly hostile to the U.S., and furthermore, alarmed by the belligerent attitude taken by Washington towards their respective countries. Arab nationalists in Syria, for example, are inclined to lend support to the remnants of the Iraqi Ba'ath party. Meanwhile, Iranian groups like the Islamic Revolutionary Guard Corps might be inclined to support Shi'a insurgents such as the Jaysh al-Mahdi militia led by Muqtada al-Sadr.

But there are attendant risks. Firstly, neither country wants continued instability on their borders. Secondly, neither country is particularly enamored of the leading ideological elements responsible for the violence in Iraq. As a regime dominated by the minority ʻAlawis (thoroughly despised by Sunni extremists), Syria does not want to see the growth of Sunni extremism in Iraq. Nor does secular Damascus wish to see a theocratic Baghdad, despite its sympathy for and traditional alliance with the Shi'as. For its part, Iran is hardly likely to support Sunni extremists or Arab nationalists. Both are antithetical to Tehran's agenda. Instead, the Iranians continue to support Shi'a groups that are not fighting the U.S., in the plausible and logical expectation that these parties will play a leading role in Iraqi politics once the U.S. has left Iraq.

So, while the restraints of Middle Eastern realpolitik keep states from openly supporting foreign insurgents against the coalition in Iraq, there are many other factors and organizations that contribute to this continuing and complex problem.

Notes

1. Quoted in *The Washington Times*, April 30, 2004.
2. Islamist groups, on the other hand, recruited from among the growing population of disgruntled Islamists in Jordanian cities such as Maʻan.
3. Personal interviews with the author.
4. *New York Times*, January 14, 2004.
5. Quoted in *al-Hayat*, December 20, 2003.
6. Cross-border traffic between Iraq and its neighbors by smugglers and tribes existed even in the best of times when Iraq was able to police its borders. Now even though the borders are not effectively policed, foreign infiltrators are unlikely to come into Iraq on their Sports Utility Vehicles – which outrun the two-wheel drives of the border patrols – laden with large quantities of light weaponry or explosives. Nor do they have to since Iraq is one huge ammunition dump.
7. *The Independent* (London), March 07, 2004.
8. For more see *The Daily Star* (Beirut), July 16, 2004.

Terrorism and Complex Warfare in Iraq

By Ahmed Hashim
May 19, 2005
Terrorism Monitor 2 (12)

Few observers of the post-Saddam Iraqi scene expected an insurgency to break out in Iraq so shortly after conventional combat operations were officially declared to be over. When the insurgency erupted in May 2003, there was little concern on the part of senior U.S. strategic planners or the Coalition Provisional Authority (CPA). In the early days, insurgents, often amateurish and clumsy, were described as former regime "dead-enders" who would be soundly defeated. Instead, the violence escalated over the course of the summer, and by fall 2003 a series of spectacular and bloody attacks on coalition forces, non-governmental organizations and others had captured the attention of the administration, the military and the media. These deadly attacks included the assassination of Ayatollah Muhammad Baqr al-Hakim, and the destruction of the Jordanian Embassy, the United Nations headquarters, and the Red Cross building. By October 2003, administration officials began admitting that they were surprised by the intensity and resilience of the insurgency [1]. In early November 2003, dire prognostications began to appear, especially from U.S. intelligence agencies, arguing that the insurgency was gaining support among the populace [2]. By the end of that month, understanding the insurgency and dealing with it had risen to the top of the U.S. agenda.

As of May 2005, the insurgency in Iraq has derailed U.S. political goals and continues to threaten the stability of a new sovereign political entity since June 30, 2004. Moreover, the tenuous security situation in the country since May 2003 has contributed enormously to the slow pace of reconstruction and reconciliation.

The Onset of the Insurgency

The insurgency began in May 2003 with the outbreak of violence by the Sunni Arab population in what has come to be known as the "Sunni Triangle." The grievances of that minority group, including the threat to their identity in the new post-Sunni Iraq, fanned the flames of violence [3]. Challenged by the total collapse of an already ineffective police force, law and order in Iraq also faced the rise of vicious criminal gangs that terrorized the Iraqi populace and engaged in massive smuggling across the country's unguarded borders. Saddam Hussein had let out of his prisons over 200,000 hardened and petty criminals. Coalition forces simply did not have enough manpower to police Iraq, while at the same time fully engage in combating the insurgency.

The impact of the situation on the Sunni Arab commercial class aroused the fears of middle-class Sunni Arabs. Both classes would have been an invaluable asset to the Coalition had their grievances been addressed from the outset. As one Sunni observer put it: "If the Americans came and developed our general services, brought work for our people and transferred their technology to us, then we would not have been so disappointed. But it is not acceptable to us as human beings that, after one year, America is still not able to bring us electricity" [4]. The CPA initially made little effort to reach out to Sunni Arabs. This indifference to the community that had held the reins of power for over 70 years was seen as a calculated step by leading Sunnis to fully marginalize that community in the new Iraq [5].

But what do the insurgents want? At a basic level they want a redress of their grievances, both material and non-material. At a more complex level, they want the U.S. to leave Iraq, because only then, do they feel that these grievances can be redressed. While many of the groups have articulated these issues in writings and statements, almost none have articulated a vision of a free, post-U.S. Iraq. The insurgency is not a monolithic or united movement directed by a leadership with a unitary and disciplined ideological vision. Moreover, some insurgents may have calculated that at this stage they do not need an elaborate political and socioeconomic vision for a "free" Iraq; that is to say, it is enough to articulate a desire to be free of foreign occupation to gain the support of the people. Furthermore, it is likely that these myriad groups who cooperate with one another and coordinate attacks at the operational level have profound political differences, and wish to avoid fratricidal conflicts. As one insurgent leader put it: "We first want to expel the infidel invaders before anything else."

Social Composition of the Sunni Insurgency

The insurgency does not have the support of all Sunni Arabs, but its range encompasses all classes, both urban and rural. Its ranks include students, intellectuals, former soldiers, tribal youths, farmers, and Islamists. It also has the tacit support of many within the Sunni Arab community. While many Sunni Arabs may not actively support the insurgents, they are not reticent about expressing their admiration for the insurgents' activities. For example, a member of the Fallujah administrative council openly stated that insurgents are "Mujahideen" or holy warriors. "We don't know them," he said, but then ventured to add, "Al Anbar (the province where Fallujah is located) has a bigger nationalist consciousness than the rest of Iraq. We are also more religious. We consider this resistance a religious duty and a nationalist one as well." [6] Similarly, some members of the Iraqi security forces have expressed sympathy and support for the insurgents. An Iraqi police officer, who works closely with U.S. forces during the day and at night offers intelligence about his day-time colleagues over to the resistance, had the following to say:

I have good relations with the American soldiers in my work, but I live in a different situation. The Americans have given us nothing – no jobs and no hopes. They are thieves. They break into our houses without warning and stand on our heads. This is why the people are getting more hurt and more angry. This is why we want revenge. The resistance here is growing stronger every day, first, because the American are occupiers and we will fight them until they leave the country, and second we fight to return Saddam Hussein to power because he is the only man who can return Iraq back to safety within an hour [7].

Evolution of the Insurgency

Professional groups undertook some of the insurgent attacks in the early summer of 2003 [8]. However, for the most part, these hit-and-run attacks were undertaken by amateurs and individuals hired by former regime loyalists. By fall/winter 2003, matters had gotten worse. The insurgents became more proficient. While U.S. forces had killed most of the amateurs, the Tactics, Techniques and Procedures (TTPs) of the surviving insurgents became more lethal as a result of experience [9]. Their proficiency also increased as former professional military personnel increasingly opted for the path of violence out of nationalistic and religious reasons. Disgruntled military personnel, with no profound sympathy for the defunct regime, but outraged over the loss of status and privilege as a result of the disbanding of the armed forces, were increasingly active in the ranks of the insurgency by fall 2003. Senior or mid-ranking officers would often mentor or advise novice but enthusiastic insurgent cells. Following the terrible losses of November 2003, U.S. forces targeted the former regime insurgents with greater vigor [10].

The decline in importance and fortune of former regime loyalists allowed for an Islamo-nationalist element to gain prominence within the insurgency. Made up of former military personnel and motivated by the preaching of the Sunni clergy, the insurgency has benefited tremendously from a fusion between nationalist and Islamist sentiments among Sunnis. This transition has been bolstered by the Sunni clergy, who have begun to shed their traditionally insignificant role in community affairs in favor of more active participation.

The Role of the Mosques and the Sunni Clergy in the Insurgency

Insurgent organization and political indoctrination is not transparent. This is not surprising, as Sunni mosques increasingly have become centers of opposition to the Coalition. Traditionally, the Sunni clergy has not been as politically active as their Shi'a counterparts in mobilization of the populace against perceived injustices or inequities. This has begun to change both in Iraq and in the rest of the Arab world. Iraq has witnessed a rising tide of political activism among the mainstream clerical establishment and the emergence of younger politically active clergymen (*imam*) with clear-cut Salafist tendencies. Friday sermons have been a traditional way of channeling political and social discontent in Muslim societies. In Iraq, the Friday sermons by both Sunni and Shi'a clerics resonate with a population that has no notable or charismatic politician or lay leadership to turn to in this time of stress and humiliation.

In this context, the statement of an insurgent leader that the "most prominent resistance is the Islamic resistance" should not be doubted. The pro-Saddam group lost considerable power and legitimacy with the apprehension of the former Iraqi leader in mid-December 2003. Moreover, many Islamic-nationalist insurgents blame the Ba'athists and the former regime for the disasters that have befallen the country. These Islamo-nationalist insurgents showed greater motivation and dedication than the free-lance insurgents of the early months of the insurgency. More ominously, new insurgents showed a dramatic improvement in small-unit fighting skills during the bloody outbreak of fighting in April 2004. They have shown an ability to stand and fight (rather than merely to "shoot and scoot" or "pray and spray" as in the past), to conduct coordinated small unit ambushes and attacks against U.S. forces, and to target on supply convoys.

Young men from the various Sunni Arab tribes have also begun to swell the ranks of the insurgency. Infuriated by what they saw as outrageous behavior by U.S. forces, tribes such as the 50,000-strong Albueissas have played a prominent role in the tribal-based insurgency; its members claimed that their fighters shot down the U.S. Army chinook, which resulted in the deaths of 17 U.S. troops in early November 2003.

While this analysis has detailed much of the Sunni components of the insurgency, it is important to keep in mind the rise of the Shi'a resistance as well. By the end of March 2004 – and to everyone's surprise – significant elements of the Shi'a community rose in open rebellion against the Coalition, when the firebrand cleric Muqtada al-Sadr unleashed his Jaysh al-Mahdi militia against the Coalition. Suddenly, the coalition was faced with the unsavory prospect of a two-front war. The precipitating factors of the Shi'a insurgency were again the mistakes and failed policies of the CPA, but as with all conflicts there were underlying causes for the Shi'a uprising [11]. Understanding this aspect of the insurgency would require a detailed and comprehensive look at Iraq's Shi'a population, its composition, and the goals of its leaders and people.

From Low-Level Insurgency to International Jihad

There is growing evidence that the insurgency in Iraq has begun to attract foreign Islamists and anti-American groups, such as al-Qaeda, for whom Iraq is a new and easily accessible battlefield. Foreign Islamists infiltrating into Iraq would be expected to make common cause with local Sunni Arab Salafis who have emerged in cities such as Ramadi, Fallujah, and Khaldiya and Rutba. One insurgent leader in Rutba – a former conscript in the Iraqi Army – told a Western journalist that his group is Islamic and has learned from al-Qaeda, although it had no direct contact with that organization: "The resistance is Islamic, we are ordered by God, we have no relation to that party…al-Qaeda is an Islamic group and we've learnt from them, and we learnt much from Osama bin Laden. He is our sheikh also" [12].

However, the mutual suspicion between Sunni Islamists on the one hand and former regime loyalists, secular-minded nationalists, and tribal elements who are actively opposing the Coalition on the other hand does not mean that the latter groups would be averse to providing logistical support for the former [13]. The attempts by "freelance jihadists" itching to fight the U.S. and by al-Qaeda elements to infiltrate Iraq can only be successful if such foreign volunteers are provided with the resources and protection needed to undertake their missions. Jihadists do not cross the border into Iraq with the provisions they need, nor can they easily blend into the local population without local support.

The number of foreign infiltrators is small and will continue to be dwarfed by local members of the insurgency. However, the infiltrators may have an impact beyond their numbers. The importance of the Salafis/foreign jihadists lies in two distinct areas. First, they have contributed to increasing the prospects for communal violence or complex war by waging a campaign of terror deliberately focused on leaders of other communities, promoters of "moral laxity," and non-Muslims. They have derided the Shi'as and their rituals and have even attacked and defaced posters of Shi'a religious figures. In fall 2003, Islamists were particularly active in Mosul, where they attacked a nunnery, killed a well-known writer, bombed a popular cinema, and torched four liquor stores.

Secondly, the rise of Iraqi Salafism and the infiltration of foreign Salafis and al-Qaeda operatives may explain the rise of massive suicide bombing campaigns in Iraq between early fall 2003 and late January 2004. The month of August 2003 saw three massive car bombings and the numbers grew that fall. Some of the most devastating suicide bombings came in mid-November 2003 against the Italians in Nasiriyah and in mid-January 2004 outside one of the gates of the CPA compound in Baghdad. The summer of 2004 has witnessed a revival of the suicide-bombing phenomenon and an increase in kidnappings and targeted assassinations. These are all tactics associated with foreign extremist groups.

Conclusion

The Iraq Government, which will take over on July 1, 2005, simply has no way of dealing effectively with the ongoing crisis within the country. This puts the burden on U.S. and other Coalition forces. It is likely that as Iraq staggers uncertainly towards a qualified sovereignty, the security situation will deteriorate. Indeed, it could worsen dramatically. Following the hand-over, Coalition forces may possibly witness the emergence of "complex warfare patterns." National resistance, politico-economic violence by organized criminal gangs, and incipient civil war pitting ethnic and religious groups against one another in a massive fight over "who gets what, when and how" could become the norm rather than an all-out war of national liberation. Should this occur, the prospects for U.S. success in Iraq in bringing about security as a stepping-stone towards reconstruction and political stability will be non-existent.

Notes

1. See Brian Knowlton, "U.S. Surprised in Iraq by Insurgents' Fight," *International Herald Tribune*, October 27, 2003.
2. See Jonathan Landay, "CIA Has Bleak Analysis of Iraq," *Philadelphia Inquirer*, November 12, 2003.
3. See "Iraq's Sunnis seethe over loss of prestige," *Houston Chronicle*, June 06, 2003 (accessed on-line).
4. Quoted in Rory McCarthy, "False dawn of peace lost in violent storm," *The Guardian*, April 08, 2004.
5. Interviews in Karrada, Baghdad, November 2003.
6. Quoted in Charles Glover, "Smiles and Shrugs Speak Volumes About Nature of Attacks On American Troops," *The Financial Times*, September 25, 2003, (accessed on-line).
7. For the story and quotes see Damien McElroy, "This is Jabir: Policeman By Day, Terrorist By

Night," *Sunday Telegraph*, October 19, 2003.

8. See William Booth and Daniel Williams, "U.S. Soldiers Face Persistent Resistance," *Washington Post*, June 10, 2003.

9. Interviews in Baghdad, Ramadi, Balad, Tikrit, and Mosul, November 2003.

10. Only April 2004 has been worse in terms of U.S. casualties.

11. For an extensive and authoritative analysis of CPA missteps – simply one of many made by that organization over the course of its existence – vis-à-vis Muqtada see Rajiv Chandrasekaran and Anthony Shadid, "U.S. Targeted Fiery Cleric In Risky Move," *Washington Post*, April 11, 2004.

12. See James Hider, "We follow Usama, Not Saddam, Say Desert Guerillas," *The Times*, December 27, 2003.

13. For an analysis of growing cooperation between Iraqi insurgents and foreign Islamists see "Die irakische Guerilla wird immer schlagkraftiger," Neue Zurcher Zeitung, October 23, 2003 (accessed on-line).

Anbar Province and Emerging Trends in the Iraqi Insurgency

By Mahan Abedin
July 15, 2005
Terrorism Monitor 3 (14)

The recent upsurge of fighting in Iraq's restive al-Anbar province is one of many indicators that some of Iraq's insurgents are evolving into organized guerilla formations. This comes at a time of daily multiple bombings in Baghdad and other cities, which have elevated the insurgency to a new level of intensity. Since early May 2005, the U.S. military has been conducting a series of extensive operations in al-Anbar, particularly along the border with Syria, which allegedly serves as the primary infiltration point into Iraq. But given the size of this western province, and the implacable enmity of a great majority of its inhabitants to the U.S. military presence in Iraq, these operations are unlikely to stem the tide against the insurgency.

The sheer significance of the U.S. Marines (around 1,000 strong and supported by air power) having to fight near-conventional battles with well-armed and determined rebels along the Syrian border near the town of Qaim in early May 2005 was not lost on the newly elected Iraqi government. In a typically knee-jerk reaction, and one in which will likely prove to be of little consequence, the Iraqi authorities announced the creation of a new anti-terrorism unit, to be managed jointly by the ministries of defense and interior [1]. In yet another attempt to show their determination to get to grips with a worsening insurgency, the Iraqi authorities announced the capture of a leading bomb expert who allegedly supplied car bombs to insurgent groups in the Mosul area. According to the Iraqi security forces, Ali Salim Yousef is a confidant of the leader of the Abu Talha organization, an insurgent group with loose links to the al-Zarqawi network [2].

Defiant and hard to verify pronouncements by the fledgling Iraqi government notwithstanding, the battles of early May 2005 and subsequent joint operations by the U.S. military and Iraqi security forces in al-Anbar point toward emerging trends in the Iraqi insurgency. Many villages and outposts in the province are under effective insurgent control and this is clearly boosting the organizational capabilities of the rebels. The most ominous implication of this revolves around the very real possibility of insurgents cohering into organized guerrilla formations and possibly inflicting serious casualties on the U.S. military in Iraq.

That the latest trend in the evolution of the Iraqi insurgency is unfolding in the al-Anbar province is not in the least surprising. From the opening shots of the insurgency in May 2003 to the present, almost every development of consequence, in terms of the insurgents' tactics and strategy, has unfolded in this vast and sparsely populated western region of Iraq. The first serious demonstrations against the occupation occurred in Fallujah, where several demonstrators were shot dead by U.S. forces, an event that deepened the animosity of the local population toward the American occupation. In due course Fallujah was transformed into the epicenter of the insurgency and in April 2004 was completely seized by the insurgents, who held onto the city for more than six months.

Al-Anbar: A Brief History

While Arab nationalists in Iraq and beyond have historically touted the al-Anbar as a bastion of Arabism in the country, the region has a more complex history. Ironically the word "Anbar" is Persian for "warehouse" – it was given this name by the ancient Persian Sassanid Empire, since the whole area served as a massive warehouse for its troops.

From the 16th century onwards, while Mesopotamia was gradually brought over to the Shi'a branch of Islam by the missionary zeal of the Iranian Safavid Empire, the al-Anbar region remained mostly Sunni. At the same time the region's close proximity to two important Arab capitals, Amman and Damascus, underpinned its status as a gateway to the Arab world. These two facts shaped the region's distinctive political and religious culture.

In the 20th century the al-Anbar region emerged as a bastion of modern Iraqi nationalism. In 1920, a rebellion against nascent British rule erupted in Fallujah, the so-called city of mosques. The British sent the brilliant explorer and distinguished colonial strategist, Lt. Colonel Gerald Leachman to defeat the rebels. In a remarkable battle that resonates to this day, rebels led by local leader Sheikh Dhari killed Leachman and a sizeable number of his troops on the southern outskirts of Fallujah.

In subsequent decades both Fallujah and the province's capital Ramadi produced some of the Arab nationalists that determined the political destiny of modern Iraq. In this respect, the region's close proximity to Syria (which in the 1930s and 1940s was the intellectual center of Arab nationalism) was a decisive factor. While a significant constituency amongst the prominent tribes and the more urbanized elements of al-Anbar society were against the Ba'ath party (primarily because of its links to the Iraqi Communist Party), the advent of the second Ba'ath regime in 1968 was broadly welcomed.

Al-Anbar and the Ongoing Insurgency

Aside from the nationalism and religiosity of its people, there are two other factors that make the al-Anbar region the heartland of the Iraqi "resistance". Firstly the region has historically provided many of the most competent officers in the Iraqi military and security forces. The dissolution of the Iraqi military and security forces in the aftermath of the 2003 invasion effectively made tens of thousands of experienced officers jobless. Today, some of these officers are connected to the insurgency, particularly in planning, networking and connecting the insurgents to wider regional support networks. Secondly, the al-Anbar province is usually the first port of call for jihadis and other foreign (and in some cases Iraqi) elements that infiltrate into the country through the border with Syria.

The infiltration of jihadis and other elements from the Syrian border is often cited as the most worrisome factor in the insurgency. The Western press is fixated on "foreign" fighters infiltrating into Iraq to plan and execute some of the more dramatic attacks. Up until the early parts of 2005, the Iraqi media and government spokesmen echoed the same fears. But recently there has been a trend toward making a more dispassionate assessment of the infiltration from Syria. There is now wide recognition that, in terms of numbers, the level of infiltration is insignificant compared to the many thousands of Iraqi insurgents who comprise the vast majority of the "resistance." But the infiltration is important insofar as expertise and logistics are concerned. Many of the car bombs that explode on Baghdad's streets on a daily basis are driven to the capital from al-Anbar. Moreover, many of the suicide bombers who blow themselves up against hard and soft targets alike on a scale that is beginning to surpass the suicidal exploits of Japan's Kamikaze pilots of World War II, are believed to be motivated by specially trained religious instructors, some of whom are foreign.

In order to stem the flow of car bombs and suicide bombers in Baghdad, the Iraqi authorities launched operation "Lightening," involving up to 40,000 troops and security personnel, and aimed at denying rebel access to the Iraqi capital. The Iraqi authorities also announced the creation of a new counterinsurgency force, designed first and foremost to deal with infiltration into the capital from al-Anbar. The so-called "Tiger" unit was initially given control over the Rasafa quarter of Baghdad [3]. Judging by the continuing near-daily bombings in the Iraqi capital, these measures have clearly not been effective enough. In any case it is important to put the security assessments and ambitions of the Iraqi authorities in their proper context. In 2005, Laith Kubba, spokesman for then Prime Minister Ibrahim al-Jaafari, predicted that coalition forces would "disappear" from the streets of Iraqi cities within "weeks" [4].

Wider Trends in the Insurgency

Aside from the worsening situation in al-Anbar (and its inevitable impact on security in Baghdad), two other developments are worth noting. The first involves recent statements that the U.S. authorities in Iraq have held talks with the "representatives" of the insurgents. Although much speculation has followed these rumors and statements (which were confirmed by then U.S. Defense Secretary Donald Rumsfeld), the Jamestown Foundation's sources in Iraq believe that the statements are designed to sabotage the morale of the insurgents, who have shown no real signs of engaging in dialogue with anybody, let alone the U.S. military in Iraq. It is interesting that most of the news relating to the alleged talks is leaked by *Baghdad*, a daily newspaper belonging to Ayad Allawi's Iraqi National Accord, which has close links to the U.S. military and intelligence apparatus in Iraq. The self-appointed middleman of the insurgents is former Electricity Minister Ayham al-Samarrai, who is believed to be close to Allawi. In early June 2005, al-Samarrai told *Baghdad*, that the Islamic Army in Iraq and the Mujahideen Army, which according to him constitute 50% of the insurgency, had signaled their readiness to disarm and start negotiations with the government [5].

Not surprisingly the insurgents immediately threatened to assassinate al-Samarrai, making it clear that he represents nothing but his own interests and ambitions.

It is indeed unlikely that there have been any meaningful contacts between the insurgents and the U.S./Iraqi authorities. The insurgents have not yet developed a strong enough ideological and political infrastructure to be able to participate in the political process. Moreover, insurgent organizations are numerous, and as of yet, no single organization can claim to speak on behalf of any strand of the insurgency. According to the Jamestown Foundation's sources in Iraq, there are around 100 insurgent groups in the country. Their size varies from small groups composed of half a dozen men, to the largest insurgent organization, the Islamic Army in Iraq, made up of around 2,000 full-time and part-time insurgents. The latter is believed to be controlled from a safe distance by former Iraqi military intelligence officers based primarily in Syria, but also in Cyprus, Jordan and the United Arab Emirates.

The second development relates to calls by Iraqi President Jalal al-Talabani and Abdul Aziz al-Hakim, then leader of the Supreme Council of the Islamic Revolution in Iraq (SCIRI, later renamed the Islamic Supreme Council of Iraq), to deploy Kurdish and Shi'a militias against the insurgents [6]. This call comes at a time of worsening sectarian tensions in the country, with Harith al-Dhari, the head of the Association of Muslim Scholars, accusing the Badr organization (the armed wing of SCIRI) of assassinating Sunni Muslim clerics [7]. Despite subsequent denials that there are any plans afoot to deploy the militias, the initial announcement by al-Talabani and al-Hakim is profoundly important. It points toward the eventual deployment of the Badr organization (originally established and trained by Iran's Islamic Revolutionary Guard Corps in the early 1980s) against the insurgents. The Kurdish militias are unlikely to be deployed outside the Kurdish regions, for fear of igniting a wider ethnic conflict in Iraq.

The Badr organization is already involved in counterinsurgency operations, albeit indirectly. For instance, *al-Liwa al-Dheeb* (Wolf Brigade), widely believed to be the only effective and motivated component of the Iraqi Security Forces, is largely led by former Badr organization commanders. Despite their profound misgivings toward SCIRI and the Badr organization, the U.S. authorities in Iraq are reluctantly incorporating the latter in the country's security structures. As the extent of insurgent penetration of new Iraqi military and security structures become more apparent, with recent reports that top officials in the interior ministry had been passing highly sensitive information to the rebels [8], calls will inevitably grow for the direct deployment of the Badr organization in counterinsurgency operations. In any case, the Badr organization remains a primary target for the insurgents; a senior officer in the organization was assassinated just over a week ago [9].

In the midst of this worsening security situation, the U.S. and its allies in Iraq are increasingly reliant on the political process for good news. But even on this front, there are serious and potentially fatal problems. While the success of the January 2005 provincial elections is open to debate, it is readily apparent that the political process is not having any meaningful impact on the ordinary lives of Iraqis. Given that there are regular power blackouts, water shortages and mass unemployment, the project to "democratize" Iraq is, at best, irrelevant insofar as the great majority of the population is concerned. Moreover, deepening the political process runs the risk of further empowering SCIRI and other Shi'a Islamist organizations, whose vision for Iraq is very different to that of the United States, and who in due course may become more serious adversaries than the numerous and implacable guerillas of al-Anbar.

Notes

1. *Al-Sabah al-Jadeed* (independent daily published in Baghdad), May 16, 2005
2. *Baghdad* (daily, published by the Iraqi National Accord), May 18, 2005
3. *Addustour* (independent daily), June 2, 2005.
4. *Al-Mada*, June 6, 2005.
5. *Baghdad*, June 9, 2005.
6. Al-Mutamar (daily, published by the Iraqi National Congress), June 9, 2005.
7. *Asharq al-Awsat*, May 19, 2005.
8. *Baghdad*, June 27, 2005.
9. *Al-Mashriq*, July 7, 2005.

Assessing the Impact of Iraq's 2005 Parliamentary Election on the Insurgency

By Mahan Abedin
December 21, 2005
Terrorism Monitor 3 (24)

As Iraq staged its first election for a full-term parliament since the fall of Saddam Hussein, there are increasing hopes in Washington and London that the pace of the steadily growing insurgency may have at long last been stunted. But if previous elections in post-Saddam Iraq (i.e. the January 2005 provincial elections) are used as a template, it is clear that such elections do not have a decisive impact on the terrorist and insurgent movements in Iraq. Moreover, the December 2005 parliamentary election, insofar as it incorporates representatives and sympathizers of the insurgents into the political process, may in fact lead to a deterioration of security in the short term.

Overview

Broadly speaking, three features of the 2005 parliamentary election will directly impact the insurgency. First, despite predictions to the contrary, the religious Shi'a parties (as was represented by the United Iraqi Alliance) are expected to do well in the elections, possibly even better than their performance in the January 2005 provincial elections. This was contrary to the wishes of then U.S. Ambassador Zalmay Khalilzad and the U.S. military and intelligence apparatus in Iraq, who were hoping to diminish the influence of the religious Shi'a parties, partly to appease the Arab Sunni guerilla movement and partly owing to fears of growing Iranian influence. The ongoing political dominance of the religious Shi'a parties means that Iraq's security forces (namely the National Guards, the various police outfits and the security units attached to the Interior Ministry) will continue to be dominated by the Shi'a. This will make it more even more difficult for Khalilzad and his Iraqi allies to reach out to elements of the so-called "nationalist" insurgency.

Second, Muqtada al-Sadr's large and popular movement participated in the elections and will have "official" representation in the new parliament. Sadr's representatives also served in the previous parliament, but in an unofficial capacity. Moreover, this time around, the Sadrists will have a much larger stake in parliament and the government. Given the Sadrists' implacable opposition to the U.S. military presence in Iraq, they will likely use their newly acquired electoral clout to lobby for the withdrawal of coalition forces. Again, this is worrisome for Khalilzad, who needs to ensure that the Iraqi government does not even begin to talk about a U.S. withdrawal before the U.S. initiates it.

Third, the new parliament will contain elements which are either directly tied to the insurgency or are, at the very least, sympathetic to it. A new list composed of three Arab Sunni parties (dominated by the Iraqi Islamic Party), called the Iraqi Accordance Front (IAF), is expected to do well in the elections, most likely receiving the majority of votes in the three key provinces of Ninawa, Salah al-Din and al-Anbar. These areas constitute the Arab Sunni heartlands of Iraq, where the insurgency is rooted. The rise of the Iraqi Islamic Party (IIP) is particularly problematic for the U.S., not only because the IIP is openly supportive of what it calls the "nationalist resistance," but also because the party has strong links with Islamic parties outside Iraq and is trusted by several Arab regimes. The IIP is expected to use its electoral clout to promote two interrelated agendas: first, to "legitimize" the so-called resistance inside government circles, and second, to work with regional forces and Arab governments to make Iraqi democracy "safe" for the Arab world. This entails keeping the Shi'as in check and ensuring that Iraq does not develop liberal democratic institutions and practices. The growing respectability and influence of the IIP, coupled with the rising fortunes of the Sadrists, make it less likely that the U.S. will be able to eventually leave Iraq on its own terms.

Insurgent Strategy and Tactics

As a general rule, elections in Iraq have not had a significant impact on the insurgency, as demonstrated by the previous two elections. In terms of tactics, the recent election is likely to lead to three new developments. First, insurgent representation in the new government, in the form of the IAF, will likely result in more attacks on coalition armies, particularly American forces in the Baghdad province. This is designed to give teeth to greater political calls for an early U.S. withdrawal from Iraq. There is already evidence that the Arab Sunni political parties coordinated their electoral strategy with several insurgent organizations. Indeed several insurgent groups have called for a ceasefire during the elections, and virtually the entire "nationalist" insurgency (save for a few hardcore Ba'athists) was in favor of Arab Sunni participation in the elections. This policy was endorsed by the hardline Association of Muslim Scholars (AMS) whose representative in the south of Iraq, Sheikh Yousif al-Hassan, urged Arab Sunnis to participate in the elections and vote for the IAF (*al-Iraq al-Yawm*, December 12, 2005). The AMS is considered by many to be the public face of the insurgents.

Attacks on U.S. forces in and around Baghdad are particularly effective not only for symbolic reasons, but also because they highlight the impotence of Khalilzad and the Americans. But increasing attacks on Coalition forces in Baghdad will rely heavily on the active connivance of elements in the security forces. It remains to be seen whether the Arab Sunni political parties have enough clout to convince the security forces (and their religious Shi'a masters) to allow the insurgents to target Americans without fear of detection and harassment. This kind of pressure seems to have started in earnest with the AMS launching a thinly veiled attack on SCIRI and the Badr organization, but adding that aggressive tactics will not deter people from fighting the "occupation" (*al-Mashriq*, December 8, 2005). Previously Hadi al-Amari, the head of the powerful Badr organization, had for the first time made a distinction between "terrorism" and "resistance," which could be interpreted as a cryptic message to the Arab Sunni guerilla movement (*al-Adala*, November 24, 2005).

Second, the elections will most likely strengthen the "nationalist" insurgency at the expense of the Salafi-jihadis. By nearly all accounts, the former already comprise well over 95% of the insurgency, but their overwhelming numerical strength has been overshadowed by the ideological and propaganda prowess of the jihadis. This is likely to change mainly because post-war Iraq has now turned a corner. Indeed, no matter how imperfect the emerging Iraqi regime is proving to be, it is now clear that the political process is irreversible. The jihadi aspiration of perpetuating Iraq as a failed state under American occupation and engulfed in sectarian conflict was always overly ambitious. Moreover, the primary conflict in post-war Iraq has been centered on the enmity between the organized religious Shi'as – who were at the forefront of the long struggle against Saddam – and the former security and military elites who lead the insurgency. But this feature will become more pronounced and complex as the political stakes rise in Iraq.

Third, the increasing alienation of the Salafi-jihadis will likely lead to more outrageous attacks. Indeed, as the jihadis become more desperate they will resort to sensational and highly provocative terrorist attacks to maintain their relevance. The Jamestown Foundation's sources in Iraq claim that the Badr Organization has already foiled an assassination attempt on Grand Ayatollah Ali al-Sistani. Moreover, these sources claim that the al-Zarqawi network may strike at the shrines of Imam Ali and Imam Hussein (at Najaf and Karbala, respectively) in order to inflame Shi'a passions both in Iraq and beyond and create wider rifts between the religious Shi'a and other political forces in the Iraqi government. If the Najaf and Karbala shrines are destroyed in terrorist attacks, the repercussions will be truly awful, particularly for Shi'a-Sunni relations in Iraq.

A Shi'a Insurgency?

As predicted by the Jamestown Foundation's *Terrorism Monitor* (November 7,

2003), SCIRI and its paramilitary wing, the Badr organization, have maintained their working relationship with the U.S. authorities in Iraq. Even now, as the U.S. is showing increasing signs of wanting to diminish SCIRI's influence, there are no signs that either SCIRI or Badr would want to directly confront the U.S. military.

But the same cannot be said of other religious Shi'as who are as adamant as the Arab Sunni guerilla movement that Coalition armies should leave Iraq immediately. The Sadrists and their numerous offshoots have shown a greater willingness to decisively confront British authority in the south of Iraq. The British claim that an offshoot of the Sadrists – with possible help from Iran – is responsible for recent deadly attacks on their forces in and around Basra. The uneasy détente between the British and the religious Shi'as – whose militias have heavily penetrated the new security structures – seems to have broken down. This was partly confirmed by Amara's provincial council chairman, Abdul Jabbar Waheed (a Sadr loyalist) who called for a general strike in mid-November to protest at random raids and arrests by British forces (*al-Mada*, November 16, 2005). The fear is that the elections, which have strengthened the hand of Muqtada al-Sadr and his allies, will embolden renegade and extremist Sadrists to increase their attacks on the British and possibly start targeting U.S. forces in eastern Baghdad (which has been a Sadrist stronghold since the downfall of Saddam).

A full-scale insurgency by al-Sadr's forces (on a par with the rebellions of April 2004 and August 2004) is unlikely, simply because the Sadrists now have a credible political stake in the new Iraq. Like the Iraqi Islamic Party, they will seek to promote the insurgent cause within the government and lobby influential Iraqi officials to increase pressure on the Americans.

What is likely to happen in the next decisive 18 months is greater Shi'a opposition to the Coalition presence in Iraq. Contrary to what many U.S. analysts believe, the Iraqi Shi'a in general have no particular affinity for the United States. They have gone along with American designs in Iraq because, broadly speaking, these have coincided with their own interests. But now that the Arab Sunni Islamists have been officially incorporated into the government and more broadly the new power and influence structures in the new Iraq begin to take definitive shape, the Shi'as might resort to violence and other spoiling tactics to maintain their position.

The one thing the religious Shi'as fear most is what they privately call the "Turkification" of Iraq. This is a reference to the type of political system that held sway in Turkey from the early 1920s to the late 1990s, where the military was the ultimate arbiter in political affairs. The religious Shi'as are suspicious of the fact that the Americans have monopolized the training of the new Iraqi army. The fear is that the Americans want to develop a pro-Western military, which will keep the new Iraqi Islamic state (dominated by the religious Shi'as) in check. This will arguably be the greatest point of contention between the religious Shi'a and the U.S. in 2006, but whether it will spark terrorist attacks against U.S. forces remains to be seen.

Conclusion

While the elections were held successfully and the political process in Iraq now seems irreversible, there is also little doubt that the country is being steadily transformed into an Islamic state. The "Islamization" of Iraq is taking place at all levels, but most noticeably at the very top where the new Iraqi parliament is poised to be dominated by Shi'a and Sunni Islamists. The former are backed by Iran and the latter are inspired and backed by the Muslim Brotherhood and other Islamist forces in the Arab world.

The irreversibility of the political process notwithstanding, the scope and intensity of the insurgency is unlikely to diminish in the foreseeable future. In fact, as the political stakes rise in Iraq, there will be a greater temptation on both sides of the sectarian divide to stage sensational attacks on U.S. interests in Iraq, on a par with the October 1983 bombing of the U.S. Marine barracks in Beirut.

The best option for the United States is to resist calls for an early withdrawal and continue with the training of the new Iraqi army. It is this army, which will contain the jihadi threat in Iraq after the U.S. leaves the country. As for the broader insurgency, this will only diminish when the Shi'a and Sunni Islamists begin to agree on the details of power and influence sharing in the new Iraq.

Chapter 2

Evolving Trends and Insurgent Groups

Divisions Within the Iraqi Insurgency

By Lydia Khalil
April 30, 2007
Terrorism Monitor 5 (7)

With so many actors in the Iraqi insurgent theater, it is hard to keep track of the various permutations of militant Islamic groups and their alliances. It is going to become all the more difficult given recent splits and conflicts between and within indigenous Iraqi groups and al-Qaeda affiliates. The violence in Iraq has not abated, but the cohesiveness of the insurgency is certainly challenged. Iraqi insurgents are concerned about this given the recent fissure of a prominent indigenous group, the 1920 Revolution Brigades, and the fighting between al-Qaeda and their former allies within the Sunni Arab tribes. All militant groups within Iraq have been frantically calling for unity and insisting that recent splits are amicable, while al-Qaeda has been aggressively and violently demanding allegiance from all involved. Despite their best efforts, the Iraqi insurgency continues to splinter.

1920 Revolution Brigades Splits over Islamic State of Iraq

The most obvious example was the mid-March 2007 announcement by the 1920 Revolution Brigades that they have split into two groups—one retaining the name of the 1920 Revolution Brigades, and the other calling itself Hamas-Iraq. The division was not just the result of internal disputes within the organization, but also accelerated by disagreements over the group's relationship with al-Qaeda (*al-Hayat*, March 31, 2007).

On March 27, 2007, for example, the leader of the 1920 Revolution Brigades,

Harith Dhahir Khamis al-Dhari, was killed by al-Qaeda for his reported negotiations with the government and his refusal to pledge allegiance to al-Qaeda's Islamic State of Iraq (http://mohajroon.com, March 27, 2007; *Terrorism Focus*, April 10, 2007). While members of his tribe and the 1920 Revolution Brigades denied that he had any dealings with the government, it turns out that the off-shoot organization, Hamas-Iraq, is advocating more political activity, perhaps even modeling itself after the original Palestinian organization Hamas (http://mohajroon.com, April 2007). The 1920 Revolution Brigades, however, denounced strongly Hamas-Iraq's advocacy of political participation and defended the Islamic State of Iraq. The recent debate in Iraq mirrors the larger disagreement that Ayman al-Zawahiri had with the Palestinian Hamas, in which he criticized their participation in elections (http://muslim.net/vb, March 12, 2007).

Islamic Army in Iraq Ridicules Al-Qaeda

The elements of the 1920 Revolution Brigades that are now Hamas-Iraq are not the only ones to have quarreled with al-Qaeda's Islamic State of Iraq. The Islamic Army and Ba'athist elements within the insurgency, along with tribes making up the al-Anbar Salvation Council, have also conflicted with al-Qaeda (*Terrorism Focus*, March 28, 2006). The Islamic State of Iraq has come out so forcefully against those who have not submitted allegiance to its leader Abu Omar al-Baghdadi that it has created a backlash within indigenous elements of the Iraqi insurgency who resent al-Qaeda co-opting their indigenous struggle for global Islamic goals in which they do not necessarily believe.

In a lengthy statement posted on their website in April 2007, the Islamic Army accused al-Qaeda of killing many of its members and of being behind attempts to discredit the Islamic Army within the insurgency. They even accused al-Qaeda of operating outside the bounds of Islamic law and robbing and killing innocent Sunni civilians. They refuted Abu Omar al-Baghdadi's claim that the Islamic State of Iraq is the most powerful force operating in the insurgency and claimed that al-Qaeda has killed members of other insurgent groups like Ansar al-Sunna and the Mujahideen Army.

The Islamic Army's posting states that al-Qaeda rushed to label fellow Muslims as infidels without clear proof and calls on the "leaders of al-Qaeda, especially Osama bin Laden…to purify his faith and honor…it is not enough to declare disavowal of these deeds, but to correct their path" (http://iaisite.info). It is significant that the Islamic Army, after remaining silent about its disputes with al-Qaeda, is now choosing to go public. It even defended its position of being open to negotiating with the coalition under certain circumstances. In fact, the Islamic Army has become so disenchanted that it is now reported by Iraqi government sources that it is also bringing in other insurgent groups like the al-Rashideen Army, the Umar Brigades and the Black Banners to join the fight against al-Qaeda (*al-Quds al-Arabi*, April 2, 2007).

Ba'athist elements of the insurgency have also come out against al-Qaeda in Iraq. On March 18, 2007, al-Jazeera carried an interview by Dr. Abu Mohamed, spokesman for the Ba'ath Party in Iraq. On al-Jazeera, Mohamed denied any relationship with al-Qaeda, saying, "their doctrine, vision and strategy differ from those of the Ba'ath Party and remaining national resistance factions." The Ba'ath Party has quarreled publicly with the Mujahideen Army and the Islamic Army in Iraq, who resent the Ba'ath Party inflating their role within the insurgency. Both groups have issued statements on their websites and on jihadi forums diminishing the role of the Ba'ath Party and their relationship to it, prompting a rebuttal by Ba'ath leaders (al-Basrah.net, March 24, 2007).

Cohesion Challenged

Ansar al-Sunna, a powerful group within the insurgency and with past ties to al-Qaeda, has cautioned the insurgent groups against airing their disagreements publicly, warning Iraqis that reports of division are a new deceptive tactic by the Iraqi government and Coalition forces (*Terrorism Monitor*, December 20, 2005). Abu Abdullah, a leader within Ansar al-Sunna, stated that the U.S. and Iraqi governments "found they were left with no other option but to resort to deception, misguidance and playing with words through the media" (Islamic Renewal Organization, March 30, 2007). At the same time, Ansar al-Sunna has responded to recent statements that it has allied with the Islamic State in Iraq and denied reports that it has joined a "coordination group" made up of other insurgent elements. Ansar al-Sunna's message is inconsistent in that it calls for unity, while it has fiercely retained its independence from other groups operating in the Iraqi theater.

Elements of the Iraqi insurgency routinely deny their contacts with the government and downplay the significance of splits within their respective organizations, saying they are for operational expediency. It is in their interest to maintain a public front of unity in many regards. Firstly, many insurgent groups deny contacts with the government so as not to jeopardize their jihadi credentials. Secondly, while divisions within the insurgency are very real, they do not want to air out their dirty laundry in public, believing that it will weaken their position vis-à-vis the government and coalition forces if they are believed to be capitulating. Critical statements of other groups are often couched under the banner of "advice." Thirdly, insurgent groups, regardless of their internal differences, want to portray reports of their splits as coalition propaganda attempts, revealing the Iraqi government's weak position, not their own. Nevertheless, divisions within the insurgency cannot be denied and present a critical opportunity for both the Iraqi government and coalition forces to exploit these divisions effectively.

Al-Qaeda and Iraq: Too Soon to Declare Victory

By Michael Scheuer
October 24, 2007
Terrorism Focus 4 (34)

"Al-Qaeda in Iraq Crippled" was the headline splashed across Western print and electronic media on October 15, 2007. The stories accompanying the headline described the number of Al-Qaeda in Iraq (AQI) leaders who have been killed in recent months, the downward trend in AQI car bombings and the slowing of the infiltration of Islamist fighters from Syria and Jordan [1]. The stories were sourced to both named and unnamed officials of the U.S.-led coalition in Iraq, and the bottom-line was offered by then Lt. Gen. Raymond Odierno who claimed that AQI's capabilities had been "degraded" by 60-70% so far in 2007, and then Lt. Gen. Stanley A. McChrystal was reported to be urging a U.S. declaration of victory over AQI. Last week's stories were focused on al-Anbar province and the Baghdad region, but it was unclear if generals Odierno and McChrystal were limiting their analyses to those areas or all of Iraq.

The foregoing analyses of AQI's defeat in Iraq are, of course, impossible to assess without access to the full range of intelligence reporting—both classified and open source. The militaries of the U.S.-led coalition may have firm evidence that AQI is done and finished. Yet, if they do, it means that AQI and the central command of al-Qaeda – Osama bin Laden, Ayman al-Zawahiri and others – have radically changed their approach to the war in Iraq and, indeed, to their overall approach to fighting the United States and its allies in insurgency situations.

Although this would be excellent news for the West, it is too early to accept these assertions completely.

Like most other insurgents, al-Qaeda's doctrine places first priority on the survival of its forces. The equation is simple: no forces, no insurgency. If the opinions of the above-mentioned generals are correct, al-Qaeda has abandoned its doctrine and decided instead to stand and fight to the death. Yet, the recent media coverage has provided no evidence of that. The claim by the generals that 30 AQI leaders have been killed is impressive – and hopefully true – but after capturing and killing several hundreds of AQI (since 2003) and al-Qaeda leaders (since 1995), 30 dead leaders seems a weak reed on which to hang a claim of overall victory. If AQI stood and fought to the death, there would be verified body counts that are much higher. It is possible, however, that many AQI fighters may have been killed by Iraqi Sunni tribal groups in al-Anbar, and that their deaths may not be verifiable. That said, open source reporting makes it seem unlikely that the al-Anbar Sunni leaders will push their war with AQI to the point of eliminating the latter simply because they know they will need the assistance of AQI and its foreign backers when the U.S.-led Coalition withdraws from Iraq and their war against the Shi'a-led regime intensifies.

Decreases in the number of car bombs, as well as in the numbers of Islamist fighters infiltrating Iraq from Jordan and Syria, are also good news, but they are more signs of insurgent canniness than they are of coalition victory. The decreases have been most noticeable, as the generals said, in al-Anbar province and around Baghdad. In the former, the U.S. Marine Corps have been operating full-bore for more than a year in both fighting and aiding local Sunni tribes. It should be no surprise that the Marines have had some important successes, and it should be no surprise that al-Qaeda has moved most of its forces to other provinces – or to Jordan, Syria and Saudi Arabia—to avoid the mayhem the Marines can inflict on them. Al-Qaeda leaders have long said that the U.S. Marines are the only U.S. fighters they respect, and so they have no eagerness to go toe-to-toe with them. In Baghdad, Washington's 2007 surge of forces in the capital area has brought larger numbers of dead insurgents and an overall slowing of insurgent operations. The surge would have been a failure if such results did not appear, and AQI and the insurgent groups would have been ignorant of their own doctrine had they not gotten out of the way of the more aggressive, numerous and powerful U.S. force. Moving away from, not toward strong enemy conventional forces is standard procedure for insurgents.

While not at all questioning the claims of numerous dead AQI leaders, fewer car bombs detonating and declining infiltrations in al-Anbar and Baghdad, it probably is too much to take these successes and extrapolate them into an overall, country-wide victory. The West made such an extrapolation soon after driving the Taliban from Afghan cities by claiming total victory, only to soon find itself facing a steadily intensifying insurgency with the very undefeated Taliban (*Terrorism Focus*, July 3, 2007). It is more likely – especially in al-Anbar – that AQI took some heavy losses from the U.S. Marines and then decided to sidestep their wrath by moving into the Levant, Saudi Arabia and other Iraqi provinces. The same is probably true for the insurgents who were battered at the hands of the reinforced U.S. Army units in and around Baghdad. Again, such bobbing and weaving is integral to AQI and al-Qaeda doctrine, and it must always be recalled that the insurgents are in no hurry (*Terrorism Focus*, March 14, 2006). If the coalition's military power is too overwhelming in one or more areas, the insurgents will simply move or stand down and wait until U.S. forces shift locations or begin to draw down their ranks. AQI and al-Qaeda are clearly aware from the international media that the U.S. will to stay in Iraq is dissolving, and that patience on the insurgents' part may give them victory with far fewer casualties than head-on battles with U.S. forces.

While U.S. generals are discussing whether AQI has been definitively defeated – and the media claims that many believe such a claim is premature – Western commentary is yet again outdoing military leaders in both their claims of victory and in misunderstanding AQI and its strategic doctrine. "Al-Qaeda is on the horns of a dilemma," syndicated columnist Clifford May wrote on October 21, 2007. "Last month, some 30 of its senior members in Iraq were killed or captured. Now, Osama bin Laden faces a tough decision: Send reinforcements to Iraq in an attempt to regain the initiative? That risks losing those combatants, too—and that could seriously diminish his global organization. But the alternative is equally unappealing: accept defeat in Iraq, the battlefield bin Laden has called central to the struggle al-Qaeda is waging against America and its allies."

Having discussed above the dangers of extrapolating undeniable but probably transitory U.S. military successes in al-Anbar and around Baghdad, May implicitly argues that the Islamist insurgency in Iraq will ultimately win or lose on the basis of what al-Qaeda and AQI does or does not do. While this analysis is off-base, it is an analytic line that holds sway among many Western experts. First, bin Laden, al-Zawahiri and the rest of the al-Qaeda leadership have described

Iraq as "Islam's" central battlefield in the war against the "Crusaders and Zionists," not as "al-Qaeda's" central battlefield (as-Sahab Productions, September 7, 2007). Al-Qaeda leaders deliberately describe themselves as only a part of a bigger Islamist struggle, and seldom if ever try to hog the spotlight. This, incidentally, is why there is no sadness among al-Qaeda's chiefs that Abu Musab al-Zarqawi is now a dead hero rather than a live operator; al-Zarqawi was simply too insistent on al-Qaeda playing the lead role in Iraq (*Daily Star*, April 3, 2006). Al-Qaeda's doctrine is to be the vanguard of a larger movement, not the movement itself (*Terrorism Focus*, September 11, 2007).

Second, May misses the point that al-Qaeda is welcomed on so many contemporary jihadi battlefields – Iraq, Afghanistan, Chechnya, Kashmir, Mindanao, southern Thailand, Algeria, among others—precisely because it is determined to play a supporting and not a leading role in those insurgencies. Rather than leading insurgencies, al-Qaeda's fighters have a long record of arriving in the battle zone and playing a subordinate role that is meant to make the local insurgency better and more effective militarily, politically and media-wise. The West would be very fortunate if al-Qaeda were fielding multiple al-Zarqawi clones that have caused internal dissension in all the insurgencies for which they joined, but such is not the case. Again, al-Qaeda doctrine is to support and guide, not to lead.

Third, and finally, no matter what al-Qaeda doctrine says, the historical reality is that insurgencies win or lose based on their authenticity; national insurgencies, such as the one in Iraq, must be led, supported and overwhelmingly manned by local inhabitants. Outsiders – as were bin Laden and other Arab mujahideen during the Afghan-Soviet war – can assist the locals in valuable ways by providing such things as arms and money, but they can never lead and command an insurgency occurring in a country where they are not natives. Bin Laden made this point explicitly in October 2007 (al-Jazeera, October 22, 2007). In speaking to the Iraqi insurgent groups, he praised them – and not AQI – "for carrying out one of the greatest duties that few people could carry out; namely, the duty of repelling the enemy…The infidels have become confused and soon will flee." Looking to the need to govern the country after a U.S. defeat, bin Laden also admonished the "brother amirs of the mujahid [Iraqi] groups" for being slow "in carrying out another duty…namely, the duty of unifying your ranks as God, be He glorified and exalted wants." The al-Qaeda chief told the Iraqi mujahideen "the Muslims [worldwide] are waiting for you all to be united under one banner to uphold right," warning them that disunity could yield the squandering of their military victory over the U.S.-led Coalition, as it did for the Afghan mujahideen after they defeated the Soviet Union (al-Jazeera, October 22, 2007).

Simply put, foreigners cannot win the popular support base indispensable to a durable and ultimately successful insurgency, and al-Qaeda learned that lesson well in Afghanistan in the 1980s and is rehearsing it again there and in Iraq today. The bottom line is that even if AQI is defeated, the Iraq insurgency – because it is authentic – will continue. In this light, current U.S. successes against AQI – while worthwhile and to be applauded—will not be a major factor, let alone determinative, in defeating the Iraqi insurgency.

Notes

1. Typically, the unnamed U.S. officials promoting this story did not mention the continuing flow of veteran and would-be mujahideen into Iraq from Saudi Arabia.

Sufi Insurgent Groups in Iraq

By Rafid Fadhil Ali
January 25, 2008
Terrorism Monitor 6 (2)

The mystical approach to Islam known as Sufism has deep roots in Iraqi society. Adherents to Sufism normally stress prayer, meditation and the recitation of the various names of God as part of their effort to create a mystical communion between themselves and Allah. Yet at various times and places – such as 19th century Africa or the 19th and 20th century North Caucasus – Sufi orders have formed the core resistance to colonial and imperial occupation efforts. Heavily criticized within Iraq during the first two years of the current U.S. occupation for focusing on spiritual matters rather than resistance, Iraq's Sufis have begun to take up arms against Coalition forces.

In the early days of Islam, Sufis tended to be lone ascetics known for wearing suf (rough wool garments), but gradually they began to organize around spiritual leaders known as *sheikhs*, or pirs. One of the greatest Sufi orders, the Qadiria, was founded in Baghdad by Abd al-Qadir al-Jilani, who lived from 1078 to 1166. The second most prominent Sufi order in Iraq is the Naqshbandia, introduced to Iraq from India by Sheikh Khalid Naqshbandi in the early 13th century. Despite the common perception that Sufism is a strictly non-violent form of Sunni Islam, there are at least three insurgent groups in Iraq today that claim to be Sufi:

> *Jaysh Rijal al-Tariqa al-Naqshbandia* (The Men of the Army of al-Naqshbandia Order, or JRTN) is the largest Sufi insurgent group. The group announced its formation in December 2006, right after the execution of Saddam Hussein.
>
> *Katibat al-Sheikh Abd al-Qadir al-Jilanin Al-Jihadia* (The Jihadi Battalion of Sheikh Abd al-Qadir al-Jilani) was announced in August 2006.
>
> *The Sufi Squadron* of Sheikh Abd al-Qadir al-Jilani was founded in April 2005.

For hundreds of years the founders and leaders of various tariqas (Sufi orders) developed special rituals, chants and even dances to pursue the spiritual dimension of Islam and praise God and his prophet Muhammad. Sufis have been frequently criticized by Salafist Muslims for syncretism with pre-Islamic religious practices, innovation in methods of worship and the veneration of their sheikhs and their burial places, which tend to become places of pilgrimage.

In Iraq, the Qadiria – both Arab and Kurd – are divided into several branches. The largest branch, the Kasnazania, is headed by Sheikh Muhammad Abd al-Karim al-Kasnazan, who lives in the city of al-Sulaimania. The Naqshbandia is led by Sheikh Abdullah Mustafa al-Naqshbandi, who lives in the city of Arbil. A third important group is the al-Rifa'ia order, whose branches do not acknowledge the leadership of a single sheikh. According to Nehru al-Kasnazan – son of Sheikh Muhammad al-Kasnazan – there are currently three million adherents to the various Sufi orders in Iraq (al-Arabiya.net, August 23, 2005).

The Sufis enjoyed many freedoms when Saddam Hussein was in power. Izzat Ibrahim al-Douri, his Vice President and the current head of the banned the Ba'ath party, is a well-known Qadiri Sufi. The former sheikh of the Iraqi Qadiria, Muhammad al-Hallab, was strongly criticized by other members of the order for the haste with which he advanced al-Douri through the spiritual teachings of the order without adequate preparation (*Mafkarat al-Islam*, August 24, 2006).

Reaction to the Collapse of the Ba'athist Regime

After the fall of the Ba'athist regime in April 2003 and the development of a large-scale Sunni insurgency, none of the leading Sufi groups called for violence during the first years of the occupation. Sufis watched the insurgency being dominated by their historical opponents, the Salafis. Militant groups affiliated to al-Qaeda have attacked Sufis and their sacred places – including the demolition of tombs of Sufi saints – but on one remarkable occasion Sufis and Salafis fought together in the battles for Fallujah in 2004. The insurgents were under the leadership of Sheikh Abdullah al-Janabi, who is an adherent of a minor Sufi order called al-Nabhania. Al-Janabi was the head of the Mujahideen Shura Council, which controlled the Sunni city until December 2004. The Council was an umbrella organization of Salafi, Sufi and Ba'athi groups.

With the escalation of Sunni-Shi'a sectarian violence in post-invasion Iraq, Sufis started to complain of attacks by Shi'a militias. The Kasnazani Qadiris called for civil peace through a *fatwa* proclaimed on their website, television station and the *Mashriq* newspaper. Other Qadiris had a different response to the growing violence. In April 2005 the Sufi Squadron of Sheikh Abd al-Qadir al-Jilani announced their formation as an anti-American armed group. According to statements in jihadi websites and forums, the group is especially active in and around the northern city of Mosul, where it is involved in setting road-side improvised explosive devices (IEDs) and sniper attacks against U.S. forces. Statements issued directly by the group are issued by the authority of the "General commanding the jihadi armed forces" and are published by the Ba'ath website, al-Basra.net.

Later the creation of the Jihadi Battalion of Sheikh Abd al-Qadir al-Jilani was announced in the town of al-Haweeja near the northern city of Kirkuk (*Mafkarat al-Islam*, August 23, 2006). The Qadiri Sufi lodge in Kirkuk has both Kurdish and Arab members. The head of al-Qadiria in Kirkuk, Sheikh Abd al-Rahim al-Qadiri, ordered his followers to suspend their usual Sufi rituals and practices to form a battalion to fight U.S. troops, Iraqi government forces and the Shi'a militias of Badr Corps and Jaysh al-Mahdi. Al-Qadiri disappeared several days before the announcement was made, though it is believed that he may have gone underground to lead the combat operations of his followers. Little activity from this group has been observed since their leader's disappearance, but the area in and around Kirkuk is still one of the most volatile in Iraq.

Formation of the JRTN

On the same day as the hanging of Saddam Hussein on December 30, 2006, the Men of the Army of al-Naqshbandia Order (JRTN) announced their formation. The JRTN is clearly the most organized of the three aforementioned groups. In a sign typical of Ba'athist and Arab nationalism – but one that contradicts the pan-ethnic nature of Sufism – the main page of the JRTN's website is headed by a map of the Arab homeland of 22 countries stretching from the Middle East to North Africa. The terminology used on the website also indicates that the JRTN is a Ba'athist-dominated organization that reflects a growing trend within the party towards Islamism since the early 1990s. This trend is represented today by the wing led by Izzat Ibrahim al-Douri more than the rival wing led by Muhammad Yunis al-Ahmad, which is hosted and sponsored by Syria and its secular Ba'athist regime.

The target of the JRTN attacks is the Coalition forces, "the unbeliever-occupier" as they are referred to in the group's doctrine. The following principles form the JRTN canon:

> *The individuals, equipment and supplies of the Coalition forces are to be targeted anytime and anywhere in Iraq.*
>
> *Iraqis have not been and will not be targeted unless they fight with the Coalition.*
>
> *There will be no confrontations with other jihadi groups; the JRTN will cooperate with them as long as they remain committed to "the legitimate constant principles and the national agenda," which likely means the Baath agenda and policies.*
>
> *Funding is accepted from Muslim supporters, but not from any other external resource that might apply conditions.*
>
> *Secrecy is a vital principle in planning and implementing operations.*
>
> *There will be no participation in the political process in Iraq under the occupation.*

The al-Naqshbandia website and the monthly online magazine regularly release videos of the group's military operations as well as statements outlining their military and political positions (see *Terrorism Focus*, January 8, 2008). According to the JRTN website, the backbone of the militant formations is the followers and supporters of the Naqshbandia order, who follow operational doctrines formed during the first week of the 2003 invasion by a gathering of Naqshbandia clerics, military men and professionals.

The lightly-equipped JRTN have used guerrilla tactics to launch a long war of attrition against Coalition forces armed with the most developed weapons and communications systems. During the early stages of combat, the fighters arranged themselves in small groups of 7-10 fighters, each with a local Amir (commander). There were commanders in every province, each connected to the "Amir al-jihad," who was the grand sheikh of al-Naqshbandia. Military staff worked under the sheikh. These jihadi groups used light and medium rifles, road-side bombs and anti-tank RPG-7 grenade launchers in urban warfare against the Coalition. They were involved in the first battle of Fallujah in April 2004, where a number of Naqshbandia clerics were among the JRTN casualties.

Mortar and rocket assault groups were formed to attack Coalition bases at the Baghdad airport and the Green Zone, in addition to air bases in al-Anbar, Tamin, Ninawa, Salah al-Din and Diyala provinces. The JRTN also claim responsibility for a series of bombing operations, including the October 2003 attack on the Green Zone's al-Rasheed hotel by a rocket array during a visit by then Deputy Secretary of Defense Paul Wolfowitz. They also claim attacks on the headquarters of the Ministry of Oil and hotels used by foreign companies operating in Baghdad.

After two years of using small-group tactics, the commanders of JRTN formations decided after strategic study to reorganize their units to form a corps based on the standards of the old Iraqi Army. These preparations are being taken to prepare for a coming battle to control Baghdad and eventually the whole of Iraq. This transformation brought the following benefits:

The range of operations has been expanded with the help of other small local groups.

It has become possible to implement brigade-size operations, according to plans set by commanders assisted by military staff.

It has become possible to launch division-wide maneuvers to deploy troops through any sector for support purposes or to implement a joint operation in another sector.

The JRTN also indicates that they have the skilled personnel and workshops needed to maintain, develop and modify different types of weapons and ammunition. The group has lately joined The Supreme Command for Jihad and Liberation Front, a Ba'athist umbrella group. On the Supreme Command's website, the JRTN is listed first of the 22 affiliated insurgent groups.

Conclusion

Joining the insurgency was not the decision of the recognized leaderships of Iraqi Sufi orders. The pressure of attacks by Salafis and Shi'a militias appears to have played a major role in convincing Sufis in some areas to defy the non-violent doctrine of their traditional leaders. In response to sectarian violence and military occupation, few of the Sufis turned to Salafist groups like al-Qaeda in Iraq, but those who decided to fight joined the more familiar Ba'athist-led resistance.

Al-Douri's wing of the Ba'ath Party continues to wield its traditional influence on the Sufis. Many Sufis were originally Ba'athists, so it was not difficult for the party to recruit them. In most areas of Iraq, Sufi insurgents are either Ba'athists or controlled and directed by al-Ba'ath. Efforts to take the Sufis out of the insurgency will have little success without first breaking the bond between the Sufis and Izzat Ibrahim al-Douri's organization. Easing the Sunni-Shi'a sectarian conflict would be a significant step toward removing the Sufis from the frontlines.

Uncertainty Facing Iraq's Awakening Movement Puts U.S. Strategy at Risk

By Ramzy Mardini
February 22, 2008
Terrorism Monitor 6 (4)

As Iraq's security situation deteriorates in the midst of resurgent violence, an increase in internal and external pressures facing the *Sahwa* (Awakening) Movement may jeopardize the prospects and goals set forth in the American counterinsurgency strategy led by U.S. General David Petraeus, then the commander of Multi-National Force – Iraq.

The formation of the Awakening Councils seemed a promising linchpin to the "surge" strategy, which has shown concrete signs of improving Iraq's security sector. Though the rise of the Awakening movement contributed substantially in limiting al-Qaeda in Iraq in the short term, its forces face uncertain and problematic long-term challenges. If the dilemmas confronting the Awakening members continue to be marginalized by Prime Minister Nouri al-Maliki's government, Iraq's improved security situation is likely to revert back to sectarianism and civil war-like conditions.

Formation of the Awakening Councils

The Awakening movement began in al-Anbar province in 2006. The governorate was then described as "an impregnable garrison" of al-Qaeda in Iraq (AQI) (*Azzaman*, January 3, 2008). The terrorist organization, then led by the late Abu Musab al-Zarqawi, suppressed the local population and killed thousands of tribal members in an effort to impose an Islamic authority over the province. Though many of the members representing the Awakening today were at one time or another part of the insurgency killing U.S. soldiers, al-Qaeda's use of vicious intimidation tactics eventually led tribal leaders to shift their allegiances by cooperating with the U.S. military.

Since 2005, the *Sahwa* has spread outside al-Anbar province, with fighters joining or forming Awakening councils across the country. With the support and nurturing of the U.S. military, the Awakening has grown to at least 80,000 members, with Sunnis representing four-fifths of the force (*Asharq al-Awsat*, January 23, 2008). The movement represents one of the main factors in the decrease of violence and one of the very few Iraqi success stories. But in September 2007, AQI had assassinated Sheikh Abdul Sattar Abu Risha, the charismatic leader of the Awakening movement (*Aswat al-Iraq*, January 14, 2008). Killed just days after meeting with then President George W. Bush, Abu Risha's death promoted uncertainty as to what would come of the Awakening movement without the sheikh's leadership and credibility.

Security/Political Dilemmas

Though the *Sahwa* councils are credited to a large extent for the decline in the total number of Iraqi casualties, all three of Iraq's major political groupings—Shi'as, Sunnis and Kurds—are wary of the Awakening's role in state affairs.

The Kurdistan Regional Government (KRG) is opposed to the formation of

Awakening Councils in its region and areas subject to Article 140 of the Iraq Constitution, which calls for a reversal of the Ba'athist "Arabization" process in Kirkuk and other disputed areas (*Kurdish Globe*, January 23, 2008). The Sunni Arab makeup of the Awakening forces conflicts with Kurdish interest in sustaining security autonomy, especially in Kirkuk and parts of Ninawa province. The major concern for Sunni Arab leaders such as Iraqi Vice President Tariq al-Hashimi and Iraqi Accordance Front (IAF) leader Adnan al-Duleimi is that the Awakening Councils will gain political power at the expense of Sunni politicians. The increasing influence of the Awakening tribesmen has begun to challenge the Sunni bloc for a share in political power—a prospect many Sunni leaders want to avoid. The boycott by IAF ministers of al-Maliki's government last August prompted rumors that the Awakening Council would nominate candidates to replace them (*Asharq al-Awsat*, November 29, 2007).

A dilemma has emerged in the current relationship between the United States and the Awakening Council concerning the prospect of integrating *Sahwa* tribesmen into Iraqi security and police forces. The Shi'a political community is uneasy with what they perceive as U.S. control over the Sunni-dominated militia. The Awakening forces are autonomous and unaccountable to the Iraqi government. Depending on their rank, members are paid from $300 to $1200 every month by the U.S. military (*The Independent*, January 28, 2008). The Sahwa leaders are demanding that they be integrated into Iraq's national defense forces, assuming permanent positions with permanent payrolls.

In addition to the suspicion of the *Sahwa* held by Iraq's Shi'a leaders, the Awakening leaders have a reciprocal mistrust of the Shi'a-dominated government, often defining it as a puppet of Iran. But concern over the Awakening's political agenda is perhaps not necessarily the major reason why some Sunni and Shi'a lawmakers have been reluctant to embrace the movement. Rather it may be suspicions over the past history of *Sahwa* members. According to Sheikh Harith al-Dhari, head of the Sunni Association of Muslim Scholars: "Many of those who have joined the *Sahwa* Councils have been members in al-Qaeda. They joined al-Qaeda in the first place for the sake of money, and when more money became available in a different direction, they rushed to it" (*Aswat al-Iraq*, January 9, 2008).

Many of the *Sahwa* fighters are former insurgents, Ba'athists and al-Qaeda terrorists. The rapid growth of the tribal coalition has led many in the Shi'a government to assume that the Awakening Councils could not possibly have inspected every member thoroughly—suggesting the organization suffers from mass infiltration. Rumors of infiltration have lately been advanced through a series of Shi'a newspaper articles. Even the idea of infiltration helps discredit the Awakening Councils in the eyes of Iraqi officials. Prime Minister al-Maliki said in an interview: "We, as a government, have intelligence information: the Ba'ath party has ordered its members to join the Awakening Councils, and al-Qaeda has ordered its members to infiltrate the Awakening Councils" (*Asharq al-Awsat*, January 5, 2008).

Threat from the Shi'a Militias

The secular and Sunni-oriented makeup of the expanding Awakening Movement has led to deep anxiety in Shi'a circles in southern Iraq. Referring to Iraq's powerful Shi'a religious leaders, the current *Sahwa* commander in al-Anbar, Kamal Hammad Abu Risha, said in an interview that Islam has "an active role in our society but we reject clerics' interference in politics. The power of the clerics should not exceed the mosques nor affect the political decision-making process" (*Aswat al-Iraq*, January 14, 2008).

Statements like this have produced anxiety in powerful Shi'a clerics such as the anti-American firebrand Muqtada al-Sadr and Abdul Aziz al-Hakim, then leader of the Islamic Supreme Council of Iraq (ISCI). Though the men are intense rivals for the Shi'a sphere of influence, the two leaders share a mutual concern for the Awakening's increasing threat towards Shi'a hegemony in Iraq. Al-Hakim and al-Sadr lead the two most powerful militias in Iraq: the Badr Brigade and the Jaysh al-Mahdi (JaM), respectively. Both organizations are Iranian-backed and trained by the Islamic Revolutionary Guard Corps (IRGC).

The formation of a secular and Sunni-dominated force of over 80,000, spread out across Iraq, supersedes both JaM and the Badr Brigade—effectively defining them now as second-class militias. While both Shi'a militias are forced to work covertly in their funding and armament activities, the *Sahwa* profits from being openly supplied and backed by the U.S. military.

Terrorist Pressures

The Awakening Councils have received threats from outsiders for their collaboration with U.S. forces. In November 2007, Syrian Sheikh Abd al-Munim Mustafa Halima—also known as Abu Baseer al-Tartousi—condemned the Iraqi tribesmen for cooperating with the U.S. occupiers. Residing in London, al-Tartousi is considered one of the leading theoreticians of the Salafi-jihadist trend in Islam. He writes that, "the so-called Awakening Councils [*Majalis al-Sahwa*], which preferred to join ranks with the invaders and aggressors against the jihad fighters, should be called the Councils of Stupor and Oblivion." When addressing the suggestion that the Councils' collaboration is a reaction to al-Qaeda's brutal tactics against their members, al-Tartousi suggests that, "one injustice does not justify a greater injustice" (MEMRI, January 15, 2008).

In late December 2007, Osama bin Laden also condemned those joining the Awakening movement, claiming that, "they sold out their religion in return for a mortal [monetary] world" (RFE/RL, January 4, 2008). Since this statement was made, there has been an exceptional spike in al-Qaeda's attacks against members of the Awakening Council. In the month of January 2008, the tribal coalition experienced the loss of well over a hundred members, including the assassinations of at least six senior Awakening leaders.

Awakening Returning to Insurgency?

The U.S. military and intelligence community is alarmed by the possibility of the Awakening Council strategy backfiring, essentially leading to an unfortunate path similar to that experienced in Afghanistan. This is the likely scenario if the United States is unable to keep paying the Awakening members and/or the central government fails to meet their demands. U.S. officials are concerned over the recent increase in killings of *Sahwa* members and the possibility that some *Sahwa* fighters might rejoin the insurgency.

"If the Americans think they can use us to crush al-Qaeda and then push us to one side, they are mistaken," says Abu Marouf, the commander of 13,000 fighters who formerly fought U.S. soldiers. As a member of the powerful Zubai tribe, he was part of al-Qaeda's defeat in the stronghold of Fallujah. While discussing his demand for the integration of his fighters into official Iraqi forces, Abu Marouf stated: "If there is no change in three months there will be war again." According to local sources, Abu Marouf is a former commander in the insurgent 1920 Revolution Brigades (*The Independent*, January 28, 2008).

Many politicians recognize a return to insurgency as a possible consequence if terrorist pressures continue. Senior Sunni politician Omar Abdul Sattar warned that if the Awakening Councils were disbanded, the security situation in Iraq will "deteriorate precipitously" (*Azzaman*, January 3, 2008). Unfortunately, despite the risk of reversing Iraq's security progress, there is no apparent urgency in al-Maliki's government to integrate Awakening members. U.S. officials point to Shi'a politicians as the main source of obstruction to the integration program. According to Brig. General Jim Huggins, of the 3,000 recruits of the Awakening Council he sent to a Shi'a leader's office to apply for integration, only 400 names received approval—all Shi'as (*USA Today*, February 1, 2008).

Prospects: al-Sadr and Iran

To add to the dilemma plaguing the U.S. counterinsurgency strategy, the rise of the Awakening councils may risk reigniting the JaM. Since August 2007, Muqtada al-Sadr's self-imposed ceasefire has contributed tremendously to the decline of violence throughout Iraq. On February 22, 2008, the ceasefire was extended for another six months. But if the Awakening movement becomes too powerful or rejoins the insurgency due to unsatisfied demands, al-Sadr may be inclined to end the ceasefire or concede further fragmentation of the Jaysh al-Mahdi. Rogue factions within the Shi'a militia have already targeted *Sahwa* fighters, especially in Baghdad.

The Islamic Republic of Iran seems to be reasserting itself in Iraq. Reports published by the Iraqi Islamic Party and the pro-Ba'athist website "Quds Press" cited unidentified intelligence sources stating that brigades comprised of rogue JaM elements were being formed by the Iranian Quds Force to assassinate Awakening Council members (RFE/RL, January 4, 2008). This was later corroborated by sources belonging to the Awakening Councils: "Special groups supported by the Iranian Quds have started armed activities against elements of the Awakening forces in various parts of Baghdad" (Al-Sharqiyah TV, January 28, 2008).

The success of counterinsurgency in Iraq is contingent on many elements of the security environment that the U.S. has little control over. One of the major factors contributing to recent security improvements is the Awakening's formation against AQI in al-Anbar province. Another major part of the success story is Muqtada al-Sadr's militia ceasefire. However, the security and political dilemmas facing the Awakening Councils may lead these organizations to fragment, split and rejoin the insurgency. This would effectively force al-Sadr to reinstate an active JaM—a prospect likely to diminish the security progress achieved in 2007.

VOLATILE LANDSCAPE
Mergers and Acquisitions within the Iraqi Insurgency

By Pascale Combelles Siegel
February 28, 2008
Terrorism Focus 5 (8)

For the U.S. military, 2007 was the year of the surge in Iraq. The controversial troop increase – along with the rise of the Sunni Awakening councils and Muqtada al-Sadr's truce – has combined to help tame both sectarian and insurgent violence. As for the insurgents, 2007 was a year of mergers and acquisitions, with groups consolidating into new fronts and alliances. This process of consolidation has gone remarkably unnoticed, possibly because its first order of business has been to take on al-Qaeda in Iraq (AQI) and its Islamic State. But does this evolution bode well for the future stability of Iraq?

The consolidation began when AQI decided to unify the insurgent groups under its leadership. A pair of umbrella organizations were formed: first the Mujahideen Shura Council, then the Islamic State of Iraq. For the better part of two years (2005-2006), AQI touted the virtues of unity and called on other insurgent groups to join forces under its leadership (*al-Fajr* Media Center, October 13, 2006; *al-Furqan*, December 22, 2006). The call was to no avail. Some groups cooperated with AQI fighters on a tactical level, but no major insurgent group decided to ally itself with AQI. Major insurgent groups stayed away from the umbrella organizations grossly dominated by AQI. When coaxing and cajoling failed, the group began attacking fellow insurgents to force their acquiescence. That tactic led to a public backlash spearheaded by the Islamic Army in Iraq (IAI) (iaisite.org, April 5, 2007) and seemingly initiated a process of consolidation around four poles:

The Islamic State of Iraq (ISI) is a group of eight Salafist organizations dominated by AQI. The ISI's project is to restore the Caliphate under a puritanical brand of Islam and use it as a launch-pad to liberate Jerusalem. It is characterized by adhesion to Salafism, belief in jihad and by an internationalist agenda. The army of Ansar al-Islam has cooperated with the ISI, but not joined it. It adheres to the same brand of ideology; however, it has not, as of yet, unveiled international ambitions.

The Reformation and Jihad Front (RJF) was formed in May 2007 by the

IAI, the Mujahideen Army and the Muhajideen Shura Council of the Ansar al-Sunna (iaisite-eng.org, September 15, 2007). The front is primarily concerned with the situation in Iraq where it wants to end the U.S. occupation, end Iranian influence over Iraqi officials, and make tabula rasa of the post-invasion political framework. Rhetorically, it mixes Salafist and nationalist references. However, the front – and particularly the Islamic Army in Iraq – has increasingly discussed international issues such as the fate of Palestinians and the Muhammad cartoons, calling for jihad to avenge the sullied honor of Muslims. The RJF has formed the Political Council of the Iraqi Resistance (PCIR) with two of the more nationalist groups, Hamas-Iraq and the Islamic Front of the Iraqi Resistance (JAMI) (al-Jazeera, October 13, 2007). The PCIR is also expressing concern with international issues such as the Israeli blockade of Gaza.

The Jihad and Change Front (JCF) was formed in September 2007. It is composed of eight groups led by the 1920 Revolution Brigades and the Rashideen Army. Ideologically close to the Muslim Brotherhood, the front embraces a moderate Islamist agenda and seeks to end the occupation and nullify the acts taken by the post-invasion Iraqi government.

The Supreme Command of Jihad and Liberation (SCJL) is a consortium of 22 factions formed by the Ba'ath Party under the leadership of Izzat Ibrahim al-Douri in October 2007 (al-Basrah.net, October 7, 2007). The command wants to end the occupation of Iraq and nullify all laws and decisions adopted since 2003.

There is good news in this process. The forging of fronts and alliances is a sign the insurgency is maturing from paramilitary groups to politico-military entities with political programs and more explicit visions of the future. This type of change is a prerequisite for engaging in a process of national reconciliation. In spite of their often-fiery anti-American rhetoric, some of these groups and fronts have cooperated at the local level with U.S. forces to enforce local ceasefires. They have also decided for the time being that fighting AQI is more important than fighting the United States. These local processes might help jump-start a more durable reconciliation.

However, there are also grounds for concern. All these fronts remain adamantly opposed to the current government of Iraq both in words and actions.

Each also wants to be considered as the sole legitimate representative of the Iraqi people, not just the Iraqi Sunnis. This demand makes it more difficult to actually engage in a formal reconciliation because under such a framework, Shi'as would have to agree to be represented by Sunni insurgent groups. When these fronts hint at a willingness to open negotiations, it is with the United States and not with the Iraqi government. Lastly, another ground for concern is the willingness of the ISI and the RJF to take on international issues and advocate jihad in other struggles, most notably on behalf of the Palestinians.

In 2007, the insurgents began to articulate political visions. In 2008, the challenge would be to draw their visions toward reconcilable positions with Iraq's other communities.

Iran Charged with Infiltration and Sabotage of Iraq's Awakening Councils

By Rafid Fadhil Ali
April 9, 2008
Terrorism Focus 5 (14)

General Muhammad al-Shahwani, then head of Iraq's intelligence service, released a statement on February 27, 2008 accusing the Iranian intelligence services of planning to sabotage the largely Sunni tribal-based Awakening Councils that have formed in Iraq to combat al-Qaeda. The statement was placed on the formal website of the Iraqi intelligence service only days before the visit of Iranian President Mahmoud Ahmadinejad to Baghdad in early March 2008 (*Azzaman*, February 28, 2008).

Although Iran has been frequently accused by U.S. officials at every level of destabilizing Iraq, it has rarely been criticized by the Iraqi government, which is formed from a coalition of Shi'as and Kurds—the Sunnis withdrew from the cabinet in August 2007. The ties between Iran and the current Iraqi governing parties go back to the 1980-1988 Iran-Iraq War, when those parties were the exiled opposition to the Ba'athist regime of Saddam Hussein.

President Ahmadinejad's visit was boycotted by the Sunni politicians and there were rallies in some Sunni towns denouncing the visit (*Azzaman*, March 2, 2008). The Sunnis have always looked at Shi'a Iran as an enemy, but this could not disturb the visit or the warm welcome that Ahmadinejad received from the

Shi'a and Kurdish politicians in Baghdad. Hoshyar Zebari, the Iraqi Foreign Minister, said that the Iranian president came with a defiant message to the United States: "You [America] have your presence [in Iraq] and I have mine" (*Asharq al-Awsat*, March 11, 2008).

The statement of General al-Shahwani – who rarely speaks to the media or releases public statements—indicated that Iraqi intelligence had information that the Iranian intelligence services had deployed operatives all over Iraq to sabotage the Awakening Councils. Al-Shahwani stressed that people should be vigilant and urged them to support the Awakening movement in order to preserve hard-won security improvements. Al-Shahwani is a Sunni and a former officer in Saddam's military. He left the army in 1990 to enter the U.S.-backed opposition and was heavily involved in a failed coup attempt in 1996. Three of his sons were executed in retribution. He maintains close links with the CIA, which continues to exert tight control over the *Mukhabarat*, Iraq's overwhelmingly Sunni and Kurdish secret intelligence service.

Al-Shahwani did not reveal any details about particular operations the Iranians might have participated in, but he called on the Iraqi security services to monitor and pursue any suspect activities. General Abdul Kareem Khalaf, spokesman of the Ministry of the Interior, agreed with al-Shahwani, saying that the head of the intelligence service would not have made his statement without having decisive evidence. A U.S. military source, speaking under condition of anonymity to an Arab newspaper, agreed with General al-Shahwani and added that forces connected to the Iranian al-Quds force had targeted the Awakening movement (*Asharq al-Awsat*, February 28, 2008). Sheikh Ahmad Abu Risha, a prominent Awakening leader from al-Anbar province, also stressed that General al-Shahwani's statement should be taken seriously. Abu Risha did not rule out that there were Iranian efforts to foil the awakening movement (*al-Malaf Press*, February 29, 2008).

Tamir al-Tamimi – also known as Abu Azzam al-Tamimi – a former member of the Islamic Army insurgent group and head of the Awakening Council of Abu Ghraib, west of Baghdad, commented on the information by making the surprising statement that Iran targets the Awakening movement directly and indirectly through organizations like al-Qaeda. The attacks come by explosive devices, car bombs or suicide attacks (*Azzaman*, February 28, 2008).

It is interesting that a wide range of Sunnis in Iraq believe that Shi'a Iran has a link with the Sunni extremist organization of al-Qaeda. Two prominent leaders of Awakening groups in western Baghdad, Abu Elabid and Shujaa al-Adhami, believe that Iran supplies al-Qaeda and the Shi'a militias with weapons and money to target their movements (Radiosawa.com, January 11, 2008).

Many Sunnis point to individuals like former Badr Brigades commander Abu Mustafa al-Shaibani, who is charged with running a network to smuggle Iranian-made improvised explosive devices (IEDs) and explosively formed projectiles (EFPs) into Iraq. According to a source from the Iraqi Ministry of Defense, al-Shaibani, who was arrested by Coalition forces in 2007, admitted that the Iranian bodies that supported him had given him instructions to widen his network to as many insurgent groups as he could reach. He revealed that in addition to the Shi'a militias he had tight relations with insurgent groups affiliated with al-Qaeda (*al-Malaf Press*, May 22, 2007). U.S. sources allege that al-Shaibani works under the supervision of Iran's Islamic Revolutionary Guard Corps, operating a network whose "first objective is to fight U.S. forces, attacking convoys and killing soldiers. Its second objective is to eliminate Iraqi politicians opposed to Iran's influence" (U.S. Treasury Department, HP-759, January 9, 2008).

As part of his reservations about the Awakening Councils, Iraqi Prime Minister Nouri al-Maliki justified his reluctance to recruit Sunni fighters to the government forces by indicating that the banned the Ba'ath Party and al-Qaeda had ordered their members to infiltrate the Awakening groups (*Asharq al-Awsat*, January 5, 2008). According to what the Sunnis believe about the relation between Iran and al-Qaeda, Iran may be partly behind the infiltrating tactics of al-Qaeda and the Ba'ath, or the Iranians might be using such infiltrations to serve their strategy of attacking the Awakening movement.

The Awakening movement started in al-Anbar where its organization was based on tribal formations led by tribal leaders. This has made it very hard for infiltration efforts to succeed. In Baghdad the Awakening movement spread in almost every Sunni neighborhood, but here the population is not from one tribe and the tribal bond in general is weaker. This offers more opportunities for infiltration. While the tribal bond protects al-Anbar Awakening from a specific type of infiltration, the continuing rivalries among the Sunni powers (see *Terrorism Focus*, March 11, 2008) might open the way to another type. A leader of one the Awakening groups in al-Anbar expressed his concern about the repeated visits of Sheikh Hamid Farhan al-Hays, a Grand Sheikh and Awakening leader, to Iran (*al-Hayat*, October 8, 2007). Al-Hays was once seen as a possible successor to the leadership of the al-Anbar Awakening Council after Sheikh

Abdul Sattar Abu Risha was killed by a car bomb in September 2007 (see *Terrorism Focus*, March 11, 2008).

Whether the theory held by some Sunnis that there is a link between Iran and al-Qaeda is right or wrong, any possible evidence and indications should be taken seriously and carefully considered. Iraqi Sunni sources point out that breaking up the Awakening Councils has become a priority for Iranian policy in Iraq. The Awakening groups armed by the U.S. army have become dangerous for the Iranian-backed Shi'a militias (thirdpower.org, January 6, 2008).

Rows over pay have become frequent between the U.S. army and the Awakening Councils. This is not an encouraging sign as most of these Sunni fighters lost their old jobs as officers in Saddam Hussein's army and security forces and have not yet been absorbed into the new Iraqi Army. This type of situation would be of great assistance to infiltration efforts by Iranian or other foreign intelligence services.

The Iraqi Sunnis believe that there is coordination between Iranian intelligence and al-Qaeda to attack the Awakening movement in order to reverse its role in the security improvement in Iraq. Iran is not willing to stabilize Iraq in order to keep the United States under pressure and prevent it from putting pressure on Iran (Tamir al-Tamimi to newsabah.com, March 16, 2008). With the allies of Tehran dominating the political scene in Iraq, the ambition of some Sunni leaders might push them closer to Iran.

Kurdish Islamist Groups in Northern Iraq

By Rafid Fadhil Ali
November 25, 2008
Terrorism Monitor 6 (22)

A spokesman of the Kurdish arm of al-Qaeda in Iraq (AQI) recently announced the group's intention to eliminate Iraq's Kurdish leadership: "To the two Kurdish puppets, Jalal al-Talabani and Masoud Barzani, I swear by God that we have no mercy or sympathy towards the traitors who sold themselves to the enemies of God. Your throats will be slit." The challenge from the Kurdistan Brigades came in an October 2008 video released by *al-Furqan*, the media arm of the Islamic State of Iraq (ISI). The Kurdish-language video shows group members doing military training and chanting in Kurdish while masked men read a statement condemning the top Iraqi Kurdish and Shi'a leaders. The statement expresses the group's opinion that the religion of the Kurdish people is in danger, as Kurdistan is under the control of the United States, the UK and the Jews. Entitled "Eid Gift #4 - The Kurdistan Brigades," the video contained footage of attacks with small arms and road-side bombs on patrols of the security forces of the Kurdistan Regional Government (KRG) (muslm.net, October 8, 2008; paldf.net, October 4, 2008).

KRG officials usually refer to the Kurdistan Brigades as a group linked to the Salafi-Jihadi Ansar al-Islam movement, the insurgent group bombed by U.S. forces during the 2003 American invasion. The stance of the Brigades differs from the conclusion reached recently by the exiled leader of Ansar al-Islam, Mullah Fatih Krekar, who said he saw no reason to clash with the ruling parties in Kurdistan at the moment, suggesting patience while waiting for this stage in Iraq's political evolution to pass (*Islam Online*, November 5, 2008).

Beside the Kurdistan Brigades, there are four major Islamist political movements active in Iraqi Kurdistan:

The Islamic Movement in Iraqi Kurdistan (IMIK) – Formed in 1987 in Halabja. IMIK fought against Saddam's regime in the 1980s. In the 1990s IMIK engaged in fighting with Jalal al-Talabani's Patriotic Union of Kurdistan (PUK). The movement is led by Mullah Ali Abd al-Aziz Halabji. In its last conference, IMIK announced reforms and elected women for the first time to its supreme command. A pledge was also made to play the role of the political opposition in Kurdistan.

The Islamic Group of Kurdistan (IGK) – Headed by Mullah Ali Bapir, the IGK formed in 2001 as an offshoot of the IMIK. The movement participates in the regional government and parliament. The group does not currently advocate jihad and has announced its willingness to work with Sufi as well as Salafist forms of Sunni Islam.

The Islamic Union of Kurdistan (IUK) – Unlike the Salafist IMIK and the IGK, this group, which is the biggest Islamic party in Kurdistan, represents the Muslim Brotherhood in Kurdistan. The IUK is headed by Salah al-Din Muhammad Baha'a al-Din and is considered the third party in Kurdistan, with members in both the central and regional parliaments.

Ansar al-Islam – A Salafi-Jihadi group founded by radical elements of IMIK in 2001 with the name of Jund al-Islam. The group is headed by Mullah Krekar, who lives in Norway. In 2003, the movement was driven from its base in Iraq by PUK *Peshmerga* and U.S. Special Forces units. Most members fled to Iran but are believed to have now regrouped in Iraqi Kurdistan. Although the group denies any link to al-Qaeda, it has called for jihad against Coalition forces and still advocates jihad in the Muslim world.

Right after the Iraqi parliament passed a law to pave the way for the formation of autonomous regions within Iraq, al-Qaeda in Iraq declared the formation of the Islamic State of Iraq in the Sunni areas of central and western Iraq. The justification was that the Kurds had their autonomous region in the north, while the legislation paved the way for the Shi'as to form their own region in the south and center. Nevertheless, the Islamic State, which was initially supposed to extend over the Sunni-Arab part of Iraq, turned out to have a Kurdish wing.

Emergence of the Kurdistan Brigades

In the first half of 2007, the name of the Kurdistan Brigades started to appear in jihadi Internet forums. On April 21, 2007, a letter signed by Haji Arif, who claimed to be the leader of the Brigades, was placed on a number of jihadi forums. In his letter Arif declared clearly that his group is part of al-Qaeda and presented his group to the public as a Salafi-Jihadi group:

> *People of Kurdistan, We promise to carry Allah's message and keep it pure by not mixing it with any infidel legitimacy such as democracy and secularism... You will see how we will destroy the enemies of Allah and restore dignity for the bearers of Allah's religion... your brothers in the Kurdistan Brigades will prevent Kurdistan from being a pastureland for the Jews, the Crusaders and their agents (majdah.maktoob.com, April 21, 2007).*

Arif went on to condemn the Kurdish leaders, Masoud Barzani, KRG president, and Jalal al-Talabani, the president of Iraq. Arif called on the moderate Islamists in Kurdistan, some of whom are involved in the parliament and the regional government, to change their course:

> *Our demands are for those movements that carry Islamic slogans but are*

aligned with the secular parties and are part of the so-called regional government of Kurdistan... they are not ashamed of sitting with the American occupiers as if they have no relation with the war between America and Islam, as if jihad does not include them. We tell them, leave the Americans and their agents and refer to the Quran verses about belief and infidelity.

Arif ends his statement by calling on Muslims everywhere to support his group with funding. Arif also confirmed his group's loyalty to al-Qaeda leader Osama Bin Laden and to the leader of the Islamic State in Iraq, Sheikh Abu Omar al-Baghdadi.

The vast majority of the population in Iraqi Kurdistan is Sunni Muslim. Nevertheless, AQI could not operate freely in that area in post-war Iraq. Unlike the rest of the country, Kurdistan was already beyond the control of Saddam's central government. The area was secured by the Regional Government, controlled by the two main Kurdish parties; Barzani's Kurdistan Democratic Party (KDP) and the PUK, headed by Jalal al-Talabani. For most Kurds the invasion was a historic opportunity to get rid of Saddam's threat, but al-Qaeda did not give up its attempts to influence the Kurds. In an interview published earlier this year on al-Sahab, the media wing of al-Qaeda, Dr. Ayman al-Zawahiri, al-Qaeda's second-in-command, gave his views on the Iraqi Kurds:

The Kurds are a genuine part of the Muslim nation, every Muslim is proud of their sacrifice and history. All Muslims sympathize with the Kurds for the oppression they suffered under the fanatical Ba'athist regime. I think that their brothers the mujahideen in Iraq, whether Arab, Kurdish or Turkman, sympathize with the Kurds and understand many of the Kurds' demands as stated by Sheikh Abu Omar al-Baghdadi (may Allah protect him). But what no Muslim, Kurdish or non-Kurdish, can possibly accept is that Iraqi Kurdistan be ruled by a secular government, loyal to the Crusaders and cooperating with the Jews (Al-Sahab Media Productions, December 2007; see also Terrorism Focus, June 24).

The Kurdistan Brigades are active in the border sector between Iraq and Iran, especially around the town of Halabja. This area east of al-Sulaymaniyah is traditionally the main stronghold of the Kurdish Islamists. It was the gateway for the first group of al-Qaeda fighters who came from Afghanistan and set up their camps there. One of those fighters was the then little known Abu Musab al-Zarqawi, the late leader of AQI, killed in 2006.

Marwan Naqshabandi, a Kurdish researcher specializing in armed groups, believes that Iran supports the Brigades. In an interview with Dubai's al-Arabiya satellite TV, he indicated that Shi'a Iran could get over the sectarian barrier with the Sunni Salafi-Jihadis: "Iran is not a sectarian state but a national one, they are clever in dealing with armed groups out of their territories. Iran is helping the Kurdistan Brigades of al-Qaeda to the extent of hitting the targets set by Iran against its political opponents. I do not believe that the Brigades are strong enough to embarrass Iran or to create trouble inside it." (al-Arabiya TV, November 16, 2008).

Conclusion

It is hard to find concrete evidence that Iran is supporting the Kurdistan Brigades, though the Brigades' need for bases in Iran is crucial. They are isolated geographically from their comrades in the Arab part of Iraq; for example, Mullah Krekar described the long journey his followers in Ansar al-Islam had to undertake when they fled their bases in Iraqi Kurdistan after the American bombing in 2003:

More than 80 fighters were killed and the two major Kurdish parties captured the same amount. Fifteen were captured in Iran and the rest disappeared in the Iranian Kurdish villages until they managed to forge identification documents [that] enabled them to pass the Iranian-Iraqi borders through Shi'a southern Iraq. They then reached Baghdad, Ramadi, Diyala and Mosul, where they are now (*Islam Online*, November 5, 2008).

The Arab and Kurdish branches of al-Qaeda in Iraq will likely work to bridge the geographical gap between them. Full coordination between the regional government of Kurdistan and the Iraqi central government will be required to prevent this. There was a big row recently when Iraqi Prime Minister Nouri al-Maliki wanted to form tribal armed groups backed by the central government in Kurdistan and the surrounding areas, with the Kurds strongly condemning the move. Kurds, worrying that the Sunni Arabs might turn against them, have opposed forming Awakening councils in disputed areas where the population is a mix of Kurd and Sunnis Arab (Moheet.com, November 18, 2008). If this dispute develops into a crisis, it would present a golden opportunity for al-Qaeda to connect the mountain bases of the Kurdistan Brigades along the Iranian border east of al-Sulaymaniyah with one of the few remaining AQI strongholds west of al-Sulaymaniyah in the Himreen Mountains.

While the Brigades are urging the moderate Islamists in Kurdistan to turn violent, moderate Kurdish Islamists must try to influence the members of the Brigades, especially those whom they knew and worked with in the past. Both the central and regional governments should support such initiatives in an effort to curb the spread of radical Islam in the relatively secure Iraqi Kurdistan.

Iraq's Islamic Mujahideen Profiled by Jihadi Websites: Part One

By Abdul Hameed Bakier
November 26, 2008
Terrorism Focus 5 (40)

The profiles of a number of Iraqi jihadi groups were prepared and released by al-Haq news agency (haqnews.net August 7, 2008). According to al-Haq, the material was collected through interviews with field commanders, jihadi forums and pertinent websites. The files accumulated by al-Haq, entitled, "The Media Jihad: a Reading of the Jihadi Media in Iraq," were also distributed in some jihadi forums, prompting forum participants to add their corrections, additions and revisions (alboraq.info, November 8, 2008). Al-Haq decided to release these profiles in the jihadi forums after Arab media refused to publish them.

Islamic Resistance Movement / 1920 Revolution Brigades

The core members of this group are a mixture of Salafis, Muslim Brothers and independent Islamists, backed by a few Iraqi tribesmen and the Association of Muslim Scholars. The group claims no alliance with any political party and has an independent decision-making process. The political wing, the Islamic Resistance Movement (IRM), includes a political office, an Islamic decrees office, a jihad security office and a media section. The military wing is called the 1920 Revolution Brigades (1920-RB) and is comprised of over thirty battalions (according to al-Haq). The name of each brigade and its field of operations are given. The profile does not give the name of the group's general leader, called only "the Amir," but names the head of the political office, Mujahid Abdul Rahman, and the official spokesman, Abdullah al-Omari.

Ideology

The group emphasizes its Islamic identity and religious justification for fighting the occupiers by relying on the teachings of the holy Quran and Sunna as a source of guidance in their religiously mandatory "defensive jihad" to evict the enemy from Iraq before moving on to "occupied" neighboring Muslim countries. The main objectives of the group are to expel the enemy and establish an Islamic Caliphate in Iraq.

The IRM reiterates that its jihad is complimentary to other groups' jihads against occupiers. The group says, "We don't claim to be the only jihadi group, but ask all our members to obey the leadership." Abu Qodama, one of the field commanders of 1920-RB, says, "We cooperate with all jihadi groups, except the Ba'athist groups whom we deem non-Islamic polytheists." Although an al-Qaeda onslaught on the IRM/1920-RB resulted in the death of some of the group's leaders, the movement opted not to retaliate (ktb-20.com July 3, 2007).

The movement rejects the political process in Iraq and does not recognize the Iraqi government that resulted from this process. The group's Amir believes peace is not possible in Iraq under U.S. occupation; therefore, any elections or referendums are irrelevant. Along with four other jihadi organizations, the IRM/1920-RB released a statement declaring any Iraqi government illegal during American occupation.

The movement affirms that their jihad is conditioned on not harming any civilians and rejects the principle of "the end justifies the means." The group aborts any attack on U.S. forces that might result in killing innocent bystanders. The group also renounces all forms of sectarianism and judges people individually on the degree of their collaboration with the occupiers.

Military Activities

1920-RB fighters are deployed in the Sunni governorates of Iraq, using rocket and mortar attacks, light weapons ambushes, sniper attacks and roadside bomb attacks. The group also claims the downing of a British C130 Hercules in February, 2005, and the kidnapping of the American director of the Baghdad airport in April 2005 (*Telegraph*, February 2, 2005).

Media Activities

The group's statements and video messages are broadcast by Arabic-language satellite channels such as al-Jazeera, al-Zawra and al-Rafidayn. The group also releases communiqués, video clips and *al-Katayb,* an internet magazine covering its military and political activities. Besides using jihadi websites such as al-hesbah.info, alboraq.info, hanein.info and muslm.net, 1920-RB has websites of its own - kataeb20.com and ktb-20.com.

Ansar al-Sunna Army

Founded in 2003 as a Salafi-Jihadi movement, this group is considered an outgrowth of the Kurdish-Sunni Arab Ansar al-Islam. The group includes former members of Ansar al-Islam and volunteers from Arab countries, although the original core was formed from members of al-Taifa al-Mansoura Mujahideen Brigades (TMMB). The TMMB later withdrew from Ansar al-Sunna and joined the Jaysh al-Islami. Abu Abdullah al-Hassan Bin Mahmoud is the Amir of the group and Sheikh Abdul Wahab al-Sultan is the religious mentor.

Ideology

As the name implies, Ansar al-Sunna is a Sunni group following the Salafist path. The legitimacy of its insurgency operations is based on the religious duty of "defensive jihad." In the founding declaration of the group, Amir Abu Abdullah Mahmoud said, "after the occupation of Iraq, jihad became a divine obligation on every Muslim. The objective of jihad is to expel the enemy and implement an Islamic *Shari'a* government."

Ansar al-Sunna's operations and objectives are in conformity with all other Sunni jihadi groups, and, like many other groups, Ansar al-Sunna refrained from retaliating against al-Qaeda's attacks on the group members. In a statement released in June 25, 2006, Ansar al-Sunna rejected the democratic process in Iraq as illegitimate and blasphemous, condemning Prime Minister Nouri al-Maliki's national reconciliation initiative and identifying members of Iraq's parliament as apostates.

Military Activities

The group is militarily active in northern Iraq, the Sunni governorates and in some southern cities, where it targets national guards, police and the militias of the two Kurdish parties led by Jalal al-Talibani and Masoud Barazani. The group claims the bombing of offices belonging to Kurdish political parties in February 2004; the bombing of an American military base in Mosul on December 21, 2004; and the bombing of the Turkish Embassy in Baghdad in October 2003.

Media Activities

Like many other Iraqi jihadi groups, Ansar al-Sunna does not have continuous coverage of its activities in major news channels other than al-Jazeera, al-Zawra and al-Rafidayn satellite television channels. The group publishes Ansar al-Sunna magazine, the *Mujahideen Harvest* news bulletin and has its own website (ansar11.org). Ansar al-Sunna posts almost daily reports of allegedly successful attacks on U.S. forces in Iraq, along with other political and religious statements. Ansar al-Sunna rejected the U.S.-Iraqi security agreement in a religious decree released by the group on November 20, 2008.

Jaysh al-Islami in Iraq

The existence of this Salafi-Jihadi group backed by Sunni tribes and ex-military officers was first announced in late 2003, but the group claims it was actually formed before the occupation of Iraq. The group's "defensive jihad" aims to rid Iraq of the U.S. occupation before setting up an Islamic *Shari'a* government. Regardless of discord with some jihadi groups and internal fighting with al-Qaeda, the Jaysh al-Islami declares it has no animosity with any jihadi group, but rather endeavors to unite with them under a single leadership. Dr. Ibrahim Yusuf al-Shamari is the group's official spokesman, Dr. Ali al-Naimi the media spokesman, and Imad al-Din Abdullah the Director of Central Media Information.

Ideology

Like many other Sunni groups, the Jaysh al-Islami rejects the current political process in Iraq but accepts any process within the framework of Islamic constraints. It also believes the occupier should compensate Iraqis for moral and physical damage inflicted by the occupation.

Military Activities

The Jaysh al-Islami is considered the biggest jihadi group in Iraq and deploys in the Sunni governorates in Baghdad, al-Anbar, Salah al-Din, Mosul, Kirkuk, Diyala, Babel, central Basra, and Amara. The group's military targets include U.S. forces, the Iraqi military, Iraqi police and the Badr (Shi'a) militias. The group is well known for it use of roadside bombs, snipers and rocket attacks. The intelligence unit of the group is responsible for a number of notorious hostage-takings and the kidnapping and killing of American civilians working with Iraq's housing ministry. Abu Moshtaq al-Zebaidi is the group's military commander.

Media Activities

The group has a number of regular publications of its military operations under names such as *Aydo* (Prepare); *Sout al-Jihad* (Voice of Jihad); *Fi thikra al-ihtilal* (On the Anniversary of Occupation) and *Alyoum wa ghadan ya Amerika* (Today and Tomorrow, O America). Special publications of the group cover unique subjects, such as weapons of mass destruction and the activities of the "Baghdad Sniper." The different formations of the Jaysh al-Islami also release their own accounts of attacks on the occupiers with videos bearing titles such as Sawaeq al-Fallujah (al-Fallujah Detonators) and Istamiro Ya Asood al-Anbar (Continue al-Anbar Lions). The group's best-known regular publication is *al-Fursan* magazine, with 16 issues so far. The Jaysh al-Islami probably leads all Iraqi jihad groups in the number of websites and Internet forums it maintains. Its official website, iaisite.org, is run by the group's media corps, along with alboraq.info, alboraqmedia.org, baghdadsniper.net and lee-flash.com.

Iraq's Islamic Mujahideen Profiled by Jihadi Websites: Part Two

By Abdul Hameed Bakier
December 3, 2008
Terrorism Focus 5 (41)

The preceeding article examined the profiles of three Iraqi jihadi groups based on information compiled by al-Haq – an Islamic news website and later distributed through a number of jihadi Internet forums (haqnews.net August 7, 2008). This issue will cover four remaining major insurgent groups mentioned in al-Haq's research.

al-Qaeda in Iraq (AQI)

AQI began insurgency operations in Iraq immediately after the occupation, under the name *Jama'at al-Tawhid wa'l-Jihad* (Monotheism and Jihad Group). In October 2004, the late leader of the group, Abu Musab al-Zarqawi, pledged allegiance to al-Qaeda's leader Osama bin Laden and changed the name of the group to al-Qaeda in Iraq (also known as al-Qaeda in Mesopotamia). Al-Zarqawi also joined the Mujahideen Shura Council in Iraq. AQI later became the core of the so-called Islamic State of Iraq (ISI).

The objectives of AQI are not limited to the liberation of Iraq. Similar to al-Qaeda's global stance, AQI aims to wage international jihad against the United States and its Arab allies and to establish a pan-Islamic Caliphate.

Ideology

AQI is a Salafi-Jihadi extremist group. "We believe the *umma* (Islamic nation) must come under one flag, especially that of the mujahideen," which is what the group tried to accomplish with the declaration of the Islamic State of Iraq (*al-Furqan*, October 15, 2006). The reluctance of other resistance movements to come under the umbrella of al-Qaeda leadership consequently led to confrontations between AQI and almost all other jihadi groups. The 1920 Revolution Brigades and *al-Jaysh al-Islami fi'l Iraq* (The Islamic Army in Iraq) became AQI's arch foes (see *Terrorism Focus*, November 25, 2008). AQI not only rejects the political process in Iraq, it targets all Iraqi parties that joined the process, including the Sunni entities. Any dealing with the occupiers is deemed blasphemy and apostasy, therefore AQI attacks the Iraqi government and its military, intelligence units and police without any exception. No party or individual is spared by AQI unless they pledge allegiance to the ISI. Internationally, AQI considers Muslim countries "infidels," stating: "We believe if infidel legislations prevails in a country and the dominance is for infidel rulers as opposed to

Islamic rule, the country is infidel. All forums of secularism, such as nationalism, socialism, communism and Ba'athism are stark blasphemy" (*al-Furqan*, October 15, 2006).

Military Activities

In the beginning, the military activities of AQI concentrated in the western areas of Iraq such as al-Anbar. After the second battle for Fallujah in October, 2004, the group spread through the Sunni governorates, central Iraq and a few areas in southern Iraq. The group is notorious for suicide attacks using vehicles filled with explosives, assassinations and the direct engagement of enemy forces.

Among AQI's most notorious attacks are the bombing of the Jordanian Embassy in Baghdad in August 2003; the bombing of UN headquarters in Baghdad on August 19, 2003; the Najaf bombings on August 29, 2003, that killed Shi'a leader Muhammad Baqr al-Hakim; the bombing of the Italian military headquarters in al-Nasiria on October 12, 2003; the Amman hotel bombings of November 9, 2005; and the September 2007 assassination of the head of al-Anbar's Awakening council, Sheikh Abdul Sattar Abu Risha. AQI also kidnapped and killed American Nicholas Berg, four Egyptian diplomats, one Algerian diplomat and two local staff from the Moroccan Embassy in Baghdad. AQI also formed the Omar Legion to confront the Shi'a Badr Brigades.

Media Activities

AQI activities enjoy extensive coverage from almost all major news channels. The video and audio messages of group leaders are monitored and broadcast all over the world. *Al-Furqan*, the ISI media agency, continuously releases video clips of attacks perpetrated by AQI under names such as "From the Mujahideen Harvest" and "American Intelligence in Baghdad's Streets." Audio lectures on religious topics by AQI leaders are also released on the Internet. The group publishes regular magazines called *Tharwat Sinam al-Jihad* and *Nashrat al-Marsad.* Al-Furqan and al-Fajr are AQI's media agencies, though they make use of many jihadi websites and forums such as al-hesbah.info, al-firdaws.info, al-ekhlaas.net, muslm.net, and m3ark.net, just to name a few.

Islamic Front for Iraqi Resistance (JAMI) / Salah al-Din Brigades (SDB)

JAMI (*al-Jabha al-Islamiya li'l Moqawama al-Iraqiya*) was proclaimed on April 28, 2004, as a political party with the Salah al-Din Brigades as its military wing. Lately the group has joined a jihadi front with Iraqi Hamas.

Ideology

JAMI is a moderate Islamic jihadi group affiliated with the Muslim Brothers of Iraq. Although the group doesn't recognize the Iraqi government and rejects the political process in Iraq, it shows flexibility in dealing with political developments.

Military Activities

SDB operates mainly in the Sunni governorates and has about twenty small formations launching rocket and mortar attacks on Coalition bases. Although the group aims to expel the occupiers from Iraq by military means, the official spokesman of the group, Dr. Saif al-Din Mahmoud, renounced the use of booby-trapped vehicles in cities, suicide bombings, abducting and killing hostages and attacks on civilians in a 2005 communiqué. SDB cooperates with all Iraqi jihadi groups except al-Qaeda. The group refused an al-Qaeda ultimatum to hand over its weapons.

Media Activities

Videotapes of the group's operations are released over the Internet. Printed communiqués and political statements are distributed on the streets, in mosques and posted in public places. Electronically, the group posts its publications on its official website (jaami.info) along with jihadi forums such as hanein.info, alboraq.info and hisbah.net

Mujahideen Army (MA)

The Mujahideen Army is an Islamist group believed to be associated with the Jaysh al-Islami in Iraq. According to official MA spokesman Abdul Rahman al-Qaisi, the group was founded before the occupation of Iraq, operating as a relief agency helping students and preaching Islam in mosques. Although the first objective of MA is to liberate Iraq by waging "defensive jihad," MA considers implementing Islamic *Shari'a* after liberation a long-term strategic goal rather than an immediate objective (like most other Iraqi groups).

Spokesman Abdul Rahman al-Qaisi has appeared in news programs and documentaries on a few Arabic news channels, but MA's video clips of insurgency operations are mostly released through the Internet. The group doesn't have any regular publications other than political and military communiqués uploaded to the group's websites (al-tamkeen.com, tamkeen.iraqserve.com). MA also uses other jihadi forums for propaganda, such as al-hisbeh.info, alboraq.info and muslm.net.

Al-Rashideen Army (RA)

The existence of this Sunni Islamist group was made public in 2005, but the RA carried out its first attack on Coalition forces in April 2003, according to RA spokesman Adil al-Zahawi. RA operates in concordance with 1920 Revolution Brigades policies and objectives. The group legitimizes the killing of occupation forces, collaborators and anyone having a political or military affiliation with the occupiers. RA rejects the political process in Iraq, doesn't recognize the Iraqi constitution or government and aims to set up a just and democratic government after the withdrawal of U.S. forces.

Military Activities

RA is composed of different battalions, such as al-Kawthar, al-Firdaws, Junud al-Rahman, al-Fajr al-Sadiq and the Muslim Bin Aqil battalion, among others. RA battalions operate in the Sunni areas of Iraq and Baghdad. The group uses rockets, mortars, roadside bombs and snipers in its attacks.

Media Activities

The group's insurgency video clips have appeared on al-Zawra and al-Rafidayn television channels. Other statements and communiqués are posted in RA's websites (alrashedeenarmy.com; al-rashedeen.info).

The United Fronts

Almost all Iraqi insurgency groups have attempted to unite under one common front against the occupation – so far the process has yielded a number of different fronts and sub-fronts, with the membership as given by al-Haq below:

Islamic State of Iraq

1. Mujahideen Shura Council – The council is made up of al-Qaeda in Iraq, al-Taifa al-Mansoura Army, Saraya al-Jihad al-Islami, al-Ahwal Brigades, Saraya Ansar al-Tawhid and Saraya al-Ghoraba.
2. Jama'at Jund al-Sahaba
3. Saraya Fursan al-Tawhid
4. Saraya Milat Ibrahim
5. Kurdistan Brigades
6. Ansar al-Tawhid Wa al-Sunna Brigades

The Political Council for Iraqi Resistance

1. Jihad and Reform Front – The front is made up of the Jaysh al-Islami in Iraq, the Mujahideen Army, Jama'at Ansar al-Sunna, and the Jaysh al-Fatiheen.
2. Hamas of Iraq
3. Islamic Front for Iraqi Resistance

Jihad and Change Front

1. 1920 Revolution Brigades
2. Al-Rashideen Army
3. Jaysh al-Muslimin in Iraq
4. Islamic Movement of Iraqi Mujahideen
5. Saraya Jund al-Rahman
6. Saraya al-Dawa wa'l-Ribat
7. Al-Tamkeen Brigades
8. Muhammad al-Fatah Brigades

Jihad and Liberation Front

1. Jaysh al- Naqshabandi
2. Jaysh al-Sahaba
3. Jaysh al-Morabitin
4. Jaysh Hamza

5. Jaysh al-Risala
6. Jaysh Ibn al-Waleed
7. United Mujahideen Leadership
8. Al-Tahrir brigades
9. Jaysh Tahrir al-Iraq
10. Saraya al-Shohada
11. Jaysh al-Sabirin
12. Jihad Ala Ard al-Rafidayn Brigades
13. Jaysh al-Faris
14. Saraya al-Jihad in Basra
15. Saraya al-Fallujah
16. Popular National Front for the Liberation of Iraq
17. Saraya Altaf al-Husseinia Revolution
18. Saraya Tahrir al-Janub
19. Jaysh Hanein
20. Saraya Diyala for Jihad and Tahrir
21. Saraya al-Majd for Liberation of Iraq

There are over twenty-five smaller and mostly unknown groups mentioned in al-Haq's study that have not been mentioned in the media, nor have they been known to perpetrate significant attacks on U.S. or Iraqi forces.

Al-Awda Party and the Ba'athist Dream of Return in Iraq

By Rafid Fadhil Ali
January 21, 2009
Terrorism Focus 6 (2)

Iraq's al-Awda party first emerged in the weeks following the demise of Saddam Hussein's Ba'athist regime in 2003. Al-Awda means "the return" in Arabic, in this case the "return" of the Ba'athists. In those days, pro-Ba'athist graffiti appeared in some areas in Iraq, with slogans like "Saddam will be back," and "Al-Awda party is coming."

Though no clear identity emerged for this organization in Iraq's post-war insurgency, the name "al-Awda" has been in the headlines lately, as the Iraqi government confirmed the arrest of 23 Iraqi officers from the Interior and Defense Ministries on suspicion of being members of the Ba'athist party (Al-

Arabiya [Dubai], December 18, 2008; *Asharq al-Awsat,* December 19, 2008). The officers were said to be members of al-Awda and were conspiring to overthrow the Iraqi government. Two days later the men were freed because of a lack of evidence. Shortly afterwards, Iraqi Prime Minister Nouri al-Maliki denied the existence of any coup attempt (Radio Sawa, December 21, 2008). The arrests took place while Minister of the Interior Jawad al-Bolani was out of Iraq. When he returned to the country, al-Bolani condemned the accusations against the arrested officers and denied any plot: "Some of the political parties did not like the success that the Ministry has achieved in minimizing their influence over the Ministry. The whole operation was due to political purposes. It was not about security" (al-Manar.com, December 20, 2008).

Al-Ba'ath is believed to have split into several different wings. The most active among those is led by Izzat Ibrahim al-Douri, the former Iraqi vice-president and one of Saddam's most trusted aides (this organization will be referred to as al-Ba'ath in this article). Oddly, the name al-Awda has not appeared on the pro-Ba'ath websites. Al-Awda has also not been listed among the many insurgent groups that formed the Jihad and Liberation Front formed by al-Ba'ath in 2007.

A spokesman of the Ba'ath denied any involvement in the recent plot:

> *Al-Awda has been said to be the alternative [form] of al-Ba'ath; this is completely incorrect. Al-Ba'ath, with its cultural ideology and history of six decades of struggle does not need to change its name and come up with another name. All of the members of the party are proud of the name and ideology of al-Ba'ath... Al-Ba'ath's goal is to resist the occupiers [the Coalition forces] and drive them out of Iraq and emancipate the country from the occupiers and their subservient collaborators [the Iraqi government]. The party is not about to stage coups that help the occupiers' project (almansore.com, December 19, 2008).*

The Iraqi constitution, ratified in October 2005, banned the Ba'ath party under any name. According to the Iraqi authorities, membership of al-Awda equals membership of the Ba'ath – both are considered a crime (al-Jazeera, December 19, 2008).

The alleged plot in the Iraqi Ministry of the Interior was the biggest accusation against al-Awda but it was not the first. Over the last two years Iraqi security forces reported several raids on groups affiliated with al-Awda. In December

2006, the Iraqi Ministry of the Interior revealed it had discovered offers to join al-Awda had been extended to a number of senior Iraqi officials. The ministry said the party's agenda was to spread terror and destabilize the country (Kuwait News Agency, December 5, 2006).

A year later the Sunni tribal fighters of the *Sahwa* (Awakening) councils of the al-Anbar province captured a group of al-Awda members. The group was reported to be linked to the smaller and lesser-known wing of al-Ba'ath led by Muhammad Yunis al-Ahmad. Sheikh Khattab Ali Sulayman, the head of the local council of the city of al-Ramadi, told the Baghdad-based *al-Sabaah* newspaper:

> *The security forces [of al-Sahwa] arrested 27 members of a network, called the Grand al-Awda party, led by Muhammad Yunis al-Ahmad. They are linked to the dissolved al-Baath party. They were captured with documents and lists of the party members. The security forces also captured statements related to the structure of the network... They are sponsored by leading figures of al-Ba'ath based in Syria. The most prominent figure of this organization is Muhammad Yunis al-Ahmad. Some of the captured documents state that that man is leading the organization.*

The head of the *Sahwa* intelligence in al-Anbar, Rashid Jubaiyer, indicated that al-Ahmad's group tried to contact police officers, urging them to abandon the force and embrace violence (*al-Sabaah*, December 2, 2007).

Unlike the main Ba'ath organization led by al-Douri, which issues statements frequently on the Internet and has a spokesman, al-Ahmad's faction avoids the media. An Iraqi government source told al-Arabiya.net tha, "Al-Awda organization is a kind of al-Ba'ath formation under a new name. The group is active in southern Iraq, with new networking tactics such as individual contacts and clusters" (Al-Arabiya.net, January 22, 2008).

In his recent statement on the anniversary of the formation of the Iraqi Army (al-Basrah.net; January 8, 2009), al-Douri described a new initiative aimed at gaining more power and influence. Al-Douri called for the following:

1. President Barack Obama must fulfill his promise and pull out the troops from Iraq.
2. The insurgent groups must unite.
3. Exiled Ba'athists must return to Iraq and join the struggle of their party.
4. The members of Saddam's army who joined the new Iraqi army must

return to the Ba'ath. Al-Douri said his party would take the initiative and contact them.

5. The members of the Iraqi parliament who voted against the Status of Forces Agreement (SOFA) between Iraq and the United States should join the Ba'ath.

6. The members of the *Sahwa* movement should re-join the insurgency.

Al-Douri also seized the political moment in the wider Middle East, alleging that the Israeli attack on Gaza would not have taken place if Iraq had not been under occupation (albasrah.net, January 8, 2009).

Conclusion

The setback of al-Qaeda in Iraq at the hands of the Sunni tribal fighters in the *Sahwa* movement has not affected the Ba'ath. The party's new approach is to entice more groups and individuals to join the movement. Defying Iranian influence in Iraq will always be an attractive propaganda theme the Ba'ath will use, especially among the minority Sunnis. The main concern of Sunni society in Iraq (and even in the broader Arab region) is how to face the perceived Iranian influence over Iraq.

Surprisingly, the Ba'athists also appear to have been trying to gain some support among the Shi'a. Al-Douri's Jihad and Liberation Front, comprising nearly two dozen militias and insurgent groups, claims to have loyal members in Shi'a southern Iraq. Followers of Muhammad Yunis al-Ahmad are also believed to be active in that area. In August 2006, Iraqi police in the Shi'a southern city of al-Omara announced that they had arrested three senior members of the Ba'ath party on charges of re-organizing the party. According to the police, "The leader of the group had visited Syria and coordinated with members of al-Ba'ath to re-organize the party under the name of al-Awda" (elaph.com, August 16, 2006).

Iraqi government sources tend to link al-Awda organization to Muhammed Yunis al-Ahmad's branch of the Ba'ath. This branch is based in Syria and sponsored by the Syrian government. Although al-Douri's group has denied using the name of al-Awda, the concept of the return and the propaganda behind it are obviously welcomed by them. The denial came only lately and was specifically in response to charges of involvement in the recent alleged plot in the Ministry of Interior. The Ba'athists' dream of a return to power is alive and they will continue working to achieve it. An article in the constitution banning the

Ba'ath and criminalizing its members will not stop them. The Iraqi government has a limited amount of time to prove to its people that post-war Iraq has become or will soon be better than Saddam's Ba'athist regime. More must be done to integrate former Ba'athists who denounce violence – otherwise it will not be easy to rule out the threat of the Ba'athists and their dream of a return.

Chapter 3

Insurgent Tactics and Methods

Jihadi Website Advises Mujahideen on Equipment to Bring to Iraq

By Erich Marquardt
May 9, 2007
Terrorism Focus 4 (12)

On April 19, 2007, the jihadi website *alfirdaws.org* posted an in-depth article on the necessary equipment for the mujahideen in Iraq. The information was in response to a posting by a user who inquired about the most important equipment a fighter must prepare before joining the Iraqi jihad. In response, a user who goes by the alias "Terrorist 11" posted a long document from Sheikh Yusuf al-Uyayri (alternatively known as Yusuf al-Ayyiri), a Saudi-born top al-Qaeda strategist who was killed by Saudi security forces in 2003. The extensive document outlines various guerrilla tactics to be used by a mujahid fighter in a zone of conflict. Al-Uyayri describes a mujahid as a "multi-type combat businessman," who must be prepared for many different situations.

According to al-Uyayri, in the early stages of guerrilla warfare, it is critical for the mujahid fighter to be capable of fighting independently. He states, "He must not be like a soldier in a regular army who operates in conjunction with others in terms of equipment and combat. He must view himself as the commander, the navigator, the shooter and the communications or reconnaissance man...he must equip himself with everything that he needs and train on all combat tasks and appropriate weapons." The recommended equipment list for the mujahid is specific and long, including: a pocket Quran, night vision goggles, shackles for use in abductions, a GPS system, video cameras for casing targets and an extensive list of other supplies. Al-Uyayri emphasizes the importance of proper planning before joining the jihad, saying that the mujahid must be adequately prepared before entering the fight: "if he can obtain this equipment and other things that he might need and failed to do so, he violates God's commandment to do what is within his ability." Nevertheless, if the mujahid is unable to acquire the extensive list of supplies, he should still join the jihad since God "only asks a person to do what he can."

The document details the proper fighting techniques of urban warfare. When planning urban operations, "the target should be easy and simple, and the security around it should be weak. The combat action against the target should be quick and not be based on a complex plan." The idea, according to al-Uyayri, is "for the mujahideen to be like gas or air; present, but not seen." The section is detailed, outlining how to move in urban areas, methods for clearing rooms and buildings, using hand grenades in cities and rooms, choosing firing positions in urban centers, and the proper use of camouflage, among other instructions. The article explains that a mujahid defending his territory "must take all the following methods into consideration: martyrdom operations and operations involving sniping; mine-planting; laying traps and carrying out detonations by remote control; explosives and sabotage; cutting supply routes; operating behind enemy lines; attacking units that cooperate with the enemy; raiding enemy bases, especially airbases; focusing on all types of ambushes; poisoning food and drink; kidnappings or assassinations; and reconnaissance tasks."

In addition to information on the necessary equipment for the jihad, the document spends a considerable time outlining the level of cooperation necessary between various jihadi groups inside a theater of operations. While it is important for the guerrilla fighter to be completely independent in the beginning stage of the conflict, once the mujahideen become stronger, "interrelationship is essential" to prevent disagreement between groups and the fracturing of the movement. According to al-Uyayri, "jihad is a collective worship. From the military standpoint, it is a collective action aimed at defeating the enemy and deciding the battle in favor of the mujahideen…A single central command should direct operations to produce the desired results. The worst mistake is for separate groups to work in one sector without interrelationship…We must be weary and eliminate any reason for division and dispute." The concern over the fracturing of the movement is warranted considering the recent disagreements among jihadi fighters in the Iraq conflict, with various groups splitting from each other over disagreements about tactics and strategies (*Terrorism Monitor*, April 12, 2007).

Finally, al-Uyayri explains the religious duty of Muslims to defend their territory. He warns, "If the enemy invades a Muslim country, no one should say he did not make ready his strength to the utmost of his power and could not resist the enemy until he made the necessary preparations...Such words are unacceptable according to the *Shari'a*. What needs to be done immediately is to resist the invading enemy with whatever resources we have." Defending the terrorist tactics of the mujahideen, he explains that, "it is legitimate to say we will not launch a jihad until we have fighter aircraft, interception missiles, or ballistic missiles to match the enemy. However, this, in our case today, is beyond our ability. God asked us to do what we can."

The Internet is littered with similar training manuals. The depth of these documents, however, once again demonstrates how transnational groups are able to acquire training and information through the Internet to conduct jihad in disparate theaters of operation (*Terrorism Focus*, October 24, 2006). Furthermore, this latest document also shows the staying power of jihadi strategists such as Sheikh Yusuf al-Uyayri. Despite his death in 2003, his writings have lived on to make him a powerful asset in the global Salafi-Jihad.

Al-Qaeda Adapts its Methods in Iraq as Part of a Global Strategy

By Abdul Hameed Bakier
December 21, 2007
Terrorism Monitor 5 (24)

For the last few months, reports from Iraq have been indicating a tangible decline in insurgency and terrorist operations. For the first time since 2003, the Iraqi people are enjoying a sense of security in the streets of Iraq, although skeptics claim it is the calm that precedes the storm. The stabilizing security situation comes amid claims that al-Qaeda has been defeated or at least has been seriously crippled in Iraq (alerhab.net, November 24, 2007). Has al-Qaeda actually been defeated and subjugated by the coalition forces in the Iraqi arena? Taking al-Qaeda's past and current behavior into account while monitoring Iraq's jihadi websites, one is presented with strong indications that al-Qaeda is adapting to the new realities on the ground while avoiding direct confrontation with the coalition forces. The global strategy of al-Qaeda since 9/11 – as posted in al-Qaeda's internet forums – sheds further light on the terror plans it has designed to lure and engage Americans in various fronts in the region (alboraq.info, March 10, 2007).

Al-Qaeda: Defeat versus Retreat

The discourse concerning al-Qaeda's possible defeat in Iraq comes as a result of the relative drop in violent operations in the so-called "Sunni triangle." The decrease in al-Qaeda activity is attributed to many different factors, the most important of which is the mistake it made by targeting other Sunni jihadi groups such as the Islamic Army of Iraq, Iraqi Hamas and al-Rashideen Army. In August 2007, Iraqi Hamas was accused of helping Coalition forces in Diyala province against al-Qaeda. Al-Qaeda did not understand the Iraqi mentality and tried to lead the community by establishing the Islamic State of Iraq, instead of coexisting with the different Iraqi groups. The targeting of Shi'as and their shrines aggravated the Sunnis Iraqis as much as it did the Shi'as because it upset the precarious balance between the Sunnis and Shi'a. These blunders were exploited by the Iraqi government and Coalition forces, leading to the establishment of the successful Sunni *Sahwa* (Awakening) Movement (Emirate Centre for Strategic Studies and Research, December 9, 2007).

The *Sahwa* are paramilitary groups comprised of Sunni Iraqi tribes formed to fight al-Qaeda. Contextually, Sunni wrath directed at the Coalition veered towards al-Qaeda, depriving it of much needed Sunni support. In the same way, the spokesman of the Islamic Army of Iraq (IAI), Ibrahim al-Shamari, says: "The decline in jihadi operations against the occupier is due to the fact that they are engaged by al-Qaeda in the worst struggle that could exist among fellow Muslims. The attacks of al-Qaeda, in some cases, took a form of full-scale war extending from north of Babel to Latifia area and from north and west Baghdad to Samarra. In this big area of its operations against IAI, al-Qaeda didn't target a single American, Shi'a militia or the Shi'a police" (hanein.info, December 15, 2007).

Conversely, the impression that al-Qaeda has been defeated in Iraq is challenged by the continued violent attacks occurring daily in Iraq. Al-Qaeda operatives are adapting to the new situation in the Sunni triangle imposed by the *Sahwa* by moving to northern Iraq, especially to the city of Mosul where they found a new ally. The Maghawir al-Tai Mujahideen in Mosul began a year ago as a small group operating in the industrial area in Mosul. They have since grown larger and decided to join al-Qaeda in the Islamic State of Iraq, consequently providing a safe heaven for al-Qaeda to launch its new tactics. Jihadi forum chatters from Iraq claim that over 2,000 jihadis from Mosul have already joined al-Qaeda (hanein.info, December 15, 2007). It seems that a new application of the tactics of guerrilla warfare in other provinces is succeeding. These tactics include indirect confrontation, or "open grave tactics," that include road bombs, hit-and-run operations and car bombs, together with al-Qaeda attempts to take advantage of the differences between Sunni tribes on the issue of cooperation with Coalition forces. Al-Qaeda is also leaving behind sleeping operatives in the cities they flee, awaiting the right circumstances to reactivate. Evidence of this may be found in the recent bomb attacks in Diyala province that killed over 20 civilians and injured many others (almalafpress.net, December 10, 2007).

The jihadi websites responded indirectly to the reports on al-Qaeda's defeat in Iraq by posting reports and video of al-Qaeda attacks on Coalition forces, especially in areas where the Iraqi government says al-Qaeda has fled. In addition some websites re-posted al-Qaeda's future global strategy (www.alboraq.info, March 10, 2006). Moreover, al-Qaeda's second-in-command, Ayman al-Zawahiri, commented on the new developments in Iraq in general and al-Qaeda defeat in particular in a December 2007 interview published by Sahad, the media production house of al-Qaeda. According to Al-Zawahiri: "The jihadi situation is good in general, but setbacks are inevitable in jihad. The latest reports from Iraq indicate an increase in mujahideen strength and deterioration of the American situation regardless of their desperate efforts to delude by false propaganda. British withdrawal proves they are lying. Claiming victory over ISI through the collaboration of the Sunni tribes is mere cover for their big failure."

In summary, al-Zawahiri called upon the mujahideen to continue hit-and-run attacks, eradicate the hypocrites and traitors that infiltrated the mujahideen ranks, expose the traitors, call upon Muslims to stop supporting the pro-U.S. armed groups, concentrate on jihadi media and propaganda mainly through the Internet and build upon what has already been achieved by establishing the ISI. Al-Zawahiri also called for the mujahideen to unite around monotheism and reconcile with the rest of the jihadi groups, especially with Ansar al-Sunna, headed by Sheikh Abu Abdallah al-Shafi'i. On the political side, al-Zawahiri said, "After the victory of the Islamic State of Iraq, it will endeavor to establish the Islamic caliphate from ocean to ocean" (sahab.net, December 16, 2007).

Al-Qaeda's Global Strategy

The conflict in Iraq forms only part of a larger al-Qaeda plan. Before 2001, al-Qaeda devised a new strategy to fight the crusaders and Zionists what they call the "far enemy." To achieve victory over the enemy, al-Qaeda deemed it necessary to engage the enemy on many fronts in the region away from its bases. 9/11 was the spark that would bring U.S. forces to al-Qaeda's battlefield. According to jihadi forums, al-Qaeda's global confrontation strategy comprises seven phases:

1. *The Awakening* (2000-2003): This phase ended with the U.S. invasion of Iraq. The Salafi ideologues believe that the Islamic *umma* (nation) has been dormant in the 19th and 20th centuries because all the strategies implemented by the Muslims for resurrection have failed. Therefore, al-Qaeda planned to strike a blow to the enemy to induce an uncalculated reaction. 9/11 was the bait that provoked the crusaders and lured them to attack the Muslim nation.

2. *Eye Opening* (2003-2006): By occupying Baghdad in April 2003, the Muslim nation awoke to the bitter realities of occupation. Al-Qaeda's objective in this phase was to keep the U.S. forces engaged in a fight against al-Qaeda until 2006. Regardless of the results, the ability to maintain constant clashes with the enemy was considered a victory in itself.

3. *Resurrection* (2007-2010): In this phase, al-Qaeda will be capable of mobilizing jihadis productively, exploiting unrest in different hot areas to keep the U.S. forces occupied in a war of attrition that will weaken its resolve and pave the way to directly attack Jews in Palestine and elsewhere.

4. *Recuperate and Attain Power* (2010-2013): This phase will concentrate on overthrowing the infidel Muslim regimes by direct confrontation. The United States will be exhausted and unable to support all the infidel regimes in the region, hence, al-Qaeda will become more powerful and eligible to replace these regimes.

5. *Declaration of an Islamic state* (2013-2016): At this point, the Western grip on the region will loosen, paving the way for the establishment of an Islamic state that will regain control of the Muslim nation, rebuild it and utilize the nation's wealth in creating an international deterrent to foreign intervention as well as expediting the demise of corrupt and tyrant regimes.

6. *Massive Confrontation*: 2016 will witness the onset of an all-out war

between the forces of good and evil with, of course, final victory for the Islamic state.

7. *Achieving Multiple Victories*: Any victory achieved by al-Qaeda opens the door for more recruits to work with al-Qaeda in many different domains. Those who cannot join directly will establish their own centers based on similar radical Islamist theory and ideology. Al-Qaeda believes there is a direct proportion between multiple victories and repelling U.S. and Jewish aggressions [1].

Jihadis typically corroborate this scenario by citing verses from the Quran for every phase of the plan and believe that God will facilitate the victory of the Muslim nation.

Conclusion

Although the success of the United States and its partners in exterminating notable numbers of al-Qaeda leaders has significantly reduced its ability to perpetrate terror operations, it has not ended the al-Qaeda phenomenon. Rather, it has led to the creation of unpredictable, incoherent and scattered groups adhering to the Salafi-jihadi ideology. These decentralized formations will attempt to attack soft targets and wait patiently for any slackening of security on the hard targets. A complete defeat of al-Qaeda is unlikely to come about in the near future. Iraq – like other countries in the region – will suffer from al-Qaeda terrorism long after the withdrawal of the coalition forces.

Notes

1. Sources for the seven phases of al-Qaeda's global confrontation strategy are drawn from alboraq.org; al-ekhlaas.net/forum; alhesbah.com/v; alridaws.org/vb.

Al-Qaeda's Islamic State of Iraq Turns to YouTube

By Abdul Hameed Bakier
January 23, 2008
Terrorism Focus 5 (3)

In the last few years, radical Islamist jihadis have exerted substantial efforts to boost their propaganda capabilities by encouraging their followers to exploit all means at their disposal, such as the Internet, mobile phones and preaching in mosques. In his communiqués, al-Qaeda's second-in-command, Dr. Ayman al-Zawahiri, has repeatedly emphasized the importance of jihadi media, declaring that 50 percent of the "war on the enemies" is a media war. The al-Qaeda leader has followed through by initiating an unprecedented public dialogue through jihadi websites (http://vb.roro44.com, December 18, 2007). In obedience to al-Zawahiri's guidance, jihadis are now using their expertise in information technology to develop jihadi media capabilities. The most effective of these efforts is al-Qaeda's so-called Islamic State of Iraq (ISI) "TV channel," available on the video-sharing website YouTube.

Al-Zawahiri's open dialogue was announced on jihadi websites in December 2007. Questions concerning global jihad were relayed through the most prominent jihadi websites (alfirdws.org; al-boraq.org; al-hesbah.com; ek-ls.org). Al-Qaeda's media outlets are to publish al-Zawahiri's answers some time after January 16, 2008. The most frequent questions posed to al-Zawahiri so far include:

> Why has al-Qaeda not attacked Jews in Tel Aviv?
> What is the purpose of attacking peaceful countries like Saudi Arabia that have many al-Qaeda sympathizers?
> How do you justify killing innocent bystanders in suicide attacks?
> Was there unanimous religious consent by ummah (Muslim community) sheikhs to perpetrate 9/11 attacks?
> Is al-Qaeda planning to attack targets in Egypt?

The call for open dialogue is the latest effort by mainstream al-Qaeda to reach as large an audience as possible and depict al-Qaeda leaders as intellectuals rather than mass murderers. Saudi Arabia's "al-Sakinah" campaign for dialogue with extremists – headed by the Saudi minister for Islamic affairs – announced its readiness to open a religious debate with al-Zawahiri through any means of the latter's choosing, but al-Zawahiri has not responded to Riyadh's initiative (alhayat.com, December 25, 2007).

Another big stride in the jihadi media campaign is the establishment of the internet-based ISI "TV channel" on YouTube. The ISI account with YouTube was set up in January 2007 with only around 40 subscribers, but over 7,000 viewers. The site contains a large number of video clips of insurgent attacks on Coalition and local Iraqi security forces. Emotive speeches by ISI spokesmen and officials appeal to potential jihadis seeking to join al-Qaeda forces in Iraq.

In an attempt to portray al-Qaeda's concern for humanitarian issues, the ISI site also contains a clip entitled "Care for Civilians during Jihad," in which terrorists abort the detonation of a road bomb against a passing Coalition military convoy to avoid harming a civilian car parked right over the bomb. Viewers' comments posted to the ISI YouTube account vary from generally supportive statements such as "May God render victorious the Islamic Iraq and protect its Emir and Jihadis," to comments that carry operational messages between jihadis such as "Our brothers received one shipment of the subsidies you sent. Pray for us."

This first-time al-Qaeda's media effort to open public dialogue comes amid the controversy over the Salafi-Jihadist ideological reevaluations penned by the imprisoned Sayyid Abdul Aziz al-Sharif—better known as Dr. Fadl, a prominent Egyptian Salafi-Jihadist ideologue (see *Terrorism Monitor*, December 10, 2007). Dr. Fadl's recantation of major Salafi-Jihadist extremism has harmed al-Qaeda's capabilities to recruit new jihadis and secure funds for terrorism. In response, al-Qaeda is trying to counter Dr. Fadl's attacks on the legitimacy of al-Qaeda's terrorist operations.

It was once the common practice of Salafi terrorists to videotape their attacks and smuggle them from battlefields to collect money from rich Salafi-Jihadist adherents. Today, with the use of the YouTube "TV channel" and other file-hosting websites, al-Qaeda has ensured that its announcements and combat footage will reach its adherents quickly and without risk of interception.

Iraqi Jihadi Offers Online Lessons on Ambush Techniques

By Abdul Hameed Bakier
February 5, 2008
Terrorism Focus 5 (5)

As part of the military, intelligence and religious information exchanged through Iraqi jihadist Internet forums, one jihadi recently posted a training lesson for militants in the battlefield entitled "Allurement is a technique mastered by the enemy." The posting offers methods of luring U.S. forces into ambushes and urges militants to practice devising "baits" for this purpose (hanein.info, January 29, 2008).

A forum participant nicknamed "Jeel al-Aqeeda" reminds readers how U.S. forces were lured into a well-planned ambush at the beginning of the occupation, in which a bomb was detonated by a phone call in a house surrounded by 10 U.S. Humvees. Al-Aqeeda explains that the action at the house was the ambush, false intelligence regarding the presence of terrorists in the house was the bait, and feeding U.S. forces with the false intelligence was the lure. "The ambush was repeated tens of times varying the type of the bait, the enticement style or the detonation method. When you run out of tricks to bring your enemy directly into the ambush, [using techniques of] allurement is inevitable," says al-Aqeeda. The training lesson proceeds as follows:

> *Allurement*: This is the art of gradually drawing the enemy into the ambush. The equation between ambush and the time needed to get the enemy at the appropriate spot must be calculated carefully.
>
> *The Bait and Ambush*: The bait is something considered desirable by the enemy, while the ambush is a trap devised to topple him. The bait may be placed inside or outside the ambush. The more seductive the bait, the higher the possibility of destroying the enemy.

Components for a *successful* ambush:

- Type of ambush
- Location and method of lurking
- Bait used
- Method of allurement
- Method of destruction

Components for an *unsuccessful* ambush:

- Unappealing bait
- Attacking the target too soon or before he takes the bait
- The target is smart or evasive
- The ambush is too conventional
- The ambush is uncovered by spies

Jihadis should use the tips in "components of an unsuccessful ambush" to their own advantage in exposing enemy ambushes. "For instance, if we unveil the Islamic party's secrets and plans aimed at creating a kingdom in Iraq, all these plans are bound to fail. If we expose American plans to blow up Mosul dam and blame ISI [Islamic State of Iraq] and al-Qaeda for it, the enemy's plans would fail," says al-Aqeeda, reiterating that the best counter-measure for enemy conspiracies is to uncover and expose them.

The instructor further emphasizes the importance of the choice of bait in attracting the target into the trap. "If you want to lure your enemy, choose delicious bait your enemy can't pass up," says al-Aqeeda. On the other hand, the training lesson describes two types of U.S. techniques used to target Iraqi insurgents. First is military allurement, such as booby-trapped houses and cars; secondly there is political allurement, such as mind tricks, terminology manipulation and enticement. U.S. political allurement aims to include the Sunnis in the political process, enlist them in the Iraqi military, restore some Iraqi ex-military cadres and create the trick of the "Awakening Councils." According to the posting, U.S. forces are assisted in these techniques by the Sunni-based Iraqi Islamic Party, part of the Nouri al-Maliki-led government.

Finally, al-Aqeeda suggests using unconventional plans of action to assassinate or abduct Western agents as the old techniques no longer work. One such plan involves setting up a commercial entity of any type, be it real or fictional, and then communicating with Westerners, tempting them with lucrative business deals – the bait. The best method is to invite Westerners to business or construction exhibitions, such as those frequently held in the Gulf States. The alleged company representative would suggest taking the visiting Western business people to the company headquarters or a restaurant, thereafter abducting them and erasing any trace of the front company. Although the false business scenario can be modified depending on the circumstances and available assets, essential elements of the conspiracy must include the availability of a business facility, the delivery of business proposals to Westerners, an offer of persuasive deals and finally the successful abduction of the target. This scenario takes a lot of time but is compensated by the guaranteed success of the operation.

Jihadis are constantly tutoring quality intelligence techniques in forums for utilization in terror operations. The front company technique is a very effective intelligence instrument that requires significant time and effort from intelligence services to unravel and counter.

Al-Qaeda's Islamic State of Iraq Absorbing Fighters from Other Jihadist Groups

VOLATILE LANDSCAPE

By Abdul Hameed Bakier
February 13, 2008
Terrorism Focus 5 (6)

Members of Iraq's Islamist Internet forums have been delighted lately to report a possible alliance between al-Qaeda's Islamic State of Iraq (ISI) and the Ansar al-Islam group of Kurdish Sunni insurgents. A forum participant recently posted details of a joint operation by al-Qaeda and Ansar al-Islam against U.S. forces in Mosul (muslm.net, January 29, 2008). In the same context, another forum participant announced the defection of tens of Islamic Army of Iraq (IAI) jihadis to ISI (al-ekhlaas.net, February 8, 2008). The shift to ISI follows the earlier pledge of allegiance to ISI from another insurgent group called *al-Furqan* (paldf.net July 20, 2007).

A forum chatter nicknamed "Bodyguard" posted a message a day after the attack in Mosul on U.S. 4th Division troops from Fort Carson, Colorado. In a posting entitled "Ansar al-Islam claimed responsibility for the operation that annihilated American soldiers in Mosul," Bodyguard says a detachment of Ansar al-Islam mujahideen – accompanied by ISI fighters –started out on January 28, 2008 to execute an operation against "Soldiers of the Cross" and their apostate collaborators in the al-Somar neighborhood in Mosul. The operation started at 2:00 P.M. by mining one of the roads passing through the neighborhood while mujahideen loaded with light and medium weapons waited in ambush. The mujahideen blew up the first mine against a passing U.S. military and Kurdish *Peshmerga* (militia) convoy, destroying a Humvee and killing its five American occupants. Later, they detonated an additional three mines. Four vehicles of the *Peshmerga* gathered in a previously mined spot, resulting in the death of many *Peshmerga* soldiers and the destruction of some of their vehicles when the mine exploded. Thereafter, the mujahideen engaged the enemy from all sides for over an hour, giving the Coalition enemy a very hard lesson and forcing them to call for helicopter support that searched unsuccessfully for the perpetrators. "The U.S. military announced yesterday the death of five U.S. soldiers, but we confirm that the number is a lot higher," says Bodyguard (for a detailed description of the fight from the American point of view, see the *Colorado Springs Gazette*, February 11, 2008).

Other forum participants commented on the communiqué by stating that it is a strong indication that Ansar al-Islam now supports ISI, largely because Ansar al-Islam referred to their new partners as "the Islamic State," recognizing the organization as the base of a legitimate Islamic caliphate. Negative comments were posted from some forum participants who demanded that Ansar al-Islam pledge formal allegiance to ISI and its leaders: "This is not allegiance, fighting will not succeed until they pay homage to one man," says one contributor, referring to the amir of the Islamic State of Iraq, Abu Omar al-Baghdadi.

In *al-ekhlaas*, one of al-Qaeda's media forums, participant Monasir al-Mujahdeen joyously announced that tens of Islamic Army mujahideen had "comprehended the truth" and uncovered the "hidden agenda" of the IAI before joining ISI (al-ekhlaas.net, February 8, 2008). The Islamist ISI and the nationalist IAI engaged in a number of armed clashes in 2007.

The defection of IAI fighters to the ISI is the latest in a series of such developments that threaten to weaken the IAI, which is accused by some mujahideen of cooperating with the U.S. occupation. In a relevant incident several months ago, the IAI was forced to play down the importance of the Jaysh al-Furqan, a group that split from the IAI and later joined the ISI. The IAI brushed aside the importance of al-Furqan's affiliation with the ISI, saying that the group is very small and insignificant compared to the IAI. Sheikh Abu Ahmad al-Smaidai, spokesman for the IAI, said the Islamic Army is holding together solidly and the Jaysh al-Furqan splinter group is a small operation active in only one city. He reiterated that geographic realities forced the group to ally with ISI to fight U.S. and Iraqi forces: "IAI is solid and coherent with no risk of disintegration or division as speculated by some parties," affirmed al-Smaidai. Leaflets distributed at some mosques in Baghdad by al-Furqan said they seceded from IAI after accusing its leadership of going astray, instigating internal fighting among jihadis that only serves the occupiers, collaborators and occupation-allied militias. Parts of the leaflet read: "We pledge allegiance to Abu Omar al-Baghdadi to fight the occupier until the last drop of blood, without negotiations or liquidation of the jihadist project" (paldf.net, July 20, 2007).

The largest merger among jihadist groups so far was that of Osama bin Laden's al-Qaeda and Egyptian Islamic Jihad in June 2001. That merger proved to be advantageous for the jihadis in many aspects, including the pooling of human resources, funds and expertise. In Iraq, al-Qaeda is trying to lure as many Iraqi jihadist groups as possible into their self-proclaimed Islamic State of Iraq. Jihadist groups lacking funds may be expected to join al-Qaeda, but unless these groups have the same convictions as the Salafi-jihadis, the unification cannot be expected to last very long.

Jihad Wants You: al-Qaeda Seeks Skilled Recruits in Iraq

By Abdul Hameed Bakier
February 20, 2008
Terrorism Focus 5 (7)

In another example of jihadist media use, Internet forum participants posted instructions for Muslims craving a role in the Iraqi insurgency. Iraqi jihadis issued a call for skilled assistance in strengthening their self-proclaimed Islamic State of Iraq (ISI) (al-ekhlaas.net, December 11, 2007).

In this al-Qaeda-associated web forum, a participant nicknamed "Abu Dakoon" addressed potential jihadist Islamists who are seeking ways to join the jihad in Iraq by encouraging them to study what jihad requires before attempting infiltration into Iraq. Dakoon's post is entitled "Do you want to deploy? Read what they want from you." After a few lines of pep talk, Dakoon categorizes the requirements of jihad in Iraq as follows:

Preparations

Before explaining the preparations phase, Abu Dakoon gives a briefing on the situation of jihadis in Iraq in the form of an alleged insider's account of an active duty jihadi. According to Abu Dakoon, the mujahideen are fanned out almost all over Iraq but are especially strong in the Sunni areas. Their activities are not limited to engaging the enemy and setting up ambushes, but also include military, religious, media and intelligence operations requiring military and non-military cadres. The jihadis are in need of experienced preachers and religious judges to issue *fatwas* (religious decrees). Those trained in Islamic dogma and monotheism are especially needed to refute widespread polytheism and heresy.

The Military Side

Jihadis are calling upon weapons experts and military engineers to bring their expertise to the conflict. One interesting skill of need is military leadership, which may be due to the death and capture of a significant number of field commanders. Even though jihadi websites are full of training materials, jihadis in Iraq are trying to solicit explosives and electronics experts, as well as chemists and physicists. Perhaps the jihadis' most daring recruitment effort is the call for nuclear scientists to work for the Islamic State of Iraq.

Media

Iraq's jihadis require skills necessary for maintaining and improving their ongoing media campaign in the areas of general computer programming, television montage, sound engineering, radio broadcasting and photography.

Managerial Skills

The jihadis also need those with military, religious, media, security and financial management skills. They also ask political and economic experts to join the ISI as well. Ending his instructions, Abu Dakoon says: "Islamic young men and sheikhs, you have read what we need. Master at least one of the needed skills so you can serve God's religion. This is what we need. What have you decided? Islamic youth, this is not like my previous letters. I'm writing to you directly from Mesopotamia hoping to serve the *umma* (Islamic community)."

The appeal attracted the attention of readers like al-Iskafi: "I hope the brothers would post some preparation and education links concerning the aforementioned because I don't know where to go to learn it" (al-ekhlaas, February 3, 2008). Another forum contributor, nicknamed "Saad AZ," comments on Dakoon's posting by emphasizing the need for jihad, increasing the number of mujahideen and selecting a proper leadership in the Islamic community, one capable of calling everyone to jihad – an implicit call to overthrow the current Muslim regimes that restrain their citizens from joining the jihad in Iraq. "Islam is a religion of ideology and jihad. Our Islam is all about monotheism and jihad even without the presence of occupiers in our land. There is all the more reason [to pursue jihad] when infidel formations are walking all over the Islamic land, westward and eastward. Our relief is the influx of mujahideen from outside, the donations and the channels opening through all means and methods possible."

In the last few months, jihadi forum postings have concentrated on soliciting volunteers and monetary donations for insurgency operations in Iraq in an apparent effort to recover from heavy losses inflicted on them by U.S. strikes. However, exaggerated and easily exposed claims of victories over U.S. forces have had a negative impact on jihadi fundraising.

Islamic State of Iraq Gives Advice on Infiltration Routes into Iraq

By Abdul Hameed Bakier
February 28, 2008
Terrorism Focus 5 (8)

In the previous article called "Jihad Wants You: al-Qaeda Seeks Skilled Recruits in Iraq," we examined the attempt by Iraq's Islamist insurgents to recruit trained professionals for jihad in Iraq. In this follow-up, we examine the use of jihadist Internet forums to present would-be jihadis with safe routes to infiltrate into Iraq (al-ekhlaas.net, January 28, 2008). Maps, orthophotos and other materials are included on the website. The orthophotos are aerial photographs that have had normal photographic distortions removed while being geometrically corrected for use as highly accurate maps.

On January 28, 2008, a jihadist Internet forum member nicknamed "al-Battar al-Salafi" posted a set of instructions entitled: "Urgent: How to migrate to Iraq and reach al-Qaim and Mosul provinces; Migration road." The posting pointed to safe routes for entering Iraq illegally from Syria. The roads are not safe for those on the security services' watch lists, notes al-Salafi, before giving detailed descriptions of the following infiltration routes:

> *First Route*: For those with ample funds, it is preferable to fly to Syria through Lebanon and travel by bus to the Syrian-Iraqi border city of al-Bukamal through the city of Hims. From al-Bukamal, the infiltrator should walk at night along the Euphrates River to the Iraqi city of al-Qaim, 18 kilometers from al-Bukamal. Upon arrival, the jihadi must proceed to the nearest mosque in Mosul. Without entering, the jihadi should watch for men from the forces of the Islamic State of Iraq (ISI).

> *Second Route*: A less secure route is through the Syrian city of Qamishli to al-Yarubia, the main city on the border of Syria and Iraq. With a heavy Iranian and Syrian intelligence presence, the border city is a security chokepoint the potential jihadi has to pass with extra caution, says al-Salafi. The jihadi should proceed by walking along the Tigris River until he reaches Mosul, 70 to 75 kilometers from al-Yarubia. At Mosul, the jihadi should avoid police and military personnel and report directly to the

nearest mosque, for Mosul is the cradle of the Islamic State of Iraq.

> *Third Route*: Traveling by land, the road is safer due to security slackness at the Syrian border crossings with Jordan and Lebanon. There is also the convenience of not needing to have a visa to enter Syria – Arab nationals are allowed to enter and transit Syria without entry or transit visas, provided they are properly registered in arrival and departure records. This is a cheaper route that only requires $300, as opposed to a cost of $1,000 to travel the first route. When in Syria, the jihadi should travel to the Syrian border cities mentioned earlier and proceed on foot to Iraq.

Ending his posting, al-Salafi lists the names of jihadi safe heavens in Iraq such as Rawia, a stronghold of the ISI; al-Tharthar village, where many ISI men reside; Arab al-Jubur; al-Mansuria district in Baghdad; al-Tarmia; and al-Yusufia.

For a week after al-Salafi's original posting, other forum members made inquiries about these access routes, varying from Syrian visa requirements to the availability of desert survival manuals. Another forum participant nicknamed "Irhabi dot com," posted a link to a very useful orthophoto of the pertinent area from Wikimapia.org. Yet another important contribution came as a critique of al-Salafi's infiltration instructions from an Iraqi forum member nicknamed "Wilaiat Ninawa." Ninawa affirms that anyone seeking to join jihad in Iraq has to have a local coordinator before arrival, since not all mosques in Mosul would prove welcoming. Moreover, the new arrivals might end up in mosques dominated by the Islamic Party, antagonists of the ISI. "My advice to you [is] if you don't have coordinators in Iraq, don't attempt to come here. I'm from the land of steadfastness and telling you your entrance is very difficult," says Ninawa.

U.S. pressure on some neighboring countries has had a positive effect, preventing a large-scale jihadi influx into Iraq, but it would be unlike the Salafi-jihadis to abandon attempts to infiltrate the country. Furthermore, jihadis who were already in Iraq and fled the concentrated Coalition counter-terrorism campaign are expected to regroup and cross back into Iraq to get back into the fight, bringing with them jihadi novices eager to engage U.S. forces.

Jihadi Forums Detail Tactical Use of Silenced Weapons in Iraq

By Abdul Hameed Bakier
March 25, 2008

Terrorism Focus 5 (12)

The latest insurgent technique of using silenced handguns to kill U.S. and government forces in Iraq, is discussed in two different jihadi Internet forums (hanein.info, March 18, 2008; ek-ls.org, March 17, 2008). Over five days, Islamist forum participants discussed the use of silenced weapons in killing Iraqi and U.S. personnel at checkpoints and other security controls, the types of silenced handguns, and accounts of successful insurgent attacks using silenced weapons.

Even though jihadis have enjoyed a freer hand in the Sunni districts of Iraq, they still needed extensive planning before attacking fortified security installations, like security checkpoints and police stations. A typical operation involved preparing eight jihadist assailants and backup teams with up to five AK-47 assault rifles and one PKC (the Iraqi name for the Russian-made PK machine gun) to perpetrate a two-minute attack that might kill, at most, only three security personnel due to the quick response of the well-protected security forces. According to a forum participant nicknamed "Ashiq tahat rayat al-Dola," these attacks became costly and difficult to carry out as the security situation improved in Iraq with an increasing number of Sunnis supporting government policies. Hence, says al-Dola, jihadis switched to a new technique using silenced pistols. "Today's jihadist operations against security controls have become a lot easier than yesterday.... An attack requires two jihadis at the most with one pistol of the smallest caliber," says al-Dola. The jihadi walks past the checkpoint like any other citizen and assassinates the closest security personnel with a 7mm silenced pistol, giving the assailant enough time to retreat before any response from the security forces. Another chatter nicknamed "Shamil al-Baghdadi" reaffirmed al-Dola's posting, saying he knew of a jihadist cell of about 10 fighters with a decade of experience in Afghanistan that operated in Khan Bani Saad in Diyala. In four months the cell carried out over 20 attacks on security stations using silenced guns and swords.

Many other Islamist forum chatters showed interest in the silenced pistol attacks and contributed to the subject with long and short comments. A forum participant nicknamed "Obaid al-Baghdadi" recounted an attack by two jihadis on an Iraqi military barracks in the al-Saidia district of Baghdad where silenced weapons were used prior to an unnoticed withdrawal. "They perpetrated the operation quietly. The [other Iraqi soldiers] didn't find out the two were shot until lunchtime. May God grant the two jihadis heaven and beautiful virgins," says al-Baghdadi.

Responding to complaints about the inconvenient size of the silencers, a few chatters posted links to small, lightweight integral suppressors such as the U.S.-made Gemtech Oasis-R. Moreover, jihadis are inventing their own designs for small-sized silencers with fewer baffles in the barrels. Further information is found in the *Mawsu'at al-I'dad* (Encyclopedia of Preparation), still one of the main sources for jihadist weapon-manufacturing know-how. The fourth edition of the manual includes a video clip showing how to manufacture silencers.

The switch from mass attacks to assassinations using silenced weapons is an indication that jihadis are responding to an improved security situation in Iraq following the ongoing U.S. training of Iraqi security forces and the creation of tribal security support units such as the Awakening Councils. Nevertheless, the use of silenced weapons against security and military personnel reflects the adaptability and determination of the insurgents and poses a new challenge for Iraqi government and Coalition forces.

Ex-Ba'athists Turn to Naqshbandi Sufis to Legitimize Insurgency

By Abdul Hameed Bakier
July 28, 2008
Terrorism Focus 5 (1)

The "Men of the Army of al-Naqshbandia Way" (*Jaysh Rajal al-Tariqah al-Naqshbandia*, or JRTN) is a Sunni jihadi group that first announced insurgency operations against the Coalition in Iraq in December 2006 in response to the hanging of Saddam Hussein (albasrah.net, December 30, 2006). Since then, the Naqshbandi army has claimed numerous attacks against the Coalition, posting links to video clips of these attacks in various jihadi forums. Like some other insurgency groups, JRTN publishes a monthly magazine promoting the group's ideology and enumerates its operations against Coalition forces while soliciting donations (www.muslm.net, December 28, 2006).

The Naqshbandia, founded in 1389 by Sheikh Muhammad Baha' al-Naqshbandi, is one of the major Sufi orders of Islam (forums.ikhwan.net, July 5, 2007). The Naqshbandia magazine contains both religious and secular articles promoting Sufism and jihad, such as "A series of facts about Sufism," "Military lessons derived from the prophet's migration," "The Internet in the service of Jihad" and "The American Embassy recommends the use of mice instead of dogs to sniff out explosives." The magazine includes other articles pertinent to Naqshbandi insurgency operations in Iraq, including a section on religious questions concerning jihad in Iraq sent by adherents of the faith and answered by Naqshbandi religious authorities. Three articles in the latest edition of the magazine help form a better perspective of the extent of JRTN's insurgency in Iraq:

Chronology of JRTN's operations against the Coalition in November 2007

The Naqshbandia army claims to have carried out jihadi operations against the Coalition in Baghdad, al-Anbar, Ninawa, Diyala and Salah al-Din provinces, where they launched over 17 rocket attacks using Katyusha, Grad and Iraqi-made Tariq rockets, five mortar attacks, 14 road bombs, four sniper attacks and two massive assaults with light weapons on U.S. military bases. In regular military fashion, the JRTN attributes these attacks to platoons and detachments attached to certain brigades of the JRTN.

The Big Escape of Collaborators

With every announcement about the U.S. intention to withdraw forces from Iraq, pro-U.S. Iraqis – whether civilian or military – hastily leave Iraq on long and short visits to neighboring countries in an attempt to flee before U.S. forces withdraw from the country. The Naqshbandia army believes that U.S. forces will be forced to make an undeclared pullout from Iraq as a result of heavy mujahideen strikes. The writer of the article, engineer Hatim al-Isawi, alleges that 2,745 translators from southern Iraq have already fled to the United Kingdom, where they face a grim future as a result of British refusal to grant them refugee status. In the same context, the United States granted refugee status to only 700 Iraqi spies and agents out of over 50,000 applicants. Al-Isawi reiterates: "He who knows America does not deal or ally with it. America is a country of interests with no principles or morals. The tragedy of American agents will recur and that is America's religion."

Guerrilla War of Attrition

The writer of this article, identified as Major General Ahmad al-Naqshbandi, acknowledges U.S. military might and the inability of the mujahideen to directly confront and defeat U.S. forces. Therefore, the mujahideen must aim to wage a war of attrition to wear out U.S. forces through protracted guerrilla tactics. To achieve victory, jihad has to begin with defensive strategies before moving on to a balance of power and a final assault phase. Major General al-Naqshbandi lays out the tactics needed in the first phase as follows:

1. Concentrate on attacking small, soft targets instead of hard targets even if they are attackable in order to avoid heavy casualties. The loss of large numbers of jihadis is unsustainable as it takes a long time to replace them. The preference in this phase is to rocket-attack the enemy from distant points.

2. Exert more effort in training and gradually gain fighting skills while observing the occupiers' tactics, reactions and weaknesses. The longer jihadis are able to hold their ground, the better the chances are for overcoming the threshold of their fear of the enemy.

3. Widen the jihadi base to prolong resistance operations, consequently prevailing over the enemy.

According to al-Naqshbandi, "When the *umma* (Islamic community) sees that jihadis are an equal match to the enemy by prolonging the confrontation, more fighters will start joining the jihadis or forming new jihadi entities."

Finally, the JRTN calls upon Muslims to donate money to fund jihad operations, asserting that donating money is equal to fighting and fulfilling the religious imperative of jihad.

It is a common perception that Sufism is a non-violent form of Islam, guiding its adherents away from political confrontation toward a more spiritual facet of the religion. Hence, Sufism was tolerated by totalitarian regimes such as in Iraq, and in some cases, practiced by the statesmen in such regimes. It is apparent from the regular military terminology used in the Naqshbandia magazine that ex-Iraqi military officers are the main core of JRTN and are using the Naqshbandia order to legitimize their insurgency. Although Sufism is in stark contrast with Salafism, both sects push their religious differences aside to unite against a non-Muslim enemy. However, any Sufi-Salafi alliance is not expected to survive in the absence of a common enemy, possibly even emerging as a new and bitter conflict in strife-torn Iraq.

Persuading the Uncertain and Punishing the Recalcitrant: Al-Qaeda Seeks to Absorb Iraq's Awakening Councils

By Murad Batal al-Shishani
November 7, 2008
Terrorism Monitor 6 (21)

There are indications that al-Qaeda's struggle with Iraq's U.S.-sponsored tribal Awakening Councils is far from over. An attack on the Baquba home of Awakening Council militia leader Sheikh Abdul Karim Hassan al-Dahlaji on October 29, 2008 left three family members dead and 14 others injured. A police source, speaking on condition of anonymity, said the raid was likely to have been carried out by al-Qaeda (*Aswat al-Iraq*, October 30, 2008; Press TV, October 29, 2008). Four days later, a roadside bomb killed Sheikh Abbas al-Tami and his family near Baquba, the capital of Diyala province. The sheikh was the head of the Majmaa tribe and a prominent Awakening council leader (AFP, November 2, 2008).

These incidents appear to be part of a strategy imposed by al-Qaeda in Iraq (AQI) in their fight with the *Majalis al-Sahwa* (Awakening Councils). AQI's announcement of the establishment of a so-called "Islamic State of Iraq" (ISI) in the Sunni areas of the country reflected the latest stage of disengagement between the organization and its incubator, the Sunni tribes, as al-Qaeda tries to impose its own understanding of Islam by targeting civilians (including Sunni Muslims) and "hijacking the national Iraqi resistance," as their opponents put it. This approach inflamed the Sunni tribes, leading them to organize themselves, with American support, into armed groups based on geographical and tribal distribution.

Dismantling the Awakening Movement

The Awakening Councils were founded in the predominantly Sunni al-Anbar province in January 2006 by Sheikh Abdul Sattar Abu Risha with the aim of confronting al-Qaeda. After their success in forcing AQI from al-Anbar, other Sunni provinces and areas started to form their own councils, often incorporating former Iraqi insurgents. Although a suicide bomber assassinated Abu Risha in September 2007, one can safely conclude that the Awakening Councils were the major factor behind the reduced threat posed by al-Qaeda in Iraq, as indicated by the decrease in its attacks over the past two years.

In September 2008, a new situation was created by the U.S. announcement that responsibility for 54,000 of the roughly 100,000 members of the Awakening Councils would be handed over to the Iraqi government the following month. The government has pledged to absorb 20% of these members into the police and armed forces, paying them $250 in monthly salaries rather than the $300 they now receive. The remaining 80% are to be recruited to civilian government posts (*al-Hayat*, October 19, 2008).

As the Iraqi government has done little to support the Awakening Councils from the beginning, the movement's leaders have concerns about the government's will to commit to its pledges. They are also rejecting the deal to incorporate only 20% of movement members into the security forces, arguing that the government should assimilate all members of the Awakening Councils into the police and armed forces, as they are unable to pursue any careers not related to security work. In this context, Sheikh Shoja'a al-A'azami, leader of the Ghazaliyah Awakening, and Sheikh Hamid al-Hays, leader of al-Anbar Awakening, have both cautioned the government about the consequences of not absorbing the gunmen of the Awakening Councils, arguing that 20% is not enough. Al-A'azami warned that, "terrorist groups could use this situation to present tempting offers [to the 80% without security work]" (Radio Sawa, October 4, 2008). Al-A'azami also warned that if Awakening Councils are not absorbed into the security bodies there is a "possibility that they will stage a coup and turn into anti-American, anti-government armed groups, or will be polarized by al-Qaeda" (*al-Hayat*, October 19, 2008). The current situation has encouraged al-Qaeda in Iraq to find ways to punish Awakening leaders and alienate Awakening fighters from the government in the hope they will join al-Qaeda.

Al-Qaeda's Strategy

Since Awakening Councils control most Sunni areas, al-Qaeda's strategy has been based on assassinating the movement's leaders. The most significant of these was the assassination of Sheikh Abdul Sattar Abu Risha, one of the Awakening founders, in September 2007. On September 11, 2008, jihadist Internet forums posted a list of more than 40 assassinated Awakening Council leaders. Other leaders and Awakening Council affiliates were also threatened [1]. The recent attacks on Sheikh al-Dahlaji and Sheikh al-Tami, as mentioned above, show that this strategy continues. However, at the same time, it is obvious that al-

Qaeda in Iraq realizes the changing situation of the Awakening Councils and aims to benefit from it.

On October 24, 2008, jihadi web forums circulated an audio interview with the leader of al-Qaeda in Iraq, Abu Hamza al-Muhajir (also War Minister of the ISI), conducted by "Al-Furqan Institute for Media Production." The interviewer asked al-Muhajir whether al-Qaeda would accept the "repentance of al-Sahwa members." Al-Muhajir replied:

> *Sure, the door to repentance is open, and the Amir of the Believers [Abu Omar al-Baghdadi] stated that many times, but this repentance should be according to the known shari'a regulations that govern the repentance of militant groups who abandoned the Islamic shari'a ...Again I advise al-Sahwha soldiers to repent to Allah, to be remorseful and return to righteousness. I am telling them, "Hey drunk [man], you will live sadly as a spy and you will die as an infidel, an apostate, and your son will inherit nothing but shame and disgrace. Tell me, by God, if you still remember him, who will marry your daughter? What will your children say about you? What will your grandchildren say about you? Be careful nobody points to them and says; 'Hey, children of a traitor.' And be careful that your son might spit on your grave when he experiences the humiliation that survives you. By God, we are certainly going to kill you, God willing, if you do not return to God. Therefore, you, the miserable, repent! Be careful of the fatwas issued by imams of misguidance! [2].*

It is obvious here that al-Muhajir is combining threats with an appeal to the tribal and religious pride of Awakening members with his questions, suggesting they transfer their allegiance to al-Qaeda.

Despite continued strikes against Awakening leaders, a recent newspaper report claims secret orders to halt most attacks on Awakening Council members have been distributed by al-Qaeda to its fighters (*al-Hayat*, October 19, 2008). Security sources in Baghdad confirm there is a considerable decrease in al-Qaeda attacks against Awakening Councils in the last couple of weeks, whereas Awakening members had previously been the target in 70% of al-Qaeda's total attacks.

Although al-Qaeda aims to attract Awakening Council members, which will probably play a major role in any resurgence of AQI, there are still some constraints in accepting them into their organization. Abu Omar al-Kurdi, a regular contributor to jihadist forums, posted a warning about "repented al-Sahwa," suggesting that the U.S. aim in handing over responsibility to the Iraqi government is to use them to spy on jihadi factions. Al-Kurdi suggests that these "repented" members form a special faction and wage attacks on American troops to prove the sincerity of their "repentance" (Haneen Network Forum, October 17, 2008).

The Problems Faced by the Awakening Councils

Given al-Qaeda's eagerness to attract Awakening Council members, there are two factors that could create a fertile environment for pushing Awakening Councils members into the arms of al-Qaeda or other Iraqi insurgent factions. Both factors relate to integrating the Awakening fighters into the Iraqi state.

Firstly, regarding their integration into security bodies, *Sahwa* members think that the Iraqi government is reluctant to accept them because of the influence of Shi'a militants on the security bodies (*al-Hayat*, October 7, 2008). The Sunnis' feelings of marginalization have been used by al-Qaeda in Iraq in the past to recruit young men.

Secondly, while the leaders of the Awakening movement intend to play a political role in the new Iraqi state, divisions among them have accelerated since emerging several months ago (see *Terrorism Monitor*, March 11, 2008). There are now two major and newly created political blocs among the Sunni tribes - the "Iraq Awakening Movement," led by Ahmad Abu Risha (brother of the late Abdul Sattar Abu Risha), and the "Anbar Salvation Council," led by Hamid al-Hays, who accused Abu Risha of creating alliances with the Iraqi Islamic Party against the interests of Awakening council members (*al-Hayat*, October 19, 2008; Radio Sawa, October 18, 2008). It is worth mentioning that the division between al-Hays and Abu Risha is not based solely on political disagreements, but personal conflict as well (see *Terrorism Monitor*, March 11, 2008).

With many Awakening leaders attempting to create personal fiefdoms in Sunni areas, the present situation is creating frustration among Awakening Council members and may leave them without leaders to defend their demands. These frustrated young fighters will be the focus of al-Qaeda recruitment efforts.

Conclusion

While Awakening Council forces have played a major role in decreasing al-

Qaeda's activities in Iraq, it is possible that the same forces will play a role in re-activating al-Qaeda unless the U.S. and Iraqi governments consider their demands. For this to be achieved, it seems essential to emphasize the importance of an Iraqi secular state based on re-establishing a national identity, which has been beset by sectarian violence over the past four years. This is a long-term project, which can be launched by integrating Awakening Councils members into the Iraqi state and finding ways to fund this procedure, as it will serve to promote the overall integration of Sunnis, a process essential to the survival of the new Iraqi state.

Notes

1. www.muslm.net/vb/showthread.php.
2. Ibid.

Insurgent Attacks on the Iraqi Energy Sector

By Rafid Fadhil Ali
March 13, 2009
Terrorism Monitor 7 (5)

With the recent reduction in political violence, the Iraqi government is looking to make greater use of the nation's formidable oil wealth, a frequent target of Iraq's varied insurgent groups. Iraq and the Coalition have set out a new strategy aimed at protecting the oil industry, including the 7,500-km network of pipelines that cross all over the country. A force of 17,000 military personnel supported by helicopters and advanced communications equipment is responsible for securing the oil sector. General Hameed Abdullah, the Iraqi commander of the force, said that by 2012 his men would be able to handle the security of Iraq's oil infrastructure and stop the existing smuggling and sabotage (elaph.com, November 6, 2008).

Last year, the Iraqi Minister of Oil, Hussain al-Shahristani, indicated that the monthly average of attacks on the oil sector had dropped significantly, from 30 in 2007 to only 4 in 2008. Al-Shahristani attributed the drop in sabotage to the participation in security operations of Sunni tribal fighters of the *Sahwa* (Awakening) councils (nahrannet.net, June 25, 2008).

INSURGENT TACTICS AND METHODS

History and Background

The Iraqi economy has always been dependent on oil revenues. None of the governments in Iraq's modern history have worked to change that situation despite the oil sector's vulnerability. Conflicts with Iran and the United States have caused significant damage to the oil industry since 1980. After the U.S.-led invasion in 2003, Iraqi oil installations became attractive targets for different insurgent and armed groups. More than 500 attacks took place between 2003 and 2008. The country had lost 12 billion dollars, while reconstruction efforts stumbled (elaph.com, June 6, 2008). The armed threat on the oil sector can be explained by recognizing the acts and ideologies of the following five categories of insurgents:

Al-Qaeda and Affiliate Groups

Targeting oil is a major element of al-Qaeda's global strategy. In 2004, Osama bin Laden called for an intensification of attacks on the energy infrastructure in Iraq and the Gulf:

> *Exhausting America in Iraq today economically and morally is a golden opportunity. Do not miss that opportunity. One of the biggest reasons behind our enemies' domination over our countries is to steal our oil. Do the best that you can to stop the biggest robbery in history. The oil price should be at least 100 dollars a barrel. Work hard and concentrate your operations on oil, especially in Iraq and the Gulf... I urge you to strike the support lines and the oil lines, plant the double mines that kill and leave no wounded and assassinate the companies' owners, who supply the enemy with what it needs, whether in Riyadh, Kuwait, Jordan, Turkey, and elsewhere (al-Hesbah, December 15, 2004; Al-Quds al-Arabi, December 17, 2004).*

Al-Qaeda affiliate groups played an effective role in targeting the oil industry in post-invasion Iraq. Most of the attacks occurred in the Sunni areas where the Salafi-Jihadis were active.

Despite the retreat of the Salafi-Jihadi groups in Iraq, it is expected that the oil sector will always be an attractive target for them. An article by a Salafist writer using the name "Abu Musa'ab al-Najdi" was posted in many Salafi forums, hailing the mujahideen's success in preventing the Americans from controlling

Iraq's oil. Al-Najdi described the prospects for the near future: "I expect that al-Qaeda's operations will concentrate on the oil targets in Kuwait, Venezuela and the so-called Saudi Arabia in addition to the possibility of targeting Wall Street in one way or another. Al-Qaeda will continue, but with more concentration and specific accuracy, in preventing the American thieves from taking advantage of Iraqi oil, especially with the possibility of a withdrawal of part of the American forces" (banor.net, May 10, 2007).

The Iraqi Insurgent Groups

Iraqi insurgents have always believed that oil was one of the main reasons behind the U.S.-led invasion. When the Iraqi government approved a draft of the hydrocarbon framework in February 2007 known as the Oil and Gas Law, all of the insurgent groups opposed the move. The Jihad and Reform Front issued a statement labeling the legislation as the new face of the economic occupation. The statement suggested that control of Iraq's oil was America's primary goal (before securing Israel and attacking Islam) following the invasion. The front, which includes the Islamic Army in Iraq and a wing of Ansar al-Sunna, called on the insurgents to take the following measures:

1. Target all of the betrayers and brokers and everyone who participates in passing the Oil and Gas Law.
2. Target all the monopolizing oil companies and their staff.
3. Strike all of the export crude pipelines to cut the enemy's artery but avoid striking the internal fuel pipelines, which serve the Iraqi people.

The Ba'ath Party

In 1972 the Iraqi Ba'ath government announced the nationalization of the oil industry. Saddam Hussein, who was Vice President of Iraq at the time, played a major role in the decision. The economy entered a boom for about ten years. Even for those who opposed the Ba'ath party, it is very hard to deny the popularity of the nationalization of oil and the public success of the Ba'ath government's economic policies in their early years in power in the 1970s.

After the invasion, insurgent groups aligned with the Ba'ath took part in attacking the oil industry. The pro-Ba'ath websites reported those attacks, justifying them as "part of the strategy of preventing the occupying forces from exploiting and stealing Iraq's oil wealth" (e.g. albasra.net, October 26, 2003).

When the Oil and Gas Law emerged, the Ba'ath party opposed it, issuing a statement carrying slogans like "Oil is for the people of Iraq and we will cut the hand that delivers it to America" and "No free Iraq without free oil." The statement declared, "Preserving the nationalization of oil is one of the most important goals of the resistance" (albasrah.net, July 10, 2007).

Militias, Gangs, and Tribes of Southern Iraq

Most of Iraq's oil reserves are located in the south. Al-Basra province has the largest reserves in Iraq but suffered only a few al-Qaeda style attacks after the invasion. Al-Basra, however, was subject to smuggling activities and various types of sabotage. In an exclusive interview with the Jamestown Foundation, Assim Jihad, the spokesman for Iraq's Ministry of Oil, referred to these activities as "the other terror." Jihad indicated that gangs have frequently punctured the pipeline network to steal crude oil and other fuels, adding, "Oil smuggling has been an effective economic activity in this area for years. Many gangs attack the oil institutions when the government tries to crack down on their illegal behavior." However, Jihad points out that there have always been fewer attacks on the pipeline network in the Shi'a south than in the Sunni areas.

At the peak of their confrontation with the Coalition in 2004, a group of supporters of radical Shi'a cleric Muqtada al-Sadr threatened to destroy 75 percent of the oil pipelines in the south if the Americans did not cease military operations directed at al-Sadr's followers in the Shi'a holy city of Najaf (*Asharq al-Awsat*, August 22, 2004). The threat was not implemented, but the intention of targeting the oil sector demonstrated that Shi'a militias considered such attacks a military option in the conflict.

Lately, the tribes have played a generally positive role in the stabilization of Iraq, but General Abdullah, the commander of Iraq's oil protection force, criticized some of the tribes in al-Basra, describing them as uncooperative and accusing them of failing to help the police to stop oil smuggling carried out by fellow tribesmen. General Abdullah said members of his force work under difficult circumstances, as the government supports and arms the tribes, but no law exists to protect the law-enforcement body (*al-Quds al-Arabi*, December 28, 2007).

The Kurdish PKK

As part of their ongoing conflict with Turkey, the cross-border Kurdish rebels of the Kurdistan Workers Party (*Partiya Karkeren Kurdistan* - PKK) frequently attack the export pipeline, which links Kirkuk and the Turkish port of Ceyhan. So far the PKK attacks have occurred inside Turkey. In November 2008, the PKK carried out an attack in Turkey's Mardin province, though it had no effect on the flow of the crude in the pipeline (*Yeni Ozgur Politika*, November 24, 2008; iraq4allnews.dk, November 22, 2008). The presence of the group in northern Iraq and its conflict with Turkey will remain a potential threat for the Iraqi oil industry (see *Terrorism Focus*, December 12, 2008).

Conclusion

The consolidation of the Iraqi security forces was not the only reason behind the drop in attacks on the Iraqi oil industry. In his interview with the Jamestown Foundation, Iraqi Oil Ministry spokesman Assim Jihad identified four key factors behind the security improvement:

1. The growing social awareness among the population of the importance of the country's natural resources; the propaganda of the insurgents has not been as successful as it once was; and the exhortations to attack the pipelines because they pump oil to Israel no longer have much effect.
2. The role of the tribally-based and U.S.-armed *Sahwa* councils in improving regional security.
3. The U.S. counterinsurgency strategy and improved coordination between the American military and Iraqi provincial forces and authorities.
4. The increase in the size and capability of the Iraqi security forces.

The threat posed by the five groups specified in this article to Iraq's oil industry is unlikely to dissipate any time soon. These groups criticize the industry's corruption and the rivalries among political factions over oil exploitation in Iraq. They refer also to the frequent fuel and electricity shortages in Iraq and the suffering of the people [1]. A lack of transparency has eroded the people's confidence in the oil sector, creating frustration that can lead to radicalization. No longer enjoying the advantage of having the world's third-largest oil reserves (or first-largest, as many Iraqis believe), many Iraqis remember the era of oil-funded development in the 1970s as the "good old days," even if they were under Ba'athist rule at the time. Translating security improvements into development and job opportunities will mark a major step forward for the central government in Baghdad.

Notes

1. See a statement by the Ba'ath party on alrafedean.com, February 14, 2008; and an article by Dr. Ashraf al-Hilli on aliraqnews.com, June 23, 2007.

Islamic State of Iraq Brings Internet Propaganda to the Streets

By Abdul Hameed Bakier
April 24, 2009
Terrorism Monitor 7 (10)

The Jihadi Media Support Battalion (JMSB), an Internet-based jihadi propaganda group, has announced the launch of a new propaganda campaign entitled "ISI: The Gate to Liberate Extorted Palestine." The goal is to acquaint as many Muslims as possible with the so-called Islamic State of Iraq (ISI) and the Salafi-Jihadi creed (al-mohagr.com, March 13, 2009). The campaign has attracted many positive responses from jihadi forum members.

The JMSB campaign's objectives and instructions were posted in many jihadi forums and websites by forum members claiming to be JMSB reporters. The posting called upon Salafi-Jihadi adherents to participate in distributing leaflets about the ISI to as many Muslims in the world as possible. The first leaflet to be distributed is a communiqué regarding the establishment of ISI and the appointment of its Amir, Abu Omar al-Baghdadi. The message also encourages Muslims to migrate to the Islamic State of Iraq and deploy there to conduct jihad. The campaign endeavors to counter the anti-jihadi Western and Arab media efforts. JMSB praised other existing jihadi online media outlets, such as *al-Sahab* Media Productions, *al-Fajr*, *al-Furqan*, *al-Somod*, the Islamic Global Media Front, *al-Malahim*, the Media Jihadi Battalion, and *al-Yaqeen* Media for their continuous support of jihad. JMSB urges volunteers to bring to the streets the Internet-based jihadi propaganda from the aforementioned media groups. A JMSB reporter claimed that since the setup of JMSB in October 2008, 16,000 leaflets featuring the ISI and its Amir have been distributed. The leaflets urge Muslims to fight the Zionists and Crusaders who "want to wipe out Islam."

JMSB lists the main objectives of jihadi media propaganda. The campaign is intended to:

1. Inform as many Muslims as possible about ISI and the state of the jihad, which Muslims
are religiously obliged to migrate towards and support financially.
2. Counter enemy propaganda, especially the Jewish news networks.
3. Communicate with the mujahideen through the Internet and spread their achievements.
4. Encourage jihadi media supporters to move to the next phase: jihad field operations.

The JMSB instructs each campaign volunteer to print 1,000 copies of the leaflets on private, non-color printers and distribute them to randomly selected addresses from different post offices, direct to mail boxes, on walls and utility poles, in schools, universities and marketplaces, and to parked cars or drivers. The post included video clips of armed men stopping cars and handing out leaflets to the drivers.

The volunteers should distribute 1,000 copies each and do the same through the Internet in forums, chat rooms and emails. The JMSB warns volunteers to take the following security precautions while handing out the leaflets:

- Avoid places monitored with CCTV networks.
- Avoid public places adjacent to government buildings.
- Volunteers work individually and never tell one about their activities.
- Keep the leaflets in an easily accessible place.
- Distribute the copies immediately after printing.
- Do not hand out the leaflets in residential areas.
- Distribute the leaflets to Muslims only.
- Do not keep copies at home or in the computer after distribution.

Finally, JMSB calls upon graphic designers to design logos for this campaign and future campaigns, as this is the biggest jihadi media project ever. "Be it known to you, media jihadist, with this activity you are waging jihad similar to what the mujahideen are doing in the battlefield. Be honest with God and He will facilitate a passage for you to join the Mujahideen in the battlefield," says a JMSB reporter. He also recommended a number of websites for communicating with the jihadi media and the JMSB for information about mujahideen achievements censored by the international media (katebatnusra.arabform.com)

Many jihadi forum members responded to the JMSB campaign with comments on the wording of the leaflets and questions about security precautions. One forum member, nicknamed Nashid al-Irhab, revealed his participation in the campaign but asked for further security instructions from JMSB concerning printing and distribution procedures (al-mohagr.com March 26, 2009).

Another forum member said he is very enthusiastic about the campaign and suggested inserting the leaflet between false business advertisement brochures to fend off suspicions and use gloves so as not to leave fingerprints on the leaflets.

Another forum member complained other jihadi outlets were not included in the campaign, but declared that the importance of the campaign had encouraged him to participate, even though he "is not the jihadi type" (almnbr.info, March 18, 2009).

Jihadi propaganda materials are a key indication for security forces of terrorist activities. They are usually confiscated and scrutinized for possible intelligence that would lead to the arrest of terrorists exposed by the materials. Compartmentalizing jihadi propaganda activity to an individual level, as recommended by JMBS, would lessen the chance of exposing the jihadis behind the ISI's propaganda campaign.

Chapter 4

Faces of the Insurgency

A Profile of al-Qaeda's New Leader in Iraq: Abu Ayyub al-Masri

By Abdul Hameed Bakier
June 20, 2006
Terrorism Focus 3 (24)

It did not take al-Qaeda in Iraq long to name the successor to Abu Musab al-Zarqawi, contrary to speculation that the killing of al-Zarqawi would disrupt al-Qaeda's operations. In a defiant spirit, al-Qaeda announced the name of the man it appointed to the helm of its operations in Iraq less than a week after the death of al-Zarqawi: Abu Hamza al-Muhajir, who the U.S. government says is Sheikh Abu Ayyub al-Masri (al-Jazeera, June 15, 2006).

Al-Masri, an Egyptian in his 40s, has been one of al-Zawahiri's disciples since 1982 and lived in Sudan until 1995. From there, he moved to Pakistan and stayed with the Osama bin Zaid Mosque group in Peshawar; the mosque, apparently, is frequented by extremists. In 1999, al-Masri went to Afghanistan and trained at the al-Farouq camp where he met al-Zarqawi. Al-Masri became an expert in making roadside bombs and explosives. In 2001, al-Masri traveled to Iraq and worked with Ansar al-Islam in the north. Later, he joined al-Qaeda and became very close to al-Zarqawi, directing suicide bombers from Fallujah (al-Arabiya, June 12, 2006).

Although al-Masri is unknown to many observers, what little is known suggests that in the last three years he was in charge of the intelligence operations for al-Qaeda in Iraq and was mainly responsible for soliciting new recruits and insurgent groups to al-Qaeda's corral. To fulfill this task, he traveled, using fake names, to countries all over the Middle East and North Africa. Also, being well educated in *Shari'a* law, al-Masri was tasked with receiving and teaching the Salafi-Jihadist ideology to new recruits. At one stage, he was based in al-Qaim, 380 kilometers northwest of Baghdad (al-Arabiya, June 12, 2006).

In his first communiqué on June 13, 2006, al-Masri vowed to revenge the killing of al-Zarqawi and threatened to punish the United States and its allies, saying the fortresses in the green area would not protect them. Furthermore, al-Masri pledged to wage formidable battles in the coming days against the U.S. "crusaders" and the Iraqi "apostates" and proselytes collaborating with them. He also sent a strong warning to Shi'as, calling them the blasphemous grandchildren of Ibn al-Alqami—the Shi'a minister in the last Islamic regime that ruled Iraq who betrayed the Caliph—promising to carry through what al-Zarqawi started. The historic reference to Shi'as indicates deep-seated animosity toward them and the continuity of al-Qaeda's endeavors to fuel sectarian violence and, consequently, to induce civil war in Iraq. In the same statement, al-Masri pledged allegiance to Osama bin Laden, testifying that al-Qaeda soldiers in Iraq were awaiting bin Laden's orders (al-Arabiya, June 13, 2006).

Although not much information is known about al-Masri, he sounds just as violent, if not more violent, than his predecessor. The one letter he released on the Internet in 2004, titled The Samiri of our Age, reaffirms his adherence to the Salafi-Jihadist extremist ideology. In this 2004 letter, al-Masri exhibits a strong grasp of the Quran and Quranic teachings. He cites a verse from the Quran that tells the story of the Jew (Samiri) who went against the will and teachings of the Prophet Moses and carved a calf from gold to worship instead of God. God bestowed on the renegade Jew wisdom and grace, but Samiri showed ingratitude and antagonism toward God and the Prophet Moses. Accordingly, al-Masri talked about today's Islamic scholars and clergymen, who have learned the true word of God that was revealed to Prophet Muhammad, yet flatter political leaders for a few dinars and dirhams. In al-Masri's opinion, today's leaders are materialists and not true adherents of Islam. He compares these "bad Muslims" with Samiri, in the verse he cites, and calls them the Samiris of our age.

Additionally, in his letter he accuses moderate Muslims, or the non-Salafis, of being more like Samiri and far more astray than Jews. His accusations against moderate Muslims demonstrate his likely fanaticism and potential for violence. He cites additional verses to consolidate his points, calling upon Muslims to declare an Islamic state according to the Prophet Muhammad's teachings; only then, according to al-Masri, will Muslims be victorious (the entire document can be found at: www.alokab.com/quran/details.php.

The connotation of al-Masri's letter is superficial in Islamic ideology and does not necessarily illustrate deep understanding of Islamic doctrine. Regardless of al-Masri's background as an ideologue tasked with non-violent activities during al-Zarqawi's tenure, his communiqué and letter reveal a very extreme, fanatical mindset. Significantly, being an Egyptian and one of al-Zawahiri's disciples – or the so-called Egyptian Mafia composed of Egyptian nationals aligned with al-Zawahiri – al-Masri could be prone to target Iraqis, Shi'a and Sunni government forces, as opposed to bin Laden's Saudi mafia – Saudi nationals – whose priority is U.S. and Western targets.

The Shi'a Zarqawi: A Profile of Abu Deraa

By Lydia Khalil
November 16, 2006
Terrorism Monitor 4 (22)

Depending on whom you ask, Abu Deraa is either considered a Shi'a hero or the Shi'a version of Abu Musab al-Zarqawi. The legendary militant, notorious for his brutal tactics and hatred for Sunnis, is known to operate out of Sadr City, yet he remains a mysterious and elusive presence. He is feared by many Iraqis because of his reputation for cruelty as a death squad leader. The U.S. military has launched numerous operations recently to capture or kill Abu Deraa, but have so far come up empty-handed. Nevertheless, while Abu Deraa's fable is great, the facts on him are slim.

"Abu Deraa," his *nom de guerre*, means "Father of the Shield." His real name is Ismail al-Zerjawi. Other than his name, little else is known about him or his whereabouts. It is believed that Abu Deraa was a refugee who came to Sadr City from the southern marshes where he had worked as a fishmonger. During the rule of the Ba'ath Party, Saddam Hussein drained the marshes and destroyed Shi'a villages as punishment for their uprising after the first Gulf War—this caused many Shi'as, like Abu Deraa, to move to the Sadr City slum in Baghdad. Abu Deraa is allegedly in his forties and is married with two children.

Many of the tidbits of information on Abu Deraa used for this report were gleaned from various Western and Arab news reports covering the practices of Iraq's Shi'a militias. The Iraqi media have remained largely silent on Abu Deraa. He has granted no interviews nor released any statements to the Iraqi or foreign press, preferring to remain elusive and have his legend speak for itself. Any member of the Iraqi press that conducts too many inquiries about Abu Deraa would likely suffer a fate similar to his victims. His associates and the Shi'as he lives amongst are protective of him.

Until recently, his appearance was disputed, but oddly enough a video clip surfaced of him on YouTube. Short, stocky and bearded, Abu Deraa is pictured feeding a baby camel. His bodyguards were reported as saying that the video of Abu Deraa and the camel was a message to Iraqi Vice President Tariq al-Hashimi. According to his bodyguards, when Abu Deraa captures and kills al-Hashimi, he will sacrifice this new camel. The accuracy of the video cannot be confirmed.

Abu Deraa's Operations

Iraqi Sunnis accuse Abu Deraa of killing thousands of Sunnis, not just political figures and militant Salafists, but ordinary civilians as well. One of his associates recounted to an Australian newspaper how Abu Deraa lured Sunni men to their deaths. The associate explained how Abu Deraa commandeered a fleet of ambulances and drove them into a Sunni neighborhood in Baghdad calling on all young men to come and give blood, announcing on a loud speaker that "the Shi'as are killing your Sunni brothers" (*The Age*, August 22, 2006). The young men went to the ambulances and were trapped and killed. According to one of the many rumors circulating around the country, Abu Deraa offers his victims a choice in their murder—suffocation, shooting or being smashed to death with cinder blocks. Many of the murdered victims have been found in the al-Seddah sector of Sadr City, an area for which Iraqis have nicknamed the "Happiness Hotel." Victims are found in shallow graves, many with signs of torture.

Yet Abu Deraa has also captured and killed high-value targets. A video recorded on a telephone camera and circulated in Shi'a areas shows a man believed to be Abu Deraa conducting the kidnapping and assassination of Saddam Hussein's lawyer Khamis al-Obeidi. The video shows al-Obeidi emerging from a private residence, where he was undergoing interrogation, into a narrow alleyway. Al-Obeidi pleaded with his captors on the video, saying that he would lie beneath their feet and do whatever they wanted. Abu Deraa then tied al-Obeidi's hands behind his back and placed him in the back of a white Toyota pickup truck. Al-Obeidi was paraded through Sadr City, where the crowd threw stones at him and taunted him with Shi'a slogans. He was hit on the back of the neck, an extreme insult in Arab culture. After being paraded through the slum, the vehicle stopped and Abu Deraa fired three shots into al-Obeidi's skull (*The Age*, August 22, 2006). Abu Deraa is also thought to be responsible for the July abduction of female Sunni Member of Parliament Tayseer Najah al-Mashhadani. Unlike al-Obeidi, she is still believed to be alive.

VOLATILE LANDSCAPE

The Sunni leadership is understandably nervous. Last summer, an anonymous letter was distributed to Sunni mosques in Baghdad, titled "The Reaper of al-Rusafa." It warned Sunnis living in the area about Abu Deraa. The letter reads:

> *His name is Abu Deraa and he is a professional killer who is not any less dangerous than al-Zarqawi...Some of the Sadr City police force works under his command and under the command of other forces from Muqtada al-Sadr...Everyone in Sadr City knows this madman but they do not say his name; it is whispered in Sadr City when they wake up to the news of the blindfolded dead bodies thrown out at al-Seddah...which the Interior Ministry officially made as a place for Abu Deraa's victims.*

Connections to Shi'a Militias

Reportedly, Abu Deraa was a forger during Saddam's rule, but he now makes his living doing the dirty work of Shi'a militias and political parties, whose leadership publicly disavowed him. His connection to Muqtada al-Sadr's Jaysh al-Mahdi (JaM) militia is unclear. He may have, at one point, taken orders from al-Sadr, or alternatively played up his connection to the JaM for his own legitimacy and standing within the Shi'a community. Either way, he is most likely now working as a free agent whose actions are publicly denounced by the Shi'a leadership but who privately are not altogether unhappy about the "justice" he is inflicting on the Sunni community. Since he mostly operates out of Sadr City and neighboring Shula, he must have at least the tacit approval of al-Sadr since the latter's organization regulates human traffic in the entire area (*al-Sharqiyah*, November 3, 2006).

Abu Deraa has mostly been associated with the al-Sadr trend, but it is also rumored that he is supported by Iran (Tehran, not knowing who will emerge as the dominant Shi'a group in Iraq, has been supporting all of the Shi'a parties). It is also possible that he is supported in some way by the Supreme Council for the Islamic Revolution in Iraq (SCIRI, later renamed to the Islamic Supreme Council of Iraq), a powerful party within the United Iraqi Alliance (UIA). SCIRI and the JaM are rival Shi'a groups that are competing for dominance in the UIA. SCIRI has a powerful backer in Iran and is a strong proponent of federalism based on three large regional blocs. SCIRI's power base is mostly in southern Iraq, while al-Sadr is more powerful in Baghdad. Al-Sadr is a nationalist and is opposed to the strong federalization of Iraq. Although he has recently flirted with Iran, his group's connection to Iran is not anywhere near as strong as is SCIRI's.

Yet, where does Abu Deraa fit into this picture? There is much confusion about the labyrinth of connections and competing interests among Shi'a political parties and Abu Deraa is a piece of that puzzle. Abu Deraa is married to the sister of Hadi al-Amari, the SCIRI Badr Corps commander (author interview, senior Iraqi advisor, November 6, 2006). It is not altogether clear what other connection between Abu Deraa and SCIRI exists beyond family ties, but it is safe to assume that the SCIRI's Badr Corps commander is at least aware of Abu Deraa's actions and whereabouts. SCIRI has publicly condemned the sectarian killings conducted by Shi'a gangs and militias, despite incidents committed by their own Badr Corps. It is in SCIRI's interest to have Abu Deraa associated with the JaM. This connection damages the JaM's and Muqtada al-Sadr's reputation by associating them with such a ruthless figure. It also keeps the political heat on al-Sadr and the JaM and away from SCIRI. SCIRI is also aware that the U.S. military has been intent on capturing or killing Abu Deraa, and it has not raised any public criticism against these operations.

Nevertheless, for both al-Sadr and SCIRI, Abu Deraa is a useful tool because he remains a disposable one. If he is killed or captured, as will likely happen sooner or later, he will have served his purpose in avenging Shi'a deaths without tainting the more established political parties, especially SCIRI and Da'awa. For Muqtada al-Sadr, it is in his interests to maintain a murky connection to the death squad leader. The Shi'a community applauds Abu Deraa's actions against their former oppressors, making it important for al-Sadr to appear on Abu Deraa's side; at the same time, al-Sadr must distance himself from Abu Deraa's distasteful methods so as not to damage his growing political reputation.

Al-Sadr understands that the U.S. military seeks to capture or kill Abu Deraa. He has calculated that it is not in his interests to stick out his neck for Abu Deraa and has ordered his followers to avoid confrontation with U.S. troops in Sadr City. Al-Sadr's spokesman said on *al-Sharqiyah* television on November 3, 2006 that "Al Sayyid Muqtada al-Sadr and the jihadist al-Sadr trend distance themselves from the deeds that were committed, and are being committed, and which are attributed to the al-Sadr trend."

Abu Deraa has been reportedly pushed further and further out of Sadr City. Previously based out of the Lost 70's area of Sadr City – a desolate, largely abandoned area of the poor slum – military operations have forced him to go to the al-Amin district, according to some sources. Others have even speculated that

Abu Deraa crossed the eastern border into Iran. Military forces conducted two recent raids targeting Abu Deraa, one in July 2006 and most recently on October 25, 2006. He escaped in both instances, but in October 2006, his son and an associate were killed (al-Jazeera, October 30, 2006). Abu Deraa may be able to evade capture for a period of time, but the pressure on him is intense. That same pressure is also on his tacit Shi'a backers. Nevertheless, the established Shi'a parties, particularly al-Sadr's movement, are still unwilling to take action against him. Al-Sadr, for example, recently released a list of blacklisted members of his party and individuals he claims are acting on his behalf but are not associated with the JaM – Abu Deraa is not on that list.

Conclusion

Abu Deraa, however, is only a small part of the larger issue facing Iraq—the splintering of militia groups into uncontrollable gangs. The JaM may have unleashed Abu Deraa and others like him, but now they are unable to rein him back in, even if they had the will to do so. This development is a serious threat to al-Sadr. Al-Sadr's movement is considered the only legitimate, national, grassroots movement to have emerged out of Iraq since the fall of Saddam Hussein. Having criminal gangs and individuals like Abu Deraa not only associated, but uncontrolled by al-Sadr, marks a serious danger to his legitimacy. If this trend continues, then Muqtada al-Sadr will no longer be viewed as an Iraqi nationalist, but as another partisan Shi'a leader beholden to Iran.

Harith al-Dhari: Iraq's Most Wanted Sunni Leader

By Lydia Khalil
December 27, 2006
Terrorism Monitor 4 (24)

According to Iraqi President Jalal al-Talabani, Harith al-Dhari has "nothing to do but incite sectarian and ethnic sedition." Al-Dhari, the leader of the Association of Muslim Scholars (AMS), has been an outspoken critic of the Shi'a-led Iraqi government and is rumored to be affiliated with the 1920 Revolution Brigades, an indigenous Iraqi insurgent group. In November, the Iraqi Interior Ministry issued a warrant for the arrest of the controversial Sunni leader for "inciting terrorism and violence among the Iraqi people." The Iraqi government has been critical of him in the past and it is unclear what finally triggered the Interior Ministry to issue a warrant for his arrest. Al-Dhari's published statements and numerous interviews, however, give us a clear window into his attitudes and actions regarding the insurgency. He is certainly a supporter of what he labels the "resistance" and what others label as "terrorism."

Arrest Warrant Issued

Harith al-Dhari was believed to be in Jordan when the arrest warrant was issued on November 16, 2006. The surprise announcement of the warrant was made by Jawad al-Bolani, Iraq's Shi'a Interior Minister. He stated that it is "the government's policy that anyone who tries to spread division and strife among the Iraqi people will be chased by our security agencies…We have to prove to everyone that the government…is going forward with major steps to achieve security." Al-Bolani even stated that the government was asking international police to arrest al-Dhari if he does not return to Baghdad. Yet, according to al-Dhari and his supporters, the arrest warrant has nothing to do with the Interior Ministry's desire to achieve security in Baghdad, but rather it was an attempt to silence and marginalize the cleric. The AMS, which al-Dhari leads, issued a formal statement on its website on November 17. The statement read: "The warrant issued by the Interior Ministry against Dr. Harith al-Dhari…is clear evidence that this government has lost its balance and declared its bankruptcy." Al-Dhari flatly denied the accusation of inciting terrorism. He speculated that the timing of the arrest warrant had to do with his visit to Saudi Arabia, which angered Shi'a members of the Iraqi government. He has also repeatedly challenged the legitimacy of any government that was formed "under the occupation," which has further encouraged the government to come out against him.

The political timing of the announcement for his arrest is certainly controversial. It has elicited a strong backlash among Iraq's Sunni community. Faced with overwhelming evidence implicating Shi'a militias attached to the government with sectarian violence, the arrest warrant was viewed as a sectarian attack by a biased government—regardless of the objective justifications for the arrest warrant. After the initial outcry against the Interior Ministry's announcement, the ministry quickly softened its stance and announced that the government did not issue an "arrest warrant" but an "interrogation warrant" (al-Arabiya, November 17, 2006). Harith al-Dhari remains outside of Iraq, traveling in the region. He was last seen in Syria.

There is no doubt that Harith al-Dhari has made public statements against the government and called on all Iraqis to resist the occupation and its Iraqi partners. He is also reported to have ties to certain groups that make up the indigenous Iraqi insurgency such as the 1920 Revolution Brigades and the Islamic Army in Iraq. The question, however, is whether he has directly supported or directed the violent insurgency, rather than simply made public statements encouraging resistance. Is he a vociferous advocate of Sunni rights and anti-sectarian tendencies? Or is he a rejectionist with links to the insurgency, as many U.S. and Shi'a leaders claim? Who is Harith al-Dhari? Where did he come from and can he claim to represent Sunni and Iraqi interests?

Al-Dhari's Past and the Role of the AMS

Harith al-Dhari was born in Baghdad in 1941 and hails from a prominent Iraqi family of the al-Dhari clan. He is considered Iraq's most notable Sunni scholar with degrees from Cairo's al-Azhar University. He is related to the famous Sheikh al-Dhari who became a national hero when he killed a British officer in 1920, sparking a revolution. He spent much of his adult life teaching Islamic law and history at various Arab universities. Harith al-Dhari organized the AMS on April 14, 2003 as an anti-occupation movement, a nationalist force, and as a nucleus for Iraq's Sunni religious authority (*al-Manar al-Yawm*, September 5, 2004).

The AMS is largely a response to the marginalized role of the Sunni community. It has a strong nationalist bent but its message mostly resonates with Iraq's disenfranchised Sunnis. It is a clerical body, but has been vocal on political issues and has provided religious cover for the resistance. Yet, because of its refusal to fully enter the political fray due to al-Dhari's opposition to the occupation and the U.S. sponsored political process, the AMS' political influence is limited. The coalition has tried repeatedly to negotiate with the AMS, but it has remained adamant that it will not engage substantively with the United States while the military occupation remains. It did, however, negotiate in ending the siege of Fallujah in 2004. The fact that Harith al-Dhari has mediated with certain insurgent groups for the release of hostages and mediated to end the siege of Fallujah suggests that he has strong ties to elements in the insurgency. Nevertheless, he insists that, "we did not negotiate or mediate because we have no links to those parties. We only appealed to them and our appeals succeeded in freeing the hostages" (*al-Dustur*, November 2, 2004).

Harith al-Dhari's son, Muthana Harith al-Dhari, is also an active member of the AMS. He serves as the organization's spokesman. He is reported to be the leader of the 1920 Revolution Brigades, but he publicly denies this. The AMS, through both father and son, has been an enthusiastic supporter of the Iraqi resistance and has defended Iraqis' right to resistance and has even stated that it is a religious duty that needs no *fatwa* for justification (*al-Manar al-Yawm*, September 5, 2004). The AMS has repeatedly called on the government to resign. Al-Dhari has made a link between occupation and sectarianism in Iraq—two developments that have weakened the position of the Sunni minority. Since he has rejected political participation, however, all that is left is promoting the resistance. It is this support of the resistance that prompted the arrest warrant.

While promoting resistance, al-Dhari has also discounted the political process in all its forms. He has rejected the constitutional process, boycotted elections and disparaged participation in government. Al-Dhari has stated, "The political process, irrespective of the way they describe it, has brought nothing good to Iraq...they have divided Iraq on a sectarian and ethnic basis...Iraq today belongs to the occupation, to those who benefit from it, who serve it and who are collaborating with it to oppress their Iraqi brothers" (al-Jazeera, November 25, 2006).

The Islamic Army in Iraq, the Islamic Front for Resistance, and the 1920 Revolution Brigades have all condemned the arrest warrant against Harith al-Dhari, all groups that the Iraqi government claims he supports. It is not clear whether he directly leads or supports Iraqi insurgent groups, but al-Dhari is certainly an articulate spokesman for their cause.

Resistance or Terrorism

Harith al-Dhari has made an effort to establish a clear distinction between resistance and terrorism—which he claims the Iraqi government, the United States and the media have lumped together to further their aims. According to al-Dhari, "The resistance is the party that targets the occupation, the occupation alone. It has not harmed any Iraqis because it is a rationalized resistance and is defending something called the liberation of Iraq" (al-Quds Press Agency, April 26, 2006). Terrorism, on the other hand, is something entirely different according to al-Dhari. He blames the occupation and the ineffective Iraqi government's security policies for terrorist activity. During an interview published earlier this year on Egypt's Muslim Brotherhood's website, al-Dhari outlines which Iraqi groups he considers part of the resistance and which he does not. He divides the resistance into several groups, the most important of which he says are the Islamic Army, the Islamic Resistance Movement, the Mujahideen Army and the Islamic Resistance Front.

Al-Dhari also classifies the Mujahideen Shura Council, an umbrella group of al-Qaeda affiliated groups, as part of the legitimate resistance. Other groups, which he labels as part of the legitimate resistance, are the Iraqi Mujahideen and the al-Rashideen Army, among others. He explains, "I must point out that these factions attack the occupation forces and do not target the civilians because it is a resistance that broke out immediately at the beginning of the occupation. These factions do not receive support from any foreign party" (Ikhwanonline, March 6, 2006). He has gone so far as to say that actions known to be taken by Sunni insurgent groups – such as the attack on an Egyptian diplomat and violent bombings that killed Iraqi civilians – were not the responsibility of the insurgency, but instead the work of intelligence agencies (Ikhwanonline, March 6, 2006). He also believes that the bombing of the United Nations headquarters in Baghdad in 2004 was either the work of the "occupation" or groups they encouraged.

He has admitted that members of the resistance have made mistakes, but is more forgiving of their actions and blames "media exploitation" for the distorted image of the resistance. He has stated that tactics like kidnapping and car bombings were exploited especially by the U.S. media to tarnish the resistance (*al-Misri al-Yawm*, July 9, 2005). In an article published in the Baghdad newspaper *al-Zawra*, he writes, "Some Iraqi resistance factions have made mistakes that gave a faulty impression about the resistance as a whole. This is not strange. What is strange is to expect the resistance to be perfect and free from error at all times. No resistance movement has succeeded in doing that."

Al-Dhari has tried to avoid characterizations of him as a spokesman for the resistance, preferring to be considered as a representative for national Iraqi interests. He states, "The voice of the Association is not a voice that speaks on behalf of the resistance. It is the voice that speaks on behalf of all of Iraq and on behalf of all those that reject the occupation." He also states, however, that he seeks recognition of the resistance: "The resistance should not be disregarded. It should be recognized as an effective party that has its weight in Iraq. The problems of Iraq cannot be resolved without listening to the resistance and involving it in the affairs of the country" (*Asharq al-Awsat*, May 13, 2006).

Al-Dhari has given religious cover to many insurgent tactics. He has justified kidnappings by saying, "Many scholars, including [Yusuf] al-Qaradawi, have issued *fatwas* sanctioning the kidnapping of combatants in times of war because it is permitted by religion and according to the practices of the Prophet Muhammad." He asserts that kidnappings are akin to taking prisoners of war and that their killing is justified if the "commander of the people deems those prisoners war criminals and sentences them to death" (*al-Dustur*, November 2, 2004). Even though al-Dhari has recognized the legitimacy of the Mujahideen Shura Council, he has also stated that Abu Musab al-Zarqawi's importance, when he was alive, was exaggerated by the United States to justify its occupation of Iraq. Al-Dhari accuses the United States and the Iraqi government of building a myth around al-Zarqawi in order to hijack the resistance, attributing it only to al-Qaeda so that when al-Zarqawi was killed, they could claim they killed off the resistance (*al-Dustur*, November 2, 2004).

Conclusion

Al-Dhari's ability to unify the Sunni community in a constructive way has certainly been hampered by the arrest warrant and by his own tactics. He has alienated an important tribal constituency—the al-Anbar tribes who are now committed to fighting against al-Qaeda and the insurgents. They have even gone so far as to ask the AMS to remove him as leader. They have even filed a lawsuit against him. In an announcement on *al-Iraqiya*, "In the name of the al-Anbar Chieftains Council, we tell Harith al-Dhari that if there is a bandit, it is you. If there is a murderer or kidnapper, it is you." While some other Iraqis have rallied around him, he is not in Iraq to lead them and has rejected government participation. His voice is limited by the arrest warrant since this prevents him from returning to Iraq, unless he is willing to face arrest, and by his own refusal to support the government so as to change its policies from within.

Becoming an Ayatollah: The New Iraqi Politics of Muqtada al-Sadr

By Babak Rahimi

February 25, 2008
Terrorism Monitor Volume: 6 Issue: 3

VOLATILE LANDSCAPE

As a political and military force, Iraq's Shi'a Sadrist movement has undergone a number of radical transformations since 2003, when its leader, Muqtada al-Sadr, surprisingly emerged as a leading political figure. Al-Sadr's recent decision to continue with his seminary studies and graduate as an ayatollah at the conservative seminary school of Najaf underpins a major change in the movement's structure that could have serious repercussions for the future of Iraq. Against the backdrop of changing political alliances between Kurds and Sunnis, al-Sadr is transforming his movement into a new political phenomenon with implications for the country's political structure and security dynamics. The consequences are also immense for Shi'a Iraq, posing serious challenges to the conservative clerical establishment in Najaf.

Al-Sadr's attempt to become an ayatollah follows his earlier call to suspend operations by his militia, the Jaysh al-Mahdi (JaM) in the summer of 2007. Together with his decision to study in Najaf, this has marked a decisive new beginning in the organizational structure and leadership dynamics of the JaM militia. The decision to suspend JaM was made largely because of the outbreak of violence between JaM forces and the rival Badr Organization in Karbala in August 2007 (Aftab-e Yazd [Iran], August 30, 2007). The incident was a major embarrassment for al-Sadr, who had been seeking the support of Grand Ayatollah Ali al-Sistani, Shi'a Iraq's grand cleric, and the conservative establishment in Tehran against the rebellious splinter groups within his own militia since 2005. The suspension, which came in August 2007, was a way to ensure his Shi'a partners that he was willing to restructure his forces for the sake of Shi'a unity at a time when US—or Israeli—forces seemed to be on the brink of starting a major military conflict with Iran.

The call was welcomed by al-Sistani, who had been encouraging al-Sadr to arrive at such a decision since January 2007 (author's interview with a representative of Ayatollah al-Sistani, Qom, August 29, 2007). The two met in June 2007 to discuss the problem of JaM splinter groups (*Aftab-e Yazd*, June 14, 2007).

Najaf and Tehran both share an interest in containing al-Sadr and his militia, as well as bringing his paramilitary organization—and other shadowy anti-Najaf movements—under the control of the Shi'a clerical establishment. For Najaf and Tehran, the best way to tame al-Sadr is to chip away at his popular base through the electoral process and intra-Shi'a negotiations, such as the October 2007 cooperation pact with rival Shi'a leader Abdul Aziz al-Hakim (Fars News Agency,

October 6, 2007). This would, accordingly, diminish his status as a charismatic militant leader defiant of existing institutions.

Al-Sadr's decision to become an ayatollah, along with his suspension of JaM, is an indicator of more complex transformations occurring within the Sadrist movement. Al-Sadr is not merely trying to gain religious legitimacy by becoming an ayatollah, but also access to a major source of religious and financial capital that is primarily under the control of high-ranking Shi'a clerics in Najaf. Since his family legacy alone would not entitle him to what his father had acquired as a senior jurist (*marja taqlid*, or "source of imitation") in the 1990s, becoming an ayatollah would guarantee al-Sadr access to religious capital that has been solely in the domain of high-ranking clerics for centuries. The attainment of religious credentials through the traditional seminary complex can provide al-Sadr with enhanced authority over spiritual matters, such as the ability to issue a *fatwa* (religious verdict) and control religious taxes, powers he now lacks as a junior cleric. If successful, al-Sadr could extricate himself from the authority of Najaf with its strict hierarchical set of power relations and close familial ties to Iran and beyond. It could also help him get rid of the influence of Iranian-born clerics by refusing al-Sistani's mentorship, instead studying under an Afghan-born senior cleric, Grand Ayatollah Sheikh Ishaq Fayyaz (*Shahrvand-e Emrooz* [Tehran], December 30, 2007).

Al-Sadr's New Political Strategy

How could these developments impact Iraq's security politics? First off, with an inflated religious authority, al-Sadr could wield greater power in regions where he lacks influence. In Basra especially, al-Sadr prepares to tackle his most powerful rival, the Badr Organization, by propagating his new image in tribal and urban regions of the province (author's interview with a seminary student of Ayatollah al-Sistani, Qom, August 28, 2007). In a significant sense, al-Sadr wants legitimacy in places where he is mostly viewed as a young cleric of low-ranking scholarly status. By flexing his muscle as a high-ranking spiritual leader, Basra may witness a new series of conflicts between rival Shi'a groups with equal claim to religious legitimacy in the traditional Shi'a sense.

But al-Sadr also aims to consolidate his power by bringing together his followers and identifying himself as their sole spiritual leader. This would ultimately undermine al-Sistani's influence among his younger followers who may revere al-Sadr but obey al-Sistani on matters of religious and potentially political importance. By further consolidating power in terms of attaining religious authority, al-Sadr is preparing to revitalize his organization as a new religious-political movement with a highly centralized military branch. Under this new leadership, the political branch of the Sadrist movement will most likely be strengthened and the unruly JaM subordinated to the civilian – i.e. clerical – leaders of the movement.

Second, al-Sadr's rise to the rank of ayatollah will reinforce his Iraqi identity. The move towards nationalism should be seen as a way to challenge the transnationalism of Najaf by creating a new form of Shi'a politics free from non-Iraqi influence. Aside from their plans to centralize control over oil reserves, one of the reasons al-Sadr and his parliamentarian representatives have sided with the secular National List of former Prime Minister Ayad Allawi and Sunni leader Saleh al-Mutlaq's National Dialogue Front is to create a new parliamentary bloc to challenge Najaf and its influence over the four-party alliance of Nouri-Maliki by carving out a new political front of nationalist parties (al-Jazeera, January 14, 2008). Al-Sadr is playing a delicate game of balancing his position between nationalism and sectarianism, though his appeal to Shi'a factionalism is mainly aimed at bolstering his base where he is now seeking a new constituency and a more centralized political movement.

The focus on a nationalistic leadership strategy can also be attributed to the ongoing political transformation of Sunni politics on the parliamentary level. The new agreement signed between the Patriotic Union of Kurdistan (PUK), the Kurdistan Democratic Party (KDP) and the Sunni Iraqi Islamic Party (IIP) – which led to the formation of a new Kurdish-Sunni alliance (see *Terrorism Monitor*, January 11, 2008) – can further push al-Sadr to the nationalist camp. With the possibility of Ninawa province and the city of Mosul coming largely under the administrative control of Iraqi Kurdistan – as one of the key points of agreement between IIP leader Tariq al-Hashimi and the Kurdish parties and the ascendancy of Kurdish nationalism marked by symbolic events like the display of a Kurdish flag by the regional parliament of Kurdistan (*al-Sabaah*, January 16, 2008) – al-Sadr and his followers are bound to move to the nationalist and anti-federalist camp of the Iraqi parliament.

In this altered political setting, the new JaM could emerge as a powerful militia, a fully organized, disciplined paramilitary force, vying not only for domination over other Shi'a militias in the southern regions, but possibly challenging the Kurdish militias in Baghdad and northern Iraq. Due to the shadowy network apparatus of the militia, the military might of the new JaM should not be underestimated. It may help to better understand how the new JaM may emerge as a new military force by briefly reviewing its formation since 2003.

The Transformation of a Militia

When dozens of young Shi'a volunteers responded in June 2003 to a fiery call by the maverick cleric to join JaM, the U.S. administration and the Coalition authorities dismissed the new paramilitary force as nothing more than a nuisance. The militia, the Coalition Provisional Authority (CPA) argued, would disappear—along with the insurgency—once the Coalition troops completed the process of de-Baathification and the institutionalization of democracy in the country. But this was a major understatement. In reality, al-Sadr's armed forces were not just a "gang," but a newly formed unit of militants drawn largely from former Shi'a infantry from Saddam's army and downtrodden unemployed young people based in the slums of Sadr City.

Surprisingly, the militia grew into a sizable force of more than 6,000 nearly a year after the U.S.-led invasion of Iraq. Its expanding network of operatives grew in parts of the country where Coalition and Iraqi security forces failed to protect civilians against insurgent attacks and criminal activities. To many military analysts who truly realized the growing importance of the up-and-coming militia, JaM represented a complex set of social and religious currents in Shi'a Iraqi society that were largely forced underground during the Ba'athist era. Its appearance after the fall of Saddam's regime underlined the formation of a momentous social movement with real and legitimate grievances that merited serious attention at a time when Iraqi politics was undergoing major transformations under the occupation.

From late 2003 to spring 2004, JaM quickly grew in size and strength. From 2005 to 2006, JaM's rapid expansion in size and influence astonished even those observers who correctly predicted the rise of the Sadrists as a major military force in the post-Ba'athist era. By December 2006, JaM had an estimated membership of 60,000 armed men, constituting a major military force competing for power in the streets of Iraq.

The two main reasons for JaM's initial success can be identified as follows. First and foremost, the Sadrist armed forces were effective in providing security for the local population in exchange for loyalty and allegiance to the movement. In the neighborhoods of Sadr City, where the militia's headquarters is based, JaM is revered as a vigilant public institution that operates to safeguard the economic, legal and political interests of the Shi'a community. In light of the bombing of the Sammara shrine in February 2006, which unleashed a new wave of sectarian violence in the country, JaM gained even more prestige among the Shi'a inhabitants of the slums for their ability to protect the community against *Wahabi* militants. The Sadrist militias were also able to provide security for the Shi'a population in diverse places around the country, especially during religious festivals in shrine cities like Karbala and Najaf when members of the Badr Organization were primarily busy protecting officials of the Islamic Supreme Council of Iraq (ISCI).

Second, under the leadership of its politically shrewd leader, JaM was successful in combining its populist ideology with social programs aimed at supporting the lower-income strata of the Shi'a population. The Sadrists are avid advocates of social justice and try to represent the more economically disenfranchised Shi'a Iraqis, who make up a considerable portion of the southern urban regions and parts of the capital city. The Sadrist militants are inspired by the apocalyptic teachings of Muqtada al-Sadr's father, Grand Ayatollah Muhammad Sadiq al-Sadr, whose execution by Saddam in 1999 elevated his prestige to a cultic figure of immortal status. The core of these teachings is a belief in the millenarian notion of the return of a messianic figure, in this case the twelfth Imam and Mahdi, Muhammad ibn Hassan (born in 868 C.E.), whose reappearance – as he is already on earth but concealed from view – will establish justice in a world infected by sin and oppression. The spiritual mission of the militia is to hasten the Imam's return through various heroic enactments of self-sacrifice, though at times these acts may merely mean offering selfless service to the Shi'a public. In this ideological spirit, JaM is known to operate both as a military unit and a charity group.

The New JaM(s)?

Although it remains to be seen whether JaM will re-emerge as a more disciplined militia under the full control of al-Sadr, February 2008 will most likely witness the rise of a new JaM with a better trained military corps, a centralized command apparatus and tightly watched areas of operation. Iran's Islamic Revolutionary Guard Corps – or perhaps Lebanese Hizballah – may play a more direct role in the organizational restructuring process, though much of this may depend on the future of U.S.-Iranian relations. With Hizballah of Lebanon serving as a model for the new JaM, the result could be an impressive, newly equipped and armed military force, unlike its origin as a populist militia with limited abilities (*Shahrvand-e Emrooz*, December 30, 2007).

But this new development contains the danger of upsetting many Sadrists who may feel left out from the reorganized militia, inflating the number of existing splinter groups. Those members of al-Sadr's militia who are desperately seeking new leadership from a charismatic leader who can bravely uphold the movement's nationalist and anti-establishment ideology have the greatest risk of splitting from the existing militia. The new JaM unveiled in February 2008 may give way to an upsurge of new Sadrist movements, all claiming to represent the authentic ideals of al-Sadr's father, though all differing in the ways in which they operate in the militia-ridden landscape of Shi'a Iraq.

All in all, al-Sadr's choice of strategy is significant. It signals a new era of Iraqi politics that will likely revolve around control over resources, like oil and territorial domination, and militia power rather than identity politics of the ethnic and sectarian sort witnessed in the earlier years of the post-war period. Although the decline of sectarianism is certainly good for Iraq, the rise of a new factional struggle for control over resources may only breed new forms of militia politics. The appearance of the new JaM may serve as a sign of an ominous future.

Reviving the Iraqi Ba'ath: A Profile of General Muhammad Yunis al-Ahmad

By Rafid Fadhil Ali
February 9, 2009
Terrorism Monitor 7 (3)

The U.S.-led invasion of Iraq not only toppled Saddam Hussein, but it also put an end to three and a half decades of political domination by the Ba'ath party over Iraq. Despite a proliferation of political parties and militant organizations eager to take or at least share power in a new Iraq, the Ba'athists, who once held a monopoly on power and remain convinced they are the only legitimate government in Iraq, are still active and reorganizing. The Iraqi Ba'athists, however, have split into two factions, one based in Iraq and the other in Syria. The latter group is led by General Muhammad Yunis al-Ahmad, a once relatively obscure member of Saddam's general staff who has emerged as a claimant to the leadership of the Iraqi Ba'ath party.

From Pan-Arabism to Regional Rivalry

The Arab Ba'ath Socialist Party was founded in Syria in the mid-1940s as a pan-Arab nationalist organization with the aim of unifying all the Arabic-speaking countries. The party first ruled Iraq in 1963 after a successful coup attempt against then Prime Minister General Abd al-Karim Qassim. A few months later the Ba'athists were overthrown and suppressed by General Abdul Salim Arif. The party returned to power in 1968 after another coup, led by Ahmad Hassan al-Bakr, where Saddam woud became his deputy. In 1979 Saddam became president of Iraq until the Ba'athist reign ended with the U.S. invasion in 2003. Although Saddam was not popular in Iraq, hundreds of thousands of Iraqis were members of his party. Many were sincere party members, but others had to join the organization to pursue their education or keep their jobs as government employees.

Since the late 1960s, Iraq and Syria were ruled by two rival wings of the Ba'ath. The personal and political animosity between Syria's President Hafiz al-Assad and President Saddam Hussein dominated regional politics for decades. The pan-Arab party command was split in two, with Ba'athists around the Arab world having to choose between the Iraqi or Syrian faction. The Syrians, however, were unable to welcome the fall of Saddam as it put them under direct American pressure. As a result, Syria became a gateway for foreign fighters on their way to Iraq.

Ba'ath entities were outlawed after the war. The members of the top four levels of the party were excluded from public life by order of Paul Bremer, the administrator of the Coalition Provisional Authority. Saddam and most of the leading figures of his regime were captured one by one. Some Ba'athists, however, did not accept the defeat easily and formed underground organizations. One of those is led by Syrian-based General Muhammad Yunis al-Ahmad, a senior member of the Ba'ath party under Saddam.

Reviving the Party in Syria

General al-Ahmad's highest post under Saddam was his membership in the supreme command of the Ba'ath party. The general seems to have an ideal resume for someone who would want to build a Ba'athist paramilitary organization, having worked in the so-called Political Guidance Directorate of the former Iraq Army. That department was in charge of ensuring the complete control of the Ba'ath over the Iraqi armed forces through a network of loyal officers in every unit. After that, General al-Ahmad occupied a senior post in the military bureau of the party [1].

Al-Ahmad was not one of the 55 most-wanted Iraqi officials depicted in the famous set of playing cards distributed by the U.S. Army during the invasion. A few months later the Coalition acknowledged their oversight by issuing a million dollar reward for information leading to his arrest (*Middle East Online*, February 18, 2004).

General al-Ahmad was mentioned when Moyayad Yaseen Ahmad, the leader of the Jaysh Muhammad (The Army of [the Prophet] Muhammad) insurgent group, was arrested. The government said the captured insurgent had visited Syria, where he met with General al-Ahmad to coordinate joint efforts in the insurgency (*Asharq al-Awsat*, November 17, 2004). On December 6, 2004 the Iraqi government-owned *al-Sabah* newspaper reported:

> *A group of fugitive members of al-Ba'ath held a conference in the Syrian city of al-Hasaka lately. They elected the (criminal) Muhammad Yunis al-Ahmad as secretary-general of the party in Iraq. The attendees offered to stop the insurgency in six hours if the Iraqi government allowed them to participate in the political process. It was not clear how serious the offer was. But the Iraqi government continues its effort to capture al-Ahmad, labeling him as a terrorist who leads and funds insurgent groups.*

The Ba'ath after Saddam

Saddam Hussein was the Secretary General of the Arab Ba'ath socialist party since 1979. Even after his capture in 2003 he was still recognized by the Iraqi Ba'athists as the supreme leader. Following Saddam's execution in December 30, 2006, General al-Ahmad made his most serious attempt to succeed the late party leader by calling for a general conference of the party in Syria to elect a new leadership. The move was condemned by the followers of former Iraqi Vice President Izzat Ibrahim al-Douri, who had already claimed Saddam's succession. Unlike the conference of 2004, this meeting ignited a huge controversy among the Ba'athists. Al-Douri criticized Syria for supporting an American conspiracy against the Iraqi Ba'ath, though shortly afterwards his spokesman played down those remarks (al-Arabiya, January 22, 2007).

The conference was held without any direct media coverage; no pictures were available from the event. General al-Ahmad ordered the expulsion of al-Douri from the party, but al-Douri had already ordered the dismissal of al-Ahmad and 150 other members. The Iraqi Ba'ath party has since split into rival wings (Almalafpress.net, April 25, 2007).

Although the supporters of al-Douri accused al-Ahmad's group of being keen to contact the Iraqi government, this has not yet been proved. Former Iraqi presidential advisor General Wafiq al-Samarai was reported to have met with al-Ahmad's aides in Jordan in 2007 (alnazaha.org, April 28, 2007), but denied ever meeting with any of al-Ahmad's representatives in an interview with the Jamestown Foundation. Al-Samarai said that he believed al-Ahmad's organization would remain a secret armed group and its leading figures would stay in Syria.

Al-Ahmad's Role in the Insurgency

In two television interviews in 2007, General Gazwan al-Kubaisi, the second man in al-Ahmad's group, portrayed the strategy of his party in the insurgency:

> *We asked our supporters in Iraq to join other groups as our abilities are still weak… We do not care who is leading the insurgency, whether the Islamists or the Ba'athists, [so long as] the Islamist armed groups are filled with Ba'athists... We are open to cooperation with any armed group that targets the occupier enemy [the Coalition forces] and the collaborating government but not the Iraqi people.*

Al-Kubaisi also called for the Americans to withdraw their troops from Iraq and claimed his party could help in securing such a withdrawal:

> *They should leave and not stay for years - we could help them to withdraw without losing face. Our conditions are: They should release all the Iraqi prisoners from their jails and from [those of] the collaborating government. They have to hand over the collaborating government to be tried by Iraqis. They must rebuild everything that was damaged in Iraq. They must apologize to the Iraqi people, to the Arab nation, to all Muslims and to humanity for the crime of letting Safavids execute Saddam Hussein (al-Arabiya, August 29, 2007; Al-Baghdadiyah TV [Cairo], December 9, 2007)*

[2].

In addition to General al-Ahmad and General al-Kubaisi, the Syrian-based Ba'ath faction is believed to include most of the remaining leading figures of the party, including Mezher Motni Awad, To'ma Di'aiyef Getan, Jabbar Haddoosh, Sajer Zubair, and Nihad al-Dulaimi.

Aside from the military representation in al-Ahmad's group, the organization is also believed to have made some inroads among the majority Shi'a. Although al-Ahmad and his senior aides are Sunnis, his organization has many Shi'as in the middle level. Al-Douri has held to conservative Islamic policies based on his Sunni faith. Al-Ahmad, however, took the opportunity of returning to the party's original pan-Arab nationalist secular ideology. This has proved attractive to some former Ba'athist Shi'as from southern Iraq, especially those who have not been integrated into post-war Iraq as a result of their party membership (Almalafpress.net, April 25, 2007; see also *Terrorism Focus*, January 21, 2009).

Still, al-Ahmad seems to have failed to overthrow al-Douri. Al-Douri's followers are more active on the Internet and most of the pro-Ba'athist websites recognize al-Douri as the head of the party. Al-Ahmad does not even have exclusive support from the Syrian government and his group is susceptible to Syrian interference in Iraqi Ba'athist affairs. Also, Syrian support is not necessarily an advantage for the Iraqi Ba'thists. In addition to the historical animosity between the Ba'ath membership in the two countries, the Iraqis could not ignore that Syria is the main ally of their rival, Iran.

Conclusion

Despite their differences, both factions of the Ba'ath party have the same ideology and goals. Al-Ahmad will have to work hard to gain the support of what is left of the Ba'athist base. The image of being under the influence of the Syrian government will not help him in this context. Al-Ahmad probably will focus on the military side where his experience and contacts lay. The strategy used against al-Qaeda in Iraq will not automatically work against al-Ba'ath. Iraq and Syria have recently ended a twenty-four year break in diplomatic relations, which should encourage the two countries to raise the level of security coordination between them. This will deny General al-Ahmad and his group the safe haven they have been enjoying for years. The Iraqi government's efforts to integrate more former Ba'ath loyalists will make it harder for al-Ahmad or any other

Ba'athists to re-structure an influential organization by recruiting segregated former comrades.

Notes

1. Information on al-Ahmad from an interview with General Wafiq al-Samarai, head of Iraqi military intelligence in early 1990s. General al-Samarai fled the country and joined the opposition, eventually becoming the top military advisor to current Iraqi president Jalal al-Talibani. Al-Samarai points out that the main area of al-Ahmad's activities is in and around the northern city of Mosul, with a presence in al-Anbar, Kirkuk, and Diyala.

2. "Safavids" refers to the Safavid Dynasty that ruled Iran and large areas in west Asia in the 16th and 17th centuries. The Iraqi Ba'athists use the term to refer to the Iranians and their allies in the Iraqi Shi'a parties. As secularists, the Ba'athists do not deny Shi'a Islam, but by using the term Safavid they show their disrespect for the Iranian interpretation of Shi'a Islam. The Ba'athists believe that the origin of Shi'a Islam is Arab, not Persian.

Muqtada al-Sadr's Radical Rival: A Portrait of Qais al-Khaz'ali

By Rafid Fadhil Ali
January 29, 2010
Militant Leadership Monitor 1 (1)

For most observers, the link between the release of British hostage Peter Moore, held in Iraq for two and a half years, and the nearly simultaneous release of Iraqi militia commander Qais al-Khaz'ali by Iraqi authorities was clear and obvious. Al-Khaz'ali, a Shi'a cleric, was moved from an American military prison in Baghdad to Iraqi custody in late December 2009. American and British authorities denied the existence of any prisoner exchange deal. Moore, an IT consultant who was kidnapped in Baghdad along with his four body guards, was released on December 30, 2009. On the same day, the Iraqi government announced that al-Khaz'ali had been handed over to the Iraqis. A few days later, al-Khaz'ali was reportedly set free by the Interior Ministry, though the Iraqi government's liaison officer on hostage issues claimed al-Khazali was still in custody facing various charges (al-Manar.com, January 5, 2010; Reuters, January 5, 2010).

Al-Khaz'ali is the leader of Asa'ib Ahl al-Haq (League of the Righteous - AAH), the group that abducted the British men in a raid on the Iraqi Ministry of Finance building. Three of the bodyguards were killed and their bodies were previously traded for the release of other AAH figures. The fourth bodyguard, Alan McMenemy, is also believed to be dead. The American army classifies the

AAH as one of the "Special Groups" – Iranian-backed Shi'a militias that split from the Jaysh al-Mahdi (JaM) militia of Muqtada al-Sadr.

Qais al-Khaz'ali was arrested on March 22, 2007 along with other leaders of AAH. All were accused of being responsible for killing five American soldiers in Karbala (see *Terrorism Monitor*, June 25, 2009). Currently in his mid-thirties, al-Khaz'ali comes from the southern city of Diwaniya. In the 1990s, Qais al-Khaz'ali was one of the young clerics who joined the movement led by Muqtada's father, the late Ayatollah Muhammad Sadiq al-Sadr (assassinated in February 1999 by Saddam Hussein). After the fall of Saddam, al-Khaz'ali became very close to Muqtada. One of his first posts was heading the regional office of the Sadr movement in al-Rusafa (East Baghdad). The Shi'a district of Sadr City, Muqtada's most important stronghold, was within his area.

In the second Battle of Najaf between U.S. forces and the Sadrists in the summer of 2004, al-Khaz'ali was a field commander and the spokesman for Muqtada. According to the account of al-Khaz'ali's deputy, Akram al-Ka'abi, the idea of forming AAH emerged after that battle:

> *A few days after the battle of Najaf, I sat with brother Qais al-Khaz'ali and decided to change the resistance tactics based on experiences in the battles of Baghdad and Najaf. We made use of both the successes and mistakes and set a new strategy. We followed the tactics of guerrilla warfare. This was different than our old fighting style, adopting the principle of maneuvering, attrition and preserving the resistance elements. By Allah's will, we saw how big the difference was. For example, in one of the old battles we lost 150 fighters in six hours from the enemy's bombardment. But now, after applying the new tactics for four and a half years, we lost only a very few martyrs. Most of the casualties are on the occupier's side (Islamtimes.org, November 11, 2009).*

Al-Khaz'ali and the other AAH leaders avoided appearing in public. They did not issue statements regularly. In the beginning they did not stress their differences with Muqtada al-Sadr and the wider Sadrist movement he leads. AAH does not have an official website but has started to place videos of their attacks on Coalition forces on the internet. Most of the attacks were carried out through the use of improvised explosive devices (IEDs). AAH has a sister organization, Hizballah in Iraq, led by another previous spokesman of Muqtada, Ahmad al-Shaibani. The rhetoric and the attack styles of the two groups are similar.

AAH has not denied getting support from Iran. Salam al-Maliki, former Minister of Transportation and an AAH figure explained in an interview, "AAH has relations of accord and coordination with Lebanese Hizballah, Hamas, influential parties in the Iranian government and Shi'a figures from the Gulf. We have things in common, including religion, sect, resisting the occupation and rejecting the American presence in the area" (*Asharq al-Awsat*, August 10, 2009).

The capture of Qais al-Khaz'ali did not seem to have any effect on the operational capabilities of AAH, but he did manage to retain his influence as the leader of the organization. At the beginning of 2009 it became known that there were negotiations between the Iraqi government and al-Khaz'ali, who was being held in the American detention center at Camp Cropper near Baghdad International Airport. The purpose was to settle the issue of the British hostages in return for the freedom of al-Khaz'ali and his associates (*al-Hayat*, March 28, 2009).

Al-Khaz'ali extended his influence inside the prison. He led Friday prayer and made Friday speeches. In one of those speeches he called on the Iraqi government to release the resistance prisoners, offer an amnesty to those who fled the country and reconsider the sentences of death or life imprisonment given to Shi'a insurgents (eljnub.com, May 17, 2009).

The expanding presence of AAH seems to have upset Muqtada al-Sadr. He denounced AAH leaders and denied that they were affiliated with his movement anymore. The Sadrists also criticized AAH over their negotiation with the government (Roafd.com, June 12, 2009). AAH responded by saying that they were not part of Muqtada's group but an independent entity (*Asharq al-Awsat*, August 10, 2009).

The Shi'a web forums published a letter that al-Khaz'ali wrote to Muqtada. AAH did not deny it and the style sounds authentic. In the letter, al-Khaz'ali points out the following:

"The negotiation was with the government, not the occupiers. Yet it was not against Islam to negotiate directly with the occupation."

"Our goal is to release the prisoners, not to end the resistance. That is what happened in Lebanon and Palestine."

"We declared a ceasefire to give the government a chance to end the

occupation. The international and local circumstances are suitable to end the occupation by peaceful means, while you [Muqtada] declared your ceasefires under unsuitable circumstances."

"We were not negotiating under your [Muqtada's] name. We have our [own] names and figures" (iairaq.com, October 19, 2009).

Since June 2009, the Iraqi government has started to deal with AAH as a political group. The release of al-Khaz'ali will support that, though many Sunnis accuse the AAH of being responsible for attacks against civilians. AAH has always claimed that it only targeted foreign forces. The debate will not end until the facts are revealed through an inquiry. Such a move seems very unlikely as the Americans themselves did not charge the AAH leaders with attacks against their forces. Meanwhile, Iraqi Prime Minister Nouri al-Maliki needs any support he can find within the Shi'a community. He will have to face a coalition of the main Shi'a parties (including Muqtada's) in the general election in March 2010. Sunni politicians criticized the government's friendly approach towards the AAH while refusing similar treatment for Sunni insurgent groups.

The events of the last year have led to the public break of the AAH from Muqtada's movement. All the indications suggest that AAH has special relations with Iran. The terms of those relations are not clear, but most of the Sunni media label them as controlled by Iran's Islamic Revolutionary Guard Corps. Throughout the saga of the British hostages, Qais al-Khaz'ali has proved that he has tight control of the AAH. He definitely lacks the political charisma of Muqtada al-Sadr, but the AAH has demonstrated that it possesses very well trained fighters who have adapted various tactics to serve specific goals. The AAH is an example of the effectiveness of a relatively small insurgent group with high quality training and performance, surviving the hardest years of the Iraqi insurgency without losing any of its prominent leaders in the fight or in the courts.

Part II

Instabilites of the North and South

Chapter 5

The Security Scene in Southern Iraq

Understanding The Roots Of The Shi'a Insurgency In Iraq

By Ahmed Hashim
June 30, 2004
Terrorism Monitor 2 (13)

By the end of March 2004 – and to everyone's surprise – significant elements of the Shi'a community rose in open rebellion against the coalition when the firebrand cleric Muqtada al-Sadr unleashed his so-called Jaysh al-Mahdi (JaM) against the Coalition. Suddenly, the coalition was faced with the unsavory prospect of a two-front war. While the precipitating factors of the Shi'a insurgency were the policies of the Coalition Provisional Authority (CPA), as with all conflicts, there were underlying causes for the Shi'a uprising [1].

In analyzing the Sadr phenomenon as an insurgency, we cannot ignore these underlying causes or relegate them to the background. A proper analysis must recognize that the phenomenon was not primarily a religious movement; rather, it was a populist one. Attacking the non-existent religious credentials of this young firebrand, who had not yet reached a level of religious learning within the Shi'a clerical, did little to dampen his appeal. To be sure he draws support from the fact that he is both a Sayyid – descendant of the Prophet Muhammad – and the son of one of the leading Ayatollahs of Iraq, Muhammad Sadiq al-Sadr. However, his appeal has been mainly to the disenfranchised within the Shi'a community.

Though Shi'as did not welcome Coalition forces with open arms (despite promises by the civilian architects of the war and their exiled Iraqi advisers), without a doubt, the Coalition did have considerable goodwill within the community in the early days of the occupation [2]. This author's analysis of the situation from the ground in Iraq and from statements of various Shi'a clerics concludes that over the course of the several months before June 30, 2004, Shi'as were prepared to challenge the authority and legitimacy of the Coalition only if the gap between its promises and its achievements were too great. As Hasan Zirkani, a pro-Sadr cleric in *Madinat al-Sadr* (Sadr City), bluntly put it in a November 2003 prayer meeting: "We had hoped that some of the problems might have vanished by now." What were these problems? The lack of law and order, rampant unemployment, lack of basic services in Shi'a urban areas – and coalition disregard for the cultural and societal norms of the population. The Shi'a political leader best able to undertake that challenge was none other than Muqtada.

Saddam Hussein assassinated Ayatollah Muhammad Sadiq al-Sadr in February 1999, after he had begun a strategy of politically mobilizing dispossessed Shi'as, particularly in what used to be called Saddam City [3]. Not only was the Ayatollah, a man of pronounced religious learning (a native Iraqi religious scholar), he was a man of political activism. His son, Muqtada, is a populist with xenophobic tendencies and a particular disdain for Iranians. Indeed, among the reasons for Muqtada's distaste for Grand Ayatollah Ali al-Sistani is the fact that the latter is Iranian by birth [4]. In this context, the Muqtada uprising must also be viewed as an internal struggle within the Shi'a hierarchy for political and socio-economic paramountcy over the Shi'a population. Waged largely between "nativist" Iraqi Shi'as such as Muqtada on the one hand and returning exiles on the other, this battle is, by extension, over the future of Iraq itself [5].

Initially, Muqtada focused his energies on revitalizing his father's extensive political network among the poor Shi'as and the younger clerical establishment. He created a militia (the JaM), a major step in itself, but cleverly argued that it would not be armed and would devote itself to social work in the neighborhoods. Members of the militia merely hid their arms, which they had acquired from looted Iraqi military stores, at their homes; the central offices of the Sadrist movement supplied ammunition. They were able to practice marksmanship in the numerous garbage-filled open fields that dot Sadr City. Few of the "rank and file" within the lower levels of the militia – often young illiterate kids who had migrated from rural areas into urban centers – had any training in arms or small-unit tactics whatsoever.

Recruits to the Muqtada insurgency indicate the clear class and social basis of the movement. Muqtada catered to the most dispossessed elements within the long-suffering Shi'a community. Disgruntled and unemployed young men, who would stand at street corners for hours on end every day, would eventually be enticed into attending Friday sermons, after which their entry into the movement began. His constituency was derived from towns such as Sadr City – a large, sprawling, squalid and fetid suburb of Baghdad where the unemployment rate hovers around 70%, and the city of Kut, which faces a similar unemployment problem [6]. For months as Muqtada built up his organization, the Coalition and the CPA had debated what to do about the Sadrist movement, particularly after his sermons began to sound like they were preaching violence against the Americans. In March 2004, when the CPA decided to close down Muqtada's paper and then proceeded to arrest one of his chief aides, Muqtada concluded that the U.S. was going to move against him. He decided to preempt the CPA by calling out his supporters, arming them, and throwing them into battle against the Coalition forces.

Thus the Muqtada uprising should not be viewed merely as a radical religious movement outside the context of contentious Iraqi politics. Rather, it is simply one of many different movements vying for control within the country. As each of these movements pursue their various agendas, the potential for conflict with the new Iraqi government and Coalition forces persists – however, the potential for intra-Iraqi conflict also becomes greater, and can threaten to destabilize an already vulnerable central authority.

Is Civil War in Iraq's Future?

More ominous than a Shi'a uprising, is a possible rise of violence by ethnic and sectarian-based socio-political movements against one another and against the Coalition forces. Already, ethnically Turkic Iraqi Turcomen minorities in the north have clashed with Kurds in the vicinity of the oil-rich town of Kirkuk over the "correct" division of resources and political power. While traditional conflicts between Iraq's Arab majority and large Kurdish minority over the level of Kurdish political autonomy have not yet flared, localized violence between Arabs and Kurds over land and resources has occurred in northern Iraq. The prospects of a civil war between Arabs and Kurds are quite high should the latter decide that they would prefer to secede. Most troubling to observers, however, is the dire possibility of an inter-Arab civil conflict between Sunni and Shi'as. Tension between the two sectarian communities can be found at three distinct levels.

First, each community maintains a traditional disdain for the other and their respective rituals. This has been compounded by Sunni Arab's view of the Shi'as as either actual or potential fifth columnists for their co-religionists in Iran. Such sentiments are nothing more than ingrained Sunni prejudice against the Shi'as, which existed at the time of the Ottoman Empire (1300-1900), was magnified for much of the monarchical era (1921-1958) and reappeared in a thinly veiled manner under the republican and Ba'athist eras (1958-2003). Prejudices, however, can lead to vicious sectarian clashes and fulfill significant roles in civil wars. While mutual historical prejudices are not enough to begin a civil war, they add fuel to the fire when groups clash over concrete political, material, and resource issues, and over the future direction of the state itself. All of these ingredients for civil war exist in present-day Iraq.

Second, tensions still exist over the role of the Sunni Arab community in the oppression and wholesale massacre of Shi'as under the Saddam regime. Shi'as have little reason to forget these recent events, and first-hand observations in Iraq over the course of November and December 2003 indicate that many Shi'as are not too eager to forgive either [7]. Though the collapse of a regime which had brutalized them for over thirty years was a key victory and has opened the way for their rise to power, there may still be attempts by individual Shi'as or parts of the community to seek vengeance against Ba'athists or former regime members.

Last, but not least, is the struggle over the political future of the country and its reconstituted identity. Sunnis believe that they are entitled to rule as the authentic voice of the country. They are the most skilled and most educated segment of the population, and see themselves as having the country's best interests at heart [8]. For many Sunnis, the rise of Shi'as means domination by Iran, a country for which they have excoriated for decades under Saddam. For their part, Shi'as fiercely resent any aspersions cast on their "Arabness," their alleged subordination to Iranian interests and their supposed inability to rule Iraq. To many Shi'as, these views smack of a colonial mentality on the part of their Arab brethren.

The Muqtada uprising is one element within the complicated and dangerous landscape of Iraqi politics. Simultaneously an intra-Shi'a conflict and a struggle over the future identity of Iraq, it is representative of the multi-faceted nature of the various competing interests in the country. While tensions between these interests have yet to spill over into a civil war, the possibility exists, as Sunnis and Shi'as, radicals and conservatives, rich and poor, Arabs and non-Arabs all fight for a place at the table in occupied and post-occupation Iraq.

Notes
1. For an extensive and authoritative analysis of CPA missteps – simply one of many made by that organization over the course of its existence – vis-à-vis Muqtada see Rajiv Chandrasekaran and Anthony Shadid, "U.S. Targeted Fiery Cleric In Risky Move," *Washington Post*, April 11, 2004.
2. See, for example, Scott Calvert, "In Najaf, regime's symbols tumble," *Baltimore-Sun*, April 04, 2003 (accessed on-line).
3. Muqtada's uncle Ayatollah Muhammad Baqr al-Sadr was one of Iraq's leading Islamic thinkers. He was executed by Saddam in April 1980.
4. Muqtada alternates between statements that ostensibly show respect and disdain for the senior Iranian-born Ayatollah al-Sistani. On occasions Muqtada's disdain shows through clearly though. When al-Sistani suggested that Muqtada take his fight against the U.S. outside of the holy city of Najaf, Muqtada retorted that, "if there is one man who needs to leave, that is precisely al-Sistani. He is an Iranian. I am a child of this country. I was here when he was safe and sound in Tehran. I, my family, and my people have paid a very high price in blood under Saddam," quoted in Renato Caprile, "The United States can kill me, but Iraq will turn into an inferno," *La Repubblica*, April 26, 2004, p. 5, cited in Foreign Broadcasting Information Service, EUP20040426000085, April 26, 2004 accessed at https://portal.rccb.osis.gov/. On the origins of the Muqtada phenomenon see, "Moqtada al-Sadr, la voix radicale des chiites irakiens," *Le Monde*, April 04, 2004; Patrice Claude, "Moqtada Al-Sadr, l'imam rebelled," *Le Monde*, May 13, 2004.
5. For more detailed discussions of the dynamics of internal Shi'a factionalism and strife in the post-Saddam era see Faleh Jabar, "The Worldly Roots of Religiosity in Post-Saddam Iraq," *Middle East Report*, No.227, Summer 2003, p. 12-18.
6. I visited al-Kut in early March 2004 (it is located in one of the poorest of Iraq's provinces) and had a long conversation with an Iraqi who revealed the extent of the unemployment problem and growing support among the young for the movement of Muqtada al-Sadr.
7. Interviews in Hilla, November 29, 2003.
8. Interviews with Sunni Arabs, Baghdad, November 2003.

The Sadr-Sistani Relationship

By Babak Rahimi
March 30, 2007
Terrorism Monitor 5 (6)

One of the oddest developments in the recent history of Iraq has been the growing connection between the young firebrand cleric, Muqtada al-Sadr, and the highest-ranking Shi'a cleric, Grand Ayatollah Ali al-Sistani. Earlier in 2003, the erratic politics of al-Sadr, with his mix of Arab nationalism and militant chiliastic ideology, was considered to eventually collide with al-Sistani's quietist form of Shi'ism, which advocates that clerics should maintain a clear distance from day-to-day state politics. Since 2004, however, an unlikely alliance has gradually taken form between the former adversaries, which is bound to reshape Iraqi Shi'a politics in the years to come.

By and large, the relationship between the two clerics has been one of asymmetrical partnership, in which al-Sistani plays the superior partner, guiding the younger and less experienced al-Sadr in his quest for becoming a legitimate leader of the Iraqi Shi'a community. In doing so, al-Sistani has tried to tame al-Sadr by bringing him into the mainstream Najaf establishment in order to form a united Shi'a front against extremist Sunnis and the United States. In return, al-Sadr, who lacks religious credentials, has been using al-Sistani's support to legitimize his religious authority and expand his influence in southern Iraq. The relationship is mutually opportunistic, but also pragmatic, since the two clerics have not been able to ignore each other.

In broad terms, such an alliance signals two significant changes: first, a dramatic shift in the balance of power in Shi'a Iraq in terms of the revival of the Hawza, as a cluster of seminaries and religious scholarly institutions in Najaf, and, second, an increase of tension between Shi'as and Sunnis in Iraq. Moreover, the growing alliance between al-Sadr and al-Sistani also underlines another vital feature tied to the Shi'a ascendancy in Iraq: the rise of Iran as a regional power. Iran has been playing a crucial role in the shaping of Sadr-Sistani relations, since any alliance between Shi'a leaders is intertwined with the Qom-Tehran nexus and Iranian politics in the greater Middle East.

Against the Najaf Hawza: 2003-2004

Since the U.S.-led invasion of Iraq, the Sadrist movement, mainly dominated by Muqtada al-Sadr, has emerged as one of the most populist and grassroots currents in the post-Ba'athist era. Yet the militant movement has also posed the most serious threat to clerical orthodoxy and its conservative and quietist tradition, best embodied by Grand Ayatollah al-Sistani.

Much of the "heterodoxy" of the Sadrist movement lies in its early (2003–04) rejection of clerical monopoly, led by some young clerical students and followers of al-Sadr who accused al-Sistani of transforming the shrine city of Najaf into a "sleeping house of learning." The heretical tendencies of the Sadrist movement entailed rejecting the religious authority of a living, high-ranking cleric in favor of the rulings of a deceased *marja* (religious scholar), a blasphemous idea according to the orthodox thinking that al-Sistani and his Hawza represent. Yet there is also the factor of Arab nationalism. Ideologically, the Sadrists are Arab nationalists and resent the presence of any non-Arab cleric in Iraq, especially those of Iranian descent, like al-Sistani, who have been residing in the shrine-cities for decades.

The origin of the movement dates back to the early 1990s, when Ayatollah Muhammad Sadiq al-Sadr, the father of Muqtada, led an anti-quietist campaign by accusing al-Sistani and other leading clerics in Najaf of abandoning ordinary people and allowing Ba'athist oppression to take place [1]. When Muqtada emerged as the leading figure in the movement four years after the assassination of his father by Saddam's regime in 1999, he continued his father's legacy and expanded his anti-quietist movement in the slums of Baghdad and southern Iraq. In spring 2003, al-Sadr refused to accept al-Sistani's leadership, and declined his invitations for a meeting [2]. Tensions between the outspoken al-Sadr and the quietist al-Sistani were at their highest when the cleric followers of al-Sadr criticized the Grand Ayatollah for his Iranian origin and even urged him and other quietist clerics to leave Iraq [3]. The conflict between al-Sadr and al-Sistani culminated in the August 2004 showdown between the JaM and U.S. troops in Najaf, when al-Sistani saw the clash as an opportunity for the eradication of his young rival [4].

Nevertheless, eventually al-Sistani decided to intervene and offer protection to al-Sadr and his followers. After three weeks of intense fighting between the JaM and U.S. and Iraqi forces around the Imam Ali Mosque in Najaf, al-Sistani was finally able to broker a ceasefire deal with al-Sadr in late August 2004 [5]. Although his change of position was partly aimed at ending the destruction of the shrine complex and protecting Najaf's inhabitants, al-Sistani saw the JaM as a major asset in dealing with anti-Shi'a Sunni groups and U.S. forces in Iraq. Due to the encouragement from Hizballah and Tehran, the agreement signaled an opportunity to tame al-Sadr and his JaM, militarily weakened by U.S. forces, by bringing his troops closer to the mainstream Shi'a establishment [6].

Post-2005 Elections and the Iran Factor

The 2004 deal signaled a tipping point in Sadr-Sistani relations, bringing the two leaders closer together with the aim of advancing Shi'a interests in the democratic arena. Despite a period of tension with the Supreme Council for the Islamic Revolution in Iraq (SCIRI, later renamed the Islamic Supreme Council of Iraq) and the Badr Organization, the largest Shi'a militia that backed al-Sistani, al-Sadr finally joined forces with a Shi'a-led political party approved by al-Sistani, the United Iraqi Alliance (UIA), in the December 2005 parliamentary election. The move advanced a new stage in Sadr-Sistani relations, which underlined how the two clerics saw the importance of a centralized democratic government as a means to solidify Shi'a power in a country with a long history of Sunni-dominance.

Since 2004, al-Sadr and al-Sistani have met a number of times to discuss issues related to elections, including a major meeting in mid-September 2004 that included the late Abdul Aziz al-Hakim, then al-Sadr's main rival [7]. In early September 2004, in a potentially explosive incident, al-Sistani helped al-Sadr by asking the Iraqi police to end the siege of his office in Najaf [8]. Al-Sistani's growing relations with al-Sadr continued to evolve when he appealed to Abdul al-Saheb-e al-Khoei to delay the search for his slain brother, Sayyid Abdul Majid al-Khoei, who was allegedly murdered by al-Sadr's followers in 2003 [9]. This was a major move by al-Sistani since it basically extricated al-Sadr of any wrongdoing in the case of al-Khoei's murder.

After the January and December 2005 elections, al-Sistani refused to call for the disarming of the JaM militia. This decision was made in connection with the rise of sectarian tensions unleashed after the bombing of the Shi'a al-Askari Shrine in Samarra in February 2006. With the absence of a strong centralized government in Baghdad, al-Sistani considered al-Sadr's militia as a major force to protect the Shi'a community and its sacred shrines against Sunni extremist attacks. He even used al-Sadr to negotiate with the Sunni clerics about the looming problem of sectarian violence. After a major meeting in March 2006, al-Sistani dispatched al-Sadr to discuss the escalation of Sunni-Shi'a tensions with a number of Sunni clerics at the Azamiyah mosque in Baghdad [10]. At this stage, al-Sistani appeared to have gained considerable influence over al-Sadr, while his JaM militia was gradually breaking into subgroups, challenging their former leader for his compromising stance toward the Sunnis and the Americans—perhaps partly due to al-Sistani's influence.

In an important meeting in early January 2007, al-Sistani persuaded al-Sadr to end his boycott of the UIA and return to the parliament [11]. Al-Sadr agreed, and his followers returned to the parliament later that month. In another major meeting mid-February 2007, al-Sadr sought the counsel of al-Sistani about attacks and death threats he was receiving from his own militia [12]. Following al-Sistani's advice, al-Sadr reportedly left Iraq for Iran and he is now staying at his cousin's house, Jafar al-Sadr, in Qom [13]. This final meeting highlights the growing dependence of al-Sadr on al-Sistani's religious and intellectual authority, which has increased considerably since the toppling of Saddam's regime. For now, al-Sistani appears to have tamed al-Sadr, especially by helping him in becoming a major figure to advance an anti-sectarian platform.

Both al-Sadr and al-Sistani share the common interest of protecting the Shi'a community against the ongoing sectarian war and, simultaneously, promoting a unified Iraq governed by a centralized government in Baghdad. In this sense, the two are against a federalist system of government, particularly the sectarian-provincial model of federalism advocated by Abdul Aziz al-Hakim. This common objective has brought them closer together, while facing opposition from pro-federal factions, such as the Iranian-backed SCIRI, which continue to push a sectarian agenda in the revised version of the constitution expected to be proposed by the constitutional committee in mid-May 2007.

Here the role of Iran in the making of such an alliance should not be ignored. Although al-Sadr and al-Sistani do not want Iranian influence in Iraq, they also realize that Tehran cannot simply be ignored. Both clerics recognize that Shi'a empowerment in Iraq can only be ensured by Iranian support, and challenging Tehran could only lead to the consolidation of Sunni power, with the backing of the United States, in Iraq and the region.

Given the fact that the financial center of his religious network is based in the Iranian city of Qom, al-Sistani has been careful not to upset the Iranian authorities. He refuses to challenge the authority of Iran's Supreme Leader, Ayatollah Ali Khamenei, despite their differences in theological outlooks. For instance, al-Sistani has so far declined to declare a *fatwa* on the production of a nuclear bomb since he wants to avoid a confrontation with Tehran [14]. Al-Sistani has also criticized the student reformist movement in Iran for its disregard of Iranian national interests and warned the students against foreign influences [15]. He has even praised the Iranian president, Mahmoud Ahmadinejad, for his travels to local regions in Iran and getting involved in the daily problems of his constituency. He has even urged Iraqi officials to follow in Ahmadinejad's footsteps in Iraq [16]. Like al-Sadr, al-Sistani considers the backing of Iran as something necessary in a period of foreign aggression (i.e. Israel and the United States) and increasing anti-Shi'a currents in the Sunni world. Iran, too, recognizes the influence of the Najaf Hawza and the Sadrists in Iraq, and continues to ride the rising tide of the Shi'a revival. Tehran knows that al-Sadr and al-Sistani can play a major role in advancing Iran's interests in Iraq and the region in case the

United States decides to attack Iran's nuclear facilities.

Implications of Sadr-Sistani Ties

The changing relationship between Muqtada al-Sadr and Grand Ayatollah Ali al-Sistani signals a dramatic shift in the political landscape of the Shi'a Iraqi community since the fall of the Ba'athist regime in 2003. While new conflicts have emerged between Shi'a groups, especially between the opposition groups that left the country (Da'awa and ISCI) and those who stayed in Iraq under Saddam's reign (Sadrists), old adversaries are now becoming new partners as a result of the sectarian conflict engulfing the country.

There are two main implications involved. First and foremost, despite theological and ideological differences between Shi'a groups and leaders, sectarian identity is playing a major role in the shaping of future alliances and conflicts in Iraq. It is an undeniable truth that with the rise of Salafi Sunni attacks against the Shi'as, rivalry amongst the Shi'a groups subsides, and loose alliances are formed to protect the community. Yet while creating such alliances, each rival group also prepares to protect its own particular economic and political interests in various localities throughout Baghdad and southern Iraq [17]. In short, Shi'a relations in Iraq should be considered as both political and sectarian. Theological and ideological differences play an important role, but not a prominent one, as Sadr-Sistani relations best demonstrate.

Such a dramatic shift, however, also underlines the unpredictable political situation in the country, signaling certain unforeseen challenges that may arise in the years to come. In this sense, it is hardly an overstatement to claim that with the death of Ayatollah al-Sistani, who is 76 (as of March 2007), new unforeseen problems will likely emerge in the form of competition among leading Shi'a groups to control the Shi'a community. Since the Grand Ayatollah has not yet appointed a successor according to the traditional clerical succession process, it remains unclear what sort of political vacuum his death could create. Nevertheless, a political vacuum will certainly be created. No other cleric in the post-Ba'athist era has had so much authority in Iraq, and it is very likely that his absence will be deeply felt.

The leading candidate to replace al-Sistani is the Afghan-born, Najaf-based Grand Ayatollah Muhammad Ishaq al-Fayadh. He is an old seminary student friend of al-Sistani since the 1950s and a staunch ally since 1992. Ayatollah al-Khoei, the mentor of al-Sistani, reportedly recognized al-Fayadh as one of his most trusted and loved students, and it is likely that al-Sistani will soon appoint him as his successor. As a successor, al-Fayadh is more likely to deal directly with the United States and get involved in the transition process; however, he is also likely to antagonize the Sadrist nationalists, who view him as an Afghan foreigner who should not have a say in Iraq's politics. Two other Najaf-based clerics, the Grand Ayatollahs Bashir Hussein al-Najafi and Muhammad Said al-Hakim, are also potential candidates. It is unlikely that they will be the successors, however, because they are considered lesser scholars than al-Fayadh, who is highly respected by many Shi'a Iraqis, particularly by the tribal chieftains of Najaf.

With the vacuum of authority in Najaf, new conflicts between Shi'a groups will certainly come to light, especially in the oil-rich province of Basra, where SCIRI and the Sadrists, especially the Fadhila Party, compete for territorial control. With spawned rivalries among various Shi'a groups (and subgroups), Iraq may also see an increase of sectarian conflict as anti-Shi'a Salafi groups begin to increase their attacks on Shi'as with the aim of creating more chaos in a community devoid of a central religious authority. Tehran can also extend its religious network in Najaf in order to establish the authority of Supreme Leader Khamenei in the Najaf Hawza [18]. Khamenei's increase of influence in southern Iraq could seriously jeopardize the independence of the Hawza. These scenarios could also cause major problems for a transitional government in Baghdad that is seeking to establish authority in southern Iraq.

Therefore, what are the implications of a Sadr-Sistani partnership? First and foremost, the United States should be aware of the unpredictable politics of the Shi'a community. The swing of alliances merits serious attention, despite the fact that sectarian identity will play a central role in the intra-Shi'a relations in years to come. Second, the United States should also recognize the enduring authority of the Najaf Hawza and its sphere of influence in Shi'a Iraq. This influence is so significant that even the defiant al-Sadr failed to challenge the establishment, let alone muster enough support to lead the Shi'a community among the poor and the youth for his anti-occupation and nationalist image.

It was the common consensus in the academic and policy communities that after the Samarra bombing of February 2006, al-Sistani had become a marginal figure. Despite his brief diminishing influence as a result of the rise of sectarian tensions, al-Sistani now appears to be back with even greater authority. He is supported by centuries of traditional authority and backed by an extensive financial and religious network that reaches beyond Iraq and Iran. Both Tehran and al-Sadr know that al-Sistani should not be ignored. The United States should certainly do the same.

Notes

1. International Crisis Group, "Iraq's Muqtada al-Al-Sadr: Spoiler or Stabilizer?," p. 3-6.
2. Ibid.
3. Author interview with an al-Sistani representative, Najaf, Iraq, August 7, 2005.
4. Vali Nasr, The Shi'a Revival: How Conflicts within Islam Will Shape the Future, New York: Norton, 2006, p. 194.
5. According to al-Sistani's representative in Najaf, Hamed Khafaf, the deal also included the disarming of the JaM, "Moafeqat-e Moqtada va Dowlat-e Moaqat ba Pishnahade Ayatollah al-Sistani," *Baztab*, September 3, 2004, www.baztab.com. The disarmament of the militia was never fully enforced.
6. Author interview with an al-Sistani representative, Najaf, Iraq, August 7, 2005. See also Vali Nasr, p. 194.
7. "Jalas-e Moshtarak-e Hakim va Moqtada al-Sadr ba Ayatollah al-Sistani," *Baztab*, September 15, 2004, www.baztab.com.
8. Ibid.
9. The reason behind this call was mainly to show Shi'a solidarity in the January 2005 elections. See "Inetaf-e Marjayat Shi'I dar Moqableh Al-Sadriha baraye Vahdat-e Shiaan-e dar entekhabat," *Baztab*, November 12, 2004, www.baztab.com.
10. "Didar-e Moqtada al-Sadr va Ayatollah al-Sistani," *Baztab*, March 29, 2005, www.baztab.com.
11. Hussain al-Kabi, "al-Sadr Yahath Mowaqf al-tiyar al-Sadri beshan al-Hukumat wa al-barleman ma al-Sistani," *al-Sabaah*, January 9, 2007.
12. Al-Sistani is reported to have advised al-Sadr the following: "You have two options: bear the consequences, on you and the Shi'as in general, or withdraw into a corner," Rod Nordland, "Silence of the Sadrists," *Newsweek*, March 12, 2007.
13. Reported by Diyar al-Umari on al-Arabiya TV, February 19, 2007.
14. Author interview with a seminary student of al-Sistani in Qom, Iran, December 23, 2005.
15. Abdul al-Rahim Aghiqi Bakhshayeshi, Faqihe Varasteh, Qom: Novid Islam: 2003, p. 202.
16. "Ayatollah al-Sistani: Az Amalkard Ahmadinejad Ulgo Begirid," *Baztab*, November 11, 2006, www.baztab.com.
17. The case of Sadrist and SCIRI relations since 2003 merits serious attention.
18. The control of Najaf has been one of the primary objectives of the Iranian government in Iraq since the fall of Saddam's regime in 2003. In the last four years, Ayatollah Khamenei has established a center in Najaf, which pays the highest salary to the seminary students in the city. The extent of Tehran's influence in Najaf, however, is still limited, as al-Sistani and three other high-ranking clerics remain the most revered and influential religious authorities in the shrine city.

THE SECURITY SCENE IN SOUTHERN IRAQ

Shi'a Power Struggle Unfolds in Diwaniya

By Babak Rahimi
April 26, 2007
Terrorism Focus 4 (11)

Since the political bloc loyal to Muqtada al-Sadr abandoned the parliament and government ministries on April 16, 2007—in a move to demand Prime Minister Nouri al-Maliki set a timetable for the withdrawal of foreign troops—the Sadrist movement appears to be tilting toward a more militant stance, separated from the political process and, consequently, relying more on the influence of the Jaysh al-Mahdi (JaM) militia for control over the Shi'a population. This new development entails multiple factors, one of which is primarily an apparent increase in the level of rivalry between Shi'a militias in the main urban centers in southern Iraq. The eruption of violence in the first week of April 2007 in the northern part of the predominately Shi'a city of Diwaniya, which is the administrative center of Qadissiya province, underlines the escalation of competition for power among militia organizations, as followers of al-Sadr lead the way to claim the mantle of Shi'a leadership (al-Jazeera, April 13, 2007).

Unlike previous sporadic clashes in the city, which mainly occurred between Iraqi police and Ba'athist forces, the fighting, notably after the January 2005 elections, testifies to a power struggle among Shi'a groups in Diwaniya. The most notable clash before 2006 was the case of Hazem al-Shaalan, the former Defense Minister of the Interim Government of then Prime Miniter Ayad Allawi, whose bodyguards fought against Iraqi security forces in January 2005 while campaigning for the elections (*Baztab*, February 1, 2005). Since the rise of al-Sadr's popularity after the 2005 elections in the city, the Sadrists are now demanding more power in a city that is largely dominated by rival groups, namely the Supreme Council for the Islamic Revolution in Iraq (SCIRI, later renamed the Islamic Supreme Council of Iraq) and local tribal forces. Al-Sadr has gained considerable support among the poor and the young in a city of nearly 500,000 people.

For the most part, the early April 2007 collision between joint U.S.-Iraqi forces and the JaM militia was a continuation of months of violence in the city. The origins of the conflict may be traced back to September 2006 when, after various explosions and many deaths, U.S. forces arrested a number of JaM militiamen and confiscated al-Sadr's computer equipment from his Diwaniya office (*Baztab*,

September 14, 2006). The move was aimed at decreasing the disruptive activities of the JaM militia in the form of assassinations of members of political rival groups and the brutal imposition of Islamic law on the inhabitants of the city.

Al-Sadr's call for a united Iraqi front on April 9, 2007, which immediately followed an earlier Diwaniya fighting, revealed a new strategic tactic. The display of a united Iraqi front was first aimed at the Sunni-Shi'a alliance with an aura of nationalism to symbolically oppose the presence of U.S. forces (al-Arabiya, April 9, 2007). The call was also, however, aimed at increasing his legitimacy among Iraqis, both Sunnis and Shi'as, in opposition to any form of sectarianism, mainly led by some Sunni insurgents and especially the militia of SCIRI known as the Badr Organization, which for the moment controls Diwaniya's police force and the Qadissiya provincial council (CBS News, April 7, 2007). The main threat to al-Sadr and his JaM militia has been the Badr militia. The Sadrists' recent attempts to control Diwaniya testify to such ongoing rivalry between these two Shi'a groups that seem to be unwilling to make compromises over the control of Iraq's southern cities.

There is also tension among the tribal forces in the city over the control of *khums* money, annual religious taxes of one-fifth, which is levied by Shi'as on income to be spent on the Prophet's family and the poor. For the Sadrists, the tribal forces have failed to fairly distribute the money to the people in the city, as required by Islamic law. As in the case of Karbala, the followers of al-Sadr are interested not only in military domination, but also in control of major holy sites and religious practices, hence expanding their influence in all aspects of Shi'a Iraqi life.

There are two possible reasons behind Sadrist attempts to control Diwaniya. One possible reason can be directly linked to the implementation of the Baghdad security plan, which since February 14, 2007 has forced the JaM to maintain a low-profile in Baghdad, although it appears to continue to press for power in other cities like Basra and Diwaniya. Second, it is possible that al-Sadr is trying to gain more independence from Tehran and Najaf, especially Grand Ayatollah Ali al-Sistani, by defying the idea of a united Shi'a front against anti-Shi'a Salafism, which may seem anti-Sunni to many Sunni Arabs, and the U.S. presence in Iraq. By doing this, al-Sadr is also attempting to bolster his base and reassert power by appealing to various splinter groups in his JaM who have accused him of treason for too much flirtation with the Iranians and the Iraqi government, the latter of which is perceived as an extension of the U.S. presence.

Diwaniya is the powder keg of Iraq. With vying Shi'a militias and tribal forces, the city is bound to become a site of intra-sectarian conflict, namely a clash between the Badr and JaM militias in major cities like Baghdad, Basra and Diwaniya, despite a surge of troops in Iraq.

A Shi'a Storm Looms on the Horizon: Sadr and ISCI Relations

By Babak Rahimi
May 24, 2007
Terrorism Monitor 5 (10)

Post-Ba'athist Iraqi politics is undergoing a dramatic change, and the Sadrists and the Islamic Supreme Council of Iraq (ISCI) (formerly known as the Supreme Council for the Islamic Revolution in Iraq – SCIRI), are leading the way by bringing a major shift in the balance of power. With the gradual decomposition of Prime Minister Nouri al-Maliki's National Unity Government, mainly dominated by Shi'a and Kurdish parties, Iraq is entering a new political era. As splintered political factions, such as the Sadrists, seek to form a new coalition made up of Sunni parties, formerly exiled Shi'a groups like Da'awa and the ISCI are facing new challenges in maintaining a dominant political bloc in Baghdad.

Muqtada al-Sadr's call to create a "reform and reconciliation project," which would also include Sunnis, is a radical departure from his sectarian base which was formed with the United Iraqi Alliance (UIA) and under the spiritual leadership of Grand Ayatollah Ali al-Sistani in 2004 (*al-Hayat*, May 8, 2007). In addition, al-Sadr's move is a direct challenge to his main Shi'a rival, the ISCI, which has posed the most serious threat to al-Sadr's political prestige and leadership in Iraq since 2003. For the most part, limited political mobility in the UIA and the al-Maliki government itself were the sources of frustration for the Sadrists, and most of the blame was directed at the ISCI for its political tactics to tame the Sadrist movement in the government.

Then ISCI leader Abdul Aziz al-Hakim's May 13, 2007 call to change the name of the party from the "Supreme Council for the Islamic Revolution in Iraq" to the "Islamic Supreme Council of Iraq," dropping the word "revolution" from the name, had brought to light a key move by Iraq's leading Shi'a politician in preparing for the post-coalition era (*al-Hayat*, May 13, 2007). As the leader of Iraq's largest party, backed by possibly the largest militia in Iraq, al-Hakim's new strategy also includes a renewed pledge of allegiance to Grand Ayatollah Ali al-

Sistani and his Najaf-based religious organization (al-Jazeera, May 13, 2007; *Terrorism Monitor*, November 7, 2003). The reason for this symbolic reaffirmation of the party's political position is clear. Al-Hakim aims to distance his party from its exiled past when the party was based in Iran from the early 1980s to 2003, and reconstruct a Shi'a Iraqi identity by aligning with the Najaf clerical authority. The call was also an attempt to establish distance from the Iranian shrine city of Qom, where Iran's Supreme Leader, Ayatollah Ali Khamenei, has considerable power over the religious and political institutions (http://historiae.org, May 12, 2007).

Both factions are taking new positions in a shifting political landscape. Due to the failure of the constitutional drafting process, tensions over key political issues, such as federalism and the distribution of oil, are paving the way toward a major Shi'a-on-Shi'a conflict. The two parties appear to expect some sort of a political confrontation over the constitution after a future collapse of the al-Maliki government. What these new strategies also indicate is how the weakening of the Iraqi government is forcing Sadrists to expand their military prowess for control over cities and regions that are at the moment dominated by the ISCI's militia group, the Badr Organization. A major clash between the two Shi'a parties can be expected in the future, and only a viable political solution can prevent a full outbreak of conflict.

Arch Rivals

The early history of Sadrist-ISCI conflict dates back to the competition between the al-Hakim and al-Sadr clan families over influence in the Da'awa party since its inception in 1959. When Ayatollah Baqr al-Sadr, the uncle of Muqtada, emerged as the most prominent leader of the Da'awa movement, Ayatollah Muhammad Baqr al-Hakim, as an active member of the party, was eclipsed by al-Sadr. Energetic, contemplative and charismatic, Baqr al-Sadr's impact as a political leader was so deep that after his assassination in 1980 he continued to aspire a cult-like following among the Shi'a Iraqis. However, a major split in Shi'a politics occurred when al-Hakim formed SCIRI (*al-Majlis al-A'la lil Thawra al-Islamiya fil Iraq*) in Tehran on November 17, 1982, with the help of Iran's Islamic Revolutionary Guard Corps. The formation of SCIRI in Iran was perceived by many Shi'a Iraqis, including Muqtada al-Sadr's father, Ayatollah Sadiq al-Sadr, who later formed the Sadrist movement in the 1990s, as an Iranian intervention in the native Shi'a Islamic politics, which was believed to remain a homegrown movement. Since its inception, SCIRI has been perceived as an alien, foreign agent by most Sadrists.

With the failure of the Badr Brigade's (*Faylaq Badr*) military venture against Saddam's army during the Shi'a uprising in 1991, SCIRI's chance to win the popular support of the Shi'a population was reduced considerably. The 1992 death of Ayatollah Khoei, the country's most senior cleric, opened the way for the formation of alternative native Shi'a movements to energize Shi'a aspirations for freedom from Saddam's tyrannical rule, and Ayatollah Sadiq al-Sadr emerged as a leading candidate.

Sadiq al-Sadr's power base was so deeply grounded in the plebian Shi'a population, especially in eastern Baghdad, that still four years after his assassination by Saddam's regime his movement continued to expand. On entering Iraq after more than 20 years of exile in Iran in 2003, al-Hakim witnessed the rise of a major Shi'a political rival, a young cleric named Muqtada al-Sadr, who would publicly question his bravery and Iraqi credentials for not only failing to stand up to Saddam, but also for being a foreign agent backed by the Iranian government.

Violence has frequently erupted between the Jaysh al-Mahdi (JaM) militia and the Badr Organization since 2004 in cities like Baghdad, Basra and Diwaniya, and all of these clashes have their roots in this complicated historical setting. Yet such tension also reflects how each of these two parties aim to control the future of the country. Domination of the oil production in Basra and military control of major southern Iraqi provinces, especially in eastern Baghdad, is the key problem to this growing dilemma. There is also a major ideological rift: the envisaged future of Iraq as a nation-state by the two parties.

Although Sadrists are staunchly Shi'as, they are, however, fervidly opposed to al-Hakim's August 2005 call for the formation of a nine-province Shi'a region, with Basra as the major governmental center. As Iraqi nationalists, Sadrists are highly suspicious of a federalist model for Iraq and consider al-Hakim's proposal as one that would snatch away economic and political power from supporters of al-Sadr based in Baghdad. Al-Hakim, on the other hand, opposes al-Sadr's call for an alliance with Sunni Arabs and since 2004 has been hesitant to accept a deadline for a U.S. troop withdrawal from Iraq (*Baztab*, February 2004). Al-Hakim is worried that once U.S. forces leave Iraq, the Badr militia would have to confront the JaM militia and al-Sadr's young followers in Baghdad and Basra. Distrust of the adversary remains a major problem.

Iran and the al-Sistani Factors

In the middle of this conflict lies Iran and al-Sistani. By and large, both have a significant stake in this subtle standoff between two of Iraq's major political factions. Since an outbreak of conflict between the rival groups could harm their authority and influence in Iraq, Najaf and Tehran are doing their best to prevent a clash. Iran is desperately attempting to muster enough Shi'a support for both expanding its influence in Iraq and protecting itself from potential U.S. attacks against its interests in the region. Al-Sadr could be a huge asset for Iran's regional ambitions, but he could also be a liability. For Tehran, al-Sadr is an independent Shi'a voice who needs to be tamed and brought into the Qom-based Shi'a power base with Khamenei recognized as the main source of authority.

Al-Sistani, however, shares al-Sadr's vision of a united, non-sectarian nation-state, but he vehemently opposes his youthful aspiration for power in Iraq. For al-Sistani, al-Sadr should be tamed and brought into the Najaf-based Shi'a power base with al-Sistani and the other leading Shi'a clerics recognized as the main sources of authority. ISCI's recent pledge of allegiance to al-Sistani, then, could be viewed as a shrewd way to create a rift between Najaf and al-Sadr by forcing al-Sistani to choose sides between them—even though al-Sistani would most likely refuse such factional politics. Despite al-Sadr's growing relationship with al-Sistani since the summer of 2006, al-Hakim knows that al-Sistani views al-Sadr as a potential threat to the Najaf orthodoxy (*Terrorism Monitor*, March 29, 2007). Therefore, ISCI's tactic is to indirectly force al-Sadr to become estranged from Najaf by renewing the party's allegiance to al-Sistani; at this crucial stage of the political game, it appears that alienating al-Sadr from Najaf remains a high priority for al-Hakim.

Yet, al-Hakim's political strategy is two-fold. By getting closer to al-Sistani, ISCI is building alliances with both Najaf and Tehran. Yet, he also appears to be expanding Khamenei's influence in Najaf, where the Badr Organization is controlling the shrine city, a symbol of Shi'a power. Regardless of Tehran's involvement in al-Hakim's recent change of tactics, ISCI realizes that al-Sadr is a major threat to the party's influence, and that with the rapid rise of his popularity since 2006, both al-Sistani and Iran could play a major role in backing al-Hakim's party in case of a major eruption of conflict.

Policy Implications

The potential descent into an intra-sectarian civil war poses a serious danger to Iraq and the region. This sort of civil war could contribute to the formation of new Shi'a groups, destabilization of the Iraqi government and the southern provinces, especially Basra, and lead to serious humanitarian catastrophes. Although such intra-sectarian conflict is essentially a political one, it also includes a significant religious component. Iraq is undergoing a shift in the balance of power among Shi'a militant groups, and the best Washington can do is to hope for the victory of the orthodox Shi'a institution in Najaf. It is with the authority of al-Sistani that fighting between these two militia groups can best be prevented.

The most practical strategy that the United States could adopt at this stage is to prevent the meltdown of the Iraqi government into a state of political factionalism; in reality, Iraq's worst enemy at this moment is the Baghdad government itself. The reason is that with the absence of a relatively centralized state, militias (regardless of their ethnic and sectarian associations) are bound to expand and continue to fight among themselves (and Iraqi and U.S. troops) for power. This general strategy also means that Washington should recognize the pivotal role of political integration, rather than military operative tactics (like the troop surge), against the radicalization of Shi'a groups.

Regardless of the success or failure of the surge, the post-coalition era would need to see the formation of inter-sectarian political parties. In light of his recent call for the creation of a "reform and reconciliation project," al-Sadr could possibly lead the country to a new post-Ba'athist political era, in which Shi'a and Sunni nationalists, who remained in Iraq during Saddam's reign, could unite against former exiled Shi'a and Kurdish parties like the ISCI and the Kurdistan Democratic Party. The United States should encourage such political coalitions, despite its obvious anti-occupation (or anti-American) fervor. Nevertheless, although this new coalition can lessen sectarian tensions, it will not, however, do away with the Shi'a militia competition over power and prestige. An ISCI-Sadrist clash looms ahead, and the best Washington can do is to contain it through an already fragile Iraqi government.

The Militia Politics of Basra

By Babak Rahimi
July 6, 2007
Terrorism Monitor 5 (13)

VOLATILE LANDSCAPE

Basra, the second largest and the richest city in Iraq, is at the brink of a major economic and political meltdown. Unless Baghdad succeeds in reaching a compromise over the country's governmental apparatus (especially over the issue of federalism), the southern city may become the greatest threat to the future of post-Ba'athist Iraq. Such a threat lies mainly in a struggle for power between Shi'a militias and tribal forces who compete for control over oil resources, territorial domination and public capital (hospitals and schools), which are all leading to an erosion of security in a city that is the source of Iraq's economic life. Although much of this turmoil is a reflection of the unstable nature of the transitional process, the current situation in Basra may represent a future scenario for Iraq that is made up of political factionalism and devoid of a functional government [1].

At the center of Basra's meltdown lies the ongoing conflict between different Shi'a factions, mainly vying for control over Basra's energy industry and oil smuggling. Domination over local governance through confrontation, and at times violence, has become the routine method of conducting politics in a city that appears to be breaking apart into territories governed by different militias. Such political conflict, however, also includes competing visions of post-Ba'athist Iraq, as each Shi'a militia advocates a particular ideological agenda (regionalist, nationalist and sectarian), while seeking popular support from various segments of the Shi'a community in Basra and other southern cities.

The Fadhila Party

The Fadhila Party (Virtue Party) is a case in point. An offshoot of the original Sadrist movement in the mid-1990s, when Muqtada al-Sadr's father, Ayatollah Muhammed Sadiq al-Sadr, led a nativist Shi'a movement to oppose clerical traditional authorities in Najaf and the Ba'athist regime in Baghdad, Fadhila emerged as a major Shi'a party in Basra in 2003. With its own militia and support from the city's professional class sympathetic to the Sadrist millenarian ideology, the party managed to win local elections and gained the allegiance of smaller Shi'a parties, such as *Wifaq and Harakat al-Dawa*, for the control of the provincial council in January 2005.

On the level of religious ideology, Fadhila is a millenarian nativist movement and the party has many supporters among Basra regionalists who envision an autonomous Basra province that includes Maysan and Dhi Qar governorates. Ayatollah Muhammad Yaqubi, a student of Ayatollah Sadiq al-Sadr and the head of Fadhila, who is based in Karbala, opposes Muqtada and sees him as a rogue cleric who is taking advantage of his father's legacy to gain power. Yaqubi also opposes Iranian influence in Shi'a Iraq—even the authority of Grand Ayatollah Ali al-Sistani, an Iranian-born cleric based in Najaf. Since 2003, Yaqubi has tried to form a strong alliance with Grand Ayatollah Kadhim Haeri, based in the Iranian city of Qom, who is regarded by some Sadrists as the successor to the late Ayatollah Sadiq al-Sadr, the main rival of al-Sistani throughout the 1990s [2]. The move can be recognized to highlight Fadhila's attempt to strengthen native Iraqi clerics in order to counterbalance Iranian influence in the province.

In January 2005, Fadhila moved up the political ladder in the United Iraqi Alliance (UIA) in the interim government, but only to face major obstacles from the Nouri al-Maliki-led government later in 2006. Under the tenure of former Iraqi Prime Minister Ibrahim al-Jaafari, the party was in charge of the oil ministry, but when al-Maliki's government came to power, the Fadhila minister was replaced by Hussain al-Shahristani, a prominent Shi'a politician and scientist with no ties to the militia politics in Basra. When Fadhila withdrew from the unity government in May 2006, the party began to concentrate on local politics as a way to maintain control over the oil industry and trafficking. It was at this juncture that conflict with other rival Shi'a groups, including tribal forces, began to escalate (*Azzaman*, May 16, 2006).

Fadhila Challenges Legitimacy of the ISCI

Realizing the influence of the Islamic Supreme Council of Iraq (ISCI), which was also present in the city council and the police force, Fadhila sought ways to challenge the legitimacy of the rival group. As history professor Juan Cole described, the governor of Basra and member of Fadhila, Muhammad Misbah al-Wa'ili, accused the chief of police of allowing the continuation of political assassinations [3]. The accusation was made in a way to discredit the Badr Corps, the ISCI's militia, which had maintained influence in the city's police force through the Interior Ministry. Tensions between local groups and the ISCI grew when a major tribesman was assassinated in May 2006. The Karamishah Marsh Arabs attacked the ISCI's headquarters, accusing the Badr Corps of carrying out the assassination. Immediately after the event, followers of the ISCI and militia groups linked to the Badr Corps, namely Tha'r Allah (Revenge of God), formed demonstrations against the governor [4]. With the rise in tension between Shi'a militias and tribal rivals, al-Maliki quickly stepped in later in May 2007 to establish security by declaring a month-long state of emergency in the city (*Baztab*, May 30, 2007). At present, frictions in the Basra government continue to grow, especially between Fadhila and the ISCI, as nativist political parties (such as Harakat al-Da'awa) accuse the Badr militiamen of being agents of Tehran and advancing Iranian interests in Basra.

Fadhila and al-Sadr Compete for Basra

With the reemergence of al-Sadr on the political scene in spring 2006, Fadhila faced another Shi'a contender. Although conflict between the two groups dates back to spring 2003, al-Sadr failed to establish a strong base in Basra. After the 2004 uprising against the U.S. that led to the destruction of Najaf, the Sadrists lost even more support in the city, especially among the professional class who saw al-Sadr as an uneducated, unruly cleric. When al-Sadr began to rise as a major political figure in the UIA in 2005 and Basra began to experience greater economic hardship because of corruption in the oil industry, many younger Iraqis from the poorer parts of the city, in places like the northern district of al-Hayani-e, started to support al-Sadr [5].

Fadhila-Sadr relations are as complex as Shi'a Iraqi politics. Although the two parties rely on the legacy of Sadiq al-Sadr to legitimize their prestige, they both compete for greater influence in southern politics—in the case of Fadhila, this is limited to Basra. They also share a nationalist interest, however, to curtail the influence of then ISCI leader Abdul Aziz al-Hakim, who envisions a nine-province federal state, in which Basra would be the capital of the Shi'a-dominated southern region. Fadhila, however, rejects al-Sadr's tendency for a tightly centralized government based in Baghdad (or Sadr City). Fadhila believes that Basra should become an autonomous regional power with the oil revenues under the control of the city, while distributing the wealth to the other parts of the country [6]. Competing visions of a future Iraqi government are the fundamental elements of the Fadhila-Sadr conflict.

There are also accusations of corruption and mayhem, however, which the two parties use to discredit each other. Fadhila's control over the oil industry has been a major problem for the Basra-based party. Wa'ili, the governor, functions as the head of Iraq's Southern Oil Company, which administrates the province's oil industry (*Azzaman*, April 30, 2007). He is also well connected to wealthy oil traders [7]. Al-Sadr accuses Wa'ili and his party of involvement in oil trafficking that creates shortages of oil for the country, especially in Baghdad and the Sunni provinces in western Iraq (United Press International, April 17, 2007). Accordingly, members of the JaM are accused of infiltrating the police force, which has been blamed for political assassinations since 2005 (*Azzaman*, March 27, 2007). In reality, the followers of al-Sadr also operate in the oil smuggling business, controlling Abu Flus port, which is a major center for the export of crude oil sold on the black market (*The Guardian*, June 9, 2007). Amidst such rivalry, Wa'ili's provincial government faced a major defeat when in April the provincial parliament—which included smaller Shi'a groups like Master of All Martyrs and Hizballah (an offshoot of the Da'awa party)—almost unseated him and challenged Fadhila authority in the local parliament (*International Herald Tribune*, April 28, 2007). The blow to Fadhila's power has allowed al-Sadr to increase his influence in Basra's provincial parliament and expand his popularity among the urban poor, who view Fadhila as corrupt.

As al-Sadr attempts to widen his influence in Baghdad, the two rival factions have grown more confrontational in Basra. In March 2007, after British forces departed the city, the headquarters of the Fadhila party was destroyed, later leading to urban clashes between the JaM and Fadhila militias (*Aswat al-Iraq*, March 23, 2007). The two parties have tried to play down their differences, but in reality the Sadrists will continue to push for domination over oil commerce and Fadhila will most certainly fight to retain its tenacious hold on the Southern Oil Company (*Azzaman*, March 27, 2007).

Seen in this context, the Fadhila-ISCI-Sadr feud has been largely over control of local politics. Provincial politics, especially in terms of control over territorial domination in what can also be called the politics of "fiefdom," have been central to the balance of power between vying Shi'a militia groups. Basra is now undergoing a militarization of local politics as a weakened Baghdad government loses control of its southern provinces. Such militarization processes, however, are also linked to oil trafficking, as profit made from smuggling helps the militias and preserves the factional politics of the city.

Other Factors Destabilizing Basra

Other major factors will play a role in the destabilization of Basra. One problem concerns tribe-militia relations. Many tribes face major challenges from urban militias, especially formerly exiled Shi'a groups such as the ISCI, as competition over territorial domination and oil trafficking grows with the expansion of militia power. The increase in Shi'a-Sunni conflict also represents a major factor. Since the Samarra bombing in February 2006, Sunni communities continue to face the wrath of Shi'a militias (*Baztab*, June 20, 2006). In May 2007, for example, nearly 170 Sunni mosques were closed for security reasons in response to the assassinations of a number of Sunni clerics (*Baztab*, May 27, 2006). With a long history of religious movements, Basra is also witnessing the rise of new millenarian currents, namely the movement led by Karbala-based Ayatollah Mahmoud al-Sarkhi al-Hassani, who has gained support from disgruntled Sadrists. All of these developments could trigger further instability in a city devoid of a functioning government.

What is Iran's role in this complicated political landscape? For the most part, Iran's influence in Basra has been significant yet limited. Since the 1950s, Basra has been a major hub for Iraqi nationalism (mainly the version advocated by non-Ba'athist nationalists like former Iraqi Prime Minister General Abd al-Karim Qassim), and many Shi'a (including nativist parties like Fadhila) are highly suspicious of any Iranian presence in the city. As numerous attacks on the Iranian consulate in the city indicate, anti-Iranian sentiments run high in Basra despite Tehran's efforts to create new alliances with local Shi'a factions, especially with the Sadrists (*Baztab*, June 14, 2006).

This does not mean, however, that Iran is absent from Basra's socio-economic life. Cultural and economic ties between Basra and Iran have grown strong since 2003. Farsi is now spoken as a second language, and many Iranian goods are sold in the Basra markets (*Baztab*, May 23, 2007). The Iranian toman is a major currency in the Basra banking system, and many use it in the open markets of the city. As for oil, the importation of Iranian (refined) oil has increased from 8 million to 11 million liters a day, and some Iraqi crude oil is also refined in the Abadan and Kermanshah refineries (RFE/RL Iraq Report, September 2006). As for military operations, Iranian intelligence officers are reported to reside in the city (some of them have dual citizenship), and they travel freely between the two countries through the Shalamcheh border crossing [8].

Implications

Although Iran's impact on the daily life of Basra cannot be ignored, the internal politics of Basra remain critical to the stability of the city. Overall, the problem in Basra is a localized conflict with ties to Baghdad's political process. The rapid recovery of Basra from militia politics would require the following:

1. On immediate terms, the Basra oil industry (production and distribution) should come under the direct control of Baghdad, ideally under the supervision of Basra natives who have no links to any of the militia groups. This move is crucial, as militia jurisdiction over the production and distribution of oil plays a central role in the consolidation of militia power in the city.

2. Accordingly, the containment of militia politics will depend on the strong presence of an Iraqi force trained in Baghdad and comprised of non-militia forces with no ties to local militia groups. Although a major undertaking, this could help bring some stability to the city by replacing officials linked to militia with non-militia officers who would receive their orders directly from the prime minister.

3. Baghdad should not only rely on the clerical circles in Najaf to contain the militias since much of the infighting between militant factions in Basra regards the control of local politics. Although Najaf may influence the ISCI and the Sadrists (although not necessarily enough to disarm the militias), it will most likely fail to persuade Fadhila, which is suspicious of the "quietist" school of thought advocated by leading Najaf clerics. In a significant sense, the Basra Shi'a religious community, a major part of which is comprised of Fadhila, can be described as largely regional-nationalist in contrast to the conservative orthodoxy based in Najaf or the transnational Islamists led by Tehran. This point should be kept in mind as anti-Najaf millenarian movements continue to grow in southern provinces (especially in Karbala) and anti-Iranian sentiments remain strong in Basra.

The opinion regarding the U.S. and British role in the political order of Basra is clear: it is dangerous to become involved. One of the gravest mistakes made by the British since 2003 was their overwhelming reliance on the Badr Corps to impose order on the city and its suburbs. By taking sides, Great Britain has (unintentionally) shifted the balance of power by allocating too much authority to the Badr Corps. Although British forces have contributed to most of the security in the city since 2003 (despite the argument that they have also failed to do so because of their inability to quash the militias), the stability of Basra will largely depend on a multi-sectarian Iraqi army administrated from Baghdad, not an occupied force or a militia faction. Furthermore, the main problem with overtly (or clandestinely) strengthening or arming one of the factions is that it could entail unintended consequences that most likely would harm the country rather than contribute to its stability.

Conclusion

For the time being, Baghdad remains Basra's worst enemy. The lack of a stable and relatively centralized government, at least in this transitional stage, is at the heart of the problem. Without a stable government, Basra is destined to experience the sort of violence that Beirut suffered two decades ago. A major civil-militia war in Basra seems imminent, and the consolidation of a centralized Iraqi government (including administrative and non-sectarian federated features) may possibly be the country's best solution. Basra's meltdown could well foretell the future of Baghdad as a failed state. Even worse, it could mean the unraveling of a dysfunctional city that may threaten the stability of the Gulf region and beyond.

Notes

1. For a recent study of Basra that argues this point, see International Crisis Group, "Where Is Iraq Heading? Lesson From Basra," No. 67, June 25, 2007.
2. The alliance was never formed, perhaps, as a follower of al-Sadr suggests, due to Haeri's close ties to the Iranian government. Author interview, Najaf, Iraq, August 7, 2005.
3. See Iraq: Preventing A New Generation of Conflict, edited by Markus E. Bouillon, David M. Malone and Ben Rowswell, London: Boulder, 2007.
4. Ibid.
5. Including al-Amarah, some of the Basra branch of the JaM is based in this northern district, where Abu Qadir, a major officer in al-Sadr's militia, was killed in early June 2007 by British forces, *Baztab*, June 5, 2007.
6. Reider Visser, Basra: The Failed Gulf State: Separatism and Nationalism in Southern Iraq, Münster: New Brunswick, 2005.
7. In fact, he comes from an affluent family of oil merchants. Author interview, Basra, Iraq, August 13, 2005.
8. Author interview, Basra, Iraq, August 13, 2005.

The Surge, the Shi'a, and Nation Building in Iraq

By Reidar Visser

September 13, 2007
Terrorism Monitor 5 (17)

THE SECURITY SCENE IN SOUTHERN IRAQ

Analysts have been suggesting that the Bush administration's "surge" strategy may have achieved a measure of success in certain parts of Iraq. Many highlight the tendency on the part of local tribes in the Sunni-dominated areas to stand up against al-Qaeda, in that way emphasizing their own "Iraqiness" as well as their unwillingness to join in an all-out war against Western civilization. The number of attacks against U.S. forces has declined in many of these areas, and there are signs that al-Qaeda has been forced to relocate to new areas and to choose new targets.

Perhaps the most convincing indicator of a degree of "surge" success is one that has gone largely unnoticed. Reports out of Baghdad suggest that the Sunni politicians who for the past two years or so have worked with the Americans through participating in government and parliament are now becoming increasingly nervous about internal Sunni competition from the newly emerged anti-jihadist tribal leaders of their "own" community, for example in places like the al-Anbar governorate [1]. In terms of Iraqi nation-building, this is a healthy sign. There was always a degree of doubt with regard to the true representativeness of the Sunni parties that emerged as "winners" in their fields in the heavily boycotted 2005 parliamentary elections. The fact that these parties are now worried about internal competition means that more Sunnis are interested in participating in the system, and that a group of politicians firmly attached to the vision of a unified Iraq but also enjoying solid popular backing in their core constituencies may be on the way up, assisted by the "surge." At the same time, foreign-sponsored groups, such as al-Qaeda, and office seekers whose popular legitimacy is in doubt (for instance, some members of the Tawafuq bloc) are coming under pressure or are even being weeded out.

South of Baghdad, the logical corollary to this kind of "surge" policy would have been to build local alliances with those Shi'a groups that have a historical record of firm opposition to Iran and are unequivocal in their condemnation of Iranian interference in Iraq. The principal aim would be to create a counter-balance to the most pro-Iranian factions inside the system, such as the Islamic Supreme Council of Iraq (ISCI, formerly the Supreme Council for the Islamic Revolution in Iraq, SCIRI) and their Badr Brigades—organizations that since 2003 have been successful in obtaining a disproportionate degree of formal political power in the Iraqi political system and are currently profiting from their role in the Nouri al-Maliki government to consolidate their position further [2]. In the south, there is a vast array of groupings with a long record of hostility to

Iran, above all the various Sadrist factions like Fadhila and the "mainline" followers of Muqtada al-Sadr (some of whom have even served jail sentences in Iranian prisons in the past), but also independent Shi'a tribal groups that are fiercely proud of their Arab heritage [3]. These groups also distinguish themselves from ISCI in that they maintain that any kind of clerical rule in Iraq under the principle of wilayat al-faqih (the rule of the jurisprudent) should have as its point of departure Iraqi clerics and not Iranian ones [4].

Actual U.S. policy south of Baghdad is the exact opposite of this. Pro-Iranian ISCI and its friends in the Badr Organization (now powerful in the Iraqi security forces) are being supported by the United States in their efforts to bulldoze all kinds of internal Shi'a opposition, as seen for instance in the large-scale battle against an alleged cultist movement at Najaf in January 2007, as well as in the ongoing operations against the Sadrist Jaysh al-Mahdi (JaM) militia and its splinter factions. Indiscriminate mass arrests have often accompanied these incidents, with the al-Maliki government's wholesale designation of its enemies as "terrorists" apparently being taken at face value by U.S. forces, and with the persistent complaints from those arrested about "Iranian intrigue" being ignored. Today, apart from isolated rural enclaves, the sole remaining bastions of solid Shi'a resistance to ISCI outside Baghdad are Maysan and Basra (which happen to be located outside direct U.S. control, in the British zone in the far south), but here too change may be underway: ISCI has worked for more than one year to unseat the Fadhila governor of oil-rich Basra (he remained in office by early September 2007 despite an order by al-Maliki to have him replaced), and the Badr Brigades are reportedly influential within the security forces in Maysan. Ironically, long-standing enemies of Iran like the Fadhila party are now feeling so isolated that they see no other recourse than to upgrade contacts with their erstwhile foes in Tehran, if only tentatively [5]. The apparent U.S. rationale for letting all this happen is the idea that the Sadrist JaM somehow constitutes their worst opponent in Iraq, and that some JaM factions are even being supplied with arms from Tehran.

An alternative reading is that Iran could be deliberately feeding weaponry to marginal (or splinter) elements of the Sadrists precisely in order to weaken the Sadrist movement as a whole, and to make sure that Sadrist energy is combusted in clashes with U.S. forces. Right now, from Tehran's point of view, the implementation of the "surge" south of Baghdad could not have been more perfect. Today, U.S. forces are working around the clock to weaken Tehran's traditional arch-enemy in Iraq's Shi'a heartland—the Sadrists—while Iran's preferred and privileged partner since the 1980s, SCIRI/ISCI, keeps strengthening its influence everywhere. Back in the United States, think tanks concentrate on the ties between Sadrists and Iran and consistently overlook those factions that have truly close and long-standing ties to Tehran, whereas the 2007 National Intelligence Estimate was devoid of initiatives to bring the Shi'as into a more reconciliatory mode—suggesting that few ideas exist in Washington about alternative Shi'a policies. The U.S. mainstream media also make a contribution: after having first demonized Ibrahim al-Jaafari for alleged ties to Iran back in 2005, U.S. newspapers are now using big headlines every time there is the slightest hint about some kind of connection between Iran and Muqtada al-Sadr. On top of all this, the U.S. military itself is exposed to a significant irritant through its constant encounters with militia splinter groups and the low-level conflict that comes with them—no doubt another factor that works to Tehran's advantage.

The great irony in this is that, from the historical perspective, the neo-conservative working assumption that Iraqi Shi'as can be trusted to resist Iranian domination is generally sound—with the sole exception of the particular faction on which Washington has fixed its eyes as its special partner in the country. In the 1980s, SCIRI was designed by Iran to maximize Tehran's control of the unruly Iraqi opposition. Throughout its history, it has stressed the importance of subservience to Iran's leaders, first Grand Ayatollah Khomeini and later, the current supreme leader Ayatollah Ali Khamenei [6]. In the mid-1990s, its leader Muhammad Baqr al-Hakim became one of the first Shi'a intellectuals to produce an elaborate plan for the political unification of the Shi'as from Iran to Lebanon in a federal system under the leadership of Tehran. And as late as 1999, one of SCIRI's key figures, Sadr al-Din al-Qubbanji, angrily attacked the Sadrists for daring to suggest that the Iraqi Shi'a opposition could operate independently of Khamenei [7]. Close scrutiny of SCIRI's highly publicized name change and supposed "ideological makeover" in May 2007 shows that none of this heritage has been annulled in a convincing manner: the new and much trumpeted "pledge" to Grand Ayatollah Ali al-Sistani is in reality nothing more than a non-committal expression of general praise, and there is no renunciation of a decades-long policy of subordination to Khamenei [8]. It is suspicious that ISCI and Iran still hold virtually synchronized views on the sacrosanctity of the al-Maliki government and the 2005 constitution. Both tend to describe the idea of challenging al-Maliki as "subversive coup activity," and they are unified in rejecting challenges to the constitution by what they describe as neo-Ba'athists [9].

The problem is that Washington's "surge" is framed as a straightforward counterinsurgency operation in which the nation-building component is in the far background. "The enemy" is defined on the basis of a myopic interpretation of who is directly hostile to U.S. forces while the historical dimension of alliance patterns between Iran and Iraqi Shi'a factions is overlooked. This prevents Washington from fully understanding who is friend and foe in Iraq. It is conceivable that ISCI may assist Washington in temporarily reducing the amount of noise out of Iraq, and this may well be what the Bush administration is looking for right now. Yet, even if its members are more genteel and well-behaved than the Sadrists, it is highly unclear what kind of "moderation" ISCI is really capable of delivering in Iraq, especially in terms of a political system based on true reconciliation between Shi'as and Sunnis [10]. For that to be brought about, many Iraqis, regardless of sectarian affiliation, will require unequivocal answers from ISCI on certain key questions: Does its leadership still believe in the principle of the rule of the jurisprudent (*wilayat al-faqih*) and the idea of a supreme Shi'a leader (*wali amr al-muslimin*), and if so, whom do they consider to be the current holder of this leadership role? Are they prepared to reject, squarely and explicitly, any possible role for Iran's Khamenei in shaping their policies? Can they offer reassurances to the Iraqi people that the Iran-dominated pan-Shi'a federation scheme laid out by Muhammad Baqr al-Hakim in 'Aqidatuna in the 1990s is now null and void? After all, the futility of an approach based on vague ideas about "moderate, pro-U.S. personalities" and private assurances to U.S. officials ("Iraq will never become a carbon copy of Iran") is particularly pronounced in the strictly hierarchical Shi'a context. All orthodox Shi'as who are not themselves qualified theologians (*mujtahids*) will have to defer to the higher clergy on important issues. None of the Shi'a operators in Iraq with whom Washington has been dealing is a recognized mujtahid.

Clarification of these issues would help ISCI enormously and could assist the party in finding a much more constructive role as a key mainstream, truly "moderate" player in Iraqi politics. But until answers from ISCI are forthcoming in a very public way (rather than in hazy name changes and in private meetings with U.S. special envoys), many Iraqis will remain ambivalent about the organization's ties to Iran. In that situation, the "surge" will be doomed to fail unless it can be redefined to include a credible nation-building component aimed at areas south of Baghdad: the Iraqi nationalist Shi'as will remain on the margins, and the alliance of ISCI and the two Kurdish parties will feel that they can safely continue to ignore the Sunnis, secularists and independent Shi'as and their calls for a more substantial constitutional revision (and true national reconciliation). Even the main Sadrist parties, which have invested considerable energy in presenting themselves as "made in Iraq" and ridiculing ISCI for its ties to Iran, could end up as ironic Iranian clients unless Washington starts dealing with them in a more constructive way.

Still, if the United States is willing to rethink some of its fundamental assumptions about Iraqi politics, several options for policy adjustments remain. Washington could, for instance, take a more open-minded approach to the ongoing efforts to create a more broadly based coalition in opposition to the al-Maliki government—such as, for instance, the latest efforts by Ibrahim al-Jaafari and Ayad Allawi to engineer cross-sectarian coalitions, and as seen in the recent decision by the legal committee of the Iraqi parliament to condemn al-Maliki's decision to sack the Basra governor [11]. In theory, these kinds of alliances could be capable of compromises on issues where consensus has eluded the al-Maliki government (like the oil law and federalism), and whereas the United States should certainly refrain from backroom machinations (which would only taint any alternative government), it could focus on simply recalibrating its own policies—including its "surge"—so as to ensure that the newly improved participation of the Sunni community within the system is accompanied by parallel positive developments among the Iraqi Shi'as. That, in itself, could be enough to help the Da'awa party move back to its Iraqi nationalist ideals, and thereby nudge the al-Maliki government into a more conciliatory mode. Conversely, if Washington continues to conceive of "the Iranian threat" in Iraq as exclusively a matter of security in the most palpable sense—meaning "Sadrist terrorists"—then Tehran and its ISCI allies seem set for easy sailing in Iraq.

Notes

1. Author interview with a member of the Iraqi National Security Council, June 2007.
2. According to a formal statement dated July 31, 2007, the party henceforth wishes to be referred to in English with the abbreviation ISCI; e-mail from Karim al-Musawi of the ISCI Washington office dated August 11, 2007. Separately, for a critical perspective on SCIRI's level of popular support in the December 2005 elections, see Reidar Visser, "SCIRI, Daawa and Sadrists in the Certified Iraq Elections Results," February 11, 2006.
3. An excellent source on the historical roots of the long-standing enmity between the Sadrists and

Iran is Fa'iq al-Sheikh Ali, Ightiyal sha'b, London: Al-Rafid, 2000.

4. Recent examples of such attitudes include an article penned by Fadhila member Abu Taqi, "Muqarina bayna al-nizam al-dakhili li-hizb al-fadila al-islami wa-wilayat al-faqih," January 7, 2007, with a note of approval by Muhammad al-Ya'qubi dated 20 Dhi al-Hijja 1427/January 10, 2007. The article clearly refers to a specifically Iraqi rather than an Iranian context. See also 'Adil Ra'uf, Muhammad Sadiq al-Sadr: marja'iyyat al-maydan, Damascus: Al-Markaz al-'Iraqi li-a-I'lam wa-al-Dirasat, 1999, pp. 53–57.

5. Fadhila's move to open offices in Tehran has been particularly conspicuous; see press release from the Fadhila party dated October 22, 2006.

6. The cliché that Iran had no ambition about acting as overlord in Iraq in the 1980s lacks a sound empirical basis. SCIRI leaders like Muhammad Baqr al-Hakim and Sadr al-Din al-Qubbanji wrote frequently about the need for ultimate subordination to Khomeini even if a façade of Iraqi separateness might be retained; see for instance Liwa' al-Sadr, April 28, 1982, p. 8, and Liwa' al-Sadr, October 4, 1987.

7. Muhammad Baqr al-Hakim, 'Aqidatuna wa-ru'yatuna al-siysiyya, a pamphlet published at the al-Hakim website (http://www.al-hakim.com) before 2003 but removed soon after the start of the Iraq war. Also, Al-Muballigh al-Risali, February 15, 1999.

8. SCIRI/ISCI, "Al-bayan al-khatami li-mu'tamar al-dawra al-tasi'a li-al-hay'a al-'amma li-al-majlis al-a'la al-islami al-'iraqi," May 12, 2007.

9. See for instance comments by Hasan Ruhani quoted in *Etemad*, April 26, 2006.

10. Characteristically, supporters of the ISCI scheme to create a single federal Shi'a entity have been among the most prominent critics of the (Shi'a) Fadhila party's dialogue with Sunni politicians; see open letter from Ahmad al-Shammari to Nadim al-Jabiri, January 2006, www.nahrainnet.net/news/51/ARTICLE/6968/2006-01-21.html.

11. See *al-Hayat*, August 7, 2007. Letter from the legal committee of the Iraqi parliament to Nouri al-Maliki dated July 30, 2007.

The Hakim-Sadr Pact: A New Era in Shi'a Politics?

By Babak Rahimi
October 25, 2007
Terrorism Monitor 5 (20)

The recent "pact of honor" made by two of Iraq's most influential Shi'a clerics, Muqtada al-Sadr and Abdul Aziz al-Hakim – aimed at preventing violence and helping to maintain the "Islamic and national interest" of Iraq – appears to signal a significant shift toward stability in Iraq. The two leaders have pledged to enhance relations between their respective groups, merging media and cultural projects, and to refrain from launching negative propaganda against each other (Fars News Agency, October 6, 2007). Yet, more importantly, the pact calls for promotion of the legal-political order of post-Ba'athist Iraq, a major move that could give new life to Nouri al-Maliki's government and curtail potential violence in the south.

As the first official agreement between these two prominent leaders, the forged pact can also be recognized as a huge step in improving intra-Shi'a relations. Not since the formation of the United Iraqi Alliance, which brought together a number of Shi'a political parties under the spiritual leadership of Ayatollah Ali al-Sistani in 2003, has Shi'a politics seen such a unified front. The struggle for domination between rival Shi'a groups has caused huge problems in the south, especially after the December 2005 parliamentary election. Despite a number of attempts for reconciliation, the enmity between al-Hakim and al-Sadr and their militias has remained a major security problem, especially in the provinces of Basra and Maysan, where the two factions are vying for control over oil and territory.

Disagreements only intensified after the British withdrawal from Basra in early September 2007, causing trouble for an already unstable Iraqi government seeking reconciliation over major political issues such as federalism and the distribution of oil. Seen in such a context, this new deal is made at a time when the "surge" strategy has gradually shown signs of relative military success in places like the eastern and central provinces, where al-Qaeda forces continue to lose the support of Sunni Iraqis. Yet, one important question remains to be answered: does the new pact promise any significant improvement in the country's political situation at such a crucial stage in its history?

First of all, it is important to note that the meaning of this pact sharply differs for the two rival parties. For the nationalist Sadrists, who view the members of al-Hakim's Islamic Supreme Council of Iraq (ISCI) as traitors and question their Iraqi credentials because of their close ties to the Iranian government, the deal with al-Hakim signifies an expedient move that can potentially ameliorate the group's image as an unruly, violent organization. For the leaders of the ISCI, however, who view al-Sadr's organization as a dangerous movement led by a group of unseasoned young clerics who lack any credible link with the traditional clerical establishment (*hawza*) in Najaf (or Qom), a pact with al-Sadr can be used to tame Iraq's most powerful Shi'a oppositional organization, hence chipping away at al-Sadr's popularity by diminishing his organization's anti-establishment identity.

Although the reconciliatory nature of the deal is hailed as a major rapprochement in Hakim-Sadr relations, the pact rather masks more familiar problems than reveals a new beginning for Iraq's democratic order. First and foremost, the truce lacks a genuine effort for reconciliation, as the two rival groups still maintain their ideological differences by defining each other as military foes on the street level, rather than as political competitors in the political arena. The deal also shows signs of external manipulation by other major Shi'a players, primarily Tehran (and Qom), which is seeking a united Shi'a stance against a potential U.S. attack on Iran. As the U.N. Security Council, led by Washington, seeks further sanctions against Iran's nuclear ambitions, Iranian conservatives and hardliners are raising expectations of greater cohesion between Shi'a groups under the leadership of Tehran. A new Iraq dominated by a united Shi'a force can serve as a powerful instrument to contain U.S. influence in the region, and al-Hakim and al-Sadr could play a leading role in such an endeavor.

Secondly, the pact can help increase ISCI's political weight in the parliament ahead of provincial elections planned for next year and, concurrently, decrease al-Sadr's influence in the al-Maliki government. Despite his popular support in Sadr city and southern cities like Diwaniya and Karbala, al-Sadr's absence from al-Maliki's government continues to be a huge blow to his political influence in Baghdad. On an organizational level, the movement has become disoriented and disillusioned, as al-Sadr faces serious allegations of incompetence, especially with signs of trouble in the organization of the Jaysh al-Madhi (JaM) militia that led to its six-month suspension after the breakout of violence against the Badr Organization in the summer of 2007. The pact marks a major turning point for al-Sadr's movement. For Iran (and also the United States), the ideal way to finally tame al-Sadr is to chip away at his popular base through the electoral and institutional processes, such as the deal with al-Hakim and, accordingly, diminish his status as a charismatic militant leader defiant of institutionalization.

The third factor is the threat of a Sunni-U.S. alliance. Due to the relative military success of U.S. forces in al-Anbar province, Tehran seems to be mostly worried about the recent partnership forged between U.S. and Sunni Iraqi leaders, especially the tribal chiefs. In this sense, the gradual marginalization of Shi'a factions in Baghdad—mainly as a consequence of their own internal divisions—coupled with U.S. support for Sunnis, has created a serious problem for Tehran. The rationale behind Iran's strategy is to contain the U.S. sphere of influence in Baghdad by keeping the Sunni Arab factions divided in the parliament and making them seem inseparable from militant Salafi forces. What a Shi'a united front can do is hold back a unified Sunni front that is increasingly growing closer to the United States.

The role of Najaf, however, is less clear. Although there is no solid evidence of the extent of al-Sistani's influence, it appears that the grand ayatollah supported the negotiations and most likely initiated the event after the Karbala incident in early September 2007 [1]. Al-Sistani's interest in the pact may be articulated in the following terms: Shi'a unity must be preserved under the leadership of Najaf, which is the traditional center of Shi'a authority, although Iran may also play a role in attaining this noble objective. Najaf and Tehran, in this sense, both share an interest in containing al-Sadr and his sectarian movement, bringing the organization and other shadowy anti-Najaf movements under the control of the traditional Shi'a establishment [2]. This move also signals the extent to which al-Sistani still continues to influence Shi'a Iraqi groups, despite Najaf's loss of authority after the Samarra bombing of 2006 that empowered Shi'a militia forces against the threat of militant Salafis. This is good news for Baghdad, since al-Sistani can play a positive role in disarming the Shi'a militias and improving Sunni-Shi'a relations in the government, especially in light of al-Maliki's diminishing authority since the withdrawal of a number of Sunni and Shi'a groups from the unity government in 2007.

Whether this truce will last is irrelevant to the actual development of Shi'a militia relations on the ground. What the deal shows, however, is al-Sadr's (rather uneasy) willingness to continue his cooperation with Iraq's political establishment under the influence of non-Iraqi agents, which the ISCI best represents for many disgruntled Sadrists who increasingly view al-Sadr as a traitor to his father's nationalistic legacy. This could entail the danger of upsetting many Sadrists and inflate the number of splinter groups within the already annulled JaM militia, especially encouraging those members of al-Sadr's militia who are desperately seeking new leadership from a charismatic leader who will uphold the movement's nationalistic and anti-establishment ideology. It is critical to foresee the rise of the post-JaM militia with the possible decline of al-Sadr as a charismatic leader and the resurgence of Najaf (and Tehran) as dominant players in the Shi'a political establishment.

Unwisely, a number of U.S. think tanks and some analysts have quickly rejoiced after the Hakim-Sadr pact and welcomed the new deal as a major victory for Iraq [3]. Such premature triumphalist reaction only exposes the limits of an insular understanding of Iraqi politics that continues to interpret the country's future as a teleological move (though a bumpy one) toward progress that ends with the attainment of a liberal democratic Iraq—understood in its Anglo-

American version. This is a grave mistake. The objective for understanding an Iraqi future, however, should not be limited to analysis of current events unfolding before our eyes, but should identify the undercurrents of major tides in the troubled waters of post-Ba'athist Iraq. In truth, the transition process faces an uncertain future, in which any outcome is possible.

By seeking to create Shi'a unity under the leadership of Najaf or Tehran, al-Hakim and al-Sadr have produced a pact that is superficially nationalistic and essentially sectarian. Yet, the specter of sectarianism remains a clear and present danger for Iraq, and the Hakim-Sadr pact may just be another monumental move away from nation-building and toward the consolidation of sectarian politics.

Notes

1. According to one of his representatives, al-Sistani was not directly involved in the meeting. Yet, al-Sistani appears to be a major supporter and most likely encouraged the event in the first place. Author interview with a representative of al-Sistani in Tehran, October 11, 2007.
2. See interview with Rasul Jafarian, "Fetne-he Nimeh Shaban Karbala, Tir-e Khalas be Jarian-e Moqtada bod," in *Baztab*, September 9, 2007. Also see *Baztab*, September 9, 2007.
3. See, for instance, Amir Taheri, "Al Hakim-Al Sadr Pact is Good for Iraq," *Gulf News*, October 09, 2007.

What Direction for the Jaysh al-Mahdi after the Basra Offensive?

By Babak Rahimi
April 1, 2008
Terrorism Focus 5 (13)

As Muqtada al-Sadr orders his Jaysh al-Mahdi (JaM) militia to lay down their arms in return for an exchange of prisoners and cessation of government raids against his followers, the six-day Iraqi-U.S. military offensive in Basra has reached its final stage (Al-Arabiyah, March 30, 2008). For the most part, the violence sparked by military operations against the JaM in the oil-rich city of Basra marked the most potent armed offensive to rid southern Iraq of Muqtada's influence since 2004. The operations appear to have forced the JaM to relinquish control over territories in Baghdad, Kut and, most importantly, Basra, where a number of Shi'a militias compete for domination over the oil industry.

In military terms, the offensive has been decisive and consistent, with raids ranging from Basra to the impoverished Sadr City where Muqtada maintains a popular base (Aftab, March 28, 2008). Even in the face of harsh reaction from the political wing of the movement in the Iraqi parliament, which publicly denounced the Nouri al-Maliki government for its aggressive policy in the south (Al-Arabiya TV, March 26, 2008) and a call from Muqtada for Arabs to rally behind his militia (Al-Jazeera TV, March 28, 2008), the Iraqi forces continued to crack down on the JaM by means of various urban-combat operations, aimed at driving the militia out of key Shi'a regions in the south. Muqtada's movement appears to have suffered a major military defeat, similar to what happened in 2004 when his followers unsuccessfully clashed with U.S. forces and lost many men.

But this time things are different. The six-day-old operation has failed to achieve two of its main objectives: weaken the JaM and undermine Muqtada's political influence in regions where the al-Maliki government seeks to gain control with the support of the U.S. armed forces. In fact, what the six-day offensive may demonstrate is the bolstering of Muqtada's status as a nationalist figure and the successful establishment of a grass-roots social movement, which most political factions in Baghdad lack at this crucial stage in Iraqi political history.

The purpose of the recent military operation has been described by some as an attempt to bolster state centralization and help the al-Maliki government expand its authority against the militias in light of the 2009 provincial elections. In reality, however, the causes behind the Basra fighting have less to do with state centralization than intra-Shi'a party factionalism directed at the JaM's territorial dominance in the south. The al-Maliki government, with the help of the Shi'a Islamic Supreme Council of Iraq (ISCI) and its Badr Corps militia, has engaged in a systematic attempt to marginalize the Sadrists in the absence of Muqtada, who is currently keeping a distance from politics while he pursues his theological studies (see *Terrorism Focus*, March 25, 2008). In doing so, al-Maliki has sought to reassert the influence of his Da'awa faction—which has no militia—with the support of an unlikely ally, the ISCI, whose Badr Corps is the most formidable armed rival of the JaM in Baghdad and other regions in the south.

The other main cause of the Basra fighting is the U.S.-Iraqi military "surge." As the U.S. military presence in Baghdad increased, seriously jeopardizing the expansion of the JaM's territorial control in the capital, the Sadrists began to expand southward into cities beyond the reach of U.S. forces. Basra provided an ideal place for the reorganization of the JaM, free from U.S. intervention. The

British withdrawal in fall 2007, coupled with the Badr Corps' failure to secure popular support in the city, allowed the JaM to expand its territorial control in Basra with the help of the police force, which some Sadrist militants have been infiltrating since 2004.

While the redeployment of the JaM from Baghdad and the Karbala-Najaf regions to the southern provinces provided an opportunity for the JaM to recuperate from internal divisions, the al-Maliki government has simultaneously sought to undermine the Sadrists. The move south was prompted by heightened tensions between the Sadrists and al-Maliki after Muqtada's followers in Parliament withdrew their support for the Shi'a prime minister in April 2007 to challenge al-Maliki's support for the U.S. surge. As al-Maliki grew closer to the ISCI, the Sadrists began to perceive him as another agent of the occupation, whose objective as a formerly exiled politician would be to secure his personal rather than national interests. The tensions only increased when al-Maliki described the Sadrists as thuggish remains of the Ba'athist regime in July 2007.

Amidst the factional conflict, Iran's strategy has remained clear: to remain out of the fighting so all Shi'a factions can seek the support of Tehran for their particular political interests. By staying out of the conflict, Iran also plays the role of a big brother whose absence offers consent to the al-Maliki government to weed out the splinter groups of the JaM while keeping Muqtada and his militia close to Tehran as a potential ally in case of a U.S. attack on Iran. Tehran's objective is to see the Sadrist movement weakened through military operations, but help keep it strong enough to potentially serve as an asset for Iranian interests in Iraq.

The problem with the Basra offensive is that it only adds complexity to the already fragmented state of Iraqi politics. First off, the military operation can intensify intra-Shi'a conflicts, exacerbating the factionalism that has dominated Iraqi politics since the December 2005 parliamentary election. While the United States openly backs other Shi'a militias like the Badr Corps and helps organize and arm Shi'a tribal forces in the *Sahwa* (Awakening) Movement, the Sadrists will only be motivated to reinforce their military operations against perceived American threats. Since most of the Shi'a militias are class-based military organizations, the ISCI/Maliki-backed military attacks on JaM supported by the urban poor will only bolster class tensions in a country that is already fragmented by tribal divisions (*Asharq al-Awsat*, March 28, 2008). The irony here is the way in which the expansion of factionalism and militia politics is occurring under the very surge strategy aimed at suppressing militia power in order to jump-start the political process, a key to achieving security in Iraq. Oddly, the renewed political process has only added to a conflict-ridden political situation that has poured fuel on the flames of militia rage in the southern regions.

Secondly, the Basra fighting may in fact enhance the military prestige of the JaM among the urban poor and certain tribal regions. As a nationalist, Muqtada can strategically use the Basra affair to bolster his leadership credentials and emerge stronger than before as an anti-occupation leader whose appeal may transcend beyond the Shi'a community. But the most problematic feature of this military operation is how the recent events have in fact reduced the opportunity for the Sadrists to become a fully legitimate political movement with non-violent operational activities. The most problematic aspect of the recent fighting is the possible reversal of the five-year process that saw the gradual incorporation of Muqtada and his followers into mainstream Iraqi politics.

The al-Maliki government may jeopardize its authority by comparing the Sadrists to terrorist groups like al-Qaeda as a justification for its military attacks (*al-Hayat*, March 28, 2008). Insurgent groups like al-Qaeda lack the grass-roots support and the political will to engage with the Iraqi government. The Sadrists, however, are a genuine political organization, though with a sizable militia force. It is through political negotiation that the movement's military wing can be tamed and possibly eliminated in the due course of time. A military effort without a political purpose will only strengthen the movement as an anti-occupation and anti-establishment force. In fact, any attempt to marginalize the Sadrists will only lead to greater competition between the Shi'a groups. As recent events demonstrate, the Basra fighting marks a political awakening that can only lead to increased factionalism and uncertainty for a state still in the making.

Iraqi Shi'a Factionalism and Iran's Role in the Basra Fighting

By Reidar Visser
April 14, 2008
Terrorism Focus 5 (14)

One week after the upsurge of violence in Basra in April 2008, questions about the motives and implications of the fighting still linger. The issue of Iran's involvement remains especially obscure. A recurrent explanation suggests that the operations were an attempt by Iraqi Prime Minister Nouri al-Maliki and then leader of the Islamic Supreme Council of Iraq (ISCI), Abdul Aziz al-Hakim to weaken the followers of fellow Shi'a leader Muqtada al-Sadr ahead of the next provincial elections, and perhaps to also further al-Hakim's scheme of a single Shi'a federal entity, which many Sadrists have resisted. On the surface this seems plausible. This has clearly been a political operation and not a purely security-guided one: Many militia forces in Basra unaffiliated with the Sadrists were left untouched. Also, the Maliki-Hakim axis is the sole remnant of the United Iraqi Alliance; to them it would be prudent to stick together and guard against encroachments on their local power bases. As for the United States, as long as its policy remains tied to al-Hakim's ISCI it perhaps makes sense to give the green light to operations against the Sadrists, even if the timing and the scale of the latest attacks may not have been of its own choosing.

However, the theory of a stable Maliki-Hakim alliance overlooks disagreement between the two on key issues. Crucially, al-Maliki disagrees with the ISCI on federalism. In an interview in late 2007, al-Maliki said: "There are two schools on federalism, the first moving in the direction of making the central state extremely weak, no more than a mere instrument for delivering funds and distributing them. Another school moves in the direction of federalism with a strong state capable of controlling the situation. It is this kind of federalism that we in the Da'awa [Party] support" (*al-Hayat*, November 20, 2007). Of course, that "first school," which al-Maliki went on to criticize as potentially harmful to the unity of Iraq, corresponds perfectly with the ISCI's official policy. The ISCI's recent attempt at reducing Baghdad's power as much as possible in the Non-federated Governorates Act is the exact antithesis to al-Maliki's line.

Once the existence of this kind of friction is acknowledged, it becomes possible to identify additional weaknesses in the theory of a carefully synchronized Hakim-Maliki effort. Among them is the assumption that the Iraqi military and police have already been completely infiltrated by the ISCI and that every battle fought between government forces and Shi'a discontents over the past year has been initiated at the behest of al-Hakim.

It is true that the ISCI has obtained significant fiefdoms in the security forces; the party, however, is not omnipotent. For example, the ISCI recently complained that the police in Nasiriyah—which has an ISCI governor—were becoming "politicized" (nahrayn.com, February 26, 2008). Similarly, the Interior Ministry long resisted attempts by the ISCI to sack a police commander in Hilla to whose staunch anti-militia policies ISCI leaders took exception (the commander was eventually assassinated in December 2007). And in early March 2008, al-Maliki's chief of security in Basra, General Mohan al-Firayji, faced angry demonstrators who demanded his resignation; these protestors were mostly ISCI supporters (*al-Qabas*, March 9, 2008).

The demonstrations against General al-Firayji can offer insights into Iran's role. Alongside the ISCI, another key participant was Daghir al-Musawi, leader of the small Sayyid al-Shuhada movement. Al-Musawi's critics have long accused him of close ties to the leadership of Iran's Islamic Revolutionary Guard Corps. It is noteworthy that precisely in this context, al-Maliki's man, General al-Firayji, complained about "Iranian influence" in Basra (*al-Quds al-Arabi*, March 11, 2008). Similarly, as part of the Basra operations, Iraqi forces targeted the pro-Iranian *Tharallah* militia and arrested its leader (*Aswat al-Iraq*, April 3, 2008). This less known casualty of the Basra fighting has been a loyal ally of the ISCI in its campaign to unseat then Basra governor, Muhammad al-Waili of the anti-Iranian Fadhila party. In 2006, black-clad members of Tharallah paraded through Basra identifying themselves as the "Martyr Muhammad Baqr al-Hakim Squadron" (*al-Manara*, February 21, 2006).

In sum, it appears that Iran may have had input on both sides during the Basra showdown. The smaller pro-Iranian parties within the ISCI's umbrella organization put pressure on al-Maliki and may have nudged him toward taking stronger action against the Sadrists than originally contemplated. But the conclusion of a ceasefire on Iranian soil shows that Tehran's ability to influence the other end of the spectrum—the traditionally Iraqi nationalist Sadrist movement—may now be stronger than ever before, quite possibly the result of Muqtada's relocation to Iran at the beginning of the surge, when he may have felt cornered by U.S. policy.

To the United States, the good news is that al-Maliki still seems to insist on a certain independence vis-à-vis the ISCI and Iran. A look at the composition of al-Maliki's entourage during his previous mission to Basra when he imposed emergency rule in May 2006 suggests that his power base is evolving. At that time he arrived with the chief of the ISCI-linked Badr Organization, Hadi al-Amari, as well as a former Sadrist minister from Basra, Salam al-Maliki (*al-Manara*, June 3, 2006). This time his aides consisted of independents, Interior Ministry staff and Shirwan al-Waili of the Tanzim al-Iraq branch of the Da'awa Party. The constant in all of this seems to be al-Maliki's desire to come across as a strong leader: In 2006, he promised an "iron fist"; this time he announced "the assault of the knights." Through the process, he may well have rediscovered the usefulness of siding with the ISCI, but there is nothing to suggest that al-Maliki acted as he did for the sake of the nine-governorate Shi'a federal entity.

The bad news is that al-Maliki's current survival strategy does not appear to be compatible with the declared U.S. objective of achieving national reconciliation in Iraq. Al-Maliki's vision of national reconciliation seems largely theatrical and not focused on profound constitutional revision. So far, it has failed to appeal beyond the small ruling minority of the Sunni Tawafuq bloc, the Kurds, and the Shi'a ISCI—of whom the latter two also disagree deeply with al-Maliki on federalism. Conversely, al-Maliki's view of the Sadrists is altogether unrealistic. The Sadrists are far too deep-rooted in Iraqi society to be ignored; ideologically both they and the Fadhila, which similarly criticized the Basra operations, are an important part of the center in Iraqi politics that al-Maliki is seeking.

Finally, there is al-Maliki's continued reliance on the breakaway *Hizb al-Da'awa* (Tanzim al-Iraq). Having been set afloat by Iran in 2002—rather than being a product of the Iraqi underground, as is sometimes claimed—this chameleon-like outfit may well have as its principal objective to create as much confusion in Shi'a Iraqi politics as possible. The party was probably designed as a counterweight to the mainline Da'awa movement which always maintained a certain distance from Iran; while it supported the ISCI's ideas about a single Shi'a federal region back in 2005, it has gradually reverted to an Iraqi nationalist rhetoric, raising yet more questions about its own loyalties and aims.

Current U.S. policy seems to be to unquestioningly go after whomever al-Maliki defines as a terrorist. The Iranians pursue a very different strategy, by patronizing as many Shi'a factions as possible. A third policy alternative would be to support free and fair local elections the next provincial elections, without giving in to very predictable schemes by al-Maliki and the ISCI to exclude or obstruct the Sadrists and other undesirable competitors.

Confronting the Sadrists: The Issue of State and Militia in Iraq

By Rafid Fadhil Ali
May 1, 2008
Terrorism Monitor 6 (9)

On April 26, 2008, Iraqi Shi'a leader Muqtada al-Sadr stood down from his threat to wage an all-out war against the Iraqi government and the coalition. A week before, the anti-American cleric had issued a statement threatening to declare an open war if the security crackdown by the Iraqi and U.S. forces against his loyalists was not called off. Al-Sadr said that he was giving a final warning to the Shi'a-led Iraqi government to "take the path of peace and stop violence against its own people." Al-Sadr's statement went on: "If [the Iraqi government] does not stop the militias that have infiltrated the government, then we will declare a war until liberation" (al-Jazeera, April 19, 2008).

The statement was read out in the mosques of Sadr City, a largely Shi'a district of Baghdad. There were calls for jihad against the U.S. forces and calls for the Iraqi government to release detainees and end the siege on the poor district of eastern Baghdad. Sadr City is populated by more than two million people and is a main stronghold of Muqtada's Jaysh al-Mahdi (JaM) militia.

Neither the Iraqi government of Prime Minister Nouri al-Maliki nor the U.S. forces showed any intention of submitting to al-Sadr's threat. The Iraqi-American joint operations continued, with over 1,070 people killed in Iraq in April 2008, most of them in the violence between Shi'a militias and government/Coalition forces (AFP, April 30, 2008).

Then Major General Rick Lynch, who was the commander of the U.S. Army in central Iraq, threatened to hit back if al-Sadr launched war: "If Sadr and Jaysh al-Mahdi become very aggressive, we have got enough combat force to take the fight to the enemy." General Lynch also called on al-Sadr to play a positive role: "I hope Muqtada al-Sadr continues to depress violence and not encourage it" (*Kuwait Times*, April 21, 2008). Al-Sadr, currently pursuing theological studies in the Iranian city of Qom, made his open war threat while his followers' strongholds in southern Iraq were falling and Sadr City and other Shi'a neighborhoods in Baghdad were under military pressure.

On February 22, 2008, al-Sadr renewed the six-month suspension of JaM activities. The suspension was initially imposed by al-Sadr after inter-communal clashes during a religious festival in the holy Shi'a city of Karbala were blamed on the JaM. The decision to renew the suspension was not opposed but many figures from al-Sadr's movement were ready to end the ceasefire as they claimed they were increasingly targeted by government forces.

Days after this decision, al-Sadr announced that he had retired and admitted that he had failed to achieve his main goals: "What made me retire is the continuing presence of the occupation… I have succeeded neither in liberating Iraq nor in making it an Islamic society; it might be my dereliction, it could be society's or it could be both.....Many of those who were close to me have left me for worldly reasons, and a dominant independent trend was one of the secondary reasons behind my isolation" (*Asharq al-Awsat*, March 8, 2008). Al-Sadr also revealed that he was thinking seriously of reconstructing his movement but did not clarify how he would do so while isolated in Qom. He indicated that he had undertaken advanced religious studies to become a senior Shi'a cleric (ayatollah), which will give him great spiritual and institutional influence (see *Terrorism Monitor*, February 7, 2008).

The Assault of the Knights

Basra is the second largest city in Iraq. Being the only Iraqi port and enjoying a rich oil-producing industry, it became the scene of a power struggle among the various Shi'a militias and factions after the invasion. By the end of 2007 the British Army handed over security responsibilities to the Iraqi government.

On March 25, 2008, al-Maliki himself was in Basra, where he launched "The Assault of the Knights," a security operation intended to disarm the illegal militias. It was clear that the JaM was the main target. On the threshold of the operation, the main powers in Basra, in addition to the JaM, were the Islamic Supreme Council of Iraq (ISCI), led by Abdul Aziz al-Hakim, and Fadhila (Islamic Virtue Party), led by Ayatollah Muhammad al-Yaqubi. The influential mayor of Basra, Muhammad al-Walili, is a member of the Fadhila Party.

The ISCI is the main rival of al-Sadr's movement in Shi'a Iraq. Thousands of members of the Badr Organization—the military wing of the ISCI—have joined Iraqi government forces in post-invasion Iraq, especially when Bayan Jabr, a senior member of the ISCI, was Minister of the Interior (May 2005 - June 2006). The ISCI and the Badr Organization also influence other affiliated armed groups. The ISCI currently dominates the provincial councils in central and southern Iraq as most Sadrists boycotted the provincial election in January 2005.

After the Operation

The fighting in Basra stopped when al-Sadr called on his followers to lay down their arms and clear the way for an exchange of prisoners and a cessation of government raids against his followers (see *Terrorism Focus*, April 1, 2008). 600 were killed and 2,000 injured after a week of fighting which rapidly extended from Basra to Baghdad and other parts of central and southern Iraq. Despite the call for a ceasefire, the fighting continued, with mortar and rocket attacks on Baghdad's "Green Zone." The JaM was still armed: "We are committed to [al-Sadr's] orders but we will not hand our weapons over as they are for resisting the occupation," said Hazim al-Arako, a senior aide of Muqtada (*al-Hayat*, April 1, 2008). The Iraqi and U.S. forces did not release any detainees and kept raiding al-Sadr's strongholds throughout the country.

Many looked at the operation as a victory for al-Sadr after he had shown that he still had control of his militia. Iran also appeared as another winner as the settlement for the crisis was agreed upon in the Iranian city of Qom, where al-Sadr studies (*Asharq al-Awsat*, April 5, 2008). Hundreds of Iraqi soldiers and officers surrendered to the JaM, including some who did so in front of TV cameras. In his testimony before Congress, General David Petraeus, then the U.S. military commander in Iraq, described the operation as not adequately planned (BBC, April 8, 2008).

Muqtada under Pressure

Though al-Maliki could not prove himself a remarkable military leader in the field in Basra, he nevertheless gained political support when he returned to Baghdad. The Political Council for National Security, made up of leading Shi'a, Sunni and Kurdish politicians, backed al-Maliki and called on all parties to disband their militias or risk being barred from participating in political life. Al-Maliki had the council's full support in the campaign against the militias and the outlaws (*al-Hayat*, April 6, 2008). Next al-Maliki presented al-Sadr with a difficult choice: "The decision was made that [the Sadrists] no longer have the right to participate in the political process or take part in the upcoming election unless they end al-Mahdi Army" (CNN, April 7, 2008). Moreover the Sunnis decided to rejoin al-Maliki's government—they withdrew in August 2007—and urged al-Maliki to take action against the Shi'a militias they blamed for sectarian killings.

Despite the political progress, the fighting continued. On April 11, 2008, Muqtada's right hand man and brother-in-law, Riyad al-Nuri, was assassinated in Najaf. Al-Sadr called for calm and blamed the "occupier and its tails"—referring to the Americans and the Iraqi government—though al-Nuri might have been killed by his own people (*Alalam*, April 12, 2008). On April 19, 2008, the Arabic newspaper *Asharq al-Awsat* published a letter allegedly written by al-Nuri asking al-Sadr to purify the movement and disband the JaM; a source close to al-Nuri accused extremists from the movement of the assassination. The head of al-Sadr's parliamentary bloc neither denied nor confirmed the allegations. No matter who killed al-Nuri, it was a blow to al-Sadr and his followers and it raised the possibility that Muqtada himself might be next. Al-Qaeda's second-in-command Ayman al-Zawahiri mocked al-Sadr, describing him as a dissembler who was being used by Iranian intelligence (AKI, April 18, 2008).

The Iranian ambassador to Iraq, Saeed Kazemi Qomi, denounced the American operation in Sadr City saying that it led to the killing of innocent people, but added that Iran supported the Iraqi government in its operation in southern Iraq. In Sadr City, alleged field commanders from the JaM said that the militia is now unified under the command of al-Sadr. They added that Iran had stopped sending weapons to the JaM but the weapons they already had are sufficient for a year of continuous fighting. For the first time, al-Maliki warned Iran from intervening in Iraq's internal affairs (al-Arabiya, April 25, 2008).

Al-Maliki's Four Conditions

Al-Maliki set four conditions for the JaM in order to bring an end to the military operations:

1. Heavy and medium weapons must be turned in to government forces.
2. The militia must cease interference in state affairs and institutions.
3. The militia must cease interference in the army and security forces.
4. Wanted individuals must be turned over and lists compiled of those involved in violence (al-Arabiya, April 25, 2008).

The next day the U.S. army issued a statement announcing that U.S. and Iraqi forces had taken control of Hay Hiteen, the last stronghold of al-Sadr in Basra. At the same time Iraqi forces backed by U.S. air support were raiding the last stronghold of the JaM in the southern city of al-Kut (BBC, April 26, 2008). U.S. forces were barely involved in the opening round of the operation, but by this time they had become heavily involved after some Shi'a units proved unreliable in fighting the Shi'a militias.

Despite these setbacks, al-Sadr refused to submit to al-Maliki's conditions (Radio Sawa, April 27, 2008), though he did retract his open war threat and called for an end to the bloodshed. In a statement, al-Sadr said that his threat was directed to the occupier—i.e. the U.S.-led Coalition—while calling on Iraqis not to use arms against fellow Iraqis, not to use violence to impose law and not to divide Iraq. Significantly al-Sadr called on the resistance not to use the cities as military operational fields against the occupier (*Asharq al-Awsat*, April 26, 2008). It is not clear if al-Sadr meant to make an essential change of his tactics; since the invasion, all JaM battles have been fought inside the cities and residential neighborhoods. As al-Sadr rejected al-Maliki's four conditions, the Iraqi prime minister responded: "The Iraqi government will not retreat until the JaM and other Sunni groups are disarmed and until al-Qaeda is destroyed." Al-Maliki accused JaM of using civilians in Sadr City as human shields (BBC, April 30, 2008). Baha'a al-Araji, a Member of Parliament and member of al-Sadr's movement, suggested the Iraqi presidency act as a mediator and a guarantor between the Sadrists and al-Maliki. This would be preferable to Iran, which hosted the initial peace deal in the beginning of the fighting.

The Crisis Continues

The first days of the anti-JaM operation revealed the poor performance of some Iraqi government units and a lack of coordination with the Coalition forces, demonstrating that any major campaign in the future should be well prepared politically and militarily.

The Iraqi government can bar al-Sadr's movement from participating in the upcoming provincial election but it cannot change the fact that millions of Iraqis are sincere followers of Muqtada al-Sadr. The cleric might have declined pursuing "open war" at the moment, but he is still capable of waging a popular uprising that would raise the number of casualties on both sides. April 2008 became the deadliest month in Iraq for the U.S. Army since September 2007 (BBC, April 30, 2008).

The ban on militias has focused on the Sadrists. The *Peshmerga* militias of the two major Kurdish parties and the ISCI Badr Organization have found their way into the Iraqi forces while the poor Shi'as who are the raw material of the JaM are still suffering from unemployment and negligence. The same applies to the Sunni fighters of the Awakening movement who have been trying in vain to join the Iraqi forces. A program of rebuilding the Iraqi forces on a base of national loyalty is essential to reduce violence. There may be steps in this direction—al-Maliki recently called for the recruitment of 25,000 Shi'a tribesmen to the Iraqi security forces (*al-Hayat*, April 6, 2008). To fight extreme ideologies, the Iraqi government must direct greater efforts and funding to development and reconstruction projects in impoverished Shi'a areas; otherwise, the crowded slums will continue to produce extremists and criminals.

The Mumahidun: Muqtada al-Sadr's New Militia

By Babak Rahimi
September 4, 2008
Terrorism Monitor 6 (17)

The Jaysh al-Mahdi (JaM), the Shi'a militia loyal to Muqtada al-Sadr, has recently undergone a significant transformation. On August 28, 2008, al-Sadr suspended the armed operations of the JaM (al-Jazeera, August 28, 2008). Al-Sadr's latest statement on the JaM militia follows a similar call in early August 2008 when he announced new plans to reorganize the JaM into "a cultural and religious force," charged with the responsibility of leading an intellectual jihad (IRNA, August 8, 2008). As outlined in that statement, such changes primarily involve the centralization of the command structure into a small, tight unit of loyalists, coupled with vigorous religious training for the militiamen. The new militia is called the *Mumahidun* ("those who pave the path"). The name was coined in reference to the devout followers of the Hidden Imam, who prepare the way for the Mahdi's return, believed by Shi'as to culminate in the establishment of divine justice on earth.

Origin of the Reforms

The origin of the plan to remold the JaM militia into a cultural body dates back to August 2007, when clashes between the Badr Organization, representing the rival Shi'a Islamic Supreme Council of Iraq (ISCI), and the JaM led to the death of several Shi'a pilgrims in Karbala. With the intervention of Najaf and Tehran, al-Sadr agreed to a truce and issued a decree to freeze the activities of the JaM, a ruling that was renewed in February 2008 to assure his Shi'a critics that he is sincere in bringing the unruly militia under his control. Prime Minister Nouri al-Maliki's spring 2008 military offensive to drive the JaM from the city of Basra, and later from Sadr City, ended in a ceasefire agreement on May 10, 2008 (*Aswat al-Iraq*, May 11, 2008). Yet despite the truce, the Iraqi security offensive expanded into other cities like Amara and Diwaniya as supporters of al-Sadr followed their leader's call for restraint, showing no sign of major resistance (al-

Jazeera, June 16, 2008; July 21, 2008).

Although there have been previous plans to reorganize the militia, al-Sadr's latest repackaging of the JaM into a "cultural organization" is an indication of a major internal transformation (Aftab News [Iran], June 13, 2008). First, the change of the militia's name from "Jaysh al-Mahdi" to "Mumahidun" reveals how the Sadrist movement is changing on the ideological level. Unlike its earlier form, the new militants are no longer the immediate, charismatic soldiers of the Hidden Imam, but a regular unit of organized fighters who merely anticipate the return of their savior. For the most part, al-Sadr seems no longer to consider his movement as the immediate embodiment of the Mahdi manifested in a perceived and present sacred time, but rather a mere prelude to what can be realized in a distant messianic future. The symbolic distinction between immediacy and anticipation is crucial here, since it brings to light how al-Sadr is slowly detaching himself and his movement from the earlier apocalyptic traits seen in the post-war period and moving toward a more standardized, institutionalized Shi'a-based millenarian position.

Structure and Strategy of the Mumahidun

In an organizational sense, the new Mumahidun militia signals a transition from a paramilitary unit, with a political and social presence on the street level, to a private "special force," with specific military operational tasks. While the former JaM militia represented a united citizen militia of grass-roots background, the new elite force is divided into two operational factions: one elite unit of combatants and another unit to provide public service to the community (al-Jazeera, August 8, 2008). The latter force, designed for cultural activities, is yet to be formed (*Etemad*, August 13, 2008). As a former JaM militant explains, "the new army will be only loyal to Muqtada. You will not see any dissent in this new group" (Author's interview, Qom, August 10, 2008). Such renewed confidence underlines a self-promotional strategy designed to create a restored military unit operating on par with the Hizballah of Lebanon (*Etemad*, August 13, 2008). But it also shows how in recent months al-Sadr has seriously sought to extricate himself from unruly elements within his movement.

The causes behind this organizational strategy are several, but one major factor is the likely influence of the Iranian regime, particularly the Islamic Revolutionary Guard Corps (IRGC), in taming al-Sadr's militia. The early spring detention of al-Sadr at a residential house in Qom by the IRGC highlights a major rift between the Sadrists and the hard-line establishment in Tehran (Tabnak News, May 17, 2008). Although the purpose of the arrest remains unclear, there seems to be a steady attempt by the Iranian regime to diminish the influence of al-Sadr in Iraqi politics in a way that will strengthen the al-Maliki government. This was probably done to ensure that Baghdad would thwart any American attempt to use Iraq as launch pad for military attacks against Iran. Likewise, just two weeks prior to al-Sadr's arrest, Iranian officials accepted a request from Iraqi parliamentarian delegates, led by Abdul Aziz Hakim, to exclude al-Sadr from participation in a joint Iran-Iraq meeting in Tehran to discuss the militia problem in Iraq (Tabnak News, May 4, 2008). The move signaled a shift in the Iranian strategy to give full support to the al-Maliki government, partly in order to show the Americans that Tehran can play a major role in the stability of Iraq – a central issue in the ongoing nuclear talks.

The Growing Influence of Najaf

It is important to note that al-Sadr's recent restructuring of his militia is also linked to the growing influence of Najaf in Iraqi Shi'a politics. As the power of the al-Maliki government expanded after the Basra offensive (*Asharq al-Awsat*, June 16, 2008), so did the influence of Grand Ayatollah Ali al-Sistani over the Shi'a factions, which had considerably declined after the February 2006 Samarra bombing that led to the escalation of Sunni-Shi'a violence. Since the March 2008 Basra offensive, al-Sistani and his representatives have discreetly moved to play a more active role to support the al-Maliki government in order to limit the Sadrist influence in Baghdad and the southern regions. In one of his more explicit political statements in recent months, al-Sistani directly challenged Shi'a militant factions by urging the al-Maliki government to maintain a military monopoly and disarm the militias loyal to factions outside of the government (al-Arabiyah TV, May 22, 2008). Al-Sistani's staunch opposition to the U.S.-Iraq security deal is a reminder of how the Grand Ayatollah still continues to wield major influence in Iraqi politics, especially over al-Maliki who continues to seek Sistani's counsel (and at times approval) in major legal and political issues (Hamshahrionline, August 28, 2008).

Since the 2007 Karbala tragedy, al-Sadr has become increasingly dependent on Najaf for protection against former followers who oppose his decision to become an established figure in the Najaf clerical establishment. The origin of this shift goes back to a major meeting between al-Sadr and al-Sistani, when the young cleric expressed fear of death threats from his very own militia. Al-Sistani is reported to have advised al-Sadr: "You have two options: bear the consequences, on you and the Shi'as in general, or withdraw into a corner" (*Newsweek*, March 12, 2008). Following al-Sistani's advice to leave the country and seek a scholarly path, al-Sadr traveled to Iran, where he was reported to be staying at his cousin's house in Qom (al-Arabiyah TV, February 19, 2007). This meeting highlighted the initial dependence of al-Sadr on al-Sistani's religious authority. For now, al-Sistani appears to have successfully tamed al-Sadr, especially by helping him become an active member of the Najaf-Qom clerical establishment. This intriguing development underlines how al-Sadr is gradually moving toward the traditional Shi'a authority based in Najaf, especially in his opposition toward the security pact (Hamshahrionline, August 28, 2007).

Sistani and Iran

The recent developments in Sistani-Tehran relations may have played a role in al-Sadr's change of strategy. Since 2006, al-Sistani and Shahrestani (al-Sistani's representative in Qom) have increasingly grown closer to Tehran, especially toward certain conservative factions within Iran's political establishment. The main reason for making such an unlikely alliance is that al-Sistani's financial center is based in Qom, where Tehran has considerable control over the activities of religious centers run by high-ranking clerics. Al-Sistani is fully aware of what the Iranian regime is capable of doing to those competing religious *marjas* (high-ranking scholars) who oppose Tehran's policies. After the 1979 Islamic Revolution, for instance, Ayatollah Muhammad Kazem Shariatmadari (1904-1985), a senior Shi'a cleric, publicly opposed Iran's Supreme Leader Ayatollah Ruhollah Khomeini, who saw in his radical movement a deviation from true Shi'ism. In response, the regime immediately stripped Shariatmadari of his religious authority and placed him under house arrest, a major affront to a clerical establishment that had never before seen a high-ranking jurist deposed by another cleric.

Although al-Sistani refused to give an audience to Iranian President Mahmoud Ahmadinejad during his March 2008 visit to Iraq, he welcomed the Iranian Speaker of the House, Ali Larijani, to his office in Najaf (Mehr News Agency, April 1, 2008). The meeting was a significant political event, since it provided a direct link of communication between al-Sistani and the pragmatic conservatives led by Larijani, who have grown weary of the hard-liners' support for the JaM in recent years. Al-Sistani and Tehran continue to grow closer through various formal events and family ties, such as the recent marriage between al-Sistani's granddaughter and the grandson of the late Khomeini (*Shahrvand*, May 31, 2008).

The late July 2008 string of attacks in central Baghdad and Kirkuk and the deadly August 8, 2008 bombings in the northern town of Tal Afar are grim reminders of the still unstable situation in Iraq (IRNA, July 28, 2008; al-Jazeera, August 9, 2008). Despite the presence of U.S. troops and a stronger Iraqi security force, post-Ba'athist Iraq continues to face the possibility of renewed violence on both inter-sectarian and intra-sectarian levels. It remains unclear what role the Mumahidun militia will play in a renewed conflict. What remains certain is that al-Sadr will continue to lead his dedicated followers and seek to expand his movement in order to consolidate power within the Iraqi Shi'a community.

Conclusion

In opposition to the long-term security agreement with the United States, al-Sadr can use the nationalist opposition to enhance his popularity and hence his legitimacy as a political leader, demonstrated by the fact that he demanded the Iraqi government reject the security agreement with Washington and stage demonstrations across Iraqi cities (*Aswat al-Iraq*, August 1, 2008; August 22, 2008). While retaining fierce support among impoverished Shi'as in southern regions and Baghdad, al-Sadr may use the U.S.-Iraq Status of Forces Agreement to reignite his charismatic authority and reconstitute the JaM militia.

However, the most ominous implication in the transformation of the JaM lies in the proliferation of splinter groups that may appeal to the disgruntled followers of al-Sadr as an alternative Shi'a anti-occupation movement. Nevertheless, the point to observe here is how al-Sadr is seeking to shape himself into a political figure in light of the delays in the provincial elections and the latest frictions between centralist (led by Da'awa and Sunni Arab nationalists) and federalist factions (Kurds and the ISCI) within the parliament. As tensions over the provincial election laws increase, Iraq may begin to see a new conflict between the Sadrists and the Kurdish *Peshmerga* militia, who recently called the JaM an "outlaw" militia and challenged Iraqi forces over control of major governmental buildings in Kurdish territories (*Azzaman* [Baghdad], August 26, 2008). The main question is how al-Sadr's followers will perceive the new Mumahidun Army and respond to the latest changes designed to shape the al-Sadr movement into a purely political force confined to the electoral process of

Iraq's fledging democratic order.

In the Aftermath of Iraq's 2009 Provincial Elections: Shi'a Militancy Takes a Blow from Nouri al-Maliki's Mainstream

By Babak Rahimi
February 19, 2009
Terrorism Focus 6 (5)

Iraqis cast their votes on January 31, 2009 in new provincial council elections whose outcome could shape Iraq's balance of power and set the tone for the next parliamentary election. With 440 seats contested in 14 provinces, Prime Minister Nouri al-Maliki's *Dawalt al-Qanon* (State of Law) coalition appears to be the overwhelming winner in the elections, though the final results will not be announced until later this month (*Aswat al-Iraq*, February 5, 2009; IRNA, February 5, 2009). Holding sway in Baghdad and various southern provinces, al-Maliki has now gained influence in areas where his coalition previously lacked control, especially in southern regions like Basra and Dhi Qar. For the most part, al-Maliki appears to have been rewarded for his forceful action against militia politics, which began with the spring 2008 assault on Muqtada al-Sadr's Jaysh al-Mahdi (JaM) militia. Now al-Maliki's leadership is supported by voters who desire a more centralized and efficient form of government, such as that developed by al-Maliki in the latter part of his tenure in office.

The clear loser in the elections is the Islamic Supreme Council of Iraq (ISCI). A pro-Iranian Shi'a party that was part of the Shaheed al-Mihrab list (a coalition of Shi'a political parties), ISCI lost considerable support following allegations of corruption, mismanagement, and incompetence in recent years (al-Jazeera, February 5, 2009). With the loss of seven Shi'a regions that it took in the 2005 elections, Abdul Aziz al-Hakim's party is now one of the weakest parties on the political map (*Middle East Online*, February 5, 2009). The news comes as a major blow to the leaders of the ISCI, who hoped that a victory in the elections would help them create a nine-governorate federal region in the south of the country. Meanwhile, Sunni politics saw an increase in voter participation along with the rise of new tribal-political factions in al-Anbar province like the Awakening Alliance, which won 17 percent of the votes, and the anti-al Qaeda faction of Sunni politician Saleh al-Mutlaq, with 17.6 percent of the votes (*Niqash*, February

12, 2009; al-Jazeera, February 5, 2009).

Accordingly, the Salah al-Din province, with a large Sunni population, claimed the highest level of voter participation (65 percent), a sharp contrast from 2005, when Sunnis boycotted the elections to protest the American influence in Iraqi politics (Fars News Agency, February 1, 2009). In another example, the Sunni al-Hadbaa bloc came out on top of the Kurdish factions in the ethnically mixed province of Ninawa, taking away the Shi'a and Kurdish hegemony in Baghdad and the central provinces (*Middle East Online*, February 5, 2009). With 51 percent overall voter participation, the elections have been described as a major success for a country still undergoing a significant transformation after years of single-party rule (IRNA, February 5, 2009).

The election results, however, involve a number of salient implications, which can be more complex than early readings suggest. In a sense, the elections signal a shift away from the project of regionalization (federalism) that, according to many Iraqi nationalists, put the country's political stability at risk with the promotion of ethno-sectarian identity politics (*Niqash*, February 3, 2009). But what the results primarily verify is the growing fragmentation of the Iraqi political landscape, marked by major splits between larger Shi'a parties (like ISCI) and the Da'awa. Furthermore, divisions have also emerged within Sunni parties, especially inside the Tawafuq Front, with several parties pulling out of the coalition due to the overwhelming domination of the Iraqi Islamic Party (IIP) in the Sunni coalition (*Niqash*, February 3, 2009). There is also the newly formed nationalist faction, the Iraqi National Project, which mainly ran on nationalistic rather than sectarian agenda (*Middle East Online*, February 11, 2009). On the Shi'a front, new political trends can be detected with the appearance of independent groups like the Yusuf al-Hububi party in Karbala and the decline of more established pro-federalist Shi'a parties like Fadhila in Basra, winning only 1.3 percent of votes (*Aswat al-Iraq*, February 5, 2009).

Some troubling signs that merit serious attention have emerged from the election outcome:

First, the results of the 2009 provincial elections hardly indicate that the State of Law coalition (al-Maliki's faction) has won a sweeping victory, especially in Baghdad and the southern Shi'a provinces where Sadrists still maintain some level of influence, despite the fact that Muqtada al-Sadr's group was banned from participating on the grounds that it maintains a militia (*Middle East Online*,

February 9, 2009). In Karbala, for instance, where al-Maliki's Dawa party won a clear victory in 2005, the independent Yusuf al-Hububi party surprised many when it beat out many famous Shi'a competitors in the province. So, in many ways, al-Maliki's grip on power still still seems shaky. This is partly because of the way some Shi'a voters are beginning to see al-Maliki as someone who backs certain former Ba'athists, a perception promoted by the ISCI ahead of the parliamentary election. Thus, al-Maliki's true degree of success is still unknown.

Second, there is the possibility of a backlash from the pro-federalist factions, especially the Kurdish bloc, which may lead to the emergence of a more centralized state and a considerable threat to their regional or party interests. This may complicate the political situation even more with regards to the Kurdish claim over Kirkuk, where, due to major differences between Baghdad and Arbil, the provincial elections never took place (al-Jazeera, February 1, 2009). In the southern regions, the province of Maysan has already begun to see a pro-federalist backlash. More than a week after the elections, a total of 25 parties formed an alliance to launch a civil disobedience demonstration to protest the results of the polls (*Aswat al-Iraq*, February 12, 2009).

Third, the elections shed light on a deepening rift within the Shi'a bloc, which could enhance competition and a potential outbreak of violence for control over territories. While the ISCI will likely seek to repair its losses in the general elections by becoming more competitive on the local level in provinces like Basra and Diyala, the Sadrists, who appear to have been largely marginalized as a result of Baghdad's political and military tactics in the previous year, could see the current situation as a threat and reconstitute the JaM militia. In fact, the Sadrists are already alleging voter fraud in the provinces of Maysan, Najaf, and Dhi Qar, while al-Sadr has issued a new statement that rejects negotiations of any sort with Washington, recalling the group's commitment to armed resistance (*Middle East Online*, February 9, 2009; Fars, February 1, 2009). In many ways, the Sadrist factor is still relevant and the elections bring to light how intra-Shi'a politics are entering a new stage of competition, rather than coming to an end.

Fourth, the latest string of coordinated attacks southwest of Baghdad, Karbala, and Nasiriyah suggests an existing organized insurgent movement that seeks to interrupt the fragile political situation on the ground (*Aswat al-Iraq*, February 12, 2009).

Finally, there is Iran. For the most part, Tehran's hardliners are aware of their loss of influence in Iraqi politics as a result of the ISCI's decline in popularity and the advent of Iraqi nationalism with the victory of al-Maliki. Yet Iranian newspapers maintained a low-key position on the rise of Sunni political factions and, in some instances, described the latest results as a clear victory for "Islamist" groups with the aim of keeping religion as the basis of the Iraqi political order (Fars News Agency, February 5, 2009). The ISCI's defeat in the elections was described as a major "victory," while the decline of Shi'a voter participation, especially in the province of Diyala, was primarily blamed on a lack of security in the southern regions (Fars, February 1, 2009; IRNA, February 5, 2009).

Despite the latest setbacks, Iran remains defiant. On the day the initial results of the elections were announced, Mohsen Rezaee, the Secretary of the Expediency Discernment Council (a consultative council to Iran's Supreme Leader, Ayatollah Ali Khamenei) and a leading hard-line politician in the Islamic Republic, asserted that Iran still remains the most influential force in the region (Fars News Agency, February 5, 2009). The remark could be interpreted as a warning to Washington. It remains unclear how Tehran could change its strategy in Iraq, but the Sadrists, whose leader resides in Qom, could play a vital role in such a process.

Of course, most of the above security factors and their impact on Iraq's security situation will depend on whether or not stable alliances will emerge in the post-electoral period and how such coalitions might affect the upcoming parliamentary election. If the Sadrists, for instance, join forces with al-Maliki's ruling party, the chances of internal Shi'a conflict may be reduced if the ISCI seeks to build a coalition with Kurdish factions (*Middle East Online*, February 11, 2009). The political landscape could also look very different if ISCI forms an alliance with the faction of former Iraqi Prime Minister Ayad Alawi, signaling the rise of a major political competition between exiled Shi'a factions (both secular and religious) over key positions in the parliament (*Niqash*, February 12, 2009).

In sum, the elections have exposed a sense of national stability that appears to revolve around the rejection of a decentralized and fragmented form of governance, which many Iraqis fear will put the country's fledgling democracy at risk of a resurrection of unruly militia politics. The advent of a centralist-nationalist mood underscores Iraqis' desire for restored sovereignty in a state that is efficient, centralized, and capable of providing its citizens with security and economic stability without the help of foreign forces.

Chapter 6

Iraq's Dangerous Kurdish-Arab Rivalry

Strategic Implications for Northern Iraq's Kurdish Oil Industry

By Lydia Khalil
November 26, 2007
Terrorism Monitor 5 (22)

Article 3, Paragraph 3 of the Oil and Gas Law of the Kurdistan Region seems straightforward: "The Regional Government shall, together with the Federal Government, jointly manage Petroleum Operations ... according to the provisions of the Federal Constitution" [1]. The law seems clear until one discovers that no comparable federal (meaning national) oil law has been passed and that the provisions within the federal constitution are still hotly contested by many quarters within the Iraq government. The confusion has not only stalled oil exploration and production efforts, it carries a palpable security threat as well.

Despite opposition from the national government in Baghdad and its neighbors, the Kurdistan Regional Government (KRG) has refused to be held back by the indecision and infighting that characterizes the central government. They have charged ahead, passing their own Oil and Gas Law and forming four regional oil-related companies—the Kurdistan Exploration and Production Company (KEPCO), Kurdistan National Oil Company (KNOC), Kurdistan Oil Marketing Organization (KOMO) and Kurdistan Organization for Downstream Operations (KODO)—and signed seven new exploration deals with both Kurdish and international petroleum firms (Reuters, November 7, 2007). Kurdish officials claim they are well within their legal right to go forward with the exploration deals and that fears of the KRG monopolizing subsequent oil revenues are unfounded. Iraqi President and Kurdish leader Jalal al-Talabani explained:

Regarding the Kurdistan region's contracts, they do not deal with oil production and exploitation, but with the initial stage of oil exploration. When we reach the stage of production and exploitation, we need to go back to Baghdad in accordance with Article 12 of the Iraqi Constitution. Hence the Kurdish position is misrepresented... The Kurds have not made any demand to monopolize the oil and its revenues. We implement the relevant constitutional provisions and believe that oil and its revenues should be shared and distributed equally and fairly to all Iraqi regions without exception (Asharq al-Awsat, October 27, 2007).

Using Oil to Ensure Autonomy

Despite Kurdish protestations and assurances, the oil contracts are an obvious attempt to raise the KRG's strategic and international profile, as well as a means of consolidating their current level of autonomy and relative prosperity. The Kurds have clearly stated that they will not allow indecision in Baghdad to hinder their hard won progress nor slow down any momentum towards economic development and regional autonomy.

But what Kurdish officials often fail to mention is that there are a host of other issues that impact Iraqi and regional opinion of the Kurdish oil contracts. Turkey, Iran and Iraq's Sunni Arabs all cast a wary eye over the slightest movements towards Kurdish autonomy, however legal or justified they may appear. Given this ultra sensitive environment, the new oil contracts are as much of a security risk to the KRG as they are a potential boon to its economy and strategic profile. The central Iraq government has already called the exploration contracts illegal and threatened to impose sanctions on any of the foreign companies involved in the deal, preventing them from any future work with the Iraqi state (*al-Hayat*, November 13, 2007).

Not only that, Iraqi Oil Minister Hussain al-Shahristani recently declared that any oil contracts signed with KRG officials are null and void: "The Iraqi government had warned these companies of the consequences of entering into these contracts, and the consequence is that Iraq will not allow these companies to extract the oil" (AFP, November 24, 2007).

It is not entirely clear how the central government plans to enforce this, short of stationing Iraqi military forces in Kurdistan, since KRG officials remain defiant and refuse to bow to Baghdad pressure. In a sharply worded official rebuttal, the KRG pledged to move forward with the oil exploration projects:

> *We are not deterred by Dr. Shahristani's views. Experience shows that most international oil companies (IOCs) now ignore his unhelpful interventions. We know that the KRG is doing the right thing by encouraging the IOCs to invest in Kurdistan... We would like to remind Dr. Shahristani that we neither expect nor accept threats, sanctions and punishments from partners in our coalition government in Baghdad. The Kurdistan Alliance List [a parliamentary alliance of the PUK and KDP] is a partner in Iraq, not a rogue region to be threatened or punished... Empty threats and talk of blackmail will not last. We are sure that eventually common sense will prevail in dealing with these matters (www.krg.org, November 20, 2007).*

Accusing al-Shahristani of relying on Ba'athist and Saddamist frameworks, Kurdish leaders blasted al-Shahristani's record and reminded Iraqis that oil found in northern Iraq will benefit all Iraqis because of the obligations drafted under the Revenue Sharing Law. The response of foreign companies involved in the oil exploration deals will likely resolve the rhetorical battle, but the disagreement between the national government and the KRG has greater consequences for regional security.

More pressing for the Iraqi Kurds, the oil deals threaten to exacerbate their fragile and historically hostile relationship with Turkey. Turkey has stationed thousands of troops along the border it shares with the KRG and has conducted limited incursions to flush out Kurdistan Workers' Party (PKK) fighters hiding out in the Kurdish mountains. Turkey claims that PKK units operating out of Iraqi Kurdish territory have perpetrated attacks inside Turkey and accuse KRG officials of neglect or even collusion.

While the PKK presence in Iraqi Kurdistan is a pressing security concern, the long-term regional, particularly Turkish, worry is the growing autonomy of the KRG and the prospect of eventual Kurdish secession from Iraqi territory. In the current environment, the two issues are easily conflated.

Dispute Over Kirkuk

The recent oil exploration contracts also bring to mind Kurdish strategy in Kirkuk. In the minds of many within the region, and inside Iraq, the key to Kurdish independence lies with Kirkuk, where most of the oil in northern Iraq is located. Kirkuk is not under KRG administration yet, but the Kurdish leadership is doing everything within its power to ensure that it will be. The Kurds and the

Turkomen both have historic claims to Kirkuk and want to rectify the injustice of the "Arabization" policy imposed on the oil-rich province by Saddam Hussein. No one denies, however, that Kirkuk's oil resources are the main prize. The current territory under Kurdish regional administration contains only about 0.5 percent of Iraq's proven oil reserves, while Kirkuk has 11 billion barrels of proven reserves (UPI, November 7, 2007). Iraq has a total of 115 billion barrels of proven oil reserves, though much of the country remains unexplored.

Therefore any Kurdish moves on Kirkuk are viewed with extreme suspicion. The referendum to decide whether Kirkuk should be administered under the KRG, scheduled to take place this month, has been postponed. If Kirkuk does eventually decide to ally itself with the KRG administration, Turkey will surely not sit idly by and let this happen. The Turks and Iraqi Arabs are already compiling evidence of aggressive Kurdish action in Kirkuk, such as Kurdish party officials paying Arab families to leave ahead of decisions by the Property Claims Commission and the re-settling of supporters of Talabani's Patriotic Union of Kurdistan (PUK) and Masoud Barzani's Kurdistan Democratic Party (KDP) in Kirkuk in advance of the referendum.

If Kurdish officials are demonstrating their defiance now in pursuing the oil exploration contracts despite Iraqi and regional opposition, Turkey, Iran and their Iraqi brothers will not be inclined to give the Kurdish leadership the benefit of the doubt when they claim they harbor no intentions to secede by claiming Kirkuk. But Turkey and other regional powers are not the only security threats to the KRG. Iraqi insurgents have also set their sights on Kirkuk.

In the latest attack, a suicide bomber targeted a top Kirkuk security official, killing five and wounding 20 people. As al-Qaeda in Iraq and their supporters have been flushed out of Iraq's al-Anbar province and many parts of Baghdad, they are traveling out, upwards and along the borders. Their presence is being increasingly felt at points north. The November 15, 2007 suicide attack in Kirkuk was just one of dozens, if not hundreds, of attacks on Kirkuk this year (*Asharq al-Awsat*, November 16, 2007). The new exploration fields are a promising target to incoming insurgents and an increasingly violent indigenous Kurdish opposition to the PUK-KDP power monopoly in the KRG. A recent explosion at one exploration field, though it was deemed an engineering failure, was immediately thought to be the work of saboteurs (*Hawal*, October 27, 2007).

Conclusion

Though the Kurds insist the law is on their side with regard to the recent oil exploration deals, most of their neighbors and fellow Iraqis disagree. Kurds have achieved much since 1991—a certain degree of autonomy, influence within the Baghdad government, strong economic ties with Turkey and the support of the United States. But the continuation and progress of these achievements should not be taken for granted. They threaten to unravel if Turkish suspicion morphs into Turkish aggression or if future conflicts over oil devolve into civil conflict, erasing security gains in the KRG. But the achievements in Kurdistan did not come about without the Kurdish leadership taking risky decisions. Going forward with the oil exploration deals is a gamble they are apparently willing to take, but one not without dangers.

Notes

1. The Oil and Gas Law of the Kurdistan Region is accessible at: www.krg.org/uploads/documents/Kurdistan%20Oil%20and%20Gas%20Law%20English__2007_09_06_h14m0s42.pdf

---

Iraqi Military Operation in Diyala Province Risks Renewal of Kurdish-Arab Conflict

By Ramzy Mardini
September 18, 2008
Terrorism Focus 5 (33)

As tensions rise between Iraqi Kurds, Arab Sunnis, and Arab Shi'as in ethnically mixed Diyala province during a massive and ongoing military operation by the Iraq Army, a bombing in the disputed city of Khanaqin threatens to launch the region into new convulsions of violence. On September 13, 2008, a powerful improvised explosive device killed nine members of the Kurdish *Peshmerga* militia responsible for security in the city. The dead included Colonel Zulfiqar, the local commander of *Peshmerga* forces (AFP, September 13, 2008; *Aswat al-Iraq*, September 14, 2008).

In September 2008, then exiting commander of the Multi-National Force–Iraq, General David Petraeus, noted the security progress that has begun to stabilize Iraq was "not irreversible" (BBC, September 11, 2008). The U.S. general's remarks came after last month's unexpected confrontation between the Iraq

Army and Kurdish *Peshmerga* forces in Khanaqin. Though Iraq's security and economy have radically improved since the implementation of the U.S. "surge" strategy, developments in Diyala province highlight the danger of a sudden reversion to ethnic and religious bloodshed.

During summer 2008, Diyala province had been the focal point of unusual security moves by the government of Prime Minister Nouri al-Maliki. In mid-August 2008, under the supposed direction of al-Maliki, special counterterrorism forces – known as Emergency Response Units (ERUs) – raided the office of Diyala Governor Raad Rashid al-Mullah, shot and killed his cousin, and commenced a gunfight with local police (*Aswat al-Iraq*, August 19, 2008). The raid's aim was the arrest of popular Sunni political figure Dr. Hussein al-Zubaidi, who heads Diyala's security committee. Al-Zubaidi was beaten before being carried away. A Diyala politician responded to his colleague's detention, saying, "This has sent a bad message to the people of Diyala, that the government in Baghdad is not really going after the outlaws, it's going after their elected officials" (Fox News, September 6, 2008).

But according to an Interior Ministry spokesman, al-Maliki had not authorized the raid, leading the U.S. military to assume it was a "rogue operation." Sunni politicians in Baghdad question al-Maliki's ostensible lack of participation. Salim Abdullah al-Juboori, a member of the Iraqi Islamic Party (IIP), believes "such a raid could not have taken place unless Mr. Maliki had at least prior knowledge of it." With their leadership and attributes strictly classified, the ERUs operate under the control of the Prime Minister's office. According to a Defense Ministry official, the ERUs normally operate in Baghdad, but shifted operations towards Diyala beginning in July 2008 (McClatchy Newspapers, August 22, 2008).

The Iraq Army began Operation *Bashaer al-Kheir* (Promise of Good) on July 29, 2008 in cooperation with U.S. forces. The operation is a major offensive consisting of 50,000 soldiers and police aimed at rooting out al-Qaeda and Shi'a militias in Diyala province (*Aswat al-Iraq*, September 5, 2008). Local Sunni *Sahwa* (Awakening) members complain that the operation is being waged against them – purposely undermining their prospects for a future political role. Government efforts to marginalize the province's mostly Sunni *Sahwa* fighters have increased considerably since the operation commenced. Leaders have been arrested or evicted from their posts in an effort to hasten their disbandment.

But the central and potentially explosive issue resulting from the government's military operation in Diyala was the confrontation at Khanaqin between Kurdish militias and Iraqi forces. An oil-rich city along the Iranian border of the Diyala governorate, Khanaqin is considered one of the "disputed territories" cited in Article 140 of the Iraq Constitution. Article 140 outlines a legal process intended to reverse the "Arabization" campaigns of the former Ba'athist regime and settle the territorial disputes between the Kurdistan Regional Government (KRG) in Arbil and the federal government in Baghdad. Driven by force from Khanaqin, Iraqi Kurds have been returning to the city since 2003 and now form the majority of the population. The local council has proposed integrating the city with the Kurdistan region, but like the similar cases of Kirkuk and Mosul, a reluctant Shi'a-dominated government in Baghdad has delayed finalizing Khanaqin's status.

In 2005, overwhelming violence in Diyala province led Baghdad to invite Kurdish forces to enter Khanaqin to help stabilize the area and protect its Kurdish inhabitants (*Aswat al-Iraq*, September 5, 2008). Last month, however, under al-Maliki's authority, the Iraqi Army ordered Kurdish forces to withdraw from Khanaqin within 24 hours (*Alsumaria*, September 6, 2008). Citing direct orders from the KRG, the *Peshmerga* refused and Iraqi troops entered Khanaqin under the pretense of carrying out their province-wide military operation.

To defuse the escalating rhetoric of both sides, the KRG and the federal government came to a temporary agreement calling for a reversion to the status quo, the preference of local authorities. As part of the accord, Kurdish *Peshmerga* forces withdrew from the Khanaqin affiliated districts of Qurat Taba and Jalawlaa (*Aswat al-Iraq*, September 5, 2008). Though ongoing negotiations have yet to settle Khanaqin's status, Kurdish trust of the Shi'a government has suffered considerable and risky damage – arguably reaching the lowest point since 2003.

Kurdish officials expressed suspicion of the government's reasoning behind sending the army into Khanaqin, since they believe the town had already been pacified under *Peshmerga* supervision. Salar Mahmud, an organizer of the Khanaqin demonstrations, professed: "We think the military crackdown in Diyala province is politically aimed against the will of the Kurdish area residents…These military forces should be deployed to control areas affected by terrorism, not to show their power in front of the Kurdish people" (*Kurdish Globe*, August 24, 2008). However, Iraqi Defense Minister Abdel Qadir al-Ubaidi downplayed the Khanaqin incident, claiming "it was not a crisis but lack of coordination" between Arbil and Baghdad (*Aswat al-Iraq*, September 10, 2008).

Kurdish skeptics point to Baghdad's inconsistencies. For example, Khanaqin Mayor Muhammad Mullah Hassan claimed, "there is no Al Qaeda in our city" as the local backlash of demonstrations reinforced the public's unfavorable view of the government's actions (*Kurdish Globe*, August 28, 2008). Moreover, the Kurdish *Peshmerga* constitute an effective and capable armed force – leading many to challenge why Khanaqin was ever part of the wider *Bashaer al-Kheir* operation. As KRG President Masoud Barzani noted, "Khanaqin is a safe area and it's a wonder that the Iraqi Army entered it under the pretext of combating terrorism" (*Aswat al-Iraq*, August 28, 2008).

One explanation for the Iraq Army's entry into Khanaqin was provided by acting KRG *Peshmerga* Minister Anwar Hajji Osman, who observed that the operation reflected the government's aim of controlling Kurdish inhabited areas and disrupting the KRG's political and military positions (*Kurdish Globe*, August 28, 2008). Such tactics may be directed at weakening the KRG's influence in Diyala province, hoping to marginalize its prospects in the disputed territories before the provincial elections scheduled later this year. This is suggested by the actions witnessed in the Qurat Taba area of Khanaqin, where the Iraq Army raided the headquarters belonging to the Patriotic Union of Kurdistan (PUK), the Kurdistan Democratic Party (KDP), and the Kurdistan Communist Party, as well as taking down the KRG flag (*Aswat al-Iraq*, August 24, 2008). Another accusation was set forth by Sami al-Atroushi, a member of the Kurdistan Islamic Union, who accused the central government of engaging in "political blackmailing" to force the KRG to "give up Article 140 of the Iraqi constitution" (*Aswat al-Iraq*, September 10, 2008).

According to a secret report produced by a Kurdish political party, "Al-Maliki has started to undermine the influence of those in the Iraqi military and security commanders who are classified as protégés of the Americans…The freezing of the powers of the Iraq Army's chief of staff, Babakir Zebari, is the first indication of this trend" (*Gulf News*, September 12, 2008). Masoud Barzani claimed that the Diyala operation was implemented "behind the back" of General Zebari, a Kurd, who "was not consulted" and whose presence "has become nominal" (*Asharq al-Awsat*, September 1, 2008).

The level of rhetoric surrounding the issue has reached a new and dangerous high. Barzani claimed the new Iraqi Army had "acted exactly like the former army…including the crimes that were committed during Operation Al-Anfal [a reference to Saddam Hussein's 1986-89 campaign against the Kurds]" (*Asharq al-*

Awsat, September 1, 2008). More critically, KRG representative Mullah Bakhtiyar announced: "Kurdish negotiators in Baghdad have opened 99 gates for dialogue and one gate for war," claiming that if the Iraq government picked "the gate to war, they have been told that if war happens in Khanaqin it will happen in Kirkuk, Mosul, and the other disputed areas" (*Kurdish Globe*, September 11, 2008).

More fallout from the Khanaqin crisis appeared when Kurdish authorities questioned the government's interest in purchasing 36 F-16 fighter jets from the United States. The motives behind the military buildup had created in Kurds "a justified fear," linking past atrocities and recent developments in Diyala province. When describing the Khanaqin crisis, the KRG's parliamentary speaker Adnan al-Mufti observed: "If the situation plays out in this way and there is a government or head of the government in the future who thinks of a military solution to impose their will... and if they have F-16s, they may use them" (Reuters, September 10, 2008).

Unlike past political disputes, the Khanaqin crisis provides the first incident in which the new Iraq has adopted a formalized military response towards the Kurds. This provocation reinforces Kurdish fears of past attitudes, reactivating the anti-State narrative as Barzani points to a "chauvinist Ba'athist approach" practiced by some in Baghdad (*Asharq al-Awsat*, September 1, 2008). The rapid deterioration in trust resulting from developments in Diyala increases the risk that the unfolding security dilemma could lead to open conflict and decrease the prospect of disputes being resolved at the political level. As provincial elections approach and pressures to implement Article 140 intensify, the concurrent shift of American forces to secondary responsibilities and the deteriorating situation in Khanaqin may leave Iraq in a vulnerable security position.

Arms Shipment to the Kurds May Be a Sign of Conflict Between the KRG and Baghdad

By Emrullah Uslu
November 26, 2008
Eurasia Daily Monitor 5 (227)

The *Washington Post* has reported that three C-130 cargo planes delivered small arms and ammunition from Bulgaria to Iraq in September 2008. Three U.S. military officials indicated that the weapons shipment procedure did not comply with Iraqi government regulations. Kurdish officials declined to answer questions about the shipments but released the following statement: "The Kurdistan Regional Government continues to be at the forefront of the war on terrorism in Iraq. With that continued threat, nothing in the constitution prevents the Kurdistan Regional Government (KRG) from obtaining defense materials for its regional defense" (*Washington Post*, November 23, 2008).

The news has sent a shock wave to interested parties in the region. The Bulgarian Foreign Ministry immediately denied the report through Bulgarian National Radio: "Bulgaria did not sell arms to private individuals or non-government organizations, and no such transaction ever took place" (www.sofiaecho.com, November 24, 2008).

A day after the article was published, KRG officials changed their original response, which had appeared in the *Washington Post* and had emphasized that the Iraqi constitution did not prevent the KRG from obtaining materials for its own defense. On November 25, 2008, KRG officials categorically denied the allegations of arms purchases from Bulgaria. Jabbar Yawer, the Undersecretary for *Peshmerga* (Kurdish armed forces) Affairs in the KRG, said that "As a region we don't have the right to buy any weapons without the consent of the central government, and they haven't allocated any amount in the budget for buying weapons" (Sofia News Agency, November 25, 2008). Yawer added, "Those airplanes would have to use several countries' airspace to reach Sulaymaniyah. Moreover, U.S troops search the airplane loads at Sulaymaniyah airport. Thus, it would not be possible to deliver all these weapons to the KRG region without their [the troops'] knowledge" (ANF News Agency, November 24, 2008).

The Iraqi government has ended its criticism toward the KRG that appeared in the first *Washington Post* article: "...the Iraqi government has no objection to semiautonomous Kurdish authorities purchasing weapons and ammunition to arm their security forces, but it wants to be informed, a government spokesman said" (*Washington Post*, November 25, 2008).

The background of the arms deal is interesting. The *Washington Post* indicates that the weapons were delivered to the Kurdish region in September 2008 at a time when the KRG and the central government in Baghdad were disputing the issue of arms deals. KRG President Masoud Barzani said, "Unfortunately, we seem to be still under the influence of a totalitarian regime. The one that takes over power thinks that he has the last word in everything and that it is his right to make decisions without consulting others. He forgets the coalitions, the commitments, and the constitution" (*Asharq al-Awsat*, September 3, 2008).

When the central government in Iraq revealed its intention to purchase 36 F-16 fighter jets in September 2008, Adnan al-Mufti, the speaker of the Kurdistan National Assembly (Kurdish Parliament), delivered a speech on the arms agreement, showing that a crisis of confidence existed between the Kurdistan region and the central government. "Al-Mufti has called on the United States in particular and the arms-producing major powers in general not to sell arms to Iraq unless conditions and specific restrictions are attached to such deals prohibiting the use of these arms against the Kurds in the future" (*Asharq al-Awsat*, September 11, 2008). In response Ali Al-Dabbagh, the official spokesman of the Iraq government, said, "All we can say in this regard is that Iraq is a sovereign state. The subject of arming, training, and building the capabilities of the army is one of the rights of the federal government" (*Asharq al-Awsat*, September 11, 2008).

This debate clearly underlines the mutual distrust between the KRG and the central government. At the same time the KRG officials were vehemently opposing the central government's arms purchases, the KRG government was having weapons delivered to the region.

The information about the Kurds arms deal was apparently leaked to the media during the course of yet another conflict between the KRG and the government in Baghdad. Barzani recently criticized the government of Prime Minister Nouri al-Maliki and referred to those who supported his support council plan as "enemies" (see *EDM*, November 20, 2008). Brigadier General Tony Thomas, the top U.S. commander in Mosul, observes that the Kurds are nervous about Baghdad's growing unilateralism. Al-Maliki "sees the Kurds, specifically the *Peshmerga*, as a militia, unauthorized, shouldn't be there. …They say, 'we must be armed because as soon as you leave, we see this coming ...[al-Maliki] is going to attack us as soon as you turn away,'" said Thomas (Reuters, November 12, 2008).

Given the possibility that the U.S. may have leaked the Kurdish arms deal story to the media, one can assume that American officials may be unhappy about Barzani's assertive policies toward Kirkuk and other areas where potential problems could lead to civil war after the U.S. withdrawal.

Another aspect of the arms deal is the route that the three C-130 cargo planes used to deliver those weapons. Given that Turkey has its own concerns about the KRG in the region, it would not open its territory to such a weapons transfer.

Other countries with possible alternative routes, that is, Syria and Iran, also do not want the Kurds to have such weapons. The question is: how did the Kurds under these circumstances manage to obtain the weapons with the three cargo planes?

In the Aftermath of Iraq's 2009 Provincial Elections: A Dangerous Year Ahead for Iraqi Kurds

By David Romano
February 19, 2009
Terrorism Focus 6 (5)

Some ominous signs have appeared for northern Iraq's Kurdistan Regional Government (KRG) following the January 31, 2009 nationwide provincial elections. If the elections offer an indicator of the national mood of Iraq, then in this case Iraq's Arabs seemed to show a growing preference for Iraqi Arab nationalist political parties and a strong central government, a preference at odds with the KRG's struggle for greater regional autonomy.

The biggest loser in the provincial elections was the Shi'a Islamic Supreme Council of Iraq (ISCI) party. The ISCI went from being the hegemonic party in Iraq's southern provinces to an embarrassing second- or even third-place showing in most southern provinces. Iraq's Shi'a prime minister, Nouri al-Maliki, emerged in turn as the elections' biggest winner, greatly improving on the weak following his Da'awa party attracted in previous elections. Al-Maliki even seems to have attracted significant numbers of votes from outside his Shi'a sectarian base by downplaying religious themes in favor of Iraqi nationalist slogans and the promise of security and strong government - issues with appeal to Sunni Arabs, secular voters and even Christian Iraqis. Where he was once regarded by many as an ineffective compromise choice for prime minister, al-Maliki has now managed to shape his image into that of the strong leader many Iraqis believe they need.

Iraqi Kurds view these results with concern. In Iraq's federal level of government, the ISCI has generally worked closely with the Kurdish parties and shared their goal of a highly decentralized Iraqi federalism, with a weak central government in Baghdad. If the provincial elections indicate what the national-level parliamentary elections will look like when they are held in late 2009, Iraq's Kurdish parties will need a few more political allies to compensate for the ISCI's decline. If Arab Iraqi leaders think they can get more votes and support with a platform of Iraqi nationalism and strong central government, as al-Maliki seems to have done, such political allies may become increasingly hard to find.

Part of al-Maliki's ascendance seems to be occurring at the expense of the KRG. Kurdish relations with al-Maliki went from reasonably positive in 2006-2007 (when Kurdish parties saved al-Maliki's government from collapse as Shi'a and Sunni parties withdrew their support), to increasingly tense in 2008 and early 2009. Much of the Iraqi Arab electorate appears resentful of Kurdish gains since 2003, and displays little patience or understanding for Kurdish demands. Politicians like al-Maliki have moved to capitalize on this resentment and burnish their Iraqi nationalist credentials. Al-Maliki and his ministers now increasingly criticize the KRG; at a press conference on November 20, 2008, al-Maliki questioned the activities of the Kurdish *Peshmerga* militias and accused the KRG of violating Iraq's constitution by developing an independent oil industry and opening diplomatic offices in foreign countries (*International Herald Tribune*, December 2, 2008).

The KRG struck back by citing what it described as the Prime Minister's own violations of the constitution:

> *It is unfortunate and deeply regrettable that the [November 20, 2008] press conference of Iraq's Prime Minister illustrates efforts being made to take the people of Iraq back to a period we are desperately trying to get beyond. It was a period where the excessive concentration, or centralization, of economic and political power condemned all Iraqi peoples to unimaginable suffering....Though the Prime Minister has taken the oath to promote and protect the Constitution of Iraq - as it currently exists - it is, indeed, disconcerting when he cites the Constitution in attacking others while apparently violating it when taking unilateral decisions. The Prime Minister is obligated to act within the limits of the current constitution and not in accordance with a future constitution he may prefer (KRG.org, December 1, 2008).*

KRG leaders have also condemned al-Maliki's move to recruit and arm "support councils" in their region and the disputed territories south of it. According to the KRG, al-Maliki has approached Arab tribal leaders in northern Iraq (including those who had collaborated in Saddam's military campaigns against Kurdish rebels) in an apparent effort to create a militia directly loyal to him (KRG.org, December 1, 2008). KRG President Masoud Barzani has also accused al-Maliki of marginalizing Kurds in the Iraqi army while appointing his own people to head each of Iraq's 16 army divisions, rather than following the legal parliamentary procedure of choosing such commanders by consensus (*Los Angeles Times*, January 12, 2009).

Additionally, al-Maliki has deployed Iraqi army units northwards to areas the Kurds want to incorporate into their autonomous region. The Kurdish Autonomous Region of today consists simply of the areas from which Saddam Hussein withdrew his forces in 1991, and does not include many predominantly Kurdish areas just south of 1991's "Green Line."

One such mostly Kurdish town south of the autonomous region is Khanaqin, where al-Maliki suddenly sent an Iraqi army brigade in August, 2008, to "help with security." The Arab Iraqi army unit nearly traded fire with the Kurdish *Peshmerga* sent to intercept them before mediation led both forces to agree that neither group would enter the town.

For towns just south of the Kurdish autonomous region's accidental borders - like Khanaqin, Makhmour, Kalar, and Chamchamal - the significant oil resources around them only add to the determination of both Baghdad and the KRG to control them. The multi-ethnic demography of larger towns like Kirkuk and Mosul - with Kurdish, Arab, Turkmen, and Christian populations - further complicates the issue. Kurdish leaders who would negotiate away historic claims to areas like Kirkuk or surrender any measure of Kurdish autonomy would undoubtedly be committing political suicide. Although Article 140 of the 2005 Iraq Constitution stipulates that these areas must have a referendum to decide whether or not to join the KRG region, several deadlines for the referendum (the first in December 2007) have already come and gone. Kirkuk did not even get to vote in the 2009 provincial elections, as disagreements over who gets to vote in that province still await resolution (the three KRG provinces of Dohuk, Arbil and Sulaymaniyah did not have provincial elections either, since they are functioning under a separate KRG electoral calendar). A deadline of March 31, 2009, for a special parliamentary committee to table a new Kirkuk election law will probably be missed as well. In Diyala and Ninawa provinces just south of the KRG, Kurds largely controlled the provincial councils (as they do in Kirkuk) due to a 2005 electoral boycott by Arab Sunnis. Last month's electoral results mean they will be expected to relinquish control of Ninawa (Mosul) to the Sunni Arab al-Hadbaa party (which garnered 48.4 percent of the vote to the Kurdish Alliance's 25.5

percent) and control of Diyala to the Sunni Arab Iraqi Islamic Party (which garnered 21.1 percent of the vote to the Kurdish Alliance's 17.2 percent).

These developments, combined with Prime Minister al-Maliki's increasingly tense relations with Kurdish leaders, seem to foreshadow a difficult year ahead for Iraqi Kurds and their leaders. As the security situation in the center and south of Iraq improves, an increasingly confident al-Maliki-led government appears less conciliatory and more aggressive towards Iraqi Kurdistan. According to *The Economist*, "Mr. Barzani is said to have recently told Mr. Maliki to his face: 'You smell like a dictator'" (*The Economist*, November 27, 2008). Arab Iraqi voters in turn appear to be rewarding al-Maliki for his assertiveness.

Iraq's Kurds may hope that divisions among the Arab Iraqi political parties remain serious enough to force some of them to maintain Kurdish allies. Failing the emergence of a fractious, weak, and inward-focused political scene in Baghdad, Iraqi Kurds risk a difficult time ahead. If the government in Baghdad continues to consolidate, KRG leaders may find few friends in the region (besides the mountains) to turn to in case of political difficulties, especially given the current plans to withdraw U.S. troops.

Rising Arab-Kurdish Tensions over Kirkuk Will Complicate U.S. Withdrawal from Iraq

By Ramzy Mardini
February 25, 2009
Terrorism Focus 6 (6)

Kurdish suspicions of Iraq's central government have reignited after a January 22, 2009-decision by Baghdad to deploy the Iraq Army's 12th Division north towards the disputed oil-rich city of Kirkuk. This development, coupled with U.S. military plans to gradually disengage from Iraq, had led then Kurdistan Regional Government (KRG) Prime Minister Nechirvan Barzani to declare that U.S. President Barack Obama "has said more than once that they will withdraw in a responsible manner from Iraq...What we understand by a responsible withdrawal is that the United States resolves the problems outstanding in Iraq [before leaving]" (AFP, February 18, 2009). As the U.S. military relinquishes its security role to the Iraq Army, unresolved political issues are likely to exacerbate tensions between Iraq's central government and the KRG, complicating American plans to withdraw and leave behind a stable and secured country.

VOLATILE LANDSCAPE

Since 2003, four independently motivated forms of violence have defined Iraq's security environment: the anti-Coalition insurgency, terrorism, sectarianism, and Shi'a-on-Shi'a violence. As of 2009, the threat posed by these four fronts has been dramatically alleviated due to the formation of the Sunni Awakening councils, Muqtada al-Sadr's self-imposed militia ceasefire, and the U.S. adoption of a counterinsurgency strategy of clearing and holding territory. Iraqi Prime Minister Nouri al-Maliki has taken advantage of the improved security regime to consolidate and centralize his power. However, al-Maliki's efforts have hastened a new form of instability many have characterized as inevitable, an instability that has emerged at the intersection of differing strategic interests held by Iraq's two formal governmental institutions: the KRG and the national government in Baghdad.

There are five political issues that characterize the KRG-Baghdad rift:

1. Kurdish foreign oil contracts
2. Redistribution of oil revenues
3. The role and size of the *Peshmerga* (Kurdish militia) forces
4. The growing debate over centralization and federalism
5. Article 140 of the Iraqi constitution dealing with disputed territories

In November 2008, five committees consisting of members from the Patriotic Union of Kurdistan (PUK), Kurdistan Democratic Party (KDP), Islamic Supreme Council of Iraq (ISCI), Prime Minister al-Maliki's Da'awa Party, and the Iraqi Islamic Party (IIP) were formed to tackle most of these unresolved issues. Though progress seems somewhat fruitful when dealing with differences on the gas and oil laws, progress on Article 140 seemed to be gaining no traction.

Article 140 is the most contentious issue behind the rising tensions. It refers to a constitutional provision that sets forth a framework – normalization, census, and referendum – for dealing with territories disputed between the KRG and national government. Its initial implementation deadline of December 2007 was not met by al-Maliki, which has frustrated the Kurds. During the former Ba'athist regime, the government executed an "Arabization" campaign in Kurdish territories, expelling Kurdish families from their homes while providing financial incentives for Arab families to replace them.

Today, Article 140 represents a symbolic justice to many Kurds who call for a reversal of the Arabization campaign. Though Kirkuk is the only territory constitutionally stated in Article 140, it is believed that 30 to 40 other areas are considered "disputed territories" by the Kurds in northern Iraq. With an ethnically mixed population of Kurds, Turkmen, Arabs, and Christians, the Kirkuk region holds 13 percent of Iraq's known oil reserves (*Middle East Times*, February 18, 2009). Turkey, Iran, Syria, and Arabs in Iraq believe that the Kurdish acquisition of Kirkuk will sustain the economic base for a future declaration of statehood, and fear that it may provoke their oppressed Kurdish populations to secede as well.

During a November 20, 2008 press conference, al-Maliki claimed that the Iraqi constitution was put together too hastily and supported amending the governmental provision for federalism. Al-Maliki openly called for greater centralization and for more powers to be allocated to Baghdad. The KRG immediately condemned this idea, warning that the Prime Minister planned to suspend the constitution. Al-Maliki's remarks led the Director of Kurdish Intelligence, Masrour Barzani, to make an early January 2009 visit to the U.S. Department of Defense. Barzani told his American hosts that the Kurds planned to fight any changes to the country's constitution, pointing to the implementation of Article 140 as a critical solution to Iraq's political problems (*Kurdish Globe*, January 9, 2009). Today, many Kurds fear that al-Maliki will use his upgraded political clout to call for a stronger central government, which Kurds fear would undermine Kurdish regional autonomy and any hopes of Article 140's implementation.

Regarding the Iraq Army's January 2009 military deployment around Kirkuk, *Peshmerga* leader Mustafa Chawrash said, "The movement of the division is not normal and it is a planned agenda" (UPI, January 22, 2009). The army intends to create "a military belt" encircling the city, constraining contact with the Kurdistan provinces of Sulaymaniyah and Arbil and reducing the presence of Kurdish forces in Kirkuk (*Kurdish Globe*, January 22, 2009). Acording to Chawrash, the commander of the Iraqi 12th Division is General Abdul-Ameer Ridha, an ex-Ba'athist who led the same division against the Kurds during the Saddam Hussein regime. The U.S. military imprisoned him for four months before he returned to his post. The division consists of about 9,000 soldiers – 70 percent Arab, 20 percent Kurdish, and 10 percent Turkmen. The Kurdish press claims some Kurdish officers from the 12th Division, like the 9th Brigade and 2nd Battalion commanders, were transferred from Kirkuk to Tikrit city and replaced by Arab and Turkmen officers (*Kurdish Globe*, January 22, 2009).

VOLATILE LANDSCAPE

In December 2008, then-President George W. Bush signed a Status of Forces Agreement (SOFA) with Prime Minister al-Maliki, creating a legal framework for a continued U.S. presence in Iraq. In effect since January 1, 2009, the SOFA requires U.S. forces to pull out of Iraqi cities by July 2009, with complete withdrawal from the country by the end of 2011. Many Kurds are uneasy about the prospects of the American safety-net disappearing. This fear is in large part inspired by al-Maliki's use of the Iraq Army for political ends. Last summer, under the pretext of Operation *Bashaer al-Kheir* – a military campaign directed towards militias and terrorists in Diyala province – al-Maliki ordered the Iraqi Army to invade Khanaqin (See *Terrorism Focus*, September 18, 2008). An oil-rich city, Khanaqin is a disputed territory under Article 140. Many Kurds found this military decision provocative and dangerous since Kurdish *Peshmerga* soldiers had occupied the area since 2005.

Dangerous rhetoric has also accompanied the expected American withdrawal and al-Maliki's use of the military (*Azzaman* [Baghdad], December 2, 2008). In early 2009, then Kurdistan Prime Minister Nechirvan Barzani suggested the possibility of an Arab-Kurdish civil war if Article 140 was not implemented (*Middle East Times*, February 18, 2009). Kamal Kirkuki, the KRG Deputy Speaker, went so far as to call al-Maliki "a danger to Iraq and to democracy; he is a second Saddam" (*Asharq al-Awsat,* February 19, 2009). The growing Arab-Kurdish divide is also intensifying on the basis of a classical security dilemma: as a power vacuum develops in accordance with U.S. disengagement, both sides will unilaterally attempt to fill power gaps because neither side can afford to trust that the other's future behavior will be benign. As a senior Kurdish official put it while speaking on condition of anonymity, "Kurds have made a judgment that he [al-Maliki] cannot be trusted and that's the worst part of this-it's not about the technicalities of oil law and this and that-this issue of trust was shattered" (*Christian Science Monitor*, December 11, 2008).

While the Obama administration seeks to disengage from Iraq, the transition of power is likely to increase tensions between Baghdad and the KRG as factions compete to out-leverage one another. Al-Maliki's consolidation of power and 2009 provincial electoral gains have lessened his dependence on the PUK, KDP, and ISCI - the only three factions that once saved his government from collapsing in August 2007. This may provoke a realignment of power amongst Iraq's domestic players. The surprising performance of former Prime Minister Ayad Allawi in the January 2009 provincial elections will provide an adequate challenge to al-Maliki in national elections later this year. This circumstance may lead the PUK, KDP, and ISCI to form a common alliance to save Iraqi federalism. Conversely, strong nationalists, like Shi'a firebrand cleric Muqtada al-Sadr and Sunni Arab tribesmen, may adhere to an alliance of convenience with al-Maliki when concerning the debate on federalism and Article 140.

Challenges to U.S. Proposal to Pacify Northern Iraq May Lead to Extended American Military Presence

By Ramzy Mardini
October 23, 2009
Terrorism Monitor 7 (31)

As the U.S. military prepares for rapid disengagement from Iraq following the parliamentary election held in March 2010, growing Arab-Kurdish tensions in northern Iraq over the ownership of "disputed territories" are emerging as the main threat to Iraqi stability. In response to rising violence and high-profile insurgent attacks in Ninawa province, U.S. General Raymond Odierno had announced an initiative to facilitate Arab-Kurdish cooperation. But as the election approaches, his proposal is facing political and public opposition, as well as practical challenges that complicate U.S. plans to reduce ethnic tensions ahead of the scheduled withdrawal of all U.S. combat forces in August 2010.

At one of the fault-lines of the Arab-Kurdish conflict in northern Iraq is Mosul – Iraq's second largest city and the capital of Ninawa province. Mosul is often characterized as an ethnic tinderbox, with its population consisting of 70% Sunni Arabs and 25% Kurds; the remaining residents include Arab Shi'a, Turcomans, Yezidis, and Christians. Home to a predominately Sunni population and well known as a former Ba'athist stronghold near the Syrian border, Mosul is an ideal locale for active insurgent support and recruitment. According to one report, as many as 300,000 inhabitants of the city offered to contribute to Ba'athist military, security, and intelligence efforts before Operation Iraqi Freedom [1].

Though Iraq witnessed overall improvements in security after the U.S. military adopted a population-centric counterinsurgency strategy from 2007-2009, the Mosul area continued to witness a high level of casualties. In January 2008, Iraqi Prime Minister Nouri al-Maliki deployed the Iraq Army towards Mosul in what was intended to be a "decisive" battle against the remnants of al-Qaeda in Iraq (AQI). But after multiple operations by the Iraqi Security Forces (ISF) to uproot insurgent strongholds, AQI and affiliated terrorist groups such as the Islamic State of Iraq still have the capacity to carry out high-profile attacks throughout the province. By March 2008, the chief of special operations and intelligence information for Multi-National Force–Iraq would call Mosul the "strategic center of gravity" for AQI (American Forces Press Service, March 4, 2008).

According to the U.S. military, insurgents are now exploiting the Arab-Kurdish rift in Ninawa in the hopes of inciting sectarian violence and destabilizing the political process. In late July 2009, Odierno described the ethnic conflict in the north as the "No. 1 driver of instability" in Iraq (AP, July 29, 2009). The January 2009 provincial elections had shifted the balance of power within the Ninawa provincial government away from the Kurds to the majority Sunni Arabs. The newly elected Sunni Arab governor Atheel al-Nujaifi insists on retaining full sovereignty over all of Ninawa, explicitly demanding that all *Peshmerga* (Kurdish militia) forces yield their security profile to the ISF and exit the province:

> *The existence of disputed areas in the province does not imply that the Kurdish Region can put them under its control until a resolution is reached. These areas should be under one authority, that of Ninawa Province, which is controlled by the central authority in the capital city of Baghdad (Niqash, February 24, 2009).*

In August 2009, the Kurdistan Regional Government (KRG) stated that al-Nujaifi was responsible for the recent deaths of 2,000 Kurds, claiming the new Arab leadership was "adopting a policy of national, sectarian, and religious cleansing in Ninawa." (*Aswat al-Iraq*, August 14, 2009). The KRG argues that *Peshmerga* forces in Ninawa are necessary to protect Kurdish inhabitants in "disputed territories" under the provisions of Article 140 of the Iraq Constitution. Devised to confront the "Arabization" campaigns of northern Iraq carried out by previous Ba'athist regimes, Article 140 calls for a referendum to determine whether the area under dispute will remain under the authority of the national government or the KRG. The al-Maliki government has purposefully delayed its implementation, leading Kurds to view Baghdad with suspicion.

On August 17, 2009, General Odierno announced plans for a new security framework intended to pacify the growing sectarian divide in northern Iraq: "What we have is al-Qaeda exploiting this fissure between Arabs and Kurds in Nineveh [Ninawa]...and what we're trying to do is close that fissure" (*Los Angeles*

Times, August 18, 2009). The proposed security arrangement calls for the formation of a tripartite force – consisting of U.S., Iraqi, and *Peshmerga* soldiers – to patrol the "disputed territories." The forces would begin deployment in Ninawa and extend to Kirkuk and Diyala province. Though the oil-rich city of Kirkuk is the cornerstone and the only constitutionally defined territory of Article 140. But Kurds also lay claim to 30-40 other disputed territories in northern Iraq (*Kurdish Globe*, December 4, 2008).

The joint military patrols would have two primary goals:

1. To serve as a "confidence building measure" for the *Peshmerga* and ISF
2. To prevent insurgents from exploiting the issue of "disputed territories" (*Asharq al-Awsat*, August 19, 2009).

By working in unison to protect the local population alongside U.S. forces, the initiative intends to reduce the insecurity and build upon trusting military relationships. In addition, the security arrangement would allow for the return of U.S. combat forces in urban areas where insurgents have successfully carried out high-profile operations.

Long-term political support for the proposal is mixed and uncertain, and has led Odierno to claim nearly two months after the initiative's announcement in August 2009: "we still have some ways to go" (Reuters, October 5, 2009). Key players have agreed on joint patrols in principle in Ninawa alone. Although Odierno received initial encouragement from al-Maliki and KRG President Masoud Barzani, growing political opposition will likely complicated the ongoing patrols after the parliamentary election in March 2010. While the KRG and Ninawa's Kurdish Fraternal List endorsed the proposal, al-Nujaifi and his ruling Sunni Arab al-Hadbaa coalition in the provincial government are opposed to the scheme, claiming that only the ISF can legitimately be deployed in the areas under dispute. Kurdish support for the initiative is based on the U.S. military becoming directly involved in resolving Article 140. Besides a variety of political opposition, numerous demonstrations against the proposal have emerged throughout northern Iraq amongst Sunni Arabs and Turcoman residents (*Aswat al-Iraq*, September 16, 2009; *Azzaman* [Baghdad], October 1, 2009; September 8, 2009).

In the short-term, the Odierno initiative will likely limit the escalation between Iraqi and *Peshmerga* forces. The return of the U.S. military to the urban combat theater after leaving Iraqi cities on June 30, 2009 is expected to facilitate cooperation and provide a credible arbiter, in effect reducing the feelings of insecurity between the contending factions. However, the proposal faces an array of challenges that complicate its effective implementation and prospects for long-term success. Moreover, opposition, both political and public, and lack of interest towards reducing ethnic tensions may well persist after the parliamentary election.

The Odierno initiative is also unlikely to solidify any significant level of mutual trust between Iraqi and Kurdish commanders that would persist in practice after the exiting of U.S. forces. This is to be expected for two reasons. First, the explicit withdrawal deadlines stipulated in the Status of Forces Agreement (SOFA) render such a task problematic. Assurances of benign intentions are unlikely to establish trust given the current timetable and disengaging position that the U.S. military occupies. Second, and more importantly, the dispute over territorial ownership is defined in zero-sum terms by both parties, likely eroding in the long-term any level of mutual confidence that had been achieved by the Odierno proposal.

As President Barack Obama seeks to disengage all U.S. combat forces from Iraq by August 2010, unresolved territorial disputes may force a reevaluation of that policy and a renegotiation of the SOFA to allow for a modified U.S. military posture geared towards preventing an Arab-Kurdish civil war.

Notes

1. Eric Hamilton, "The Fight for Mosul," Institute for the Study of War, April 2008.

Iraq's Security is Kurdistan's Security: An Interview with KRG Intelligence Chief Masrour Barzani

By Wladimir van Wilgenburg
January 7, 2010
Terrorism Monitor 8 (1)

According to Masrour Barzani, director of the *Ajansi Parastini Asayishi Heremi Kurdistan* (Kurdistan Region Security Protection Agency) of northern Iraq, Kurdish security agencies have the legal right to operate outside of the borders of the three provinces of the Kurdistan region. Barzani is the son of the current president of the Kurdistan Regional Government (KRG), Masoud

Barzani.

Barzani is also a leading member of the ruling Kurdistan Democratic Party (KDP), which established the *Parastin* ("Protection") agency in the late 1960s as the intelligence arm of the KDP. Barzani is also director of the *Parastin*, which became a legal institution in 2004 and focuses on intelligence gathering, while the KRG's *Asayish* counterterrorism and internal security directorate has executive power and carries out operations against security threats. After 9/11, the KRG established an umbrella organization that coordinates between the security and intelligence bodies of the KDP and the *Dazgay Zanyari* ("Information Agency") of the Patriotic Union of Kurdistan (PUK), the KDP's onetime rival and current partner, now led by Iraqi President Jalal al-Talabani.

JF: Why is Iraq's Kurdistan region so safe? You can go out late at night here, while the Kurdistan region borders with dangerous areas like Mosul, Kirkuk and the Sunni triangle.

MB: This is a collective work of all people involved in providing security for this area. But the main reason is the culture of our people and our region. The people in the Kurdistan region do not support radicals or extremism. There is very good cooperation between our agency and our people. The support we get from our people is the key.

[There is also] the good system and mechanism that we have put in place, so that all organizations that are working in this field are closely coordinating and have joint centers to share information and to perform according to different situations that come up and to respond and face the challenges that we have.

JF: The Kurdistan region borders Kirkuk and Mosul. Some say the Sunni Arabs have grievances against the Kurds. Do you have a policy of accommodation towards the Arabs?

MB: This is a political decision. The Kurdish leadership has been trying tirelessly and will [continue to] try to make sure that this conflict will never become an ethnic problem between the Arabs and the Kurds. After 1991, there were more than 70,000 Iraqi troops that surrendered to the Kurdish forces, but the Kurds did not [take] revenge despite the fact that the wounds of the chemical bombardments and Anfal campaign were still fresh in the Kurdish mind [1].

Secondly, there was a major drought here and in the rest of the country and many Arab tribes asked for Kurdish support. President [Masoud] Barzani called on the Kurdish leaders and requested that if Arabs want to come, they should make a good gesture and open our land to them.

The third instance was in 2003, after the fall of the Saddam regime, [when] the Kurds were the only organized people with the most power at hand; they could really do much more [politically] than they did. They left all disputed, outstanding issues to the political process and to the Iraqi government to solve this problem, rather than taking over. The Kurds showed that they were here to create peace, harmony with other components in Iraq.

That is the intention of the Kurdish leadership and what our agency is also advocating. We are not there to do any harm to anyone based on their ethnic backgrounds. Our mission and duty is to fight terrorists. If someone happens to be a terrorist, they are treated as terrorists, not because of their religious or ethnic background.

JF: In the last elections in January 2009 the Sunni Arab list al-Hadbaa won the majority in Ninawa Province. Is this a threat to Kurdish security?

MB: When al-Hadbaa won the majority in the last provincial election, they decided not to include any Kurdish representatives that had won votes in their districts [2]. It was the decision of al-Hadbaa that the Kurds should not be part of the Mosul government. They decided to boycott the Kurdish representatives in their own local government. The Kurdish reaction was not to participate if they are not included in the government. It was their choice.

The Kurds have not been complaining much. Despite atrocities and allegations and complaints against the Kurds, the Kurds have not been so vocal and bold, complaining about their situation. This is not widely reported in the international community, but the truth is that Kurds are still victims of ethnic cleansing in Mosul and many of the disputed territories where the Kurds are not well protected.

JF: Is this one of the reasons you also operate outside of the Kurdistan region, because of the huge attacks against Kurds in Ninawa, while the Iraqi government does not want you to operate in the disputed regions?

MB: There is not a clear indication of who should run those areas in the disputed regions, because the fate of those areas is not yet clear. So we have to expedite the process of implementing Article 140 to determine who will be responsible for the security and the political affairs of those areas [3]. For as long as these areas remain in ambiguity, there will be a problem or challenges [over] who controls these areas.

In the areas that are predominantly Kurdish, the Kurdish security forces and Kurdish administration have the right to protect their constituencies and Kurdish populations from the threats we have witnessed [bomb attacks against Kurds]. In those areas, we have tried and have expressed our willingness to closely coordinate and cooperate with other legal institutions in those areas, namely our Iraqi military, security or police and the Coalition forces, for providing security. So it is a joint effort to protect those people in these disputed territories. More recently there have been attempts to form joint committees.

JF: A *New York Times* editorial says Kurdish troops should be reintegrated into the Iraqi army, while Kurdish President Barzani has called for a unified Kurdish army [4]. The United States is also trying to integrate the Kurds into the Iraqi security apparatus. How do you see this?

MB: Most of that stems from misunderstanding the Iraqi constitution or misreading it. The President never said he is going to create an army. He said he is going to reintegrate the armed forces of the Kurdistan region rather than having different groups [with] their own forces. That is his idea of creating the unified armed forces of the Kurdistan region. That does not mean it will be an army. Iraq will have one army. The Kurds were the very first ones who formed the core of the Iraqi military when nobody was willing to become an Iraqi soldier. Some of the *Peshmerga* [Kurdish militias] already joined the Iraqi army. If there is a need to reintegrate more troops, then obviously this is something which will happen.

Now when you look inside the security of Kurdistan, according to the Iraqi constitution, Kurdistan has the right to be responsible for the internal security of Kurdistan. It is the responsibility of the Kurdistan region to provide that security. Kurdistan is part of Iraq, so if we have security [forces] operating in the Kurdistan region or other parts of Iraq, that is security operating in Iraq collectively.

Once Kurdistan is secure and you have security forces operating in Kurdistan, they should be included in the overall defense policy of Iraq because Kurdistan cannot be seen as a separate entity—it is part of Iraq in terms of rights and duties. Protection of Kurdistan in this region is therefore protection of a part of Iraq. For as long as Iraq is a united country, obviously this is the mission of all of us to protect the country in the best possible way we can. When you look at the defense policy of Iraq, there is a budget that is supposed to be spent on defense, which is distributed from the overall budget. So this also should include the Kurdistan region, but unfortunately, until now the Kurdistan region has been deprived of this budget.

JF: The White House declared it would support Article 140 and Article 142 (on constitutional amendments) of the Iraqi constitution. Some say it is a clear signal of U.S. support for the Kurdish position on Kirkuk. But on the other hand, you have people saying that President Obama wants a special status for Kirkuk.

MB: Well, I am not in the position to be speaking on behalf of the Americans, but they tell you what is right. Iraq has a constitution; this constitution determines which way we should move to solve outstanding issues with the federal government. The best solution for the disputed territories is what the Iraqi constitution laid down through Article 140; it is very clear. The constitution should be the only way forward to solve those outstanding issues.

Every other article, including article 142, whatever is in the constitution, we have accepted that constitution. Most Iraqis, 80% of the Iraqis voted for that constitution. So we cannot be selective in picking one article or ignoring another.

There is a mechanism in the Iraqi constitution on how the amendments should be made. As long as we are committed to protecting and implementing the constitution, there should be no problems. The problems arise when there are alternative solutions to the constitution that have been pushed from time to time. These types of efforts are complicating the issue and they are contrary to the principles of democracy. This is running away from the principles of the constitution. As long as the constitution is the arbitrator, I do not think anybody would have any problems with it.

JF: So in general, you are saying we should support the Iraqi constitution, while the New York Times says that the United States should not support Article 140, because the Kurds will use Kirkuk as a stepping-stone for independence [5].

MB: My question to them: Do you want democracy or do you insist that the Kurds should never get Kirkuk? My question to those people who wrote that article is this, are you against the Kurds in Kirkuk? What you are saying indicates that although there is a democratic process and the Kurds will probably win, we should not let them win. This is against democracy; this is hypocrisy… They have to make up their mind, do they believe in democracy or not?

And why it is perceived that Article 140 is pro-Kurdish, who knows? Is there any indication in Article 140 that favors the Kurds? No. Article 140 asks for normalization of the situation, which means undoing the injustice to the people in Kirkuk. Conducting the referendum means letting the people of Kirkuk make the decision of where they want to be in the end; whether part of the Kurdistan region or not, either way it will still be part of Iraq.

Why is there so much sensitivity over why Kirkuk should not be part of the Kurdistan region? Is it a separate state? Is it different? No. They have to understand that Iraq, which includes Kurdistan, is one country. Kirkuk being [part of the Kurdistan region] or not, it would not make a difference. Kirkuk would still be part of Iraq. I am calling upon the conscience of the international community to make a judgment. OK, we have a democratic process and now they say you cannot apply the democratic process to this problem because they do not like the results beforehand.

JF: The conclusion of some foreign analysts is that if Kirkuk becomes part of the Kurdistan region, Iraq could fall apart.

MB: OK, can you make important decisions based on assumptions? Then how can they give themselves the right to make such important decisions based on assumptions, but they will deprive or prevent the Kurds or forbid the Kurds to make similar assumptions. The Kurds will also assume that they do not want a solution, because they have in mind to once again overrun the Kurds or to repeat the Anfal operations [or] repeat chemical bombardments.

JF: Human Rights Watch says Kurdish security agencies mistreat minorities and Christians in Mosul, while the Christians support the Kurds in general. What's your response to this?

MB: We say, let the facts speak. Our counterargument is: the majority of the Yezidis, Shabaks, Christians and Turkmen [ethnic and religious minorities] have voted for the Kurdistan list in the Kurdistan region, in Kirkuk and in Mosul. So, I do not credit these critics, who are criticizing and accusing the Kurds of mistreatment.

OK, here is a question to them: If Kurdistan is so bad, why do so many Arabs, Christians, Turkmen, Shabak and Yezidis who are fleeing those areas which are known for violence [come] to Kurdistan to seek protection, security and stability? We have the facts to speak. Everybody can say what they want, but they have very little to prove. We have much [evidence] to prove [our case] and many facts on the ground. We are not in need of talking so much.

Notes

1. Anfal was the codename of the brutal and repressive campaign carried out against the Kurds of northern Iraq by forces of Saddam Hussein between 1986 and 1989.
2. Al-Hadbaa is a Sunni Arab political party formed to reduce Kurdish influence in the contested province of Ninawa.
3. Article 140 of the Iraq Constitution, related to the means of determining the status of contested areas of the Ninawa, Diyala, Kirkuk and Salah al-Din governorates. Article 140 also seeks to normalize the situation in these areas by undoing the administrative changes and demographic policies introduced by Saddam Hussein.
4. "Iraq, the Kurds and the Americans," *New York Times*, December 17, 2009
5. Kirkuk has significant oil reserves that could provide the financial basis of an independent Kurdish state.

The Future of Baghdad-Arbil Relations: Remaining Conflicts of Interests

By David Romano
February 24, 2010
Terrorism Monitor 8 (8)

In his February 2, 2010 "Annual Threat Assessment of the U.S. Intelligence Community," Director of National Intelligence Dennis Blair predicts that Iraq will continue making progress, although "...this forecast is dependent on the next government's effective management of Arab-Kurd tensions, continued progress in integrating the Sunni Arabs into the political process, and the ability of the ISF to combat threats to the state." The report adds that, "Arab-Kurd tensions have potential to derail Iraq's generally positive security trajectory, including triggering conflict among Iraq's ethno-sectarian groups. Many of the drivers of Arab-Kurd tensions—disputed territories, revenue sharing and control of oil resources, and integration of *Peshmerga* forces--still need to be worked out, and miscalculations or misperceptions on either side risk an inadvertent escalation of violence. US involvement—both diplomatic and military—will remain critical in defusing crises in this sphere." U.S. General Raymond Odierno echoed Blair's concerns in July 2009, telling reporters that, "while violence continues to decline overall, tensions between Iraqi Kurds and Arabs over boundaries and oil revenues represent the biggest threat to the country's stability" (*al- Arabiya*, July 29, 2009).

In 2008 and 2009, Kurdish relations with Baghdad came dangerously close to exploding into open conflict on a number of occasions, as Prime Minister Nouri al-Maliki's increasingly "strong central government" Iraqi nationalist stance threatened the Kurdish preference for autonomy and decentralization (see *Terrorism Focus*, February 19, 2009). American intervention and mediation of a number of confrontations, including two incidents where Kurdish *Peshmerga* and Iraqi Army Arab units appeared ready to begin shooting at each other, kept tensions under control (*Middle East Report*, October 1, 2009). Given that the disputes between Baghdad and Arbil remain unresolved, a looming withdrawal of U.S. forces has increased fears of what may occur in the absence of mediators. In an attempt to foster cooperation and better relations between Kurdish forces and Arab Iraqi Army troops, U.S. forces recently began managing shared checkpoints with both forces along the Kurdish region's border (*New York Times*, January 26, 2010).

During his January 2010 visit to the United States, Kurdistan Regional Government (KRG) President Masoud Barzani therefore stressed the importance of "strategic long term US engagement with Iraq and the Kurdistan Region" (KRG.org, January 25, 2010). In his January 25, 2010 meeting with U.S. President Barack Obama, he "...affirmed the necessity for Iraq's constitution to be the arbiter of internal disputes, and informed President Obama that lasting stability in Iraq can be attained if and when Iraqis abide by, and implement, all the articles of the country's constitution" (KRG.org, January 25, 2010).

Implementing and abiding by all articles of the 2005 Constitution is the Kurdish way of insisting that 1) the Kurdish region gets the opportunity to annex some heavily Kurdish and disputed territories south of its current boundaries; 2) the KRG be allowed to sign its own oil contracts and receive a proportional share of national Iraqi oil revenues; and 3) that the Kurdistan region's autonomy and Iraq's very decentralized federal structure be maintained. These three issues lie at the center of unresolved disputes between Arbil and Baghdad.

According to Article 140 of the Constitution, Kirkuk and other disputed territories were to have their demographics "normalized" (meaning the return of mostly Kurdish residents expelled under Ba'athist "Arabization" campaigns and the departure of Arab settlers), a census was to be conducted in these territories, and Kirkuk and possibly other disputed territories just south of the current KRG borders were to hold a referendum by December 31, 2007 to decide whether to become part of the Kurdistan Autonomous Region. Although normalization has been partially accomplished, parties in Baghdad managed to continually postpone the census and referendum.

The Iraq Constitution likewise grants governorates and autonomous regions all powers not explicitly reserved for the federal government in Baghdad. The exploitation of existing oil fields is regarded as a right of the central government, with resulting revenues to be divided proportionally amongst all Iraqis (after deduction of operating expenses and a percentage of revenues for federal projects and expenses). The Kurds claim the right to manage oil fields they discovered or will discover themselves, however. This position has not changed since KRG Natural Resources Minister Ashti Hawrami told a U.S. newspaper in 2006 that, "In management of new fields, we are adamant that we will not share with the federal government. Planning, coordination – no problem. But who has the right to write contracts? We can consult with the center, but the ultimate authority lies with the Kurds" (*USA Today*, November 6, 2006). Although neither Baghdad nor the KRG disputes the principle of sharing oil revenues amongst all Iraqis, management and control of oil production sites in the country offers an important source of power and leverage for both parties. Kurds would especially like such control in order to make sure that Baghdad delivers their promised share of oil revenues. Arab parties in the rest of Iraq, however, want to maintain federal control of the oil industry for both the leverage this will provide them and in order to make sure that the Kurds do not eventually secede, possibly taking oil-rich Kirkuk with them.

Most non-Kurdish parties, with the significant exception of the Shi'a Islamic Supreme Council of Iraq, also fear that the extent of decentralization in the 2005 Constitution increases the chance of Kurdish secession. Kurds in turn insist that such decentralization is precisely what they need to remain within Iraq, and serves as the best guarantee against a risky bid for an independent Kurdish state. Masoud Barzani and other leaders repeatedly warn that a failure to respect the 2005 Constitution will remove any obligation the Kurds may have to remain part of Iraq: "We must understand that everything we accepted was because of the Constitution. When we accepted to remain within Iraq and contribute to the political process, we did that with the view that we will have a constitution" (*Asharq al-Awsat*, March 14, 2009).

The Kurds therefore attached great importance to a December 7, 2009 White House statement expressing support for Article 140 of the Iraq Constitution (the article that addresses Kirkuk and other disputed territories). Kurdish media did not seem to pay as much attention to the full text of the White House statement, however, which also included a reference to Article 142 of the Constitution: "The United States reiterates its strong support for the Iraqi people and their elected government, and reaffirms its respect for the Iraqi constitution, including Article 140, which addresses the dispute over Kirkuk and other disputed internal borders, and Article 142, which addresses the process for constitutional amendments." Since Article 142 elaborates the process by which the other elements of the Constitution can be changed, including Article 140 and the various provisions for extensive autonomous Kurdish rights, the American position remained ambiguous. Nouri al-Maliki, most of the Sunni Arab parties and several of the Shi'a Arab blocs would like to utilize Article 142 precisely in order to reverse what they view as excessively "pro-Kurdish" aspects of the Constitution.

A statement by U.S. Secretary of Defense Robert Gates made shortly after the White House one appears to take a less ambiguous and more pro-KRG position. KRG official media reported that during his visit to Arbil, Gates stated that:

> *"We have made three commitments:*
> *1. To use our influence to ensure that the outstanding disputes between the KRG and the Iraqi Government, including the Kirkuk dispute and other disputed areas and the sharing of oil revenues, are resolved based on the Iraqi Constitution and Article 140.*

2. We will continue with our military efforts with the Peshmerga forces as well as with the Iraqi Army and security forces within the framework of our joint security architecture.
3. We will offer our support and assistance for a census to be conducted in Iraq next year."

Although the statement was quoted only by Kurdish sources (KRG.org, December 11, 2009) and not published by any U.S. Government sources, if accurate it would indicate a more substantive U.S. position on the lingering disputes between the KRG and Baghdad. In addition to supporting the provisions of Article 140, American support for an Iraqi census in 2010 fulfills a long held Kurdish demand. Such a census will likely show a Kurdish majority in Kirkuk province as well as many of the territories currently disputed between the KRG and Baghdad, which will bolster Kurdish demands to uphold the other key element of Article 140 – referendum(s) to determine if the people of these regions wish to join the Kurdistan. While the census seems necessary given Constitutional requirements, grossly varying estimates of various sectarian groups' size and recent disputes about numbers of Iraqi parliamentary seats to be distributed in future elections, the results of the census will almost certainly be contested and could lead to more conflict.

Much will also depend on the results of the upcoming March 2010 parliamentary election. Significant divisions have emerged not only amongst Sunni and Shi'a political blocs, but also among the Kurds – with Kurdish Islamist parties as well as the new Gorran Party (a splinter that broke away from Jalal al-Talabani's Patriotic Union of Kurdistan) promising to run separately from the previously hegemonic Kurdish List. If more statewide political alliances across sectarian lines emerge after the elections, the dialectic of Kurdish-Arab disputes might recede a little as well. Alternately, Kurdish parties in stiffer competition with each other may feel less able to compromise on core issues like Kirkuk and control of oil resources in Kurdistan.

Part III

Iraq since the June 30, 2009 Withdrawal

Chapter 7

A Volatile Security Environment

Latest Surge of Violence in Iraq Tests al-Maliki's Government

By Babak Rahimi
May 8, 2009
Terrorism Monitor 7 (12)

These are challenging times for Nouri al-Maliki. Despite the victory of his coalition, the *Dawlat al-Qanun* (State of Law) in the 2009 provincial elections, al-Maliki's government is facing major security threats and political unrest that could undermine his political authority before the 2010 parliamentery election.

On the security front, Iraq has seen an outburst of violence with a series of at least 18 attacks in April 2009. The twin bombing in the Shi'a shrine-city of Kazemayn was the deadliest of all, adding 60 people to a death toll of more than 150 in merely a week (al-Jazeera, April 24, 2009; *Etemad*, April 26, 2009). The recent string of attacks is reminiscent of the February 2006 Samarra shrine bombings that unleashed a wave of sectarian hostilities, bringing the country to the brink of civil war. With responsibility for the attacks being claimed by the Islamic State of Iraq – a coalition of Sunni militants with many foreign fighters – it may well be that a new wave of sectarian violence is about to overtake Iraq (al-Arabiya, April 24, 2009).

However, the insurgents' strategy for carrying out the attacks is mostly political rather than sectarian. The violent incidents, mostly targeted at the Shi'a (including a failed attempt to assassinate Grand Ayatollah Ali al-Sistani), have also included attacks on members of the Awakening Council, a coalition of Sunni tribes receiving money from the government for fighting against al-Qaeda insurgents (*Tabnak* [Tehran], April 27, 2009; al-Jazeera, April 7, 2009, April 11, 2009). The Sunni insurgency also continues its assault against U.S. forces, which under the terms of the Status of Forces Agreement (SOFA) are required to withdraw from Iraq by the end of 2011. The first phase of the withdrawal from Iraqi cities is scheduled to be completed by June 30, 2009 (*Tabnak*, April 22,

2009). All in all, the attacks signal an all-out military assault by the insurgency to weaken the state ahead of the U.S. withdrawal.

On the political front, al-Maliki faces two other major challenges. The first is the rise of a loose coalition of pro-federalist and Sunni factions, known as the "153" bloc, which seeks to reverse al-Maliki's political gains in the January provincial elections. The bloc challenges al-Maliki's centralist policies, which according to some, recall the days of Ba'athist rule (*Etemad*, April 21, 2009). The election of the new speaker of parliament Ayad Samarraie, a major figure in the Sunni Iraqi Islamic Party with the backing of the pro-federalist Kurdish and ISCI (Islamic Supreme Council of Iraq) parties underlines the successful coalition-building which the anti-Maliki factions have carried out in recent weeks (*Etemad*, April 21, 2009).

Although much of their success should be credited to al-Maliki's own failure to muster enough support after his provincial election victory, the 153 bloc was primarily formed in response to Baghdad's increasing centralization policies, seen as a major threat by pro-federalist Kurds and the ISCI. The political struggle between the pro-federalist and centralist factions, which includes diverse groups like the secular Iraqiyya and the Shi'a Sadrists, should also be viewed in parallel with al-Maliki's attempt to limit the activities of the Awakening movement by arresting some of its leaders and fighters under the pretext that al-Qaeda has infiltrated the Sunni group (*Azzaman*, April 3, 2009; al-Jazeera, April 6, 2009). Al-Maliki's anti-Awakening strategy has angered many Sunni members of parliament, who see this move as another attempt by the government to monopolize power (*Azzaman*, April 9, 2009).

More important opposition has come from al-Maliki's own Shi'a constituency, groups that see his softer stance on Ba'athism as a sign of appeasement that will allow a revival of Sunni power (*Etemad*, April 21, 2009). Many Shi'a factions objected to al-Maliki's earlier attempts to include the Ba'athists in the national reconciliation project. Even Grand Ayatollah al-Sistani, a major backer of al-Maliki's government, has indirectly criticized the Prime Minister for his failure to denounce Ba'athism (*Tabnak*, March 30, 2009). It is this opposition that has recently forced al-Maliki to shift his position and wage a new set of verbal attacks against the Ba'athists, accusing them of masterminding the latest string of violence (IRNA, April 8, 2009, April 27, 2009).

Finally, there is Washington, where the Obama administration has been less focused on Iraq due to its preoccupation with domestic concerns and an increase in security since late last year. The new administration's perceived lack of involvement in Iraq has opened the political field in Baghdad to new contenders from many sides and factions, who perceive al-Maliki's political power as being in jeopardy with the much anticipated departure of U.S. troops.

One positive observation can be made here. The unfolding political rivalry could open up a new chapter for the post-Ba'athist era – the formation of an autonomous Iraqi government that would need to undergo self-adjustment through internal conflict and cross-sectarian alliances between factions seeking to gain influence over the constituencies they represent. As a transitional stage in Iraq's democratization (and a move away from sectarian politics), the latest political turmoil, therefore, should not be seen as a setback for Iraq, but as progress toward non-sectarian party politics.

The problem of security on the ground, however, could render such a transition incomplete. In the coming months leading to the elections, the key for al-Maliki's regime is to contain the bloodshed by showing the government's military strength against the insurgency while bringing to his side both pro-Awakening Sunni and pro-Sadr Shi'a factions that maintain considerable support in the eastern and south-central provinces. Amidst the unrest on the ground, the anti-Maliki parliamentary factions could continue to keep al-Maliki in check in order to curtail the total centralization of power prompted by an obvious response to concerns over security ahead of the American withdrawal. Of course, the success of such political tactics would depend on whether al-Maliki could maintain reasonable distance from Washington and appear self-reliant to Iraqis, who overwhelmingly support the U.S. withdrawal (al-Jazeera, April 10, 2009).

The Implications of Abdul Aziz al-Hakim's Death for Iraqi Security

By Babak Rahimi
September 10, 2009
Terrorism Monitor 7 (27)

Abdul Aziz al-Hakim, the head of the Supreme Council of Iraq (ISCI), died on August 26, 2009 at a hospital in Tehran, where he had been receiving treatment for lung cancer since May 2007 (Fars News Agency, August 27, 2009; *Kayhan*, August 27, 2009, September 2, 2009). His death came days after the announcement of an electoral alliance led by his party and other Shi'a factions, known as the Iraqi National Alliance (*al-Ittilaf al-Watani al-Iraqi* – INA; the new coalition replaces the United Iraqi Alliance - *al-I'tilaf al-Iraqi al-Muwahhad* - UIA) (*Etemad*, August 24, 2009). The Shi'a-dominated alliance is powered by a renewed ISCI led by the young and untried ISCI deputy leader, Ammar al-Hakim. His skill and experience will be tested as the party attempts to resurrect itself after its defeat in the early 2009 provincial elections (*Tabnak*, August 31, 2009). Most importantly, the new political bloc, which also includes the Sadrists, Fadhila and other smaller Sunni, Turkmen and Christian parties, excludes Prime Minister Nouri al-Maliki's Da'awa Party, whose popular support remains relatively strong, especially in the Sunni provinces, parts of the Shi'a southern regions and in the capital city (*Tabnak*, September 1, 2009; *Etemad*, August 30, 2009).

Amidst these political developments, Iraq continues to face a surge of violence since the June withdrawal of U.S. forces from major cities around the country (*Azzaman*, August 14, 2009; al-Jazeera August 28, 2009). Although still limited in scale in comparison to 2006, the latest outburst of violence raises new concerns about the possible emergence of sectarian conflict exacerbated by ethnic tensions, especially in Kirkuk and Mosul, where Arab nationalists like Prime Minster al-Maliki seek to thwart Kurdish claims over the oil-rich region. With tensions on the rise, the changing balance of power within the Shi'a political scene points to more uncertainty with the approach of next year's general elections.

Hakim's successor, his son Ammar al-Hakim, was recently asked for his views on the increase in violence during an interview with a Spanish daily:

> *We hold Saddam's Ba'ath primarily responsible in such processes and we believe it sent a clear message regarding the invalidity of the alleged resistance to the occupier; this fact makes it imperative for each who bears his weapons to give up, especially with the troops out of the cities now. We know that the main aim [of the insurgents] is to return Iraq to square one, but this cannot be achieved; they want this effort to remove an important card from the political process because it had achieved security in Iraq, but our confidence is in a great God and in the capabilities of our security [services] and the military government (El Mundo, July 1, 2009).*

In reality, al-Hakim's demise has now created a power vacuum that could lead to major changes within Iraqi politics:

• It could provide an opportunity for more radical Shi'a groups like the Sadrists or Hadi al-Amari's Badr Organization to claim power, while more moderate factions (i.e. those without militias) may feel intimidated and marginalized within the new Shi'a-led alliance.

• Within the ISCI, Ammar might merely serve as a figurehead, while the hard-line old guard within the party, led by figures like Bayan Jabr (a former Badr Corps commander), Sheikh Jalauddin Saghir (senior cleric in Baghdad's huge Buratha mosque) and Hadi al-Amari (head of the parliamentary defense and security committee) could take charge of the party, contributing to a sectarian type of politics reminiscent of the volatile early post-war period.

• The greatest impact al-Hakim's death might have is in undermining al-Maliki's influence in the Shi'a electoral landscape, possibly leading to his downfall at the hands of the ISCI, now at the head of the new Iraqi National Alliance.

The main implication of these changes is the possibility of an increase in hard-line Iranian influence led by the Islamic Revolutionary Guard Corps (IRGC), on which the ISCI and Sadrists have become increasingly reliant for financial and military support. This is already evident in Tehran's bold attempt to reconcile the tension between Baghdad and Damascus over regional security. The Iranian diplomatic mission is led by the Iranian ambassador to Iraq, Hussein Kazemi Qomi, a former IRGC officer who maintains close ties with ISCI (Fars News Agency, September 3, 2009). A shift towards more Iranian-leaning Shi'a politics could anger Iraq's Sunnis, especially the nationalists, who might see the changing political landscape as a threat to their interests. Although it remains to be seen whether al-Maliki will eventually join the new INA, Iraq will likely witness more violence ahead of the elections as Baghdad gradually seeks to break away from the sectarian politics represented by Abdul Aziz al-Hakim and his Shi'a federalism.

Iraqi Insurgents Take the Offensive as Parliamentary Elections Approach

By Ramzy Mardini
September 17, 2009
Terrorism Monitor 7 (28)

A VOLATILE SECURITY ENVIRONMENT

Multiple bombings targeting Iraq's governmental ministries just outside central Baghdad's fortified Green Zone on August 19, 2009 left over 120 people killed and over 600 others wounded, marking the single deadliest day in 18 months. The event forced the Iraqi government to reevaluate the country's security sector, as the attacks demonstrated the inadequacies of the Iraqi Security Forces (ISF) and the efficacy insurgents maintain in carrying out high profile and coordinated operations. As the Iraq parliamentary election approaches in March 2010, insurgents and rival political factions will likely mount an aggressive campaign to destabilize the political process and undermine the central government's credibility in pacifying Iraq sans U.S. military presence.

The Instability of the Election Season

Today, Iraqi Prime Minister Nouri al-Maliki's political strategy concerning the parliamentary election is directed towards retaining his post as Prime Minister. His campaign is grounded in two critical goals in the eyes of the Iraqi public: 1) Bringing security and stability to Iraq in order to facilitate economic growth and reconstruction; 2) Solidifying his image as the national leader by achieving Iraq's sovereignty and ending the U.S. military occupation.

For much of al-Maliki's tenure, however, these two goals have been posed in zero-sum terms; security was best achieved when U.S. forces engaged the local population and patrolled Iraqi streets. The security improvement resulting from the Awakening Movement and the implementation of the 2007 U.S. counterinsurgency strategy allowed al-Maliki to consolidate and centralize his authority at the expense of rival factions and former political allies, like firebrand Shi'a cleric Muqtada al-Sadr. Al-Maliki's 2008 demonstration of assertiveness towards his U.S. counterparts by demanding explicit deadlines be stipulated in the Status of Forces Agreement (SOFA) reflected his growing autonomy and influence on the domestic scene. His political rationale for requiring U.S. combat forces to disengage from Iraqi cities only six months after the SOFA was implemented was to demonstrate to the Iraqi public his sovereignty bona fides, effectively broadening his popularity in advance of elections.

But the handover of the urban security profile to the ISF comes at the same time as three political proceedings that carry significant security concerns; the parliamentary elections, a national referendum held the same day on the continued implementation of the SOFA, and the first post-Saddam census. If the

Iraqi people reject the SOFA in the referendum, U.S. forces may be required to leave Iraq a year earlier than the December 2011 deadline currently specified. Political sensitivity and concerns over destabilization have allowed the census to be continually delayed by Baghdad (*Aswat al-Iraq*, August 31, 2009). It is now scheduled to take place after August 2010 – the time when President Barack Obama intends to withdraw all U.S. combat forces. Because of their great potential in shaping the future distribution of power and political structure inside Iraq, all three proceedings will risk the possibility that Iraqi politics may revert back to civil war-politics, when political factions engaged one another via militias.

There are indications that al-Maliki will face-off against the Shi'a political parties in the next round of elections. In the 2005 parliamentary elections, major Shi'a Islamic parties ran on a single powerhouse political list – the United Iraqi Alliance (UIA) – in order to guarantee their dominant position in Iraq's Council of Representatives. On August 24, 2009, in an effort to reconstitute a winning Shi'a coalition for the upcoming election, the Iraqi National Alliance (INA) was announced, consisting of former UIA participants like the Islamic Supreme Council of Iraq (ISCI), the Sadrists, and the Badr Organization, among others (al-Jazeera, August 24, 2009). Al-Maliki and his Da'awa Party have refused to enter into the INA because the alliance refused to guarantee him the office of Prime Minister (Al-Sumaria TV, August 25, 2009). Moreover, ISCI had dominated the former Shi'a bloc while advocating a federal administrative structure, which is now inconsistent with al-Maliki's political agenda for achieving a strong central government. The Prime Minister has decided instead to build a rival political list, consisting of a broad-based national coalition of Sunni nationalists and southern Shi'a tribes.

These conflicting agendas are concerning in that they may lead to Shi'a on Shi'a violence ahead of the election. Instead of the old ISCI-Sadrist rivalry that characterized southern Iraq, members of the INA may attempt to sabotage al-Maliki's political campaign by undermining his ability to provide security. As suggested by the comments of Abu Hamza al-Masri, a member of Muqtada al-Sadr's staff in Basra: "The party and sectarian behavior of al-Maliki has not ended, but on the contrary, has been renewed" (*Niqash*, August 19, 2009).

A VOLATILE SECURITY ENVIRONMENT

The Insurgent Rationale

Before the U.S. military switched from campaigns focusing on territory to a population-protection counterinsurgency strategy, the goal for many insurgents was to hold and defend territory. But the loss of territorial footing for al-Qaeda in Iraq (AQI), Sunni insurgents, and Shi'a militiamen has altered their strategic engagement vis-à-vis their adversaries from a partly defensive posture to a completely offensive posture. Without the option of defense, the battleground for insurgents becomes less of a resistance based on territorial fronts and more of an asymmetrical engagement that is entirely focused on offensive attacks.

Insurgents hope to undermine the Iraqi political process, reconciliation efforts, and trust in government in order to bring about the anarchical conditions necessary for their organizational survival and the achievement of their objectives. Because of their loss of capability and territory, AQI and others are likely to make better use of their existing resources and adopt cautious assessments of their operations.

Moreover, because there is no defensive line to hold, insurgents can now decide on their own schedule when to be active members of the insurgency. This was the case during al-Maliki's spring 2008 Mosul offensive called "Lion's Roar." Many Iraqi military commanders were disappointed with the lack of resistance, as they had hoped for a decisive battle against the remaining remnants of AQI. As one report indicated, "The lack of significant resistance among the hardened fighters who had been operating in Mosul suggested the insurgency was offering Maliki and his American backers a message of their own: We fight on our terms, not yours" (*Azzaman*, June 14, 2009).

With the option of engaging the ISF on an urban battlefield removed, insurgents are forced to operate in a more discrete manner. Political assassinations have remained an efficient tool for them and will likely gain popularity as they adapt their posture in advance of the election (*Azzaman*, June 14, 2009). High-profile bombings are also another tool insurgents may come to rely heavily on in the coming months. This has been the primary strategy executed by AQI insurgents in the Mosul area, as recognized by U.S. Major General Robert Caslen. "They recognize what they need to do is the high profile attacks and go after the local nationals in order to entice the sectarian violence" (VOA, August 11, 2009).

The upcoming election offers a powerful forum where insurgent attacks could provide the greatest political damage to the Iraq government, especially against al-Maliki's prospects for retaining office. With U.S. combat forces now disengaged from ISF missions in Iraq's urban areas, the trust and confidence the Iraqi people have in their security forces will be challenged by insurgents. Al-Maliki was aware of this challenge to his political credibility after the August 19, 2009 bombings, saying: "I would like to assure the Iraqi people that the security forces are still capable of continuing the battle and achieving more victories" (AP, August 22, 2009).

Regional Conflicts of Interest

Another major concern for Iraq in the context of the parliamentary election is the role of the country's neighbors. What happens in Iraq concerns many surrounding political actors, especially when considering the changing dynamics of the regional balance of power. For example, Iraq's maturing military is making advances in its capabilities and weapons systems through the U.S. foreign military sales program. The Strategic Framework Agreement, signed as a separate document alongside the SOFA, fosters a long-term strategic partnership with the United States – effectively nurturing Baghdad as a future power player in the region.

Some nearby states, however, may feel uneasy about Iraq's increasing military capability. Uncertainty prevails in the region over the direction Baghdad is actually heading - federal and democratic or a consolidated central government. Moreover, Sunni Arab leaders are not sure whether a Shi'a Iraq would ally itself with Iran.

Such security concerns give the results of the upcoming Iraqi election a strategic interest for outside states. Neighboring governments have meddled and backed political lists in the past, as was the case in the 2005 parliamentary elections. Iran may now be concerned about al-Maliki's agenda as he plans to achieve a broad-based national coalition with Sunni Arab nationalists at the expense of closer Iranian allies like the ISCI, the Sadrists, and the Badr Organization. Activity inside Iraq by Iran's Islamic Revolutionary Guard Corps appears directed towards ensuring a pro-Iranian Shi'a government in Baghdad.

Recent discoveries of new weapons caches in southern Iraq suggest that Shi'a militias are stockpiling arms in connection with the upcoming parliamentary elections (*Arab Times*, August 31, 2009). Many of the manufacturing dates on the weapons (grenade launchers, silencers, sniper rifles, automatic weapons, and explosives) were as recent as 2008, with Persian inscriptions found on the rockets.

The findings suggest that many of the weapons arrived in Iraq after al-Maliki's spring 2008 crackdown on the Shi'a militias that uprooted al-Sadr's Jaysh al-Mahdi militia from its territorial strongholds. According to Iraqi police, investigations now hint that Shi'a militias opposed to al-Maliki are recruiting fighters to undermine his electoral prospects. As one high-ranking police officer described it, "Their aims are to destroy the image of the prime minister and pull the carpet from under his feet by making it impossible for him to claim he has succeeded in improving security" (Reuters, September 1, 2009).

Surrounding Sunni Arab states may also feel compelled to undermine al-Maliki's electoral advantages ahead of the parliamentary election, as his rhetoric and consolidation of power has been of some concern to them lately. In reacting to an upsurge of violence targeting low-income Shi'a neighborhoods in June 2009, al-Maliki pointed the finger toward Arab governments for fueling the instability: "There are states which are silent on fatwas (Islamic decrees) urging killings and branding others [as] infidels." (*Azzaman*, June 27, 2009). Although al-Maliki did not mention the states he perceived responsible, it is likely his remarks were at least partly directed toward Saudi Arabia.

Suspected involvement of Syrian intelligence officials for the August 19, 2009 bombings in Baghdad has suggested conflicting interests exist between al-Maliki's re-election campaign and some factions in Syria. Iraq believes it has collected evidence that implicates AQI, Syrian intelligence officials and Iraqi Ba'athists based in Syria in the attacks. According to al-Maliki, "Confessions by conductors of this terrorist act revealed that the operation is not internally made but carried out by [foreign] countries" (*Kurdish Globe*, August 29, 2009). Both Damascus and Baghdad have recalled their ambassadors in a dispute over the bombings.

Conclusion

Regardless of the security gains made in Iraq, the country is still riddled with poor institutions, ethnic and tribal rivalries and an absence of genuine reconciliation efforts. With the gradual disengagement of U.S. combat forces, the ISF will likely be tested on their capability and integrity as a non-sectarian institution that is dedicated to the protection of all Iraqis. The trust and confidence of the Iraqi people in the ISF is essential for continuing a counterinsurgency campaign. Iraqi insurgents and terrorists alike are no longer carrying out operations intended to seize territory inside Iraq. Rather their short-term goals are now concentrated on damaging the central government's credibility, fomenting sectarian strife between the different ethnic segments of society and promoting the perception that the ISF is inadequate to protect Iraqi neighborhoods. If successful, these goals will render any counterinsurgency strategy ineffective, as collaboration and information sharing between the local population and the ISF become increasingly difficult to achieve.

Diplomacy Fails to Defuse Iraqi Anger over Alleged Syrian Role in Baghdad's "Bloody Wednesday"

By Rafid Fadhil Ali
October 23, 2009
Terrorism Monitor 7 (31)

Only 24 hours passed between Syrian President Bashar al-Assad's warm welcome to Iraqi Prime Minister Nouri al-Maliki in the presidential palace in Damascus and the attacks on the government buildings in Baghdad that killed dozens and spoiled the development of fraternal relations between the two countries. On August 19, 2009, six explosions rocked Baghdad, killing 95 people and injuring 563 others. The two largest blasts targeted the Ministry of Foreign Affairs and the Ministry of Finance with truck bombs (AFP, August 19, 2009). The attacks were big even by Iraqi standards and August 19, 2009, "Bloody Wednesday," as it became known, emerged as the bloodiest day recorded in Iraq since the U.S. army pulled out from Iraq's urban areas on June 30, 2009. Shocked by the destruction of his ministry's headquarters and the number of casualties, Iraq's Foreign Minister Hoshyar Zebari accused the Iraqi security forces of colluding with perpetrators (Alarabia.net, August 22, 2009).

The Iraqi government blamed Syria for hosting the Iraqi groups and individuals behind the bombings, though Syria denied responsibility and President Bashar al-Assad described the Iraqi accusations as "immoral" (Syria-news.com, August 31, 2009). A political and diplomatic crisis emerged and the two countries withdrew their ambassadors from each other's capitals (*Al-Quds al-Arabi*, August 26, 2009). Iraq went further and called for an international tribunal to prosecute the perpetrators of the attacks (*Al-Sabah* [Baghdad], August 28, 2009). Prime Minister al-Maliki and Iraqi President Jalal al-Talabani were united in their calls for the United Nations to establish an independent commission to investigate the bombings (AFP, September 22, 2009).

On October 13, 2009, Foreign Minister Zebari announced his government's conclusion that there was no use in pursuing further talks with Syria through the mediation of Turkey and the Arab League. Instead, Zebari intended to form a special committee of ministers under his leadership to prepare a dossier of Iraq's evidence of foreign involvement in Iraqi-based terrorist activities to present to a special UN envoy after his anticipated appointment (*Al-Sharqiyah* [Dubai], October 13, 2009; Republic of Iraq Ministry of Foreign Affairs statement, October 14, 2009).

The sixth annual conference of interior ministers from countries bordering Iraq held in mid-October 2009 also failed to make headway in resolving the crisis in relations, with Iraqi Interior Minister Jawad al-Bolani demanding those in attendance must "criminalize the aggressors" (VOA, October 14, 2009; ChamPress [Damascus], October 13, 2009).

Regional mediation has failed to contain the situation so far, but the real reasons behind the recent tension between Baghdad and Damascus are deeper than one-day events, no matter how bloody.

Who is Sattam Farhan?

On August 23, 2009, General Kassim Ata, the spokesman of Baghdad Operations Command, showed journalists a video of a detainee who admitted to being behind the attacks. The man, who was identified as Wissam Ali Kadhum, said that he received his orders from an exiled Iraqi Ba'athist in Syria, Sattam Farhan. Kadhum said that Farhan was a member of a Syrian-based faction of the Ba'ath party led by General Muhammad Yunis al-Ahmad.

The name Sattam Farhan did not ring a bell for most people. A short while later it turned out that the Iraqi authorities were referring to Sattam al-Gaoud, a well-known businessman in Iraq since the early 1990s. Benefiting from finding ways around the international sanctions that were imposed on Iraq, Sattam emerged as a tycoon in economically-devastated Iraq, building a business empire and even purchasing a football club. Sattam was not known as a senior member of the then-ruling Ba'ath party, but he would not have achieved his prominence without the regime's blessing.

During the first weeks after the fall of Saddam, Sattam al-Gaoud led protests against the U.S. forces in his hometown of Ramadi and in Baghdad. He also founded the National Front of the Masses and Intellectuals of Iraq (NFMII). Sattam, who belonged to a prominent family of the Sunni al-Dulaim tribe, was arrested by the U.S. military in 2003 and remained in custody for more than two years. He was released in early 2006 and left for Jordan but is believed to be living in Syria now. Sattam's NFMII frequently places statements on pro-Ba'ath web sites.

The Islamic State of Iraq Claims Responsibility

A few days after the "Bloody Wednesday" attack, the al-Qaeda affiliated Islamic State of Iraq (ISI) claimed responsibility for the bombings, which they referred to as *Ghazwat al-Aseer* (The Raid of the Prisoner) (Muslim.net, August 25, 2009). Even after the ISI claimed responsibility the Iraqi government not only stuck with its accusations but also became more specific. Al-Maliki said on September 2, 2009: "We gave them [the Syrians] information collected by our security devices about a meeting between members of the Ba'ath party and takfiris [Muslim extremists] attended also by Syrian intelligence officers held in al-Zabadani (a Syrian resort nearby Damascus) on July 30, 2009. Why do they insist on hosting armed organizations and people who are wanted by the Iraqi authorities and Interpol?" (*Aswat al-Iraq*, September 3, 2009).

Syria persistently denied any involvement in the attacks by the Iraqi Ba'athists who live on its soil. "They are there but the Iraqi officials expressed contradicting statements," said Faisal al-Miqdad, the Syrian deputy foreign minister, "They decided finally to accuse some Iraqi individuals who live in Syria. We confirm that there is no link between those Iraqis and the attacks at all" (Aljeeran.net, August 31, 2009).

General al-Ahmad's Group

The organization of General Muhammad Yunis al-Ahmad, implicated in Kadhum's testimony, is one of the least known insurgent groups in Iraq (See *Terrorism Monitor*, February 9, 2009). In an interview with al-Arabiya TV channel, Ghazwan al-Kubaisi, a leading figure in the group, admitted the limited capabilities of the organization but also indicated that it coordinated and worked with the other insurgent groups. The history of the insurgency in Iraq shows that groups of different, if not contradicting, ideologies have often worked together and avoided fighting each other (Al-Arabiya, August 29, 2009).

However, does that mean the Iraqi government was correct? Despite the possibilities indicated above, there were some weaknesses in the case that the

Iraqi government tried to build. The accusations against Syria originated with General Kassim Ata, the spokesman for Baghdad Operations Command, after the Iraqi security forces came under extensive pressure for their failure to provide security against such attacks (Al-Iraqiya TV, August 23, 2009). The videotaped confession of Wissam Ali Kadhum that implicated Syria has also been criticized for the possibility that it may have been generated through the use of torture.

But the main challenge to the government's story came from inside. The Iraqi Presidential Council issued a statement saying al-Maliki's call for an international tribunal was illegal. The council, which includes Iraqi President al-Talibani (Kurd), Vice-president Adil Abd al-Mahdi (Shi'a Arab) and Vice President Tariq al-Hashimi (Sunni Arab), has urged dialogue through diplomatic and political channels to resolve the differences between the two countries (*Middle East Online*, September 9, 2009).

The crisis also showed that al-Maliki's troubles are not only in the political arena. After the initial criticism of the Iraqi security forces, al-Maliki sacked General Muhammad al-Shahwani, the head of the intelligence service. Critics said that General Shahwani was dismissed because he insisted there was Iranian involvement in the attack. (*Asharq al-Awsat*, August 24, 2009; Iraqforallnews.dk, September 6, 2009).

The Iraqi Prime Minister's authority was to be challenged when he also tried to fire General Abdul Kareem Khalaf, head of the operations of the interior ministry. Al-Maliki was pinned down by his own Minister of the Interior, who refused to carry out the decision. General Khalaf remains in his post (*Asharq al-Awsat*, October 9, 2009).

Syria and post-war Iraq

Governed by two rival wings of the pan-Arab ultra-nationalist Ba'ath party, Iraq and Syria have a long history of mutual hostility since the late 1960s. Both regimes supported the other's exiled opposition and routinely exchanged accusations of inciting violence and sponsoring plots to topple each other. Despite this, Syria still opposed the American-led invasion of Iraq in 2003. The Syrians, who have been involved in the Arab-Israeli conflict since the 1940s, did not like Saddam Hussein but from a geopolitical point of view Iraq was part of their strategic depth in the struggle against Israel while Saddam's regime was an Arab and unequivocal anti-Israeli power. They would not have welcomed his topple, which put them between the Israeli army in the west and the American army in the east.

After the war the Syrian-Iraqi border became the main crossing point for foreign fighters who were joining the insurgency. In 2006, Nouri al-Maliki, a former member of the Iraqi opposition who lived in Damascus for more than two decades, became Iraq's new prime minister. Following this, the two countries restored diplomatic relations after a 24-year break (*Al-Sabah*, November 22, 2006).

These developments were accompanied by American willingness to deal with Iraq's neighboring countries for the sake of controlling the deteriorating security situation in Iraq. All of that seemed to have led to Syrian cooperation, which became a factor in reducing the violence in Iraq. The positive role of Syria was recognized by the then-U.S. commander in Iraq, General David Petraeus: "Iraq has also been helped by more aggressive action by foreign-fighter source countries and by Syria, which has taken steps to reduce the flow of foreign fighters through its borders with Iraq" (VOA, December 6, 2007).

Conclusion

The Iraqi accusation suggests the possibility of a higher level of cooperation between the Ba'athists and Salafis in the Iraqi insurgency. It also suggests a bigger role for Syrian intelligence in that alleged coordination. If proved correct this is a worrying sign for Iraq and its security. On the other hand, if al-Maliki's government is using inaccurate information for political purposes, this will complicate the efforts to stabilize Iraq.

The first wave of the Iraqi diplomatic campaign against Syria does not seem to have shaken the Syrians, while al-Maliki appears to have chosen a poor moment to take on the Syrians. He did not seem to have coordinated with the Americans. His relations with his fellow Shi'a politicians and the Kurds are at their worst. He has problems with the regional powers. The Iranians are not comfortable with his refusal to join the Shi'a coalition and the Saudis have been refusing to invite him to visit Riyadh.

The same border which let hundreds of fighters into Iraq was also open for hundreds of thousands of Iraqis who fled the violence in their country. According to the Syrian authorities, one and a half million Iraqis live in Syria. One of the main arguments of the Syrians against the Iraqi accusations is that Syria would not support attacks against Iraqis while it was hosting hundred of thousands of Iraqis who had fled to Syria to save their lives.

Whether the Iraqi accusations are right or not, Syria openly hosts many Iraqi insurgent individuals and organizations. Syria's stance is to support the "Resistance" against the "Occupation." Iraq has passed on a list to Damascus of the suspects it wants extradited to Iraq, but Syria has cited a lack of evidence as the reason for their failure to cooperate. According to an Iraqi spokesman, Iraq is also seeking the closing of militants' training camps, an end to terrorists crossing the Syrian border into Iraq and a pledge that Damascus will stop supporting terrorist groups that target Iraqis (*The National* [Abu Dhabi], September 26, 2009). Although Iraq has taken the initiative in this row, the Syrians seem to have a more stable strategy than the Iraqis. The latter will need to have more international and regional support to effectively pressure Syria on the issue of cross-border terrorism.

Al-Qaeda in Iraq Operations Suggest Rising Confidence Ahead of U.S. Military Withdrawal

By Ramzy Mardini
November 25, 2009
Terrorism Monitor 7 (36)

On August 19, 2009, coordinated explosions rocked downtown Baghdad, resulting in over 120 deaths. Similarly, in the midst of heightened security measures, twin bombings on October 25, 2009 killed over 155 people in Baghdad, marking the deadliest attack since August 2007. Involving the participation of al-Qaeda in Iraq (AQI), the operations suggest the militants' effectiveness in carrying out coordinated and high-profile attacks on supposedly secured targets. With the gradual disengagement of the U.S. military and all combat forces by August 2010, AQI and like-minded insurgents appear to have a growing level of confidence in their operations.

Among the targets of the attacks were various government ministries, along with the Baghdad provincial headquarters. The bombings suggest an attempt to undermine Prime Minister Nouri al-Maliki's re-election bid in the 2010 parliamentary election by demonstrating the government's failure to provide security. Al-Maliki has campaigned as the national leader who brought both security and sovereignty to Iraq, but insurgents are becoming increasingly aware that their high-profile operations are succeeding in undermining the population's confidence in his government.

At the moment, the goals for the insurgents are less territorially defined and more aimed at encouraging the anarchical conditions that support the survival and influence of their organizations. Today, several factors contribute to a growing operational space for insurgent activity by promoting discouragement and subverting reconciliation efforts:

1. The U.S. military withdrawal from Iraq's urban areas on June 30, 2009, in accordance with the Status of Forces Agreement (SOFA), has left behind a less capable Iraqi Security Force (ISF) to carry on the mission of ensuring protection and confronting terrorists.

2. The growing Arab-Kurdish divide over the ownership of "disputed territories," especially in Ninawa province, has provided an effective venue for insurgents to exploit security disparities and ethnic divisions (see *Terrorism Monitor*, October 23, 2009).

3. The continued reluctance of the Shi'a-dominated government to integrate Sunni fighters from the Awakening (*Sahwa*) Movement into the Iraqi security and civilian sectors has led to growing suspicions and uncertainty amongst some Sunnis over Baghdad's long term intentions vis-à-vis their status and use.

Originating in 2006, the Awakening Movement was spearheaded by Sunni residents in the al-Azamiyah area of al-Anbar province who sought to protect and defend their neighborhoods from the brutal intimidation tactics practiced by AQI (*Asharq al-Awsat*, December 29, 2007). During this time, the AQI leadership waged a vicious campaign to claim leadership over the Iraqi insurgency while demanding the loyalty of other insurgent groups. The foreign jihadists attempted to dominate the economic interests of various indigenous Sunni Arab tribes through smuggling and kidnapping while forcing marriages to tribal women as a way of legitimizing their status within the Iraqi tribal structure.

With support and funding from the U.S. military, the Sunni-dominated *Sahwa* developed into a 100,000-member force across Iraq, consisting of various tribes and former armed insurgents who once fought against Coalition forces. The Shi'a government in Baghdad views the *Sahwa* with suspicion (i.e. Sunni-dominated, mainly former insurgents, reports of AQI infiltration). Faleh Abdul Jabar, a sociologist and director of Iraq Studies Institute in Beirut claims, "There is kind of what we call "coup d'état syndrome" – you can see it clearly in the statements of so many Shi'a Islamic leaders who fear that the [Awakening] groups intend to get incorporated into the army in order to stage a coup d'état and to bring Ba'ath back to power..." (RFE/RL, April 7, 2009).

In October 2008, the control and payroll of the *Sahwa* fighters had been handed over by the U.S. military to the al-Maliki government. But Baghdad has promised only that 20% of the *Sahwa* would be integrated into the security forces, while the remainder would be financially supported until integration into the civilian and private sector. Yet the integration has been slow, allowing for suspicions to grow amongst Sunnis as the U.S. military gradually withdraws. Moreover, Baghdad has often delayed monthly payments, leading the Sunni fighters to protest in dissatisfaction (*Aswat al-Iraq*, October 6, 2009). In late July 2009, the U.S. Department of Defense reported that the al-Maliki government was unlikely to meet the objectives set for *Sahwa* integration before August 2010 (Reuters, July 31, 2009). Strong evidence also suggests that al-Maliki's government has exercised sectarian motives when favoring the placement of *Sahwa* fighters who are Shi'a, not Sunni.

AQI's deadly harassment of the Awakening Movement has long been an effort to provide a strong incentive to disgruntled and fearful Sunnis to opt out of the fight against AQI or rejoin the insurgency. Recent operations against the *Sahwa* have contributed to growing concern about AQI's reconstitution in Iraq. In a pre-dawn raid on November 16, 2009, gunmen disguised in Iraqi army uniforms apprehended 17 individuals, later killing them with execution-style gunshots to the head near Abu Ghraib district on the western outskirts of Baghdad (*Aswat al-Iraq*, November 18, 2009). The operation, reportedly carried out by AQI operatives, appears to have targeted Sunni members of the Awakening. Among those executed were three sons and four cousins of Attala Ouda al-Shuker, a well-known anti-AQI *Sahwa* leader. A statement issued afterwards by the Sunni Iraqi Islamic Party (IIP) suggested the incident was a "worrisome indication that the situation might be deteriorating and it represents a revenge against the people who had helped stabilize the area" (CSM, November 17, 2009). The massacre came a month after coordinated bombings targeted a reconciliation meeting in al-Anbar involving the participation of Sunni tribal leaders, resulting in over 80 casualties.

VOLATILE LANDSCAPE

While AQI has targeted *Sahwa* leaders in Salah ad-Din, al-Anbar, Baghdad, and other governorates, Diyala remains one of the most dangerous provinces for the former Sunni insurgents. Diyala's *Sahwa* council has demonstrated serious dissatisfaction with al-Maliki and government security forces, and hence, may be susceptible to coercing by AQI. According to Major General Abdul Hussein al-Shammari, the Diyala chief of police, "Security investigations with Arab detainees who were recently arrested confirmed the intention of al-Qaeda to destabilize the security situation in the province" (*Niqash*, October 5, 2009). The statement comes after a September 2009 announcement by AQI of the reformation of the Islamic State in Iraq (ISI) in Diyala, suggesting AQI intends to launch a new offensive.

AQI has recently opened a campaign of assassinations in Diyala. On November 17, 2009, AQI-associated operatives assassinated Hameed Khaleel al-Obeidi, the leader of the *Sahwa* council of the Bab al-Darb district of Baaquba, the capital city of Diyala province. The next day, AQI affiliates fired upon Sheikh Houssam Ulwan al-Majmaai, the commander of *Sahwa* forces for all of Diyala, after intercepting his vehicle on the major road leading to the Kanaan district (*Aswat al-Iraq*, November 18, 2009). Though the operation failed to kill al-Majmaai, it was the second assassination attempt on his life within a month. In late October, a bomb wounded the *Sahwa* leader in the Bahraz district, south of Baaquba (*Aswat al-Iraq*, October 22, 2009). Only days earlier a suicide bomber killed the Bahraz *Sahwa* leader Leith Mashaan and other members of the Awakening movement. Mashaan was reported to have contributed to the arrests of numerous AQI leaders, including the individual the Iraqi government claims to be Abu Omar al-Baghdadi – the alleged commander of the ISI (*Aswat al-Iraq*, October 13, 2009).

There is evidence that AQI is confronting the challenges of a renewed offensive against the Iraqi state. The engagement of the Iraqi public in providing intelligence to Iraqi and U.S. forces resulted in a higher demand for secrecy for militants in avoiding exposure. This, coupled with limited resources (i.e. fewer safe houses, fighters), means AQI and other insurgent groups are likely to better utilize their force-multiplier advantages and existing assets, while adopting cautious assessments of their own operational capability.

No Place Like Home: Iraq's Refugee Crisis Threatens the Future of Iraq

By Rachel Schneller
February 24, 2010
Terrorism Monitor 8 (8)

The massive upheaval of Iraq's population that occurred since 2006 threatens the long-term stability of the country, regardless of short-term gains achieved through the political process or military surges. Symptomatic of a destabilized Iraq, displaced populations are themselves a source of future destabilization. Many Middle Eastern countries experienced instability resulting from Palestinians displaced after the establishment of Israel in 1948, the last refugee crisis of comparable proportions in the Middle East. Problems originating from the Palestinian refugee crisis continue today, and the wheels of a new refugee crisis have been set in motion with over four million of Iraq's original 26 million inhabitants displaced since 2003, about 20 percent of its pre-war population [1]. An estimated 2 million Iraqi refugees now reside predominantly in Syria and Jordan, and an additional estimated 1.6 million are internally displaced persons (IDPs) [2].

Iraq has a long history of migration both inside and outside the country. Under Saddam, Shi'a Arabs and Kurds fled to Iran to escape oppression. The Ba'athist regime actively attempted to alter the demographics of the predominantly Kurdish north and the Shi'a south. In 2003, Iraqis of all ethnicities and religions temporarily fled the general violence of the U.S.-led military intervention. But the displacement that has occurred since the February 2006 bombing of the Samarra mosque affected all of Iraq's different groups in unprecedented proportions, altering the demographic fabric of the nation for the foreseeable future [3]. Sunnis fled Shi'a-dominated areas to predominantly Sunni provinces or abroad; Shi'a fled Sunni provinces for predominantly Shi'a provinces or abroad; Arabs evacuated Kurdish areas of Iraq [4]; Christians have largely left the country altogether [5]. As an unintended consequence of the U.S. invasion, Iraqis of all ethnic and religious backgrounds who have worked for Coalition Forces have been targeted for assassination.

Brain drain has particularly affected Iraq because those with education and resources have been more efficiently able to leave the country and set up residence abroad. The less fortunate have been left to fend as best they can inside Iraq. The end result is an Iraqi population made up of young, inexperienced, poorly educated, religious and political extremists than otherwise would have been the case. With a large portion of Iraq's well-educated middle class now living in Jordan, rebuilding Iraq will be even more difficult [6].

Refugees Fuel Insurgencies

Less than ten percent of Iraq's displaced have returned to their original homes in Iraq [7]. The vast majority, however, remain in neighboring Syria and Jordan with no plans to return to a still-volatile Iraq as return becomes less likely with each passing year [8]. Host countries resist granting permanent residency status to refugees and likely will remain firm on this position [9]. Concerns related to the history of displaced Palestinian Arabs in these same countries will deter Syria and Jordan from setting a precedent by accepting Iraqi refugees as legal residents. Refugee children remain largely outside the education system, which will make unemployment a growing problem in the future as they mature and attempt to enter local labor pool with few marketable skills. Even well-educated Iraqi adults work tenuously in grey markets, subject to exploitation and deportation [10].

Only a small percentage of the approximate 2 million Iraqi refugees will be resettled in third countries. As the largest resettlement destination for Iraqi refugees, the U.S. took in 33,000 Iraqi refugees from 2003 to 2009, a tiny portion of the overall 2 million Iraqi refugees [11]. European nations, which accepted thousands of Iraqi refugees from 2003-2008, are indicating they will no longer resettle Iraqis, even forcibly repatriating some Iraqi asylum seekers [12].

Even if the U.S. could increase the number of Iraqi refugees it resettles to more adequately address the Iraq refugee crisis, which is unlikely in the current economic downturn, many Iraqis do not wish to be resettled outside of the Middle East and do not register with the United Nations High Commissioner for Refugees (UNHCR), the first step toward resettlement. Caught between two unappealing options, many Iraqis choose the least-bad alternative and remain in semi-legal status in neighboring countries rather than face the lengthy and complicated resettlement process toward resettling in the United States or Europe, viewed as hostile and discriminatory toward Arabs [13]. The large numbers of Iraqi refugees concentrated in Amman, Damascus, and a few other locations in the Middle East are creating social support networks. Resettlement in the United States, on the other hand, can result in social isolation and extreme poverty because of lack of adequate support for refugees [14].

The large "grey" Iraqi population emerging in the Middle East, tolerated but not integrated, is likely to grow in the coming years. As with Palestinian refugees after 1948, stateless Iraqis will become a population ripe for fueling future insurgencies in Iraq and the region. Eventually, Iraqi refugees will seek residency rights through local integration, diminishing resettlement possibilities, or returning to Iraq, either voluntarily or through forced deportation. All of these options will be complex and probably violent. Host countries may choose to expel or deport Iraqi refugees rather than set a precedent for granting permanent residency rights to other displaced Arabs in the region. The future Iraqi government, likely to be dominated by religious Shi'a political parties, is unlikely to welcome an influx of Sunnis and moderates who could challenge their authority [15].

Iraqi refugees are already fueling insurgent activity in Iraq. Among the first to flee Iraq after the initial U.S. invasion were Ba'athists who took refuge in Syria and Jordan [16]. The Iraqi government accuses Ba'athist residents abroad of insurgent activity and for the spate of terrorist bombings targeting Iraqi government institutions in late 2009. Iraq has also accused Syria of harboring Ba'athist terrorists, an allegation Syria adamantly refutes [17]. Further tensions between Baghdad and Damascus threaten the already fragile status of Iraqi refugees in Syria, as Syria could expel all illegal Iraqi residents to retaliate against Baghdad's accusations.

IDPs Worse Off than Refugees

IDPs in Iraq face similar challenges as refugees, but without assistance from international organizations or the option of resettlement to safer countries. IDPs encounter obstacles enrolling their children in new schools, registering for public benefits, accessing health care and finding jobs. Many Iraqi IDPs are not able to access government services in their new provinces because the Iraqi government either has not been able to mobilize programs for IDPs or because what resources are available for IDPs are divided along sectarian lines, favoring Shi'a populations [18]. In the absence of central government assistance, sectarian militias have stepped into the arena. Shi'a militia groups provide resources for displaced Shi'a; Sunni militias provide similar services for displaced Sunni, providing basic food and fuel, and assistance in settling in homes abandoned by other displaced Iraqis, setting the stage for future violent property disputes divided between sectarian groups. Indeed, property restitution will likely be among the most intractable long-term problems facing Iraq in the future [19]. Even if IDPs successfully integrate into their new communities, the majority will not willingly give up all rights to their former properties and will seek restitution or compensation once conditions in Iraq have improved.

Because they are still in Iraq, IDPs must also deal with Iraq's high levels of crime and violence. Indeed, many IDPs would probably prefer to leave Iraq where at least job prospects would be better and violence levels lower. However, IDPs lack sufficient financial resources and social networks to leave the country and support themselves abroad. IDPs are a population ripe for recruitment by insurgents and militias as, having fled violence, they are focused on security and view participation in armed groups as one of the only options for defending themselves and their families against future attacks. Both Sunnis and Shi'a who have been internally displaced are joining local militias and insurgent groups, as these are the only employment opportunities available [20].

Of those refugees returning to Iraq from abroad, the large majority become part of the IDP population [21]. These refugees do not return to their original homes, but rather seek new homes where they will not be a target for sectarian violence [22]. Sunnis who fled abroad from Basra in 2006, for example, are unlikely to return to Basra and instead will likely seek new homes in regions where Sunnis are the majority. Over time, accumulated refugee returns to Iraq will intensify the division of the country along sectarian lines.

Demographic Warfare

The dynamic of Iraqi IDPs and refugees since 2006 have altered the demographic fabric of Iraq. The country in 2010 looks vastly different than it did before the Coalition invasion and the Samarra mosque bombing. Previously mixed Shi'a-Sunni neighborhoods are now almost entirely homogenous. Northern territories used to house Kurds, Arabs, Turkomen, and other ethnicities but are now less diverse, with Kurds claiming more area for the independent Kurdish region through tactics intended to chase away minorities.

One result may be greater regional stability, as ethnically homogenous populations more readily agree on social and political goals. Regional stability, however, will come at the cost of decreased national stability and greater fragility in relations between Iraq and its neighbors.

A homogenous Kurdish area will have less incentive to engage with Arabic-speaking areas of Iraq. A homogenous Shi'a region will have little incentive to listen to Sunni concerns, let alone make concessions to them. Ten years ago, many areas of Iraq were home to mixed populations of Kurds, Shi'a and Sunni who made the necessary political compromises to co-exist peacefully. The population displacement that has occurred in Iraq, however, has exacerbated sectarian and ethnic tensions and greatly decreased incentives for negotiation and compromise.

As demographically homogenous regions become stronger and more unified in their aspirations, the central government will becomes less capable of unifying the nation. Already, provincial governments have become more capable in exacting monetary tribute from the weak national government. In 2009, Baghdad bowed to Basra and the Kurdish Regional Government, according them one dollar per barrel of oil produced or refined. For each religious visitor, Najaf will receive a fee from the national government. National unity achieved through buying off provincial governments is tenuous, dependent in Iraq on unstable oil prices and a government struggling with corruption and inefficiency.

A national Iraqi census envisioned for late 2010 will reveal the extent to which the country has become divided [23]. This census is likely to be controversial, fraught with implementation challenges, and mark a new phase of instability in Iraq. Determining the status of disputed territories such as Kirkuk is linked to completing a census, which will reveal the demographic make-up of these highly sensitive areas. National elections slated for March 2010 will also expose the extent to which Iraq has changed demographically since the 2005 elections, likely triggering further sectarian violence.

Repeating History

The Palestinian refugee crisis was a recipe for disaster, and history is now repeating itself with the current Iraqi crisis, which will likely set off decades of sectarian violence, insurgent and terrorist activity, and conflicts arising from reintegration efforts. The violence occurring in Iraq has the potential to spill over into neighboring countries, which also struggle with sectarian tensions between Shi'a and Sunni Arabs, Kurds, and Christians. For many Iraqis, going home is no longer an option, and even the displaced who succeed in returning to their original geographic location within Iraq will find a nation vastly changed and a government, perhaps more democratic, but less capable of ensuring national unity.

Notes

1. Exact figures- both of refugees and of Iraq's pre-war population- do not exist and numbers are disputed by the government of Iraq and host countries. However, these figures are the ones most quoted by the United Nations High Commissioner for Refugees and other organizations involved in the Iraq refugee and displacement crisis. See UNHCR Global Appeal 2009 Update (2009) and Elizabeth Ferris, *The Looming Crisis: Displacement and Security in Iraq* (Washington: The Brookings Institution, August 2008).
2. Kristele Younes and Nir Rosen, "Uprooted and Unstable," Refugees International, April 2008. p. 1; IOM Emergency Needs Assessments Post February 2006 Displacement in Iraq," International Organization for Migration, October 1, 2009.
3. "Assessment of Return to Iraq" International Organization for Migration, November 3, 2009.
4. "Iraq's Dangerous Trigger Line," *The Economist*, February 11, 2010.
5. "Safe conditions for Christians discussed in a conference," *Al Sabah*. January 16, 2010.
6. "Iraq needs its middle-class back to rebuild," *Aswat al-Iraq*, July 1, 2009; Nathan Fisher, "The Iraqi Refugee Crisis Continues," CommonDreams.org, June 30, 2009, http://www.commondreams.org.
7. About 336,000 out of 1.6 million IDPs. IOM Emergency Needs Assessments Post February 2006 Displacement in Iraq," International Organization for Migration, October 1, 2009.
8. "Iraqis abroad between staying out and getting back in," *Aswat al-Iraq*, January 2, 2010.
9. "Refugee Crisis in America," Georgetown Law, October 7, 2009, p. 13.
10. Ibid.
11. "Refugee Crisis in America," Georgetown Law, October 7, 2009, p. 11.
12. "Protests as asylum-seekers are returned to Iraq," *Aswat al-Iraq*, October 17, 2009.
13. "Refugee Crisis in America," Georgetown Law, October 7, 2009, p. 15-19.
14. Ibid., p. 25-33.
15. "Iraq: Preventing the point of no return," Refugees International, April 7, 2009.
16. "Baathist asserts to newspaper meetings with armed groups in Damascus to coordinate attacks in Iraq," *Aswat al-Iraq*, September 28, 2009.
17. Ibid.
18. Kristele Younes and Nir Rosen, "Uprooted and Unstable," Refugees International, April 2008, p. 5-6.
19. "Iraq: Preventing the point of no return," Refugees International, April 7, 2009; "Assessment of Return to Iraq," International Organization for Migration, November 3, 2009.
20. Kristele Younes and Nir Rosen, "Uprooted and Unstable," Refugees International, April 2008, p. 3-4.
21. UNHCR found 70% of Iraqi refugees returning from Syria became internally displaced, Kristele Younes and Nir Rosen, "Uprooted and Unstable," Refugees International, April 2008, p. 14;
22. "Assessment of Return to Iraq," International Organization for Migration, November 3, 2009; "Iraq: Preventing the point of no return," Refugees International, April 7, 2009.
23. "Iraq's cabinet agrees to postpone census until October 2010," *Aswat al-Iraq*, August 31, 2009.

Chapter 8

Insurgent Strategies since the U.S. Withdrawal

Jihadis Ask How the Mujahideen Will Control an Islamic State of Iraq

By Abdul Hameed Bakier
August 6, 2009
Terrorism Monitor 7 (24)

Jihadi Internet forum members are engaged in a continuing debate on the obstacles hindering the application of Islamic law in Iraq after the U.S. withdrawal and suggest certain approaches to modify the current social and unreligious practices of the people. The debate was triggered by a posting entitled "How would the Mujahideen control the regime?" (hanein.info, July 24, 2009).

In a posting intended to start a discussion and solicit ideas to improve the deteriorating application of Islam in Iraq, forum member "al-Falahi" complains that the people of Iraq are abandoning Islam, consequently making it difficult for the mujahideen to take control of the regime in Iraq and set up an Islamic *Shari'a* state after the complete U.S. withdrawal from Iraq scheduled for the end of 2011.

Al-Falahi claims that from the time of the 2003 U.S. invasion until a few years ago, pious Sunni Islamic practices dominated in Baghdad. Currently, most Sunni dominated neighborhoods are ignorant of the Sunni creed and the majority of Sunnis support the infidel Awakening councils. Worse, people curse God and religion, bars are abundant, and young men and women are busy engaging in forbidden relationships. Iraqis are growing ever distant from committing to an Islamic state once the mujahideen take over. The 95% of people who once supported the mujahideen now support the Awakening councils. Al-Falahi says that regardless of the reasons that led to the current detachment of people from Islam, the different Iraqi mujahideen factions must now consider how to tackle the following issues before attempting to implement *Shari'a* in Iraq:

1. The weak ideological commitment of Iraqi Sunnis.

2. The absence of a suitable entity to rule the state. To establish an Islamic *Shari'a* state, there must at least be people who are capable of resisting local pressure against *Shari'a* from the Kurdish *Peshmerga* militias in the north and the well-trained Shi'a militias in the south. The Islamic state must also be prepared for regional interference from Iran, Turkey and the "pro-Western" states of Jordan, Saudi Arabia, Kuwait and Syria, all of whom would not hesitate to impose an embargo on the Islamic State of Iraq if ordered to by the West.

3. Even if the mujahideen came to power, they would need to apply certain measures to control Baghdad's Shi'a, who are 75% of the population.

4. The mujahideen also need to deal with the existing Iraqi military and police trained by the occupation and willing to engage the mujahideen. Al-Falahi put the total strength of Iraq's security forces at 500,000, along with 100,000 members of the Awakening councils.

5. The mujahideen need to tackle the many Islamic factions with international connections.

Al-Falahi ends his posting with a question: If the Americans withdraw from Iraq leaving behind only a few bases, how could the mujahideen take over and rule the country by establishing an Islamic state?

Over the following week, many forum members responded to al-Falahi's inquiry. Some members felt that al-Falahi exaggerated the number of Iraqis who had abandoned the Islamic State project. To address the problem, members believe the real reasons behind Iraq's shift away from *Shari'a* should be explored. The mujahideen must have a clear political and Islamic agenda comprehensible by common Iraqi Sunnis. Other members responded by saying the different mujahideen factions have secret military and political plans ready to implement after the U.S. withdrawal. But to make these plans a reality these same factions will have to unite under one command and keep attacking the enemy and his supply routes until the occupation is no longer sustainable.

Concerning the Awakening councils, forum members agree they will collapse just like the current government of Iraq after the U.S. pullout. Eliminating the heads of tribes that support the U.S. occupation would guarantee the demise of the Awakening councils. The Sunni factions created by the occupation will face a similar fate, but the Shi'a factor remains a big problem for the Islamic state project and should be dealt with by the same oppressive measures used by the regime of Saddam Hussein.

Forum member Abu Obaida al-Jabouri does not think the Iraqi people are shifting their support from the mujahideen to the occupation. The proof may be seen in the daily jihad operations that kill many Crusaders, Shi'a rejectionists and apostates. When the mujahideen shura council announced the Iraqi Islamic state project, the mujahideen were in control of al-Anbar, Diyala, Salah al-Din and Mosul provinces. People were very content with the rule of the mujahideen. Unfortunately, mujahideen rule did not last long because many jihadi factions were tardy in pledging allegiance to the new state.

According to al-Jabouri, the jihadis' Islamic State project began with a first phase of guerrilla warfare conducted by the mujahideen. The second phase was the establishment of the Islamic State of Iraq (ISI). The final phase of jihadi operations – the control of the whole country – has been obstructed by the Awakening councils and Iraqi traitors who conspired against the ISI.

Now the mujahideen are back to phase one and will continue jihad operations. The Awakening councils came at a time when Shi'as were killing common Sunni Iraqis. The people were optimistic that these councils would protect them from Iranian aspirations in Iraq. Therefore, the mujahideen who succeeded in defeating the Americans and forcing them to announce pullout plans must educate the people and convince them to accept the Salafi-Jihadi factions before attempting the application of Islamic *Shari'a* similar to what is being done in Somalia and Afghanistan.

Finally, al-Jabouri said, "My dear brothers, you should not underestimate the strength of the mujahideen who defeated superpowers in Afghanistan and Iraq. We are fighting [the occupation] with our convictions and faith in God." Many expect Iraq's jihadi factions to fight each other over conflicting goals and methods after the U.S. withdrawal from Iraq, much like Afghanistan's mujahideen factions attacked each other after the Soviet withdrawal.

VOLATILE LANDSCAPE

Jihadis Turn their Eyes to Syria as a Post-Iraq Theater of Operations

By Murad Batal al-Shishani
August 20, 2009
Terrorism Monitor 7 (26)

In what might be described as Syria from a jihadist perspective, an article entitled "Al-Qaeda al-Sulbah" (the Solid Base) was posted to the jihadi website al-Faloja.com on July 21, 2009 by active al-Faloja contributor Abu Fadil al-Madi. The article urges Salafi-Jihadis to reconsider the importance of the political and strategic changes in Syria. The title of al-Madi's posting is borrowed from a 1988 article by Palestinian jihad ideologue Abdullah Azzam [1].

Al-Madi claims there was a kind of agreement between the jihadis and the Syrian regime, an "unannounced agreement to stop mutual hostilities," but the situation has changed since the latter part of 2005. It was then that the regime launched a campaign against "all the components of the Sunnis in Syria; the traditional religious groups (al-Khaznawi Naqshbandiya [a Sufi order] and al-Qubeisyat for example), the *Shari'a* institutions (al-Fatah Institute and Abu Nur Institute, in particular), and even against those who were considered to be close allies of the regime, working with all their strength as a trumpet [of the regime] (Muhammad Habash, as an example) [2]. As well, there is the fierce security campaign against the Salafi-Jihadi movement, which has escalated since [Fall 2005]."

Al-Madi's post asserts that there is an alliance between the Syrian Alawite regime and Ja'afri-dominated Iran [3]. This alliance, based on the religious links of these two branches of Shi'ism (though not all Shi'as recognize the Alawis as Shi'a), created the division in the Middle East between "the Shi'a crescent" and the "moderate axis." Despite these ties, the article claims the Syrian regime is pragmatic in terms of its relations with the United States, especially when it comes to coordination against jihadis. Washington's extradition to Syria of jihadi ideologue Abu Mus'ab al-Suri is an indication of the degree of this cooperation, claims the writer. Having concluded that the Syrian regime is working hard against Sunnis in general, the writer asks, "What is the Salafi-Jihadi movement's strategic vision for Syria?... Will it remain a potential passage for supplies [to Iraq] or has the time come - or close to it - for a radical strategic change?"

Al-Madi's post states that the jihadi movement has concentrated its efforts on the Iraqi front since 2003 and "developed its political-strategic project by proclaiming the Islamic State of Iraq." However, the geographically sensitive location of Iraq and the international and regional strategic conflict over resources such as oil have pushed both the states of the moderate axis and the Shi'a crescent to try to contain the jihadi movement, penetrate its apparatus and "adapt" it by all means, "each in its own way." Accordingly, the *Sahwa* (Awakening) councils of Iraq were created by exploiting tribal relations with Jordan and Saudi Arabia. The councils also had connections to Syria, benefitting from the latter's close ties with some Iraqi Ba'athist elements. Al-Madi believes that such policies wasted the efforts of the jihadis since 2007 in a battle of attrition instead of a final battle with "the Crusaders and their supporters in Iraq."

Al-Madi continued by saying that "the fall of the Syrian regime or its collapse into chaos will have a direct impact on the neighboring Sunnis in Iraq and Lebanon, and they will liberate themselves from the constraints on their movement and will find in Syria, a free, important space for movement and supply." In such a scenario the writer thinks that the "fall of Syria" will cut off land transport of Iranian land supplies to Hizballah in Lebanon. This will equalize the strength of the Lebanese Sunnis with Lebanon's Shi'a community. According to the author, Syria will serve as a backyard to support the fight against Americans in Iraq. "More importantly, the jihadi project will be in direct contact with Israel in an area which is ideal for guerrilla warfare, namely the occupied Golan Heights, without having to fight a costly battle to overcome the Shi'a strongholds in southern Lebanon."

The writer concludes that "material interests" in Syria do not exist as they do in Iraq, meaning that international and regional actors will not become involved in armed conflict in Syria as they did in Iraq because any military invasion would be too costly. He also declared that, "the planning for change relies on a solid popular base in Syria which never existed in Iraq. The Sunnis, whose rights are prejudiced, are the majority in Syria, while the dominant and well-armed Rafidah (rejectionist) Shi'a do not form more than a quarter of the Syrian population."

Despite the "unannounced agreement" between jihadis and the Syrian regime, the enmity between the parties goes back to the early 1980s, when clashes took place between Syrian authorities and the Muslim Brotherhood. The hostility exists not because there is a close relation between the jihadis and the Muslim

Brotherhood, but because that era has played a significant role in shaping the way Islamists in the Arab world regard the Syrian regime. The negative perception of the Syrian Alawite regime can be seen in much of the Arab world's Islamist literature, but is particularly visible in the works of Abu Mus'ab al-Suri.

Al-Madi's article shows that the jihadis in the Levant region are concerned about the influence of Iran, based on their religious differences. The increasing numbers of Syrian fighters that have taken part in jihad activities in Iraq or in Lebanon since the invasion of Iraq in 2003 make the ideas presented in the article crucial [4]. The Salafi-Jihadi movement is in decline in Iraq, but it follows that those jihadis returning to their own countries or new locations could become a potential security problem. Syria is one of the countries that jihadis could aim to turn into a new front after benefitting from its use as a passage to Iraq for the last six years.

Notes

1. Abdullah Azzam, al-Qai'ida al-Salbba (the Solid Base), *Jihad Magazine*, Issue 41, April 1988.
2. Al-Madi refers here to the Syrian Kurdish branch of the Naqshbandiyya Sufi order led by Ahmad al-Khaznawi. Al-Qubeisyat is a religiously conservative women's organization. Muhammad Habash is director of the moderate Islamic Studies Center in Damascus. For the Abu Nur Institute, see *Terrorism Monitor*, June 4, 2009.
3. Al-Madi refers to the Imami Shi'a School of Jurisprudence, named for its founder, Ja'afar al-Sadiq, the sixth Shi'a imam. The Alawis are a small but powerful minority in Syria, where most of the population is Sunni Muslim. There is also a small Christian community. Murad Batal al-Shishani, *Ma Ba'ad al-Islam al-Siyasi fi Soria: Abu Mus'ab al-Suri wal-jeel al-Thaleth mn al-Salafeen al-Jihadeen* (Beyond Political Islam in Syria: Abu Mus'ab al-Suri and the Third Generation of the Salafi-Jihadists), in Radwan Ziadeh (ed), *al-Ikhwan al-Muslmeen fi Soria (Muslim Brotherhood in Syria)*, al-Misbar Studies and Research Center, Dubai, August 2009.

Jihadis Debate Methods of Financing the Mujahideen Network in Iraq

By Abdul Hameed Bakier
October 30, 2009
Terrorism Monitor 7 (32)

The main objective of jihadi websites and forums is to garner support for the Mujahideen on various levels, the most important of which is fundraising and transferring money to the battlefields, essential for the continuity of terrorist operations. To that end, Jihadi forums intermittently appeal to Salafi-Jihadi supporters to donate money while explaining secure methods of transferring money. A recent posting entitled "The Fourth campaign: Conduct Jihad with Your Money," describes methods used in a new campaign to finance Iraq's mujahideen (hanein.info, Thread of September 15, 2009 to October 9, 2009).

A jihadi forum member, nicknamed Abdullah, began the posting with a long pep talk to fellow members regarding the religious virtue of donating money for jihad that quoted verses from the Quran that equate donations to jihad with active participation in the field. Abdullah calls upon the Iraqi mujahideen to support each other financially, logistically and through the sharing of information and intelligence: "Some Iraqi jihadi formations suffer from a lack of funding. They became the poorest mujahideen on Iraqi soil for refusing conditional support. They became day laborers and jihadi lions and monks at night." Abdullah appealed to Muslim scholars and merchants everywhere to donate to jihad activities.

The new campaign has the following objectives:

1. Deal with the shortfall in jihadi funding.
2. Promote the exchange of financial support between jihadi formations. The well-funded groups must support the others. According to Abdullah, information from the inside confirms that some jihadi groups have not received a single dollar in the last 18 months while some jihadi forum members make one thousand dollars per month in salary.
3. Revive the idea of financial support of jihad as a religious duty, a concept that was abandoned by many Muslim scholars and businessmen.
4. Provide financial support to the families of martyrs.
5. Provide financial support to jihadi media efforts.

This two-month campaign, according to Abdullah, was launched by two Iraqi jihadi factions, *Jaysh al-Rashideen* and *Jaysh Sa'ad bin Abi Waqas*, and will be managed through their respective websites, al-rashedeen.info and saadarmy.com.

The first step in the fundraising process is to contact these factions through their websites to specify the amount of money to be donated and the name of the donor. The donor is given contact details for the faction's representative and a code word to identify himself to the representative through the website. After converting the money to dollars, the donor is instructed to go to a bank and specify the name of the recipient and his mobile phone number. Then the recipient is given a 10-digit wire number. Abdullah claims the banks will not question wire transfers of less than $700. The smaller the amount, the better, says Abdullah, since wires for small amounts are not monitored.

Secondly, the money wires should be sent to jihadi representatives in Syria, Jordan and Turkey. The jihadi factions' representatives in these countries will then smuggle the money into Iraq. Other forum chatters criticized Abdullah's instructions, saying intelligence services monitoring the websites could easily identify the recipient and the code word. Abdullah responded by arguing that this is only one of sixty other ways of sending money to the mujahideen that he cannot reveal over the Internet.

From the comments and deliberations of other forum members on Abdullah's posting, it is obvious that jihadis are aware their websites are monitored by security agencies. When contacted by donors they will assuredly provide safer means of sending the donations, therefore it seems that this posting attempts to serves two purposes:

1. Mislead security services into forcing further constraints on ordinary business transactions, consequently slowing down economic growth. Economic disruption is one of al-Qaeda's main goals.

2. Identify possible financial donors and contact them by other safer methods.

Al-Qaeda has proven more capable of raising and transferring money than the Iraqi factions. In last year's *Hajj* (pilgrimage) season, al-Qaeda supporters collected cash donations from pilgrims by showing videotaped appeals for financial assistance from deputy al-Qaeda leader Ayman al-Zawahiri, stored on mobile phones. The money was later carried in person through Saudi Arabia's busy borders as millions of pilgrims returned home (altwafoq.net September 28, 2009). A similar video message by Saeed al-Shahri, deputy al-Qaeda leader in Yemen, has been distributed by mobile phone in the lead-up to the November 2009 *Hajj* season.

Another unsophisticated but difficult to track means of transferring money is what could be labeled as the "verbal wire" or the "unofficial wire," a method the jihadis call *hawala*. Some jihadi websites and forums such as alnusrra.net and alboraq.inf ask donors to contact them through their websites. Once contact is made, the donor is instructed to give the donation to a certain representative in the donor's country. Then a phone call is made by that contact to another contact person in the recipient country requesting a cash payment to the jihadi group. No official wire records are made, with the whole system depending on trust between the two contact persons, both of whom usually run legitimate or front companies as part of the setup for jihadi fundraising. The verbal *hawala* is impossible to track unless the identity of the two contact persons is revealed and their calls monitored by security forces.

Militant Iraqi Nationalists Struggle with Approach to al-Qaeda's Islamic State of Iraq

By Pascale Combelles Siegel
December 23, 2009
Terrorism Monitor 7 (39)

The string of deadly bombings against government buildings and Shi'a landmarks in Baghdad that began last August provides a startling reminder that the al-Qaeda-associated Islamic State of Iraq (ISI) remains a clear danger to Iraq's long-term stability. The three sets of multiple attacks that took place in 2009 on August 19, October 25, and December 8, killed at least 362 people and wounded over 1,233, marking them as the deadliest operations since 2007 [1]. In an otherwise continuously improving security situation, the ISI claimed responsibility for the spectacular, headline-grabbing attacks in an effort to embarrass the Iraqi government, intensify Sunni disgruntlement with the current political establishment and rally former nationalist insurgents behind its banner.

The ISI Claims a New Strategy

Despite the attacks' high death tolls, the ISI proudly took ownership of the operations. The ISI argued that the attacks were designed to "crush the strongholds of infidelity and the forts of polytheism of the apostate Safavid [i.e. Iranian-influenced] government" (al-falojah,net, August 24, 2009). In each claim of responsibility, it identified its targets as government buildings and institutions:

1. August 19, 2009 bombings - the Ministry of Foreign Affairs, Ministry of Finance, Ministry of Defense, Offices of the Baghdad Governorate

2. October 25, 2009 bombings - Ministry of Justice and Baghdad Provincial

Council headquarters

3. December 8, 2009 bombings - the new Treasury building, Criminal Courts Compound, Ministry of Justice, and Ministry of Labor

The ISI argued that the ministries are legitimate targets for three reasons. First, Iraq's current governmental institutions were established by the United States according to a non-Islamic political model; these institutions are therefore those of the "infidels" (those who do not accept the Prophet's message) and should not be used to govern Muslims. Second, these institutions are currently run by Shi'a political parties, which the ISI considers to be apostate, akin to Muslims who have renounced Islam because they do not practice what the ISI considers to be the only "true" Islam. Finally, these governmental institutions are run by political parties allied with Iran, a country which the ISI accuses of seeking to dominate and subjugate Iraq like the Persian Safavid dynasty had done in the 16th century.

For the ISI, the symbolic value of the targets far outweighs any other consideration, in particular whether the toll was justified. In claiming responsibility for the August 19, 2009 bombing, the ISI argued that it targets "the pillars of this malignant and slaughtered state and those who help it, support it, and establish its pillars" (al-faloja.net, August 24, 2009). Hence, in the ISI's world, all workers who need to make a living by working for governmental institutions are legitimate targets because their daily work enables the government to function. This is a position that sets the ISI apart from most other insurgent groups who hold a much more nuanced position on targeting ordinary governmental workers or security force personnel. Groups such as the Islamic Army in Iraq (IAI), the 1920 Revolution Brigades, and the Islamic Front for the Iraqi Resistance (*al-Jabha al-Islamiya lil Moqawama al-Iraqiya* – JAMI) have long publicized their opposition to the targeting of either governmental workers and/or Iraqi civilians on humanitarian grounds. The only "collateral damage" the ISI regretfully acknowledged were those Sunni passers-by who might have been killed or injured due to "their presence at those locations" (al-faloja.net, August 24, 2009).

For the ISI, only Sunni Muslims are worthy of concern, because they are the only Muslims who practice religion "correctly." While the ISI offers religious solace to those victims, it also suggests advice to Sunnis so as to minimize future unwanted tolls: "We ask them in Allah to avoid passing by and being present in these locations as much as they can." However, the ISI warns that mass casualties are nonetheless acceptable because the ends justify the means. "We will not halt the duty of jihad against the polytheists and defense against the infidels because of those who fall as martyrs, as our scholars determined" (al-faloja.net, August 24, 2009).

Interestingly, the ISI does not feel a pressing urge to justify its targeting. The ISI only talked about the civilian victims in its first claim of responsibility for the August 19 attacks. It did not even broach the subject when it took responsibility for the attacks of October 25 and December 8, indicating that the movement feels it has satisfactorily answered its detractors.

Nationalist Insurgents Adopt a "Neither-Nor" Approach

The ISI's renewed focus on fighting the Iraqi government is putting nationalist insurgents in a difficult position. In 2007-2008, nationalist insurgents have massively deserted the anti-U.S., anti-government battlefield and have fought against the ISI because of its misguided strategy (provoking a Sunni-Shi'a civil war) and tactical excesses (anti-civilian tactics). The ISI's focus on targeting the Iraqi government fits the nationalist insurgents' stated objective of taking down the post-2003 political process, although its callous disregard for human life goes far beyond tactics the nationalist insurgents deem appropriate and legitimate. Consequently, as much as they have deplored the loss of lives, nationalist insurgents have nonetheless reserved much of their scorn for the Iraqi government and have avoided criticizing the ISI.

The Sunni insurgent groups were quick to deplore the attacks and the loss of human life, but they did so in a generic manner, avoiding blaming the ISI directly for the attacks. For example, JAMI condemned the bombings and called "the death of such a number... a humanitarian and social disaster" (jami.org, December 9, 2009). The IAI denounced "these criminal incidents and affirmed its refusal of such acts" (iaisite.org, November 21, 2009). After the October 25 twin bombings, the Political Council for the Iraqi Resistance (PCIR) wrote, "the Council condemns these blind explosions that occurred today in the al-Salihiyah area of Baghdad, and which did not differentiate between the child and the adult, or between the man and the woman" (pciraq.org, October 25, 2009).

However, the Sunni insurgents painstakingly avoided blaming the ISI for the carnage. Regardless of the fact that the attack bore the hallmark of the ISI and despite the fact that the ISI claimed responsibility for the attacks, the IAI, JAMI and the PCIR all failed to mention the ISI in their statements. Moreover, they repeatedly exonerated the "resistance," arguing that the "mujahideen" could not have carried out such bloody attacks because they act on behalf of and in the interests of the Iraqi people. As JAMI put it after the 19 August bombings, "There is no sane person who thinks that the Iraqi resistance could carry out such an act." (jami.org, August 19, 2009). The IAI went further, chiding the Iraqi government for accusing the "Ba'athists" and "takfiris" of conducting the attacks, questioning whether the groups even existed, let alone played any kind of role in Iraq's politics. The IAI argued that "the Ba'ath [has] no more existence" and charged that the government was using the term "takfiri" to describe Sunnis in general (iaisite.org, October 27, 2009). After the December 8 bombings, the IAI again proclaimed the mujahideen's innocence: "They will not have an opportunity to blame their crimes on the groups of the mujahideen because no one will believe them. The resistance proves every time that it sides with the innocent and noble sons of our people" (iaisite.org, December 9, 2009).

Rather than holding the ISI accountable for its senseless and bloody attacks, nationalist insurgents concentrated their fire against the Iraqi government and the political process. Following the August 19 bombing, JAMI questioned how powerful car bombs could be smuggled past the security checkpoints and hypothesized that the Iraqi security forces were the "perpetrators of the attacks" (jami.org, August 19, 2009). JAMI then implicitly accused the United States and Iran of responsibility, arguing that the bombings only serve American and Iranian long-term interests in Iraq. After the December 8 bombings, JAMI argued that the "occupation and its Quislings are [the ones who] shed Iraqi blood" and warned that parliamentary elections, scheduled for March 2010, could not fix Iraq's problems. In condemning the October 25 twin bombings, the PCIR accused the Iraqi government and the United States of orchestrating the attacks, arguing that "with the approach of the parliamentary elections, the conflict between the powers of the unjust [the Baghdad government] and aggression [the United States] increases, aiming to cling onto and to maintain their power and authority… Again, our people in Iraq are paying the price of these fights, as these parties are using the blood and the bodies of Iraqis as a way to maintain their authority, using the ugliest and most horrible ways of murder and destruction" (pciraq.org, October 25, 2009).

Conclusion

In an interview with *al-Jazeera*, a spokesman for the PCIR summarized the ambiguities behind the position held by the nationalist insurgents:

> *Perhaps it is too early to accuse a certain party or quarter without evidence because struggle for power among these blocs and parties exists on a large scale. The goal, however, is very clear. It is mobilizing the street on a sectarian basis, especially since the street has started to break away from them [i.e., the ISI extremists] after having tested them and [having] discovered their uselessness for the Iraqi people and even for their voters, supporters, and aides (al-Jazeera, December 9, 2009).*

As the ISI forcefully claims responsibility for its renewed anti-government strategy, nationalist-minded insurgents have chosen to give the ISI a free pass so as to not appear supportive of an Iraqi government it despises.

Notes

1. On August 19, 2009, six blasts near government ministries and other targets in Baghdad killed 95 and wounded 536. On October 25, 2009, twin car bombs targeted the Justice Ministry and the Baghdad Provincial Government office in central Baghdad, killing 155 and wounding 500. On December 8, 2009, at least four car bombs exploded near government buildings and a police checkpoint, killing 112 and wounded 197. Data compiled by Reuters AlertNet: www.alertnet.org/thenews/newsdesk/GEE5B70M6.htm.

The Changing Strategic Posture of Iraq's Insurgents

By Ramzy Mardini
February 12, 2010
Terrorism Monitor 8 (6)

The string of high-profile bombings that followed the withdrawal of U.S. combat forces from Iraqi cities on June 30, 2009 exposed not only Iraqi security shortcomings, but also the continued effectiveness of the insurgents to carry out demanding operations. These types of operations suggest the militants are choosing high-profile terrorism as a strategy for undermining counterinsurgency efforts, targeting the confidence and trust of the population in the government as a way of ensuring a climate of uncertainty, feeble governance, and organizational survival.

VOLATILE LANDSCAPE

A new security challenge emerged when U.S. combat forces exited Iraqi cities in accordance with the Status of Forces Agreement arranged by the outgoing Bush administration. Without U.S. combat forces patrolling side-by-side with Iraqi soldiers in urban areas, deterrence-by-denial becomes less credible, bestowing to insurgents a new rational basis for exploiting a weaker security apparatus.

Sunni insurgent groups and Shi'a militias invested much time and resources to gain and hold territory during the height of the insurgency (2005-2007), but militant strongholds were uprooted over the course of a population-centric counterinsurgency carried out by U.S. and Iraqi forces. The loss of territorial possession has forced a smarter, albeit less resourceful, insurgency. It has evolved from being centered on a costly and preoccupying defensive posture to a purely offensive and asymmetric terrorist campaign. As U.S. General Raymond Odierno claimed late 2009, al-Qaeda in Iraq has essentially "changed from a broad-based insurgency to a terrorist group trying to target the government" (*New York Times*, December 20, 2009).

By building confidence and trust between the population and protection forces, counterinsurgency fosters a rational framework for locals to cooperate and provide intelligence without fearing retribution. This public engagement forces upon militants a higher demand for secrecy in avoiding exposure, likely leading to a greater inclination towards political assassination operations.

This was the case on February 7, 2010, when gunmen with silencers in the Raas al-Jada area of western Mosul assassinated Dr. Soha Abdullah Jarallah – a female political candidate and part of former Prime Minister Ayad Allawi's al-Iraqiya coalition (*Aswat al-Iraq*, February 7, 2010). Preceding the December 30, 2009 twin bombings in al-Anbar that killed 30, wounded over 100 and severed the hand of Governor Qassim Mohammed Abid al-Fahdawi, a series of nearly 40 assassination attempts targeted tribal, religious, security, and political figures in the province.

With the increased need for secrecy coupled with limited resources, insurgent groups are likely to better utilize their force-multiplier advantages and existing assets, while adopting cautious operational assessments. The three highly coordinated, mass-casualty Baghdad bombings since the June 30, 2009 withdrawal (occurring on August 19, 2009; October 25, 2009; and December 8, 2009) are a testament that the adversary recognizes the effectiveness of infrequent high-profile attacks on government symbols in influencing the minds of Iraqis.

In addition, with a more capable and visible central government in Baghdad, the incentive for insurgent groups to pool resources and cooperate with one another has increased. An example may be found in the Jaysh Rijal al-Tariqah al-Naqshabandiyah (JRTN), a militant Sufi movement with ties to Ba'athist leaders including Izzat Ibrahim al-Douri. The movement is known to have formed new ties to other Sunni insurgent groups (see *Terrorism Focus*, February 21, 2007; July 28, 2008). In November 2009, U.S. General Raymond Odierno suggested that al-Qaeda in Iraq was also collaborating with Ba'athist elements, recognizing that AQI "has now become more and more dominated by Iraqi citizens" rather than foreign jihadis (Reuters, November 18, 2009).

Because no openly defined militant stronghold exists, the battleground for combating the insurgency has become undefined as well. Insurgents can now decide when and where to become active members of the resistance, rationally choosing to fight—or not fight—depending upon which side is advantaged. This was noticeable during Prime Minister Nouri al-Maliki's Mosul offensive in May 2008, codenamed Za'eer al-Assad (Lion's Roar), which disappointed some Iraqi commanders who were expecting a hardened resistance amongst the militants.

Instead of engaging armies in guerilla warfare, the insurgents favor exploiting areas of political and ethnic sensitivity with the intention of inflaming inter-ethnic tensions. Their assassination campaign against the *Sahwa* (Awakening) Movement coerces fearful and disgruntled Sunnis to opt out of the fight against insurgents, while the Shi'a-led government continues to arrest many senior *Sahwa* officials on the grounds of supporting terrorism. On January 23, all 13,000 *Sahwa* fighters in Diyala province left their posts in protest of Baghdad's harassment campaign against them (*Aswat al-Iraq*, January 23, 2010).

Insurgents are also fueling dangerous suspicions between Sunni Arabs and Kurds by exploiting the debate on the "disputed territories" in Ninawa province, compounding the rising tensions between the Sunni Arab provincial governor Atheel al-Nujaifi and the Kurdish Regional Government (KRG) (*Aswat al-Iraq*, August 14, 2009; *Niqash*, February 24, 2009; *Kurdish Globe*, February 6, 2010). Tensions have risen to the verge of armed conflict on multiple occasions, only to be defused by the intervention of U.S. combat forces.

The debate over Article 140 – a constitutional provision that aims to settle the dispute over territorial ownership between the KRG and the national government – remains unresolved and a potential rationale for a second civil war. In addition, the first post-Saddam census has been delayed until after the scheduled withdrawal of all U.S. combat forces in August 2010 (*Aswat al-Iraq*, August 31, 2009). Along with the March 2010 parliamentary election, these political proceedings offer real venues for exploitation and destabilization by insurgents.

The objectives of the insurgent groups have narrowed and become more realistic because they have ceased to be territorially defined. Strategic and tactical assessments are no longer about gaining territory, but rather to complicate counterinsurgency activities by instilling in the public a sense of uncertainty, suspicion, insecurity, and dwindling confidence in the Iraq government. The lack of a territorial baseline has now forced militants to think prudently about how to effectively confront their adversary, as the power to coerce rather than control becomes the standard for operational planning.

Chapter 9
The Changing Political Landscape

The Politics Behind Iraq's Second Parliamentary Election

By Joel Wing
January 21, 2010
Terrorism Monitor 8 (3)

Iraqis will head to the polls on March 7, 2010 in the second parliamentary election since the overthrow of Saddam Hussein in 2003. Iraqi politics are in a state of flux that is reflected in the run-up to the vote. The election law was held up over longstanding issues like Kirkuk. At the same time, the ethno-sectarian parties that dominated the 2005 polls are being challenged by a new wave of nationalist parties. This has created challenges to forming a state ruled by law, given tensions between the new parties and the old lists that are attempting to hold onto power.

Iraq's parliament passed a new election bill on December 6, 2009. Three days later, the three-member Iraqi Presidential Council approved the legislation and it became law (*Aswat al-Iraq*, December 9, 2009). That was almost two months past the original deadline of October 15, 2009 set by the Iraqi Election Commission (RFE/RL, October 7, 2009). The original version of the law was passed by parliament on November 9, 2009 after long arguments [1]. One of the disputes was over what type of voter system to use. An open list was chosen where the public is able to pick from parties, lists, and politicians. Due to disputes between Kurds, Arabs, and Turkmen, voting in Tamim province (which includes Kirkuk) was made provisional for one year while a committee looks for any irregularities that could invalidate the balloting (*Aswat al-Iraq*, September 24, 2009). Finally, the number of seats up for grabs was increased from 275 to 323, based upon population numbers from the Ministry of Trade and a requirement that there be one seat in parliament for every 100,000 people (*Niqash*, November 9, 2009).

VOLATILE LANDSCAPE

Iraq seemed to be ready for the polls when Vice President Tariq al-Hashimi vetoed the first draft of the bill on November 18, 2009. Al-Hashimi objected to the fact that Iraq's refugees, mostly from his Sunni constituency, would have their votes go towards only eight compensatory seats shared with smaller parties that did not get enough ballots at the provincial level, but did well nationally [2]. This backfired when the Kurdish Alliance, backed by Prime Minister Nouri al-Maliki's State of Law coalition and the Islamic Supreme Council of Iraq (ISCI), ignored al-Hashimi's concerns and amended the law to reduce the number of available seats in parliament by basing them upon older 2005 statistics with a 2.8% increase for recent population growth [3]. This reduced the number of seats in many Sunni areas while increasing them in Kurdistan. That dilemma was finally worked out on December 6, 2009, by giving every province an increase in seats, including three in Kurdistan, and allowing refugees to be counted as part of their home provinces. The new number of seats in parliament is now set at 325 [4].

The Iraqi Election Commission then set the voting date for March 7, 2010 (*Aswat al-Iraq*, December 9, 2009). This will cause legal problems as the constitution says that elections should be held no later than January 31, 2010 and parliament's term ends March 15, 2010 (Reuters, December 7, 2009). It is expected to take months to put together a new government, so some sort of caretaker administration will have to be assembled in the meantime.

With the election law finally passed, Iraq's many lists are left to focus upon their campaigns. In 2005 there were three main ethno-sectarian lists competing:

1. The Shi'a United Iraqi Alliance, which was made up of the Islamic Supreme Council of Iraq (ISCI), the Sadrists, and the Da'awa Party, amongst other smaller Shi'a entities.

2. The Kurdish Alliance, consisting of the Kurdistan Democratic Party (KDP) and the Patriotic Union of Kurdistan (PUK).

3. The Sunni Iraqi Accordance Front, consisting of the Iraqi Islamic Party, the General Council for the People of Iraq, and the Iraqi National Dialogue Council (BBC, January 20, 2006).

By 2009 almost all of those alliances had broken apart and there is now a mix of ethno-sectarian and nationalist lists running for office [5].

The Shi'a bloc for example, has split into two. Prime Minister al-Maliki's Da'awa Party formed the State of Law coalition for the 2009 provincial elections. The coalition calls for a strong central government and better security. The ISCI, the Sadrists, former Prime Minister Ibrahim al-Jaafari's National Reform Trend and Ahmad Chalabi's Iraqi National Congress created the Iraqi National Alliance (INA). Since they have disparate views on many issues, the INA's main selling point is its Shi'a identity. Iran played a large role in its formation in an effort to maintain Shi'a power in Iraq [6]. Tehran and the INA also wanted al-Maliki to join because he is the most popular politician in Iraq, but they did not want his leadership and refused to assure him the prime minister's post [7]. The two lists are likely to get the most votes from the Shi'a majority, but because of their split neither may even get a plurality. There are constant hints and rumors that the two may rejoin after the voting (Alsumaria TV, January 7, 2010).

The other major list is the Kurdish Alliance of the KDP and PUK. They and their constituency are still rather homogenous, which means they will probably get about the same number of votes as in 2005, when they received the second-highest number of seats after the United Alliance. In 2010 this means they will be looked at as the main element in the formation of any new coalition. The Kurdish Alliance will be asking for the retention of ethno-sectarian quotas that assure a Kurdish president and deputy prime minister in the national government, concessions to allow them to export oil, and a resolution to the Kirkuk issue. Their most likely partner is the National Alliance since the Kurds and the ISCI have a long-standing relationship predating the U.S. invasion, but this relationship is complicated by the fact the Sadrists are not friendly to Kurdish demands.

After these three larger lists, there are several medium-sized groups:

1. The *Iraqi National Movement* coalition, which includes former Prime Minister Ayad Allawi's Iraqi National List, Vice President Tariq al-Hashimi's Renewal List and Saleh al-Mutlaq's Iraqi National Dialogue Front. On January 8, 2010, the Accountability and Justice Commission (successor to the De-Baathification Commission) banned al-Mutlaq from participating in the election, accusing him of being a Ba'athist [8]. Al-Mutlaq ran in the 2005 election, where his party garnered 11 seats, and he also helped draft the 2005 constitution (McClatchy, January 7, 2010). The Commission has questionable legal standing and its decision to ban al-

Mutlaq could disrupt the voting, as other members of the list have threatened a boycott in response. It would also set a bad precedent if the Commission were able to ban parties that have actively been involved in Iraqi politics with no previous problems.

2. The *Unity of Iraq Alliance* is made up of Interior Minister Jawad al-Bolani's Constitution Party and Iraq's Awakening Conference, led by al-Anbar governorate's Sheikh Ahmad Abu Risha (*Aswat al-Iraq*, October 21, 2009). Al-Bolani has been mentioned as a possible candidate for prime minister, but his party has never done well in elections.

3. The last significant list is the *Iraq Consensus*, which is led by the Iraqi Islamic Party [9]. It is the successor to the Iraqi Accordance Front.

Most of these lists are more nationalist and secular in orientation than ethno-sectarian. Their real importance will be seen after the votes are tallied and the large parties need to put together ruling coalitions. These medium-sized lists will be crucial in getting the required number of seats to rule, and will be offered ministries as a reward for their support.

Conclusion

Iraq's 2010 election is likely to bring about both change and stasis. The 2009 provincial elections showed that voters were more interested in issues like security, services, and nationalism than ethno-sectarian identity. The 2010 vote will continue that trend, as there are more serious secular contenders this time around. At the same time, groups that still hold onto identity politics (like ISCI and the Kurdish Alliance) will have enough power to upset any broad consensus on Iraq's major issues, such as the implementation of federalism or the development of the oil industry. This was demonstrated when the Kurdish Alliance and their ISCI allies were able to hold up the election bill over Kirkuk and a closed list. The voting is also causing legal problems, as the Accountability and Justice Commission is attempting to ban parties just prior to the vote and the delay in passing the election law means that constitutional deadlines will be broken and a caretaker government will have to be formed. These are all important developments for Iraq's nascent political system. New voices are emerging, and some of the old ones are trying to intimidate them. This, along with the inability to follow deadlines, even ones set in the constitution, will test the resiliency of Iraq's government ability to move towards a more open system.

Notes

1. Reidar Visser, "The Election Law Is Passed: Open Lists, Kirkuk Recognized as a Governorate with 'Dubious' Registers," Historiae.org, November 8, 2009.
2. Reidar Visser, "Constitutional Disintegration," Iraq and Gulf Analysis, November 19, 2009.
3. Reidar Visser, "The Hashemi Veto Backfires, Parliament Ups the Ante," Iraq and Gulf Analysis, November 23, 2009.
4. Reidar Visser, "No Second Veto: The Election Law is Approved by Tariq al-Hashimi and the Iraqi Presidency," Historiae.org, December 6, 2009.
5. Marisa Cochrane Sullivan, "Iraq's Parliamentary Election," Institute for the Study of War, October 21, 2009.
6. Jeremy Domergue and Marisa Cochrane, "Balancing Maliki," Institute for the Study of War, June 2009.
7. Nimrod Raphaeli, "Al-Maliki Turns His Back on Iran, Embraces Iraqi Nationalism," Middle East Media Research Institute, September 2, 2009.
8. Reidar Visser, "Why Ad Hoc De-Baathification Will Derail the Process of Democratization in Iraq," Iraq and Gulf Analysis, January 8, 2010.
9. Ahmed Ali, "Iraq's Elections Challenge: A Shifting Political Landscape," Washington Institute for Near East Policy, November 20, 2009.

Who Speaks for the Shi'a of Iraq?

By Rachel Schneller
February 19, 2010
Terrorism Monitor 8 (7)

Iraq's Shi'a Arabs, the demographic majority with an estimated 60-70% of the population, wield the most political influence in Iraq. But the Shi'a of Iraq are a diverse group, with major regional differences between the Shi'a of Basra and the deep South and the Shi'a of the north-central region. Iraq's Shi'a hold divergent views on the appropriate role of religion in government. Other areas of internal division among Shi'a parties exist, such as a common position on cooperation with the United States, but these are secondary in their influence on Shi'a voters.

Iraq's Shi'a political parties have fought battles with each other that at times were as bloody as the sectarian war between Sunnis and Shi'a in 2006-2008. From 2005-2008, the Badr Corps of the Islamic Supreme Council of Iraq (ISCI) and Sadrists fought militia battles in the streets of Basra. In 2009, the two groups reconciled and formed a coalition for the March 2010 elections. How could two groups bent on eliminating each other become allies only two years later? Why did Da'awa—the compromise party supported by both ISCI and Sadrists in 2006 for the Prime Ministership—break from the coalition in 2009?

Secularism vs. Theocracy

Iraq's Shi'a hold widely divergent views on secularism and the role of religion in post-Saddam Iraq. Many Shi'a view secularism—a main characteristic of Saddam's regime—with distrust. Indeed, secularism and Ba'athism are synonymous in the minds of many Iraqi Shi'a. Saddam's Ba'athist agents, both Sunni and Shi'a, noted who attended Shi'a mosques and reported on Shi'a clergy and Iraqi travel to Iran. Saddam was not trying to exterminate Shi'ism from Iraq. Rather, he wanted to eradicate the Shi'a opposition that used Shi'a religious institutions and sought refuge in Iran to organize and plan attacks against Saddam. But the effect of Saddam's surveillance of Shi'a mosques and clergy was perceived by Iraq's Shi'a population as a threat to their religious identity. In spite of opposition to Saddam, many of Iraq's Shi'a were as secular in their political and social views as most Ba'athists, and opposed an Iranian-style theocratic government.

With the fall of Saddam's regime and the rise of Iraqi Shi'a political parties, advocacy of an Islamic government became an option, and one that was desired among Shi'a who viewed the incorporation of Shi'a Islam into Iraq's government as an effective way to render a Ba'athist return to power impossible. Da'awa and ISCI are among those Shi'a parties that espouse an Islamic government in order to protect Shi'a interests in Iraq. These parties rose out of the opposition to Saddam, and their leaders were among the Shi'a opposition targeted by his regime. This religious outlook, however, conflicts with the Shi'a who prefer a secular lifestyle and who do not want to live under an Iranian-style theocratic government. Ayad Allawi's al-Iraqiya and Ayad Jamal al-Deen's Ahrar are examples of secular Shi'a parties.

Religious Shi'a parties in Iraq are sometimes assumed to be "Iranian" parties because they share a similar ideology and because of the frequent travel to Iran by religious Shi'a politicians. ISCI in particular has been labeled an "Iranian" party. Contrary to this assumption, some of the most virulent opposition to Iranian influence in Iraq comes from religious Shi'a parties, including ISCI [1]. Iran provided shelter to Shi'a resistance fighters, but these Shi'a Arabs were not treated as equals by Iran and were denied residential rights (*Azzaman*, January

27, 2009). Arabic remained their primary language, and they returned to Iraq at the first opportunity. Secular Shi'a parties, such as al-Iraqiya, on the other hand, tend to espouse good relations with Iran and shy away from strong criticism of their eastern neighbor (*Asharq al-Awsat*, January 20, 2010).

A great deal of religious rivalry exists between Iraq and Iran. Both Najaf (Iraq) and Qom (Iran) are seats of Shi'a religious power. Religious Shi'a parties distrust Iran's motives for interfering in Iraqi affairs, and are particularly suspicious of Iran's interest in Najaf. Secular Shi'a parties, on the other hand, tend to focus on Iran's potential as a trading partner and how to divide natural resources such as oil and water. When viewed in this manner, anomalies such as the secular anti-Iranian Ahrar party become more comprehensible, in that Ayad Jamal alDeen, a Najaf cleric is both skeptical of Iran's motives in Iraq and committed to secularist government.

Rivalry between the major Iraqi Shi'a religious parties is understandable, given that the prize would ultimately be power and influence in a future theocratic government. The Badr/Sadr battles of 2005-2007 were not surprising as these two factions have been vying for dominance within the religious Shi'a movement in Iraq. Their rapprochement in 2009 makes ideological sense in that both parties believe a Shi'a theocratic government would best protect Shi'a interests against a possible return of a hostile Sunni dictatorship.

However, further schisms between ISCI and the Sadr movement are very likely because both desire dominance over the theocratic movement in Iraq but draw on different voter bases [2]. In the run-up to the March 2010 parliamentary election, arguments between the ISCI and Sadrist coalition partners drew attention to the fragility of the partnership, with Muqtada Al-Sadr accusing ISCI of sympathizing with the Ba'athists (*Aswat al-Iraq*, January 22, 2010).

De-Ba'athification Masks De-Secularization

The Shi'a are divided on the "de-Ba'athification" of Iraqi politics. With secularism confused with Ba'athism, selective de-Ba'athification would accomplish the religious Shi'a parties' goals of de-secularization. Some former Ba'athists may be allowed to continue to participate in Iraqi politics as long as they espouse theocratic views. [3] Secularist Shi'a, on the other hand, sometimes wax nostalgic about the Saddamist era, not because they miss Ba'athism, but because they prefer secularism to the imposition of religious dictates on personal lifestyles. Secular Shi'a parties advocate for reconciliation with former Ba'athists and reintegration of Sunni extremists into the government in the name of political stability, but these populations would also temper the influence of the more religious Shi'a parties in government (*Al-Bawaba*, January 28, 2010).

Many Iraqi Shi'a hold both positions simultaneously; they desire a secular government and wish to prevent the return of a Ba'athist government. Shi'a voters will cast their ballots according to which priority is higher at election time. A secular Shi'a voter may prefer Ayad Allawi's secularist platform but may vote for a religious party if the primary concern is preventing a return of the Ba'athists.

South vs. North Iraqi Shi'a

Iraqi Shi'a of the North/Central region differ from the Shi'a of the South, culturally and linguistically. [4] Southern Shi'a, originating from Nasiriyah, Amara, and Basra, feel entitled to a greater share of political power and resources considering their numerical strength in the most oil-rich region of the country. [5] The Fadilah Party, for example, is a Southern Shi'a party with a stronghold in Basra. Fadilah is a religious party and part of the Iraqi National Alliance (INA) of Shi'a religious parties. But while it is an INA member, Fadilah at times differs from ISCI and Sadrists on issues that pertain to the Southern Shi'a, particularly concerning oil and decentralization (*Aswat al-Iraq*, November 16, 2009).

Shi'a party positions on decentralization strongly correlate to the geographic base of the respective party's power. Southern Shi'a favor decentralization, which would result in more revenue remaining in the oil-rich southern provinces. Fadillah, for example, held a referendum in 2008 to declare Basra its own region, but failed to garner the necessary ten percent support to be brought to Parliament. Fadilah's position is not shared by nationalist Shi'a parties with strongholds outside the deep South because they would suffer if a greater share of resources were diverted to Basra. ISCI also supports decentralization, albeit a larger Shi'a region. Sadrists and Da'awa favor a strong central government that would keep revenue flowing to Baghdad, where both parties historically maintained stronger voter influence.

One of the trends to watch in the Shi'a political landscape will be the "migration" of Shi'a politics southward. In the January 2009 provincial elections, Da'awa came to power in the Basra provincial council. The Fadillah governor was replaced with a Da'awa member. Subsequently, Da'awa began moving away from its strongly centrist position and toward greater regional resource sharing, as reflected in the 2010 budget that accords the Basra provincial government a dollar per barrel of oil produced, a move that puts Da'awa more at odds with centralists but is more representative of the interests of Shi'a in Basra [6]. If Da'awa can maintain a strong power base in Basra, it may not need to ally with the "nationalist" INA to maintain primacy among the religious Shi'a parties [7].

As Iraq's population becomes increasingly divided along sectarian lines, a natural occurrence will be the migration of the Shi'a voter base southward. The Basra, Maysan, and Dhi Qar regions likely will gain in power and influence within Shi'a parties because these regions will become almost entirely Shi'a. A strong centralist political line will lose voters in the South. As internal displacement along sectarian lines continues and the country itself becomes more divided, decentralization is a more likely outcome.

	Sadrists	ISCI/SCIRI	Fadhila	Da'awa	Iraqiya	Ahrar
Year of formation	2003	1982 (from Da'awa)	2003	1957	1990	2009 (from Iraqiya)
Religious vs secular government	Religious	Religious	Religious	Religious	Secular	Secular (clergy)
South Shi'a party	No	Yes	Yes	Yes (pre-viously No)	No	No
Reconcilia-tion with Sunnis and former Ba'athists	No	No	Yes	No (Previously Yes)	Yes	Yes
Voter base	Younger (under 40), unemployed, rural, uneducated, religious/ poor	Older (over 40)/ veterans of Shi'a uprising, religious, middle and upper class	Religious, some education, linked to oil	Older (over 40), religious veterans of Shi'a uprising	Educat-ed, secular	Younger (under 40), educated
Main strongholds	Bagdhad (Sadr City), Maysan	Diyala, Muthanna, Basra, Baghdad	Basra	Qadisi-yah, Dhi Qar, Baghdad	Baghdad	Najaf, Dhi Qar
Centralized versus decentral-ization	Centralized	Decentralized	Decen-tralized	Decentra-alized, formerly centralized	Central-ized	Central-ized

Notes

1. "Shiite Politics in Iraq: The Role of the Supreme Council," International Crisis Group. Middle East Report No.70, November 15, 2007.
2. Reidar Visser, "Sadr-Badr Compromise in Tehran, the Iraqi National Alliance (INA) is Declared," www.historiae.org, August 24, 2009. The ISCI voter base draws on upper and middle class, well-educated, middle aged Shi'a. The Sadrist voter base is younger, under-employed and less educated. See "Shiite politics in Iraq: The Role of the Supreme Council," International Crisis Group: *Middle East Report* No. 70, November 15, 2007.
3. Reidar Visser, "Some More De-Baathification Metrics," Iraq and Gulf Analysis, January 22, 2010. See also Reidar Visser,. "The 511 De-Baathification cases: Sectarianism or Despotism?" historiae.org, January 20, 2010.
4. Reidar Visser,. "Basra, the Reluctant Seat of 'Shiastan'?" Middle East Report, March 12, 2007.
5. Reidar Visser,. "Decentralization Bonanza in the Iraqi Budget," historiae.org, .January 27, 2010.
6. Ibid.
7. Reidar Visser, "After Sadr-Badr Compromise in Tehran, the Iraqi National Alliance (INA) is Declared," historiae.org, August 24, 2009.

ABOUT THE AUTHORS

Mahan Abedin is a counterterrorism and security consultant and an advisor to indepedent Persian-language media. He is currently an international research fellow at the Institute for Defence Studies and Analysis in New Delhi. From August 2004-April 2006, Mr. Abedin was former Editor of the Jamestown Foundation's *Terrorism Monitor* publication. He holds a First Class Honours Degree in Politics and International Relations from the University of Reading and an MSc (Distinction) in Political Theory from the London School of Economics.

Rafid Fadhil Ali is an Iraqi journalist, writer and researcher, and currently a senior broadcast journalist at the BBC World Service in London. From 2003 to 2007, he covered the Iraq war and the events that followed. Working for different Iraqi, pan-Arab and foreign media organizations as a TV reporter, Mr. Ali is an expert in Iraqi politics and militant groups in the Middle East. He writes frequently in Arabic and English for publications such as *Terrorism Monitor* of The Jamestown Foundation, and the daily *al-Hayat* Arabic newspaper.

Abdul Hameed Bakier is an intelligence expert on counter-terrorism, crisis management and terrorist-hostage negotiations. Since 2006, he has monitored Iraqi Jihadist websites and written on insurgent tactics and techniques for The Jamestown Foundation. He is based in Jordan.

Ahmed S. Hashim is a leading authority on Middle Eastern, Central and South Asian security issues. He is Professor of Strategic Studies at the U.S. Naval War College. His previous books on Iraq include *Iraq: Sanctions and Beyond* (1997, coauthored with Anthony H. Cordesman), and *Insurgency and Counter-Insurgency in Iraq* (2006).

Lydia Khalil is an International Affairs Fellow in residence at the Council on Foreign Relations. Khalil, a specialist in Middle East politics and international terrorism, has worked in the United States and abroad for the U.S. government, international organizations, private companies, and think tanks on a variety of international political and security issues. She was recently appointed as a Visiting Fellow at MacQuarie University in Sydney, Australia, as part of the

Centre on Policing, Intelligence, and Counterterrorism. She is also a Non-Resident Fellow at the Lowy Institute as part of the West Asia Program. Prior to her appointments in Sydney, Khalil was a counterterrorism analyst for the New York Police Department, focusing on international terrorism trends and terrorism cases in the Middle East, Africa, and Europe. Previously, she worked in Iraq as a policy adviser for the Coalition Provisional Authority in Baghdad, where she worked closely with Iraqi politicians on political negotiations and constitutional drafting. Khalil holds a B.A. in international relations from Boston College and a M.A. in international security from Georgetown University. Khalil was born in Cairo, Egypt, and is a native Arabic speaker.

Erich Marquardt is the Editor-in-Chief of *CTC Sentinel*, a monthly counterterrorism journal published by the Combating Terrorism Center at West Point. Previously, he was the Program Manager for Global Terrorism Analysis at The Jamestown Foundation.

Babak Rahimi is Assistant Professor at the Department of Literature, Program for the Study of Religion, at the University of California - San Diego. From 2005-2006, he was a Senior Fellow at the United States Institute of Peace, where he conducted research on Grand Ayatollah Ali al-Sistani and Shi'a politics in post-Ba'athist Iraq. From 2000-2001, he was also a Visiting Fellow at the Department of Anthropology at the London School of Economics and Political Science. Dr. Rahami holds a B.A. from the University of California - San Diego, M.A. in Ancient and Medieval Philosophy from the University of Nottingham, and a Ph.D. from the European University Institute in Florence, Italy.

David Romano is an Assistant Professor of International Studies at Rhodes College and Senior Research Fellow at the Inter-University Consortium for Arab and Middle East Studies. In addition to numerous articles on Middle East politics, the Kurdish issue, forced migration, political violence, and globalisation, he is the author of the book, *The Kurdish Nationalist Movement* (2006, Cambridge University Press). For several years, he has studied and conducted field research in Turkey, Iraq, Iran, Syria and Israel/Palestine. Dr. Romano earned his doctorate in political science from the University of Toronto.

Michael Scheuer served in the Central Intelligence Agency for 22 years before resigning in 2004. He served as the Chief of the bin Laden Unit at the Counterterrorist Center from 1996 to 1999. He is the once anonymous author of *Imperial Hubris: Why the West is Losing the War on Terror.* His other book also includes *Marching Toward Hell: America and Islam After Iraq*. Dr. Scheuer is a former Senior Fellow at The Jamestown Foundation.

Rachel Schneller is an International Affairs Fellow in residence at the Council on Foreign Relations (CFR). During her tenure, she will be researching the implications for Iraq and U.S. foreign policy of the displacement of 4 million Iraqis from their original homes to locations outside and inside Iraq. Rachel was a Foreign Service Officer with the U.S. Department of State. From 2005-2006, she served at the U.S. regional Embassy Office in Basra, Iraq, where she reported on sectarian violence and internal displacement following the Samarra mosque bombing. She earned her M.A. from the Johns Hopkins School of Advanced International Studies (SAIS).

Murad Batal al-Shishani is a London-based analyst on Islamic groups and terrorism. He is also a specialist on Islamic movements in Chechnya and in the Middle East. Al-Shishani is a regular contributor to several publications in both Arabic and English such as The Jamestown Foundation's *Terrorism Monitor* and the London-based *al-Hayat.* His weekly column is published at the Jordanian daily *al-Ghad* every Wednesday. He is also the author of the books, *The Islamic Movement in Chechnya and the Chechen-Russian Conflict 1990-2000,* and also *Iraqi Resistance: National Liberation vs. Terrorism: A Quantitative Study.*

Pascale Combelles Siegel is a Virginia-based independent defense consultant specializing in perception management.

Emrullah Uslu is a Turkish terrorism expert and currently a Ph.D. candidate at the Center for Middle Eastern Studies at the University of Utah. He previously worked as a policy analyst for the Turkish National Police's Counterterrorism Headquarters for more than six years. Mr. Uslu has taught courses on terrorism and political violence, and regularly contributes to the Istanbul-based English daily *Toda"s Zaman* and Turkish daily *Taraf.*

Reidar Visser is a Research Fellow at the Norwegian Institute of International Affairs. He has a background in history and comparative politics and holds a doctorate in Middle Eastern studies from the University of Oxford. He has published extensively on the history of southern Iraq and the issues of decentralisation and federalism, including two books, *Basra, the Failed Gulf State: Separatism and Nationalism in Southern Iraq* (2005) and *An Iraq of Its Regions: Cornerstones of a Federal Democracy?* (2007, coedited with Gareth Stansfield). Many of his writings are available from his widely cited Iraq website, www.historiae.org.

Wladimir van Wilgenburg is a journalist and editor at the Kurdish newspaper *Rudaw* based in Iraq, and regularly writes on the Middle East for Turkish, Kurdish and English newspapers. He is currently studying political history and international relations at the University of Utrecht in the Netherlands.

Joel Wing is an Iraq analyst who runs the blog *Musings on Iraq*, which covers the daily security, political, and economic dynamics in Iraq. He holds a B.A. and M.A. in international relations from San Francisco State University.

ABOUT THE EDITOR

Ramzy Mardini is an analyst on international security affairs and the Middle East. He joined the Jamestown Foundation in 2007 as an analyst on Iraq. Prior to joining, Mr. Mardini had served at the Executive Office of the President and as Iraq Desk Officer for Political Affairs at the U.S. Department of State, where he handled the office portfolio on intelligence for the Director of Iraq Affairs. Proficient in Arabic, he has traveled extensively to the Middle East. In 2007, he served as a researcher on Iran at the Center for Strategic Studies at the University of Jordan, where he coauthored an occasional paper on the domestic politics of Iran's Assembly of Experts.

Mr. Mardini graduated *summa cum laude* with *research distinction* in political science from The Ohio State University, and holds an honors M.A. degree in international relations from the University of Chicago. He lives in Washington, DC.

INDEX